The Versailles Effect

Material Culture of Art and Design

Material Culture of Art and Design is devoted to scholarship that brings art history into dialogue with interdisciplinary material culture studies. The material components of an object—its medium and physicality—are key to understanding its cultural significance. Material culture has stretched the boundaries of art history and emphasized new points of contact with other disciplines, including anthropology, archaeology, consumer and mass culture studies, the literary movement called "Thing Theory," and materialist philosophy. **Material Culture of Art and Design** seeks to publish studies that explore the relationship between art and material culture in all of its complexity. The series is a venue for scholars to explore specific object histories (or object biographies, as the term has developed), studies of medium and the procedures for making works of art, and investigations of art's relationship to the broader material world that comprises society. It seeks to be the premiere venue for publishing scholarship about works of art as exemplifications of material culture.

The series encompasses material culture in its broadest dimensions, including the decorative arts (furniture, ceramics, metalwork, textiles), everyday objects of all kinds (toys, machines, musical instruments), and studies of the familiar high arts of painting and sculpture. The series welcomes proposals for monographs, thematic studies, and edited collections.

Series Editor:
Michael Yonan, University of California, Davis, USA

Advisory Board:
Wendy Bellion, University of Delaware, USA
Claire Jones, University of Birmingham, UK
Stephen McDowall, University of Edinburgh, UK
Amanda Phillips, University of Virginia, USA
John Potvin, Concordia University, Canada
Olaya Sanfuentes, Pontificia Universidad Católica de Chile, Chile
Stacey Sloboda, University of Massachusetts Boston, USA
Kristel Smentek, Massachusetts Institute of Technology, USA
Robert Wellington, Australian National University, Australia

Volumes in the Series

British Women and Cultural Practices of Empire, 1775–1930
Edited by Rosie Dias and Kate Smith

Jewellery in the Age of Modernism, 1918–1940: Adornment and Beyond
Simon Bliss

Childhood by Design: Toys and the Material Culture of Childhood, 1700–Present
Edited by Megan Brandow-Faller

Material Literacy in Eighteenth-Century Britain: A Nation of Makers
Edited by Serena Dyer and Chloe Wigston Smith

Sculpture and the Decorative in Britain and Europe: Seventeenth Century to Contemporary
Edited by Imogen Hart and Claire Jones

Georges Rouault and Material Imagining
Jennifer Johnson

The Versailles Effect: Objects, Lives and Afterlives of the Domain
Edited by Mark Ledbury and Robert Wellington

Lead in Modern and Contemporary Art (forthcoming)
Edited by Sharon Hecker and Silvia Bottinelli

Enlightened Animals in Eighteenth-Century Art: Sensation, Matter and Knowledge
(forthcoming)
Sarah R. Cohen

Materials, Practices and Politics of Shine in Modern Art and Popular Culture
(forthcoming)
Edited by Antje Krause-Wahl, Petra Löffler and Änne Söll

Domestic Space in Britain, 1750–1840: Materiality, Sociability and Emotion
(forthcoming)
Freya Gowrley

Domestic Space in France and Belgium: Art, Literature and Design, 1850–1920
(forthcoming)
Edited by Claire Moran

The Versailles Effect

Objects, Lives, and Afterlives of the *Domaine*

Edited by
Mark Ledbury and Robert Wellington

BLOOMSBURY VISUAL ARTS
LONDON · NEW YORK · OXFORD · NEW DELHI · SYDNEY

BLOOMSBURY VISUAL ARTS
Bloomsbury Publishing Inc
50 Bedford Square, London, WC1B 3DP, UK
1385 Broadway, New York, NY 10018, USA
29 Earlsfort Terrace, Dublin 2, Ireland

BLOOMSBURY, BLOOMSBURY VISUAL ARTS and the Diana logo are trademarks of
Bloomsbury Publishing Plc

First published in the United States of America 2020
Paperback edition published by Bloomsbury Visual Arts 2024

Selection and editorial matter © Mark Ledbury and Robert Wellington, 2020
Individual chapters © their authors, 2020

For legal purposes the Acknowledgments on p. xx constitute an extension of this copyright page.

Cover image: Regia Versaliarum [royal palace of Versailles]. Bronze medal, struck after 1700. 41mm. (© Collection: Robert Wellington.)

All rights reserved. No part of this publication may be reproduced or transmitted in any form or by any means, electronic or mechanical, including photocopying, recording, or any information storage or retrieval system, without prior permission in writing from the publishers.

Bloomsbury Publishing Inc does not have any control over, or responsibility for, any third-party websites referred to or in this book. All internet addresses given in this book were correct at the time of going to press. The author and publisher regret any inconvenience caused if addresses have changed or sites have ceased to exist, but can accept no responsibility for any such changes.

Library of Congress Cataloging-in-Publication Data

Names: Ledbury, Mark (Andrew Mark), editor. | Wellington, Robert, editor.
Title: The Versailles effect : objects, lives, and afterlives of the domaine / edited by Mark Ledbury and Robert Wellington.
Description: New York : Bloomsbury Visual Arts, 2020. | Series: Material culture of art and design | Includes bibliographical references and index.
Identifiers: LCCN 2020037685 (print) | LCCN 2020037686 (ebook) | ISBN 9781501357787 (hardback) | ISBN 9781501357763 (pdf) | ISBN 9781501357770 (epub)
Subjects: LCSH: Château de Versailles (Versailles, France) | Architecture and society–France–Versailles. | Art and society–France–Versailles.
Classification: LCC DC801.V56 V372 2020 (print) | LCC DC801.V56 (ebook) | DDC 944/.3663–dc23
LC record available at https://lccn.loc.gov/2020037685
LC ebook record available at https://lccn.loc.gov/2020037686

ISBN: HB: 978-1-5013-5778-7
       PB: 978-1-3504-3759-3
       ePDF: 978-1-5013-5776-3
       eBook: 978-1-5013-5777-0

Series: Material Culture of Art and Design

Typeset by Integra Software Services Pvt. Ltd.

To find out more about our authors and books visit www.bloomsbury.com and sign up for our newsletters.

Contents

List of Figures	ix
Notes on Contributors	xvi
Acknowledgments	xx

1 Enduring Versailles *Mark Ledbury and Robert Wellington* — 1

Part I Making the Palace

2 The Other Palace: Versailles and the Louvre *Hannah Williams* — 13
3 The *Grands Décors* of Charles Le Brun: Between Plan and Serendipity *Bénédicte Gady* — 33
4 *Artisans du roi*: Collaboration at the Gobelins, Louvre, and the *Académie Royale de Peinture et de Sculpture* under the Influence of the *Petite Académie* *Florian Knothe* — 45
5 Rough Surfaces: Etching Louis XIV's Grotto at Versailles *Louis Marchesano* — 63

Part II Versailles Life

6 Porcelain and Power: The Meaning of Sèvres Porcelain in Ancien-Régime France *Matthew J. Martin* — 77
7 Hair, Politics, and Power at the Court of Versailles *Kimberly Chrisman-Campbell* — 95
8 The Politics of Attachment: Visualizing Young Louis XV and His Governess *Mimi Hellman* — 109
9 Courting Favor: The Apartments of the Princesse de Lamballe at Versailles, 1767–89 *Sarah Grant* — 129

Part III Outsiders

10 Enslaved Muslims at the Sun King's Court *Meredith Martin and Gillian Weiss* — 153

11	A Turk in the Hall of Mirrors *David Maskill*	177
12	Cornelis Hop (1685–1762), Dutch Ambassador to the Court of Louis XV *Daniëlle Kisluk-Grosheide*	193

Part IV Versailles Now

13	Melancholy, Nostalgia, Dreams: Adventures in the *Grand Cimetière Magique* Mark Ledbury	215
14	American Versailles: From the Gilded Age to Generation Wealth *Robert Wellington*	237

Bibliography	257
Index	281

List of Figures

1.1	Regia Versaliarum [royal palace of Versailles]. Bronze medal, struck c. 1700. 41mm. Collection, Robert Wellington. Photo: Author	2
2.1	Detail of the "quartier du Louvre" from Louis Bretez, *Plan de Paris dessiné et gravé sous les ordres de Michel-Étienne Turgot* (1739). Image in the public domain	15
2.2	Frontispiece to Étienne La Font de Saint Yenne, *L'Ombre du Grand Colbert, Le Louvre, & la Ville de Paris, Dialogue* (n.p., 1752). Designed by Étienne La Font de Saint Yenne; drawn by Charles Eisen; engraved by Jacques-Philippe Le Bas. Paris: Bibliothèque Nationale de France. Photo: BNF	22
2.3	Pierre-Antoine Demachy, *Clearing the Colonnade of the Louvre*, c. 1764, oil on canvas, 41 × 52 cm. Paris: Musée Carnavalet. Image in the public domain	24
2.4	Pierre-Antoine Demachy, *Clearing the Colonnade of the Louvre*, 1772, oil on canvas, 76 × 131 cm. Paris: Musée du Louvre. Image in the public domain	25
2.5	Two maps showing the home addresses of the Academy's artists in 1680 and 1780, respectively. Maps courtesy of Hannah Williams and Chris Sparks, *Artists in Paris: Mapping the 18th-Century Art World*, www.artistsinparis.org (accessed January 8, 2018)	28
3.1	Charles Le Brun, *Order Restored to the National Finances* (detail), c. 1679, black chalk whitened with white chalk, squared with red chalk, outlines incised, on paper, 235 × 208.5 cm, Paris, Musée du Louvre, Département des Arts graphiques, inv. 29950. Image in the public domain	35
3.2	Charles Le Brun, *Study for the Arcs of the Apollo Gallery*, c. 1663, black chalk on paper, 42.7 × 56.9 cm, Paris, Musée du Louvre, Département des Arts graphiques, inv. 29484 verso. Image in the public domain	37
3.3	Charles Le Brun, *Minerva and Three Muses*, c. 1674, oil on canvas, 40.3 × 55.3 cm, Paris, Galerie Éric Coatalem. Photo: Author	39

3.4 Charles Le Brun, *Erato, Muse of Lyric Poetry*, c. 1674, black chalk whitened with white chalk, outlines incised, on paper, 141 × 92.5 cm, Paris, Musée du Louvre, Département des Arts graphiques, inv. 29847/1. Image in the public domain 41

3.5 Étienne Baudet, *Staircase of the Ambassadors* (reversed detail), c. 1679–83, engraving, Versailles, Musée national du Château de Versailles et de Trianon. Photo: RMN 42

4.1 Workshop of Charles Le Brun (1619–90), Plan du premier parterre d'eau de Versailles, black chalk, black ink, pen, wash with gray and watercolor on paper, 63 × 72cm, c. 1674, Paris: Musée du Louvre, Cabinet des Dessins, INV30326-recto. Photo: RMN 49

4.2 Workshop of Charles Le Brun (1619–90), Vue en perspective du premier parterre d'Eau de Versailles, black chalk, brown ink, pen and watercolor on paper, 15.3 × 52.7cm, c.1674, Paris: Musée du Louvre, Cabinet des Dessins, INV30321-recto. Image in the public domain 49

4.3 Charles Le Brun, *Les Quatre Complexions de l'Homme*, black chalk, gray wash on cream paper:, c. 1674, Paris: Musée du Louvre, Cabinet des Dessins. Dépôt Versailles, Châteaux de Versailles et de Trianon. Photo: RMN 51

4.4 Matthieu Lespagnandelle (1616–89), *Le Flegmatique* (*Les Quatre Complexions de l'Homme*), marble, c. 1674, Versailles, Châteaux de Versailles et de Trianon. Image in the public domain. Photo: Myrabella/Wikimedia Commons 52

5.1 Jean Lepautre, View of the interior of the Grotto of Versailles (plate 2). Etching, 1676. Image Courtesy of the Getty Research Institute 64

5.2 Jean Lepautre, View of the interior of the Grotto of Versailles (plate 7). Etching, 1676. Image Courtesy of the Getty Research Institute 66

5.3 Jean Lepautre, Pillar ornamented with seashells and rocks (plate 9). Etching, engraving, and drypoint, 1673. Image Courtesy of the Getty Research Institute 66

5.4 Conch Shell, detail of Figure 5.3 68

5.5 Étienne Picart after G. Marsy and B. Marsy, *Horses of Apollo Tended by Tritons* (plate 17). Engraving and etching, 1675. Image Courtesy of the Getty Research Institute 68

5.6 Horse and Niche, detail of Figure 5.5 69

List of Figures

6.1	Sèvres Porcelain Manufactory. Part of the Cameo service, 1778–9, State Hermitage, St Petersburg. Image in the public domain	78
6.2	Vincent Chapelle, *Le nouveau cuisinier royal et bourgeois* … in François Massialot (1660–1733). Paris: La Veuve Prudhomme, 1742. Image courtesy of the University of Utah Libraries	81
6.3	Pierre Aveline, l'ancien, (*c.* 1656–1722) *Entrée du Trianon de Porcelaine*, etching/engraving, in *Recueil de 58 planches vues de Trianon et de Versailles c.* 1690 GR104. Photo: Château de Versailles, Dist. RMN-Grand Palais/Christophe Fouin	83
6.4	*Manufacture royale de Sèvres. Façade de la cour royale*. Archives de la Manufacture. 2012.1.1637. Photo: RMN-Grand Palais (Sèvres, Cité de la céramique)/Martine Beck-Coppola	88
7.1	Nicolas Bonnart, *Habit d'Espée en Esté*, hand-colored engraving on paper, *c.* 1678, Los Angeles, Los Angeles County Museum of Art (M.2002.57.34). Image in the public domain	96
7.2	Charles Simonneau after Antoine Benoist, *Portraits de Louis le Grand gravés suivant ses differents âges MDCCIV* [1704]. Text by the poet Étienne Pavillon. Engraving, 1704, Princeton University, Graphic Arts Collection. Image in the public domain	97
7.3	*Le Perruquier Barbier* engraving by R. Bénard after J.R. Lucotte, 1762. London, Wellcome Collection. Photo: Creative Commons license CC-BY	97
7.4	Georges Jacob and J-B.S Rode, *Chaise de toilette, c.* 1787, carved beech; caning; modern silk Velvet upholstery J. Paul Getty Museum, inv. 72.DA.51. Image in the public domain	101
7.5	Jean-Baptiste Gautier-Dagoty, *Marie-Antoinette Playing the Harp in Her Room at Versailles*, gouache, *c.* 1777, Versailles, Châteaux de Versailles et de Trianon. Photo: Art Resource	104
8.1	*Seuccession [sic] du Roy Louis XV à la couronne de France et de Navarre le 1er Septembre 1715 sous la Regence de Monseigneur le Duc d'Orléans*. 1715. Paris, Bibliothèque Nationale de France. Photo: BNF	113
8.2	*Les premiers hommages rendus à sa majesté Louis XV par son eminence Monseigneur le cardinal de Noailles, présenté par Monseigneur le duc d'Orléans, regent du royaume, à Versailles le 1er Septembre 1715*. 1715. Paris, Bibliothèque Nationale de France. Photo: BNF	114

8.3	*Le roi Louis XV allant au parlement tenir son lit de justice le XII Septembre 1715* (detail). 1715. Paris, Bibliothèque Nationale de France. Photo: BNF	115
8.4	French School. *Madame de Ventadour with Louis XIV and His Heirs*. 1715–22. London, The Wallace Collection, P122. Image in the public domain	117
8.5	Charles-Nicolas Cochin, *Death of Louis XIV*. From *L'Histoire de Louis XV par les Medailles* 1753. Etching (cropped to image), Châteaux de Versailles et de Trianon. Photo: RMN	121
9.1	Karl Anton Hickel, *Portrait of the princesse de Lamballe*, 1788, oil on canvas, Vienna, Liechtenstein, The Princely Collections. © 2018 Liechtenstein, The Princely Collections, Vaduz-Vienna/SCALA, Florence. Photo: SCALA, Florence	130
9.2	The *Pavillon de la Surintendance* on the *rue de l'indépendance Américaine*, with the marked sections numbered 1 and 2 indicating the location of the princesse de Lamballe's first and second apartments, respectively. Photo: Author	132
9.3	Floorplan of the princesse de Lamballe's first apartment at Versailles in 1766, with the *entresols* flaps lifted. Paris, Archives Nationales. Image in the public domain	133
9.4	André-Charles Boulle, *bureau plat* from the princesse de Lamballe's *cabinet de compagnie* in her first apartment at Versailles, c. 1710, rosewood (palissandre), gilt-bronze, and black morocco leather. Paris, Archives Nationales. Photo: Author	136
9.5	Jean-Baptiste Sené, lyre-backed chair from the princesse de Lamballe's *salon de compagnie* in her second and third apartments at Versailles, 1787, mahogany and velvet. Private collection. Photo: Daguerre, Paris	138
9.6	*Elévation d'un projet de galerie à la suite de Madame la Princesse de Lamballe*, 1785, Paris, Archives Nationales. Image in the public domain	140
9.7	The garden façade of the *Aile du Midi* overlooking the *Parterre du Midi*, with the marked section indicating the location of the princesse de Lamballe's third apartment. Photo: Author	142
9.8.	Plan of the Apartment of the princesse de Lamballe in the *Aile du Midi*, Paris, Archives Nationales. Photo: Image in the public domain	143

List of Figures

10.1 Jacques Le Pautre (after Jean Bérain), Ballroom at Court during Carnival, 1683, published in *Mercure galant*, March 1683, p. 242, etching and engraving. Paris, Bibliothèque Nationale de France, Hennin 5282. Photo: BNF — 154

10.2 Henri Bonnart (publisher), *The Glorious Actions of the Duc of Bavaria Presented to His Sister Madame La Dauphine*, almanac print for 1688, etching and engraving. Paris, Bibliothèque Nationale de France, Hennin 5602. Photo: BNF — 161

10.3 Anonymous, *Louis XIV Followed by the Grand Dauphin Passing on Horseback in Front of the Thetis Grotto at Versailles*, oil on canvas, c. 1680–4. Versailles, Châteaux de Versailles et de Trianon. Photo: RMN/Art Resource, NY — 162

10.4 François de Troy, *Charlotte-Elisabeth de Bavière, Princesse Palatine, Duchesse d'Orléans*, 1680, oil on canvas, Versailles, Châteaux de Versailles et de Trianon. Photo: RMN/Art Resource, NY — 163

10.5 Henri Bonnart, *Dame*, from *Recueil des modes de la cour de France*, 1677, hand-colored engraving. Los Angeles, Los Angeles County Museum of Art. Image in the public domain — 164

10.6 Nicolas Arnoult, *Madame la Princesse de Conty douairière* [c. 1695], reprinted in *Recueil des modes*, 4 vol. (Paris: Menus-Plaisirs du roi, c. 1750). Engraving. Paris, Bibliotheque Nationale de France, Cabinet des estampes, RES-926 (8). Photo: BNF — 164

11.1 Charles Nicolas Cochin, *The Reception by Louis XV of Saïd Méhémet Pacha in the Grand Gallery at Versailles*, c. 1744–5, pencil and wash on vellum. Paris, Louvre, Cabinet des dessins. Reversed horizontally. Image in the public domain — 178

11.2 Unknown draughtsman, *Plan of the Hall of Mirrors, the Salons of Peace and War for the Audience of the Turkish Ambassador in 1742*, detail showing the new arrangement for the 1742 audience overlaying the earlier plan for the audience of the ambassador of the Shah of Persia in 1715, pen, ink, and wash on paper. Paris: Archives Nationales (CP/O/1/1772 dossier 2, no. 4). Image in the public domain — 179

11.3 Anon., *Audience Given by King Louis XV to Mehmed Çelebi Efendi, Ambassador of Sultan Achmet III, March 16, 1721, at the Tuileries Palace*. Etching and engraving. Paris, Bibliothèque Nationale de France. Photo: BNF — 181

11.4	Detail of Figure 11.1	182
11.5	Jacques André Joseph Aved, *Portrait of Mehmed Saïd Efendi*, 1742, oil on canvas. Versailles: Musée national des Châteaux de Versailles et de Trianon, MV 3716. Photo: RMN	183
11.6	Detail of Figure 11.5	185
11.7	Benjamin Duvivier after Edme Bouchardon, reverse of a bronze medal commemorating the Turkish embassy of 1742, *c.* 1760, bronze. Private collection. Photo: Author	188
12.1	House built for Jacob Hop at Herengracht 605, Amsterdam (façade altered in 1739; now the Willet-Holthuysen Museum). Photo: Author	194
12.2	Carriage ordered by the Count of Ribeira Grande for his official audience at Versailles, 1715, painted and gilded wood, metal, velvet, tortoiseshell, and brass. 240 × 370 × 740 cm. Museu Nacional dos Coches, Lisbon V0007. Photo: DGCP/ADF	196
12.3	Adolf van der Laan (1684–1755), *The Formal Entry of Cornelis Hop into Paris*, *c.* 1719–20, ink on paper, 13.7 × 18.6 cm. Amsterdam, Rijksmuseum, RP-T-00-1741. Image in the public domain	197
12.4	Louis Michel Dumesnil (1663?–1739), *The Formal Audience of Cornelis Hop at the Court of Louis XV*, *c.* 1720–9, oil on canvas. 104.5 × 163 cm. Amsterdam, Rijksmuseum. On loan from the Koninklijk Oudheidkundig Genootschap SK-C-512. Image in the public domain	198
12.5	Simon Fokke (1712–84), *The Formal Audience of Cornelis Hop at the Court of Louis XV*, *c.* 1747–59, etching. 18.5 × 28.5 cm. Private collection. Photo: Author	199
12.6	Snuffbox with Miniature Portraits of Louis XV and Marie Leszczyńska, Box by Daniel Govaers (active 1717–*c.* 54); Miniature portraits: Attributed to Jean-Baptiste Massé (1687–1767). 1725–6, gold, diamonds, enamel, and tortoiseshell. 3 × 8.5 × 6.5 cm. Paris: Musée du Louvre, Département des Objets d'Art OA 10670. Image in the public domain	206
13.1	Photograph of the Installation of Jeff Koons, *Split Rocker*, in Versailles: Photo, Jean Marc Fondeur, Flickr, Creative Commons License CC-BY-SA	227

13.2	Installation photograph of the Versailles exhibition of Takahashi Murakami, *Flower Matango, 2001–6*, fiberglass, iron, oil, and acrylic paint, 315 × 204.7 × 263 cm. Photo: Dimitry B/Flickr, Creative Commons License CC-BY-SA	229
13.3	Joana Vasconcelos, *Marilyn (PA)*, 2011. Pans and lids made of stainless steel, cement (2×) 290 × 157 × 410 cm. Collection of the artist; Courtesy Nathalie Obadia Gallery, Paris/Brussels and Haunch of Venison, London Work produced with the support of Silampos. Photo: Ben Harvey. Creative Commons License CC-BY-SA	230
13.4	Anish Kapoor, *Dirty Corner*, steel, stone, and concrete, 2015, installation in the park of the Château of Versailles. With graffiti erased. Photo: Fred Romero/Flickr, Creative Commons License CC-BY-SA	231
13.5	Olafur Eliasson, *Fog Assembly*, 2016, View of the installation in the Domaine de Versailles, 2016. Photo: Fred Romero, Flickr, Creative Commons License CC-BY-SA	232
14.1	The apartment of Donald and Melania Trump, Trump Tower, New York. Photo: Sam Horine	238
14.2	Richard Morris Hunt, Elevation of the Marble Staircase, Marble House, Newport. Photo: Gavin Ainsworth	242
14.3	The Palm Court, Plaza Hotel, New York. Photo John Wisniewski. Creative Commons License CC-BY	244
14.4	Atrium, Trump Tower, New York. Photo: Sebastian Bergmann/ Wikimedia Commons: https://commons.wikimedia.org/wiki/File:Trump_Tower_-_the_atrium.jpg	246
14.5	Palm Beach, Florida—March 13: The Donald J. Trump Ballroom at the Mar-A-Lago Club' in Palm Beach where Republican Presidential candidate Donald Trump spoke after the Florida primary, March 13, 2016, in Palm Beach, Florida. Photo by Brooks Kraft/Getty Images	250

Notes on Contributors

Kimberly Chrisman-Campbell is a fashion historian, curator, and journalist based in Los Angeles, CA. She is a former Andrew W. Mellon Foundation Postdoctoral Curatorial Fellow in French Art at The Huntington Library, Art Museum, and Botanical Gardens and Research Scholar in Costume and Textiles at the Los Angeles County Museum of Art. She is the author of *Fashion Victims: Dress at the Court of Louis XVI and Marie-Antoinette*, *Worn on This Day: The Clothes That Made History* and *The Way We Wed: A Global History of Wedding Fashion*. She is working on a cultural history of hair in the eighteenth-century Atlantic world.

Bénédicte Gady is a curator at the Musée des Arts Décoratifs, Paris. Gady's work has focussed on Louis XIV's first painter, Charles Le Brun, and she has written widely about, and curated many exhibitions on, the topic of this painter's work, most recently the exhibition Charles Le Brun at Louvre Lens in 2016—the first major retrospective of the artist's work to be held in over forty years. Bénédicte's prize-winning monograph, *L'ascension de Charles Le Brun. Liens sociaux et production artistique*, was published in 2010.

Sarah Grant has worked at the V&A since 2006. Her various exhibitions include: The Neoclassical vision of Ennemond-Alexandre Petitot in 2015, Fashion Fantasies: Fashion plates and caricatures 1760–1920 and Modern Masters: Matisse, Picasso, Dali and Warhol, both 2010. Her monograph, *Female Portraiture and Patronage in Marie Antoinette's Court: The Princesse de Lamballe*, was published by Routledge in 2018.

Mimi Hellman is Charlotte Lamson Clarke '53 Chair in Art History at Skidmore College (Saratoga Springs, New York). Her scholarship explores the interplay of design, visuality, and social formation in eighteenth-century France, especially in domestic interiors. Publications include essays in *Taking Shape: Finding Sculpture in the Decorative Arts*; *The Cultural Aesthetics of Eighteenth-Century Porcelain*; *Paris: Life & Luxury in the Eighteenth Century*; *Interiors and Interiority*; and *Body Narratives: Motion and Emotion in the French Enlightenment*.

Daniëlle Kisluk-Grosheide is Henry R. Kravis Curator in the Department of European Sculpture and Decorative Arts at The Metropolitan Museum of Art, New York. With Bertrand Rondot, she was the organizer of the exhibition Visitors to Versailles: From Louis XIV to the French Revolution, held at Versailles and at The Met in 2017/2018, and editor of the catalogue. She has written extensively about various aspects of the decorative arts ranging from the seventeenth-century panels inlaid with mother-of-pearl by the Amsterdam artist Dirck van Rijswijck to a pair of nineteenth-century candelabra from the famous surtout de table of Ferdinand Philippe, duc d'Orléans.

Florian Knothe teaches the history of decorative arts in the 17th and 18th century with particular focus on the social and historic importance of royal French manufacture. He has long been interested in the early-modern fascination with Chinoiserie and the way royal workshops and smaller private enterprises helped to create and cater to this long-lasting fashion. Florian worked at The Metropolitan Museum of Art focusing on European Sculpture and Decorative Arts, and on European and East Asian glass at The Corning Museum of Glass, before his current position as Director of the University Museum and Art Gallery at HKU.

Mark Ledbury is Power Professor of Art History and Visual Culture, and Director of the Power Institute at the University of Sydney. His research mostly concerns eighteenth century European art, with a focus on histories of genres, and on theatre-arts relationships. He is the author of *Sedaine, Greuze and the Boundaries of Genre* (Oxford, 2000), *James Northcote, History Painting and the Fables* (New Haven, 2014) and the author and editor of books and articles that explore the historiography of art. At the Power Institute, he convenes programmes and research projects that explore the diversity, range and depth of visual art, and the global reach of its histories.

Matthew Martin is Lecturer in Art History and Curatorship in the University of Melbourne. He was formerly Curator of International Decorative Arts in the National Gallery of Victoria, Melbourne. His research interests include the cultural history of eighteenth-century European porcelain, art collecting and patronage amongst eighteenth-century English recusant elites, and the collecting of eighteenth-century art in twentieth-century Australia.

Meredith Martin is associate professor of art history at New York University. With Gillian Weiss, she has written *The Sun King at Sea: Maritime Art and Galley Slavery in Louis XIV's France*, forthcoming from the Getty Research Institute, and she is the author of *Dairy Queens: The Politics of Pastoral Architecture from Catherine de' Medici to Marie-Antoinette* (2011), and a co-editor of *Objects in Motion in the Early Modern World* (2015). Martin is co-curating an exhibition about the Mississippi and South Sea Bubbles that will open at the NYPL in 2021. She is a founding editor of *Journal18* (www.journal18.org).

Louis Marchesano heads the Department of Prints, Drawings, and Photographs at the Philadelphia Museum of Art. His publications include *A Kingdom of Images: French Prints in the Age of Louis XIV* (as contributing editor), *The Enduring Burin in Early Nineteenth Century Paris*, and *Käthe Kollwitz: Prints, Process, Politics*.

David Maskill studied at the Courtauld Institute of Art and then took up a position as a senior lecturer in the art history programme at Victoria University of Wellington, New Zealand from 1993 to 2019. He is a specialist in French art of the eighteenth century and the history of prints. He has published his research in these areas in *Print Quarterly*, *Dossier de l'art*, *Journal18*, and the *Melbourne Art Journal*.

Gillian Weiss is associate professor of history at Case Western Reserve University. With Meredith Martin, she is the author of *The Sun King at Sea: Maritime Art and Galley Slavery in Louis XIV's France*, forthcoming from the Getty Research Institute. Her monograph, *Captives and Corsairs: France and Slavery in the Early Modern Mediterranean*, was published by Stanford University Press in 2011 and in French translation by Anacharsis in 2014. She also co-edited a special issue of French History on "France and the Early Modern Mediterranean". (2015).

Robert Wellington is Senior Lecturer and Australian Research Council, Discovery Early Career Research Fellow at the Centre for Art History and Art Theory, Australian National University. He is an art historian with a special interest in the role of material culture in history making and cross-cultural exchange at the Court of Louis XIV. He is a member of the advisory panel to the Bloomsbury Academic book series, *The Material Culture of Art and Design*. His monograph, *Antiquarianism and the visual histories of Louis XIV: Artifacts for a future past*, was published by Ashgate in 2015.

Hannah Williams is Lecturer in the History of Art in the School of History at Queen Mary University of London. A specialist in French visual and material culture of the long eighteenth century, she has particular research interests in social, urban, and religious histories of the Paris art world. She is the author of *Académie Royale: A History in Portraits* (2015), creator of *Artists in Paris: Mapping the Eighteenth-Century Art World* (www.artistsinparis.org), and co-author with Katie Scott of *Artists' Things: Lost Property from Eighteenth-Century France* (forthcoming). She is founding co-editor-in-chief of *Journal18*.

Acknowledgments

Our thanks to Dr Gerard Vaughan and our colleagues at the National Gallery of Australia (NGA) for their generous collaboration with the Australian National University (ANU), and the University of Sydney for the conference from which the chapters in this volume were first presented.

A special thanks to co-organizers of the conference, especially Dr Lucina Ward, co-curator of the exhibition *Versailles: Treasures from the Palace* (December 9– April 17, 2017) which provided the occasion to gather such an exciting group of international scholars in Canberra for that event. Lucina was a wonderful advocate for the conference and pleasure to work with. We also acknowledge the tremendous efforts of Jessica Ausserlechner and Alex Burchmore who were responsible for the logistics of the conference, and without whom that event and this publication would not have come about.

For their help in the publication of this volume, we thank our original commissioning editor Margaret Michniewicz, series editor Prof. Michael Yonan, and the members of the editorial board for the Material Culture of Art and Design series. Special thanks to April Peake, James Thompson, Frances Arnold, and the team at Bloomsbury Publishing. Thanks also due to all of the collections and photographers who made their work available to illustrate this book.

Our thanks to Professor Will Christie, who, as acting Head of the Research School for Humanities and Arts, and the Humanities Research Centre at ANU, made funds from both of those bodies for the conference. Thanks to the Power Institute at the University of Sydney, the ANU College of Arts and Social Sciences, and the ANU Centre for European Studies, for their financial support, and particularly Mark Fletcher at the ANU CASS research office. Thanks also to our colleagues at the ANU French Research Cluster for their ongoing support.

Mark Ledbury and Robert Wellington.

1

Enduring Versailles

Mark Ledbury and Robert Wellington

The palace of Versailles holds a special place in the collective imagination in the twenty-first century, perhaps more than it ever did when it was first built as a modest hunting lodge by Louis XIII, and then expanded in a seemingly endless building campaign from the 1660s on. What is it that brings the nearly 10 million local and international visitors to palace of Versailles and its domains each year? What does the average visitor hope to find? When is the Versailles of our imagination? Do we imagine the palace in the lavish heyday of the Sun King, or at the melancholy end of the Bourbon regime in the last years of Louis XVI and Marie-Antoinette?

The question, "when is Versailles?" even perplexed those who were responsible for the first phases of expansion that made it the palace of Louis XIV and the center of French government. The first medal to commemorate Versailles was struck in 1687. It carried the inscription: COLVIT MAGIS OMNIBVS VNAM [revered above all others], words taken from Virgil, to indicate the king's preference for this palace.[1] Confusingly, the date on the second Versailles medal (Figure 1.1, 1680) does not record the year that it was struck.[2] Rather, the decision was taken to provide the earlier date of 1680 as this was "close to the year when this palace reached its perfection."[3] The continual renovations of Versailles throughout the reign of Louis XIV must have posed a challenge to the *Petite Académie* who designed this medal for where to place the palace within the history of Louis XIV's reign.

That problem was redoubled when the Louis XV chose to return to Versailles in 1722 after spending much of his minority based in Paris and under the influence of his great uncle, the regent Philippe II d'Orléans. The palace and its domains saw many phases of expansion, destruction, and adaptation for

Figure 1.1 Regia Versaliarum [royal palace of Versailles]. Bronze medal, struck *c.* 1700. 41 mm. Collection, Robert Wellington. Photo: Author.

the next seven decades until the last days of the Bourbons at Versailles when a coercive Revolutionary crowd forced Louis XVI and Marie-Antoinette to return to Paris. The nineteenth century would bring a new era for the palace too, as, successively, Versailles was physically reshaped as a museum of French history under Louis-Philippe (1830–48). That tendency was reinforced under the Second Empire by the conversion of the Trianons to museological purposes—the Petit Trianon assuming its status as shrine to Marie-Antoinette in 1867—and by new commissions of paintings celebrating France's role in the Crimean War and the Mexican Wars, among others. While the 1850s saw magnificent state occasions (such as the reception of Queen Victoria in 1855) it was only really at the turbulent and violent end of the Second Empire that Versailles assumed a revived political significance. In September 1870, Prussian troops took the town of Versailles, and it became the headquarters of the third army and eventually of Wilhelm I, and one of the bases from which the crushing siege of Paris was planned and executed. The palace was closed to the public and for a time, the Hall of Mirrors became a military hospital. Versailles was the site of negotiations for the armistice in January/February 1871, and the Hall of Mirrors was once again given back its splendor, deliberately and vengefully chosen as the site of the quasi-sacral proclamation by Bismarck of Wilhelm I as emperor of a unified Germany (complete with Te Deum) on January 18, 1871. That momentous year also saw Adolphe Thiers (1797–1877) move the National Assembly and government (in Bordeaux during the conflict) to Versailles, and thus once again, politics jostled display, machinations interrupted museology at the palace, and the Revolutionary government in Paris again attempted a march on Versailles in April 1871. The bloodshed that surrounded this effort and the intense civil war of the next few months would lead to the end of empire and the foundation of the Third Republic. The new National Assembly met in the former Royal Opera House in the palace from 1871 to 1875. After the creation of the Senate, it moved to what is still known as the Congress Chamber (the only place in France where the Président de la République can now meet both houses of Parliament) in the South Wing. Resonant symbolic politics erupted sporadically in Versailles, as vengeful ceremonies recurred after the First World War with the *Treaty of Versailles* imposed on Germany in 1919. The occupation of the Château by the Nazi Regime from 1940 to 1944 was motivated by history rather than military need. The palace of Versailles, then, even as it was remade as a museum, and visited by thousands of curious tourists, continued as a deeply resonant, fraught site of cultural nationalism, of hot and cold war, of ceremonial and actual violence more than one hundred and fifty years after the end of the ancien régime.

The complex politically motivated changes to the physical fabric and the priorities and uses of the *domaine* have been paralleled by those wrought by museological and meteorological interventions in the gardens, and by the shifting priorities of curators and visitors. (We think of the early judgment of Baedeker that outside the Musée d'Histoire de France there was not much to see at Versailles.)[4] The physical changes were forced by storms from the nineteenth century to those of 1990 and 1999; weather events that led to irreplaceable losses of mature trees and plantings, and to comprehensive restoration campaigns of the Trianon and palace gardens.

The first of the great restoration campaigns of the twentieth century was initiated by the American oil tycoon and philanthropist John D. Rockefeller Jr. (1874–1960), after he visited France in 1923, and found many major monuments, including the palace of Versailles, to be in a sorry state following the First World War. Rockefeller's letter to the French President, Raymond Poincaré (1860–1934), promised the extraordinary sum of one million dollars to make essential repairs to Rheims Cathedral, Fontainebleau palace, and the buildings, fountains, and gardens of Versailles.[5] The generosity of the Rockefeller Foundation signals the deep love for the arts of France, and for the palace of Versailles in particular, of wealthy Americans. Tourists from the United States make up about 12 percent of the annual 8 million who visit the palace each year.[6] Indeed, there are two American philanthropic foundations dedicated to raising funds for the palace, The Versailles Foundation and The American Friends of Versailles. Much of the extraordinary efforts made to bring Versailles back to its former glory over the last century have been funded by international private and corporate philanthropy such as these. In more recent times, leaders of the French luxury industry, including Dior, Chanel, and LVMH (Moët Hennessy Louis Vuitton), have funded renovations, no doubt keen to form a brand association with the original emblem of French luxury.

The modern *domaine* comprising the palace of Versailles, the two Trianons, and their parks and gardens, continues to change when new campaigns of restoration are undertaken, and new facilities are provided for the ever-growing lines of visitors that snake around the outer courtyard of the palace. Such changes fuel both fantasies of perfect restoration and debates about reconstruction and revival that have continued in the "golden gates" controversy and other recent initiatives.[7] From Vanderlyn's famous Panorama of the early nineteenth century, a fantasy homage to "Restoration" of the spaces of the *domaine* whose fragments are at the Metropolitan Museum,[8] to Eugène Atget's recasting of the gardens as hybrid of ancient ruin and uncanny geometry,[9] to the sexed-up, mixed-up world of the BBC's oddly successful costume drama, *Versailles*,[10] the *domaine* of Versailles continues to stir imaginative, wayward, passionate reconstruction in and outside France.

The chapters in this volume show that Versailles was not the static creation of one man, but a hugely complex cultural space, a center of power, but also of life, love, anxiety, creation, and an enduring palimpsest of aspirations, desires, and ruptures. The splendor of the Château and the masterpieces of art and design that it contains masks a more complex and sometimes more sordid history of human struggle and achievement, which emerges, like the stench of stagnant and insalubrious water, among the splendid plantings of the Petit Trianon.[11] The case studies presented by the contributors to this book cannot hope to provide a comprehensive account of the Palace of Versailles, the life within its walls, its visitors, and the art and architecture that it has inspired. Indeed, the study of Versailles has a long and ever-expanding history stretching back to the guide books that were first written by Louis XIV's history makers to explain the complex visual program of the palace for its visitors, and for posterity. To be sure, the bibliographic list for palace and its domains would be sufficient to fill a volume of this size alone. What we hope to have achieved here is, however, a book of essays that brings together a new generation of scholars whose work is shifting our perceptions of art, culture, and life at Versailles then and now. This collection of essays showcases fresh and challenging research, and new perspectives on canon-defining works.

The contributors to this book are considered to be among the leading voices providing nuanced and sympathetic accounts of the art and design of the ancien régime. We no longer feel the need to expose hidden (or even explicit) ideologies of royal commissions as our Marxist forebears have done so persuasively. Nor are we committed to hagiographic accounts of a handful of the artist agents who have, in the past, been credited with the design of the palace without sufficiently acknowledging the vast network of collaboration that brought about this extraordinary monument. Likewise, the authors in this volume represent a new international network of collaboration in both Versailles studies, and in the field of global long eighteenth century more broadly. It may not escape the notice of some that our contributors are based around the world, and with the exception of one, mainly outside of France. This came about by chance, more than planning, but nonetheless, can be seen as further evidence of the extraordinary influence of, and fascination for the inhabitants of, Versailles and its domains not only long after its ancien-régime heyday, but well beyond its geographic bounds.

The chapters in this book have been divided into four interconnected parts: "Making the Palace," "Versailles Life," "Outsiders," and "Versailles now." The case studies presented by our authors under those topics are more generally connected through a shared interest in the social history of art and design and, moreover, to an interdisciplinary approach to the study of material culture. The chapters place what would traditionally be called the "fine arts" of painting, sculpture, and architecture in context with other media and cultural expressions such as print, porcelain, furniture, and fashion, to consider the visual culture of Versailles and that shaped lived experience of the palace and its domains past and present. The palace of Versailles became the center of government in 1682, and from that point on became the avatar of French Court society—the conceptual place of the Court, even when the king, his courtiers, and retinue were elsewhere. Indeed, this is how we use the noun "Versailles" in this study. Versailles is not simply a geographical location, the buildings of the palace and its domain, it also functions as a synonym for what Norbert Elias called "the Court society."[12]

In the first part, "Making the Palace," Hannah Williams, Bénédicte Gady, Florian Knothe, and Louis Marchesano provide fascinating insights into the practical and logistic issues relating to the creation and documentation of this enormously complex monument to the Bourbon kings. Williams reminds of the role of "the other palace"—the Louvre—with an unconventional origin story that gets us to think about the Louvre as a machine of artistic production that formed Versailles as a showpiece for French culture. Likewise, Knothe uses the design of the second *parterre d'eau* in the 1680s as a case study to demonstrate the collaborative nature of royal commissions at Versailles and elsewhere, and to dispel the common-held idea that Versailles was the vision of a "dictator of the arts," as Anthony Blunt once-famously called Louis XIV's *premier peintre*, Charles Le Brun.[13] Gady focuses in on Le Brun for her compelling account of the evidence of "serendipity and chance" in his work, to dispel the myth that he was more an administrator than artist, and that this works were the mechanical rendering of a rigidly predetermined design. Gady's study captures the spirit of human endeavor, fallibility, and opportunities grasped that bring two lost (or at least significantly re-designed) *grand décors* of Le Brun to life. Louis Marchesano's meticulous analysis of prints that recreate *Grotto of Thetis* made for the gardens of Versailles in the 1670s but dismantled shortly after when the palace was expanded to accommodate government ministers. Marchesano's technical analysis of Jean Le Pautre and Étienne Picart's *brut pittoresque* technique for these prints reveals that the project to illustrate the marvels of the Sun King's palace was more than simply documentary. It provided its own opportunity for technical innovation that demonstrated the flourishing of the arts under Louis XIV.

The second part of this book, "Versailles Life," explores the *domaine* through the material aspects of lived experience. Matthew Martin's revealing account of the Sèvres manufactory reminds us that the production of royal porcelain was never a financially lucrative exercise, nor was it especially practical. Instead, he encourages us to look upon Sèvres as a form of royal representation, not only substantially subsidized by the Crown, but literally formed from the soil of France. As Martin observes, even after the chaos of 1789, Louis XVI insisted on keeping the Sèvres manufactory running at his own expense—the notion of kingship, it seems was impossible without the material production necessitated by the office of the Crown.

Chrisman-Campbell's intimate and resonant discussion of ancien-régime hair, in its multiplicity of forms, invokes the complexity of the body politics of the French Court and the alertness of Court politics to changes in apparel and bearing that were so vital and nuanced a signal of success and failure, power and servility.

This resonates strongly with Sarah Grant's study of the habits, dwellings, and influence of the Princesse de Lamballe. The researches of William Newton and others have given new impetus to a study of the social and cultural histories of Versailles as a space of lodging. Rather than follow Elias's lead and focus on cultural histories of Court spectacles as manipulative political processes,[14] scholars following Jeroen Duindam and others have placed more emphasis on households and housing. By demonstrating the complex demands and counter-demands for proximity and space in the real estate of the domain, we have gained a deeper understanding of the political and social tensions that pervaded Court life from Louis XIV to the Revolution, (as well as part of a wider history of privilege, venality and waste that made Court life a target of reform-minded thinkers).[15] Even though Lamballe was a powerful, high-ranking courtier, she had to negotiate, and renegotiate the appearance of her apartments. It is fascinating to learn that most of her furniture derived from the Garde-Meuble de la Couronne. The idea that she was at best allowed to select from existing pieces, rather than commission new expensive items, shows her lack of agency as a "taste-maker" at Versailles, in stark contrast to the queen, who regularly commissioned expensive and elaborate pieces from the best makers gives us a fascinating insight into the hierarchy of patronage and display in the palace.

But Lamballe's complex, restricted agency was part of a wider narrative of female agency explored in Mimi Hellman's chapter, "The Politics of Attachment: Visualizing Young Louis XV and his Governess." Hellman finds a compelling story of female agency in Madame de Ventadour, and her kin, who "exercised a distinctive mode of female agency in Court society that shaped her own status and that of her extended family." In some ways the narrative of a shaping, forming of majesty by subtle, aware, and Court-savvy females that Hellman proposes is an antidote to the story we have heard many times of the enforced shaping of courtiers by Bourbon kingship at Versailles. Her attentive exploration of the maneuvers and hierarchies of her role, "shaping exceptional, God-given qualities into properly embodied kingship," brings into the light a role often left obscure or nebulous. It reminds us of the fact that while the right to rule France was supposedly God-given, the role of king, the complexity of obligations, duties and etiquette as well as the exigencies of character were learned, and taught often by surprising and little-known persons, sometimes a long way from Versailles.

The third part comprises of three chapters on "Outsiders" at Versailles, that is, visiting ambassadors, and people of foreign birth at the French Court. As Kimberly Chrisman-Campbell points out, when the duchesse de Chartres evoked her family in her *pouf*, it made reference to her enslaved black attendant. We are reminded how surprisingly frequent slavery was in this domaine where it was deemed not to exist, but black boys were given as gifts. Meredith Martin and Gillian Weiss's paper tackles the pervasive presence of slavery at Versailles through the particular phenomenon of enslaved Muslims in the *domaine* and through ancien-régime society more broadly. They remind us that Versailles's prominent aristocratic inhabitants were "perpetually shadowed by real-life subordinates whose identities have been both preserved and obscured by art." David Maskill discusses an outside presence of a very different status and valence—the ambassador of the Ottoman Court, Mehmed Saïd Pasha, a sophisticated, polyglot courtier whose fluency and familiarity with Versailles and France were as remarkable as his difference. Maskill's chapter culminates in an examination of Aved's portrait of Mehmed Said which argues for the specific agency of the sitter in the creation of a sophisticated and learned self-image. Danielle Kisluk-Grosheide's chapter, "Cornelis Hop (1685–1762), Dutch Ambassador to the Court of Louis XV," focuses on another erudite, and much longer-term ambassadorial presence, and reminds us that the Court was peripatetic and dynamic. Hop documents the return of the Louis XV to Versailles in the 1720s, but his documents are themselves agents in an economy of correspondence and copies that helped build a vision of Versailles for all of Europe.

The last part of the book changes focus from the past to the present to consider "Versailles Now." Mark Ledbury picks up on a famous century-old "Hoax" to examine an element of lived reality in contemporary Versailles and makes the perspicacious observation that contemporary art interventions at the Palace that have been commissioned since 2006 have had the effect of "Trianonisation."

That is to say, the making playful of the once-sober site of royal magnificence at the main palace site. Where the palace of Versailles was once conceived to have a properly museological, representational, and even archival function, the placement of contemporary art within its walls and precincts has the effect of imbuing these spaces with the ludic function of the Trianons. Robert Wellington's chapter moves away from France to North America to challenge the claims made in the popular media that President Donald Trump's Manhattan penthouse and his country club, Mar-A-Lago, were inspired by Louis XIV's Versailles. Instead, he argues that Trump's interior design is better understood through the lens of an American love for the arts of France. He reveals a tradition of the newly rich to signal their social ascension by quoting and collecting the art and design of old-regime France. This one not founded in the philanthropy of the Rockefellers and their like, but in the taste for French grandeur in early American politicians and wealthy industrialists alike. From the decoration of the White House in the early nineteenth century to homes and hotels of the Gilded Age robber barons, it is argued that the pseudo-French palace style that has come to be associated with President Trump echoes established patterns of interior decoration to signal financial success among certain American entrepreneurs.

Of course, a collection such as this can only probe certain moments and examples of a complex continuum of Versailles's existence as structure and community both in and beyond the ancien régime it came to exemplify. We hope, though, to have brought together fresh insights, interpretations, archives, and ways of seeing, and we hope readers of this book will appreciate the lived complexity and long shadow of Versailles, and the arts and imitations it continues to inspire.

Notes

1 *Registre Journal des délibérations et des assemblées de l'Académie Royale des Inscriptions, 1694–1702. Archives et patrimoine historique Institut de France.* MS. 8 vols. GR, in-Fol. mardy 7 Aoust, 1696.

2 The change of design, inscription, and date for this medal was part of the final campaign in 1701 to unify the designs of these medals shortly before publication. *Registre Journal*, Samedy 4 juin, 1701. Académie des inscription et belles-lettres, *Médailles sur les principaux événements du règne de Louis le Grand: avec des explications historique. Par l'Académie Royale des Médailles & des Inscriptions* (Paris: Imprimerie royale, 1702).

3   *Médailles sur les principaux événements du règne de Louis le Grand*, 84.
4   "Notwithstanding its population of 30,000 inhabitants, its extensive Palace, erected in 1660–1710 by Mansard, its gardens, villas, etc., Versailles has little to attract the stranger beyond the incomparable **Musee Historique, founded by Louis Philippe, and occupying an almost interminable suite of apartments in the palace." Karl Baedeker (Firm) (A. Delafontaine, author), *Paris and Northern France: Handbook for Travellers* (Coblenz: K. Baedeker, 1872), 182.
5   Welles Bosworth, "The Rockefeller Donation for the Restoration of Versailles, Fontainebleau, and Rheims," *The American Magazine of Art* 16, no. 11 (1925): 586–90.
6   The figure of 8.1 million visitors to the palace of Versailles in 2018 was cited in *Le Monde*: Xavier Bourgine, "La fréquentation des musées et monuments parisiens poursuit sa hausse en 2018," *Le Monde*, January 15, 2019.
7   On these, see Alexandre Gady, *Versailles: la fabrique d'un chef-d'oeuvre* (Paris; Versailles: Le Passage/Château de Versailles, 2014).
8   "John Vanderlyn's View of Versailles: Spectacle, Landscape, and the Visual Demands of Panorama Painting," *Early Popular Visual Culture* 12, no. 1, accessed November 29, 2018, https://www-tandfonline-com.ezproxy1.library.usyd.edu.au/doi/abs/10.1080/17460654.2013.876922
9   For perspicacious discussion of some of these images, see Geoff Dyer, "Eugene Atget, Mute Witness," *Aperture*, no. 206 (Spring 2012): 66–73.
10 *Versailles* (Created by David Wolstencroft, Simon Mirren. With George Blagden, Alexander Vlahos, Stuart Bowman, Evan Williams, 3 series, 2015–), accessed November 29, 2018, http://www.imdb.com/title/tt3830558/
11 See Joseph-Adrien Le Roi, *De l'état de Versailles Avant 1789* (Versailles: Imprimerie de Aubert, 1871), 38: "D'ailleurs la rivière factice du Petit-Trianon est bordée d'arbres qui y laissent tomber des feuilles; il y croît des plantes qui se putréfient; plus ces arbres et ces plantes prendront d'accroissement, plus la putréfaction en sera considérable, moins les exhalaisons, retenues par les arbres, pourront s'élever dans les chaleurs, et alors les hommes qui habiteront ou se promèneront dans ces jardins délicieux seront plus exposés aux malignes influences des eaux de la rivière."
12 Norbert Elias, *The Court Society*, trans. Edmund Jephcott (New York: Pantheon Books, 1983).
13 Anthony Blunt, *Art and Architecture in France, 1500–1700* (Harmondsworth: Penguin, 1953), 193.
14 Elias, *The Court Society*.
15 Jeroen Duindam, *Vienna and Versailles: The Courts of Europe's Dynastic Rivals, 1550–1780* (Cambridge: Cambridge University Press, 2003); Jeroen Duindam Tülay Artan, and I Metin Kunt, eds, *Royal Courts in Dynastic States and Empires: A Global Perspective* (Leiden: Brill, 2011).

Part One

Making the Palace

2

The Other Palace: Versailles and the Louvre

Hannah Williams

A quick glance through the pages of this book and no-one could be in any doubt about the resounding impact that Versailles had on French artistic production in the second half of the seventeenth century. As hundreds of artists, architects, and artisans were called upon to create the material reality of Louis XIV's vision for his royal palace, France's artistic status in Europe was transformed. Yet it could be argued that Versailles's greatest impact on the French art world came not in its own luxurious and creative interiors, but rather in the space of artistic sociability that emerged because of it, back in Paris, in the old palace that shiny new Versailles left behind. The Louvre had been one of the French monarchy's principal residences since the Middle Ages, but when Louis XIV officially moved the Court to Versailles in 1682, the Parisian palace was left to reinvent itself. What the Louvre became was the dynamic cultural center of the Paris art world: an institutional, proto-museological, and even residential space, where the arts were theorized and practiced, where objects were made and displayed, and where increasingly large numbers of the city's artists came to live and work.

Normally, when the Louvre is mentioned in the context of Versailles's history, it is in the role of catalyst or nemesis. It was, after all, Louis XIV's supposed hatred of the Louvre, and Paris more generally, that drove him out to Versailles in the first place. The Louvre's associations with the turbulence of the Fronde (1648–53), that period of political revolt that destabilized Louis XIV's minority, motivated the king to desert the palace of his youth and create a new seat of royal power just far enough away from the capital to keep his nobles at a distance from their own power bases. And while the Louvre stood as an architectural symbol of the past reigns of his grandfather (Henri IV) and father (Louis XIII), Versailles became a feat of modern design, created to encapsulate the moment of Louis XIV.

Yet whatever the political or symbolic relationship between these two buildings, when it comes to the arts, the connections between Versailles and the Louvre were more symbiotic. During the late seventeenth century and into the eighteenth century, the Louvre transformed into an artistic factory that would furnish Versailles and adorn the French state, while the material needs of Versailles and Louis XIV's reign ensured a steady demand for the Louvre's productions, and a constant coming-and-going of people and objects between the two palaces. While most chapters in this book explore the rich histories of Versailles's creation and its subsequent lives and afterlives, this chapter instead investigates one of its effects, namely, its impact on that "other palace." In doing so, however, it seeks not to force the Louvre into one of its conventional roles in the Versailles narrative, either as "ubiquitous rival" or as "abandoned old toy," but rather to tell a more affirming, if not always glamorous, story of what happened to the Parisian palace. Far from the Louvre's undoing, the Court's removal to Versailles could indeed be seen as the building's making: an act that made space for the Louvre's redefinition as the nation's artistic center, which, given the revolutionary demise of the monarchy a century later, would actually turn out to be a role with much more longevity than that of royal palace. For while Versailles still stands today as a sparkling historical monument to its erstwhile self, unable to be anything other than an ancien-régime palace, the Louvre has lived a more active and evolving life, in different guises, at the heart of the Paris art world.

Becoming the Center of the Art World

Architecturally and socially, the Louvre and Versailles had vastly different experiences in the seventeenth and eighteenth centuries. As the first phase of building began at Versailles in the 1660s and 1670s, construction at the Louvre ground to a halt for the first time since the sixteenth century.[1] The building of Claude Perrault's elegant colonnade at the Louvre's eastern façade, completed between 1667 and 1674, would be the last significant architectural intervention at the Louvre until Napoléon I began his additions at the start of the nineteenth century. As more and more money and creative energy were being poured into the king's vision for Versailles, projected works for the Louvre—much to the disappointment of Jean-Baptiste Colbert (*surintendant général des Bâtiments du Roi*, 1664–83)—were put on hold.[2] And in the 1670s and 1680s, just as Versailles was coming into being as a royal palace, the Louvre was shifting away from this identity. Gradually and then officially discharged from its function as principal royal residence, the Louvre steadily began its new life, replacing royal inhabitants with artistic ones, and swapping political purpose for cultural endeavors.

At this moment at the end of the seventeenth century, the Louvre's association with the arts and even its function as a place of residence for the city's artists was not entirely without precedent. A small number of artists had been living in the Louvre since the reign of Henri IV, the first king to grant homes and studios within the palace's Galerie, the long wing stretching hundreds of meters along the banks of the Seine (Figure 2.1). Inside, the Galerie was divided into twenty-seven separate *logements*, individual multi-storey dwellings connected on some floors by corridors. The earliest inhabitants of these *logements* were more on the artisanal than artistic side: in 1607, Antoine Ferrier, an instrument maker; in 1608, Girard Laurent, a tapestry weaver, and Pierre Dupont, a carpet weaver; and in 1611, Pierre Courtois and Marc Bimby, goldsmiths and enamellers.[3] Soon artists came to join them and, by the reign of Louis XIV, the Galerie had developed into a busy space of artistic sociability, inhabited by many of the people responsible for designing and creating the material world of Versailles,

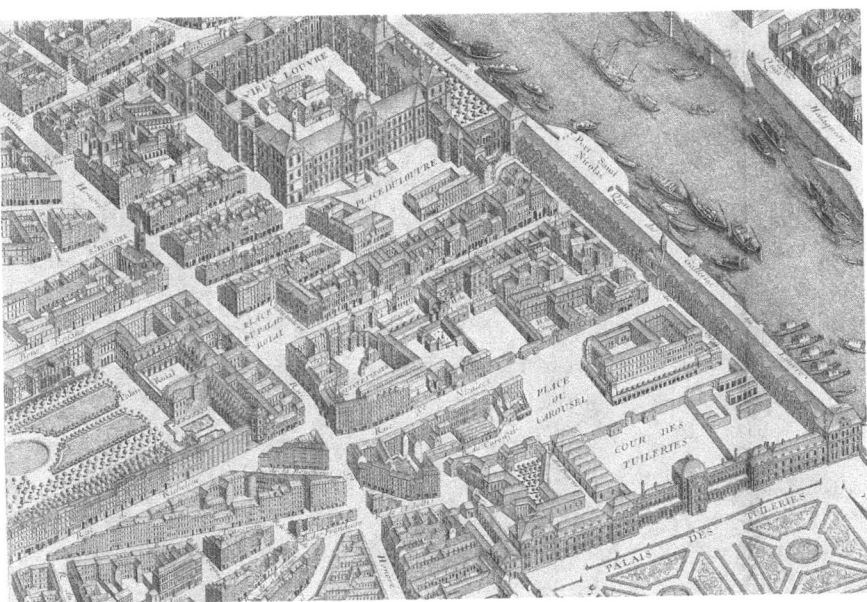

Figure 2.1 Detail of the "quartier du Louvre" from Louis Bretez, *Plan de Paris dessiné et gravé sous les ordres de Michel-Étienne Turgot* (1739). Image in the public domain.

like the sculptors François Girardon and Nicolas Coustou, the painter Antoine Coypel, and the furniture maker André-Charles Boulle.[4] The founding of the *Académie Royale de Peinture et de Sculpture* in 1648 had brought with it an art-theoretical stratification of artistic and artisanal activities in Paris, but here in the Louvre's gallery of studios—where painters, sculptors, and engravers lived side-by-side with clockmakers, cabinetmakers, jewelers, and even the odd gunmaker or optometrist—there was a more practical leveling of these hierarchies.[5] Yet while the Galerie always maintained some diversity, over the eighteenth century, the privilege of being granted a *logement* did increasingly become one enjoyed primarily by artists of the Academy.

One reason for the academicians' dominance in the living spaces of the Galerie was the academies' dominance more generally throughout the palace. After the removal of the Court to Versailles, many rooms and apartments within the main palace were given over to the royal institutions devoted to various cultural pursuits. The *Académie française*, the literary academy and bastion of the French language, had been the first to move into the palace in 1672, but in the 1680s and 1690s it was joined by the rest. The Académie des Inscriptions et Belles Lettres, responsible for composing the text for all the king's monuments and medals, took up residence in 1685; the *Académie de Peinture et de Sculpture* and the *Académie d'Architecture* were granted space in 1692; and then the Académie des Sciences arrived in 1699.[6] Gathered together into a single building, the royal academies effected the Louvre's evolution into a kind of state *Kulturforum*—a space dedicated to intellectual, artistic, and cultural pursuits.

Over the course of the eighteenth century, the Louvre's diverse individual and institutional residents served to cement the building's artistic identity ever firmer. By the time Jacques-François Blondel made his plans and descriptions of the palace for *Architecture Françoise* in the 1750s, there were few spaces within the Louvre that were not given over to some kind of cultural purpose.[7] By this point, artists were no longer just living in the Galerie, but also rubbed shoulders with the academies in the main palace. Among those artists with homes and studios in the main wings of the Louvre were François Boucher, Jean-Baptiste Pigalle, Étienne-Maurice Falconet, and Edmé Bouchardon. The building also accommodated some more practical cultural institutions, like the Menus-Plaisirs du Roi (the organization responsible for royal spectacles, events, and festivities in the city) and the Imprimerie Royale (the royal printing press). Artists' studios and these institutional workshops were functional spaces of making, characterized by all the activity and mess of artistic production. But the Louvre's neater, museological role—as a space for curating and consuming art—

also had its origins in this earlier period. Long before the French Revolution transformed the Louvre into France's first national museum in 1793, the building had already been home to parts of the royal collections of paintings, drawings, and antiquities.[8] These collections were maintained by members of the academies, and the objects were available for consultation with permission for a select audience of artists and amateurs.[9] From 1737 onward, however, the Louvre also became a space for the entire city to enjoy contemporary art. With the inauguration of the *Académie de Peinture et de Sculpture*'s extremely popular Salon exhibitions, held annually and then biennially in the Louvre's *salon carré*, the palace became the public face of the Paris art world.[10]

The Louvre: Building and Building-Site

Despite the active role that the Louvre came to play in Paris's intellectual and cultural life, and despite the presence of such elite institutions within its corridors, for most of the eighteenth century the building itself was in a fairly dire state. Descriptions of the palace from the time suggest that one of the most abiding characteristics of life in the Louvre was an experience of unrelenting construction; as Louis-Sébastien Mercier quipped, even as late as the 1780s, the Louvre seemed "condemned to be forever unfinished."[11] Life at Versailles was also affected by building works, whether during the initial seventeenth-century constructions (under Louis Le Vau and Jules Hardouin-Mansart), or during later eighteenth-century extensions (under Jacques and Ange-Jacques Gabriel). But while Versailles's building campaigns were intense and active, the experience at the Louvre was one of endless inactivity. During that architectural dead-zone for the Louvre in the eighteenth century, there were no significant developments between 1674, when Perrault's colonnade was finished, and around 1807, when Charles Percier and Pierre Fontaine began the new gallery on the north side to mirror the long Galerie along the Seine. But throughout this time, even the parts of the palace that had been built were not exactly "finished." Some sense of the building's enduring non-finito state is evident on Maurice-Étienne Turgot's *Map of Paris* (Figure 2.1), where two whole sides of the main palace do not have roofs, making the top floor uninhabitable and exposed to the elements. For those living in the palace (like Boucher, who had apartments close to the roofless section), the condition of the interiors must have posed certain challenges to daily life. But outside, the condition of the palace became an issue for everyone in the city.

Unlike Versailles, the Louvre was a problematic sight. From the outset, Versailles was designed to be looked at: whether approached along its grand tree-lined avenues; viewed from the vistas granted by its extensive parterres and formal gardens; or consumed from a distance in topographical plans and views like Pierre Patel's *View of the Château de Versailles and Its Gardens* (1668; Château de Versailles). By contrast, the Louvre was an inner-city palace, whose haphazardly developed architectural elements were completely hemmed in by their urban context. Apart from the irregularly shaped and unimposing Place du Louvre in front of the western façade and a small area of garden along the Seine (see Figure 2.1), the Louvre was otherwise claustrophobically surrounded by a dense neighborhood of streets and buildings. In its urban setting, the Louvre not only lacked any kind of grand approach or vista, but was even denied a clear perimeter, with dependent buildings encroaching upon its very walls. Major urban developments in the nineteenth and twentieth centuries would later raze this area completely, replacing it with the great artery of the rue de Rivoli, the completed symmetrical extensions of the palace, and the expansive Cour Napoléon with I. M. Pei's infamous glass pyramid. But in the eighteenth century, as Turgot's *Map* suggests, this was a heavily populated neighborhood of multi-storey apartment blocks, *hôtels particuliers*, churches, a hospital, a market, other shops and services, with a working river and ports nearby. As a lived space, this neighborhood was the epicenter of Paris's elite art world, but as a material environment, the *quartier* around the Louvre kept the palace hidden in a residential sprawl. This was perhaps nowhere more detrimental than along the eastern façade, where Perrault's great classical colonnade was blocked from view by a jumble of buildings along the rue des Poulies and the rue du Petit Bourbon.

By the middle of the eighteenth century, the state of the Louvre had become a serious concern, not least for the city's intellectuals. Voltaire, for instance, took up the palace's plight in his poem, *On the Louvre*, of 1749.

> Monumens imparfaits de ce siècle vanté,
> Qui sur tous les Beaux Arts a fondé sa mémoire,
> Vous verrai-je toujours, en attestant sa gloire,
> Faire un juste reproche à sa posterité?
>
> Faut-il que l'on s'indigne alors qu'on vous admire,
> Et que les Nations, qui veulent nous braver,
> Fières de nos défauts, soient en droit de nous dire,
> Que nous commençons tout pour ne rien achever?

Sous quels débris honteux, sous quel amas rustique,
On laisse ensevelis ces chef-d'œuvres divins!
Quel barbare a mêlé la bassesse gothique
A toute la grandeur des Grecs & des Romains?

Louvre, Palais pompeux, dont la France s'honore,
Sois digne de ce Roi, ton maître & notre appui;
Embellis ces climats que sa vertu décore,
Et dans tout ton éclat, montre toi comme lui.[12]

[Imperfect monuments to that great century,
Whose prestige was founded upon all the arts,
Will I forever see you, recalling its past glory,
Yet standing as a just reproach to its posterity?

Should those who admire you now be indignant;
And should the nations that try to challenge us,
Mocking our failings, be justified in saying,
That whatever we begin, we never complete?

Under such shameful debris, under such a rustic pile
We leave buried those divine masterpieces!
What barbarian confused gothic crudeness
With all the grandeur of the Greeks and the Romans?

Louvre, splendid palace, reflecting glory on France,
Be worthy of this king, your master and our support,
Render more beautiful the environment that his virtue adorns,
And in all your splendour, show yourself to be like him.]

Decrying the Louvre as an "imperfect monument" to the seventeenth century, Voltaire describes the palace's architectural state as "shameful debris," the entire building standing as a reproach to the posterity of France's *grand siècle*. The *philosophe* calls for action to address the Louvre's pitiful condition and make it worthy of the glory of the king and the nation, lest the palace otherwise serve only as a sign to foreign powers, that whatever great endeavors the French embark upon, they will never manage to bring them to fruition.

In 1752, an updated version of Voltaire's poem appeared in a revised edition of Étienne La Font de Saint Yenne's *L'Ombre du Grand Colbert, Le Louvre, & la Ville de Paris, Dialogue*. The changes Voltaire made to his poem suggest a growing intensity of the Louvre dilemma at this moment. One new couplet expressed outrage at the elevation of temporary buildings right in the middle of the Cour Carré:

> Mais ô! nouvel affront! Quelle coupable audace
> Vient encore avilir ce chef-d'œuvre divin?[13]
>
> [But oh! What new affront! Which audacious culprit
> Has further debased this divine masterpiece?]

Meanwhile in another line, Voltaire calls even more emphatically for the problems to be addressed, making his plea to the Louvre directly—"Sors de l'état honteux où l'univers t'abhorre" [Renounce the sorry state in which you are abhorred by the whole world]—as though the palace itself had the agency to resolve its dire condition.[14] This anthropomorphizing of the Louvre was a principal conceit of La Font de Saint Yenne's book, the rest of which is a provocative treatise bemoaning the demise of the palace, taking the form of a conversation between three characters: the Louvre, the City of Paris, and the Ghost of Jean-Baptiste Colbert (the Louvre's great champion until his death in 1683).

La Font de Saint Yenne's *Dialogue* begins with the Louvre reprimanding Paris for the hard-hearted neglect it has had to endure at the city's hands. Casting Paris in a maternal guise, the palace passionately bewails:

> Le Louvre: O Paris! Ville ingrate! si sensible autrefois à mon élévation, peux-tu l'être aujourd'hui si peu à mes gémissements & à ma douleur? Peux-tu voir mon déplorable état, & me laisser sans consolation & sans espérance? N'es tu plus ma mère?[15]
>
> [The Louvre: Oh Paris! Ungrateful city! At one time so moved by my building, how can you now be so insensitive to my pain and my suffering cries? How can you witness my deplorable state and leave me without consolation or hope? Are you no longer my mother?]

Paris responds to the Louvre's bitter reproaches with promises of reassurance and comfort:

> La Ville: Non, mon fils, je ne t'ai point entièrement oublié, puisque tu me vois accourir à tes cris pour en apprendre le sujet, & soulager ta peine, s'il m'est possible.[16]
>
> [The City: No, my son, I have not completely forgotten you; as you see I hurry towards your cries to learn of their cause & to ease your pain, if I am able.]

Defensively vindicating itself of responsibility for the Louvre's neglect, Paris lays the blame with the Crown ("que puis-je sans les ordres de mon Souverain?" [what could I do without the orders of my king?]), and laments the long-gone days of Colbert, when the Louvre (and Paris's monuments more generally) were a priority for the nation.[17] The Louvre joins the lament with more impassioned cries, this time to its paternal figure:

Le Louvre: O Colbert! ô Colbert! Ministre qui ne fera jamais assez loué ni assez regretté! O mon père! Mon créateur! Ma gloire! La gloire de la France! Où êtes-vous?[18]

[The Louvre: Oh Colbert! Oh Colbert! Minister who was never sufficiently praised or regretted! Oh my father! My creator! My glory! The glory of France! Where are you?]

At which moment, right on cue, the Ghost of Colbert appears ("Oui, c'est moi" [Yes, tis I]), to find the city of Paris unrecognizable in its current "deformed" state ("Eh! Qui êtes-vous?" [Huh! Who are you?]), and to witness incredulously the indignities that have befallen his cherished palace over the decades since his death.[19]

La Font de Saint Yenne's entertaining and emotive treatise, appealing for action on the Louvre's behalf, is encapsulated in the frontispiece he designed for the book, drawn by Charles Eisen and engraved by Jacques-Philippe Le Bas (Figure 2.2). Bringing the *Dialogue* to life, this allegorical scene is set on the rue du Petit Bourbon, with Perrault's colonnade—complete with scaffolding to indicate the ongoing building works—just visible rising up behind a dilapidated street facade of nondescript houses. The City of Paris, the female figure, bows in supplication before a bust of Louis XV, gesturing to the miserable state of the Louvre, "dishonoured" (as La Font de Saint Yenne described it), by the "mass of squalid and shameful buildings" blocking its view.[20] The Louvre, taking anthropomorphized form in the body of Genius, lies in a crumpled heap on the ground, expiring from pain and desperation, crushed by "the weight of insult and humiliation."[21] The third figure, dressed in old-fashioned costume, is the Ghost of Colbert, "by whose care and attention this incomparable monument was built," and who now turns away burying his face in his cloak, unable to bear the vision of what has become of his Louvre.[22]

With the despairing character of Colbert, La Font de Saint Yenne's dialogue in fact evokes the figurative specter of Versailles in this story of the Louvre's demise. After all, Colbert's affection for the Louvre was entirely bound up with his opposition to that other palace. In 1665, when Louis XIV had already spent more than 500,000 écus in two years on Versailles, Colbert wrote to the king

Figure 2.2 Frontispiece to Étienne La Font de Saint Yenne, *L'Ombre du Grand Colbert, Le Louvre, & la Ville de Paris, Dialogue* (n.p., 1752). Designed by Étienne La Font de Saint Yenne; drawn by Charles Eisen; engraved by Jacques-Philippe Le Bas. Paris: Bibliothèque Nationale de France. Photo: BNF.

to implore he reassess his architectural priorities.[23] The minister's advice was direct: the king should cease all spending on Versailles, and commit everything to the completion of the Louvre.[24] Colbert argued that Versailles was a frivolous venture, a building merely for "le plaisir et le divertissement" [pleasure and entertainment], that could never bring the glory that the king properly sought.[25] The Louvre, by contrast, was "assurément le plus superbe palais qu'il y ait au monde et le plus digne de la grandeur de Votre Majesté" [undoubtedly the most superb palace in all the world and the most worthy of your Majesty's greatness], and yet during this same period of excessive expenditure on Versailles, the king had utterly neglected the Louvre and with it his chance for architectural glory.[26] Evidently Colbert vastly underestimated Versailles, which proved the very encapsulation of Louis XIV's power and glory for posterity, but he was right to insist on the palaces' interdependence. The king's choice in favor of Versailles certainly determined the future of the Louvre. And for much of the eighteenth century, that future clearly looked unfairly bleak to many of Paris's residents.

Local Views

Fortunately, the tide turned for the Louvre and those protests by Voltaire and La Font de Saint Yenne eventually proved successful. In 1755, the marquis de Marigny (the new director of the *Bâtiments du Roi*, 1751–73) undertook to demolish the buildings along the colonnade (that "squalid" row visible in the frontispiece).[27] A fairly laborious task, the demolition turned the surrounding neighborhood into a building site throughout the 1750s and 1760s, slowly achieving a transformation that proved a relief for many, but which caught the attention of one inhabitant in particular.

Pierre-Antoine Demachy, an architecture and view painter, represented these mid-century building works around the Louvre on numerous occasions, capturing both the process of the demolition and its effects. Most of these paintings, made in the 1760s and 1770s, are now generically entitled *Clearing the Louvre's Colonnade*, but while they share a subject, each one offers a subtly different engagement of a scene witnessed, interpreted, and re-interpreted over many years.[28] In some, Demachy takes up a position within the construction site itself (Figure 2.3), while in others he views the works from the distance of the street (Figure 2.4). The palace is usually seen emerging majestically behind rubble, and there is often an emphasis on the labor involved in this task, with men

Figure 2.3 Pierre-Antoine Demachy, *Clearing the Colonnade of the Louvre*, c. 1764. Oil on canvas, 41 × 52 cm. Paris: Musée Carnavalet. Image in the public domain.

hammering at walls, pulling on ropes to lower beams, or loading carts with stone to be carried away (some of the activities evident in Figure 2.4). But Demachy's paintings are not naturalistic moments attempting to record or document the process. Instead, they are aestheticizing and historicizing statements about the effects of the Louvre's transformation. In their most extreme form, Demachy can turn this everyday scene of urban development into a fantastical scene of civilization-building (Figure 2.3): construction site rubble becomes broken columns and capitals—the ruins of former times; while the "Parisians" viewing the scene have a decidedly timeless look as they admire this vision of progress—Paris finally emerging as the new Rome.

Demachy was a Louvre local through and through, a long-term inhabitant living in various streets around the *quartier* until eventually, in 1769, he was granted lodgings in the palace itself.[29] Perhaps because he therefore witnessed the Louvre's transformation as both artist and resident, Demachy's paintings often reveal an interest in the palace not only as a monument, but also as a habitually frequented space. His bystanders are not always timeless peasants, but

Figure 2.4 Pierre-Antoine Demachy, *Clearing the Colonnade of the Louvre*, 1772. Oil on canvas, 76 × 131 cm. Paris: Musée du Louvre. Image in the public domain.

sometimes quite realistic city-dwellers (Figure 2.4): locals walking past on their daily passages through the neighborhood, observing and commenting upon the developing works (like the refined couple in the foreground), or ignoring them completely (like the water-carrier struggling through the mid-ground with his heavy load). In other words, Demachy intentionally shows the extraordinary as part of the ordinary. When the inveterate social commentator Mercier described the Louvre a decade later, he noted something similar, claiming that the abiding impression of the palace was a sense of contrast: the Louvre, he said, was a place where "grandeur and misery" existed side-by-side.[30] Mercier, as was his wont, was disgusted by the disjunctions between high and low, but Demachy, the Louvre inhabitant, presented these juxtapositions with more affection and intimacy. In his paintings, the Louvre becomes a place where monumentality meets mundanity, where greatness is framed by the commonplace, where a magnificent colonnade rises up, while someone's washing hangs out to dry across the street (Figure 2.4).

Despite the harmony in Demachy's paintings, for those artists living in the Louvre, palace life was not without its tensions. Having an address in the Louvre did not, for instance, always mean the same thing, as there could be extreme inequality in artists' circumstances. In the probate inventory of Charles-Antoine Coypel's numerous rooms in the Louvre, we find an abundance of luxurious commodities filling every space, from the silk shirts and gold boxes in his bedroom, to the vast quantities of wine and decorated sedan chair in his cellar.[31] Moreover, though unmarried, he nevertheless lived with no less than four servants. These decadent arrangements were a far cry from those of his half cousin, another artist and palace inhabitant. The sculptor Edmé Dumont led an entirely different Louvre lifestyle in a state of utter poverty.[32] Probably living in one of the temporary shacks erected in the middle of the Cour Carré, Dumont's pitiful residence served as both sculpture studio and family home for his wife and four children. A sense of its wretched state is suggested in a letter from the director of the Academy, Jean-Baptiste-Marie Pierre, to the current director of the *Bâtiments du Roi*, the comte d'Angiviller, which described Dumont's home as "[un] bouge" (a hovel), "sans meubles" (with no furniture), and "[un] vray nid à rats" (a true rats' nest).[33]

Within the corridors of the Louvre, where colleagues were neighbors and neighbors were colleagues, proximity no doubt inspired as much collaboration as competition amongst the palace's artistic community. But as in any lived environment, there was always conflict in the Louvre, sometimes for utterly mundane reasons. Demachy, for instance, along with his painter colleagues Hugues Taraval, Charles-Louis Clérisseau, and Louis Durameau, was once the object of an official complaint. A Louvre caretaker wrote to Angiviller to protest that he was finding it impossible to keep the building clean. Despite sweeping twice a week and flushing water through the open "conveniences" daily, his efforts at sanitation were being constantly thwarted by these artists' students, who kept defecating in the corridors and stairwells.[34] Perhaps even worse, their servants were guilty of throwing excrement out the windows of the palace, apparently with significant frequency. In a task seemingly beyond their remits, Angiviller had to ask Pierre, as director of the Academy, to step in and sort out his colleagues' households.

Conclusion: The Louvre in Context

In recent years, the social history of the Louvre has rightly become the subject of deeper research.[35] Our understanding of the Louvre's transformations and its role as a residential space for artists has been richly expanded by this scholarship, but one aspect in particular still warranting further investigation is the impact that this artistic palace had on art-world sociability more broadly. By way of conclusion, this chapter therefore pulls back to take a look at the bigger picture into which the Louvre fits.

Drawing on a largescale digital mapping project exploring Paris's artistic communities, my intention here is to consider the effects of the Louvre—that residential, institutional, and proto-museological artistic center—on the geography and demography of the art world.[36] A comparison of just two maps (Figure 2.5a and 2.5b)—showing the locations of the home addresses of all the Academy's artists in 1680 and 1780, respectively—reveals a telling story of what happened in Paris after the Court moved to Versailles and the Louvre underwent its artistic transformation. In 1680 (Figure 2.5a), before the Court's official departure, the Academy's artists were spread out fairly extensively across the entire city. From the handful of dots plotted on the Louvre, it is clear that artists were, as we know, already living in the palace at this stage, but it was far from a central location. By 1780 (Figure 2.5b), however, the Louvre has become the undeniable epicenter of this artistic community. That earlier dispersal is drastically reduced with the vast majority of the Academy's artists now living in a tiny geographic area, either in or around the palace. Though but a brief snapshot of two moments, there is enough even in these maps to suggest the dramatic reshaping of the Paris art world that occurred following the Court's removal to Versailles and the crucial role taken in that narrative by the Louvre.

Though not an essay concerning Versailles directly, this has been an effort to explore an unintended impact of the palace's creation: namely, how it might be said that Versailles made (or remade) the Louvre. Yet given what the Louvre was actually made into, the late ancien-régime life of this "other palace" is far from irrelevant to discussions of the artistic evolution of Versailles during this period. Despite its conventional narrative roles as Versailles's rival or as its abandoned forebear, the Louvre in fact had a much more intimate relationship with the new palace and a much livelier ongoing existence: as a space given a new identity by the artists of Paris; as a building figuratively and physically saved by becoming the cultural center of France; and as a vibrant neighborhood whose inhabitants—individual and institutional—formed a major part of the story of the making of Versailles.

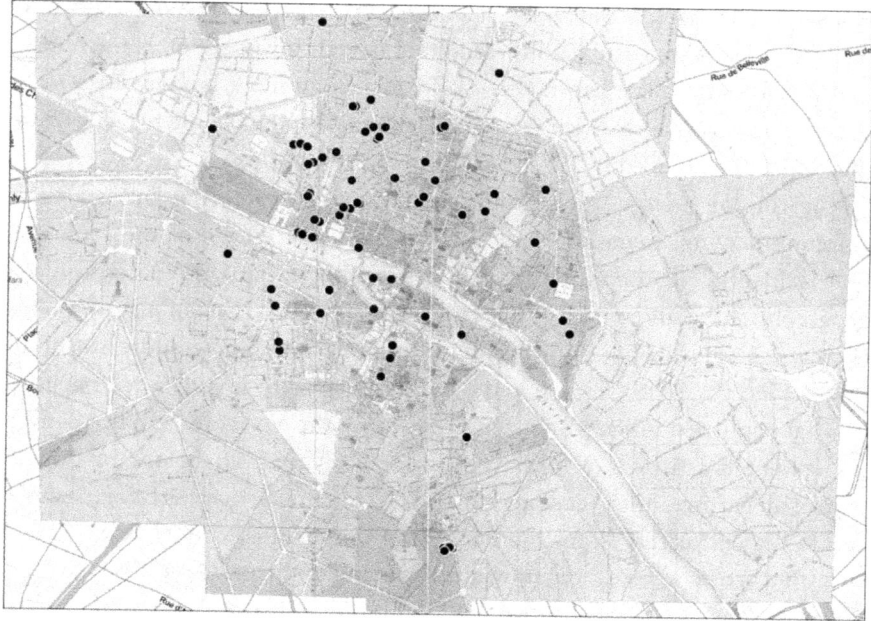

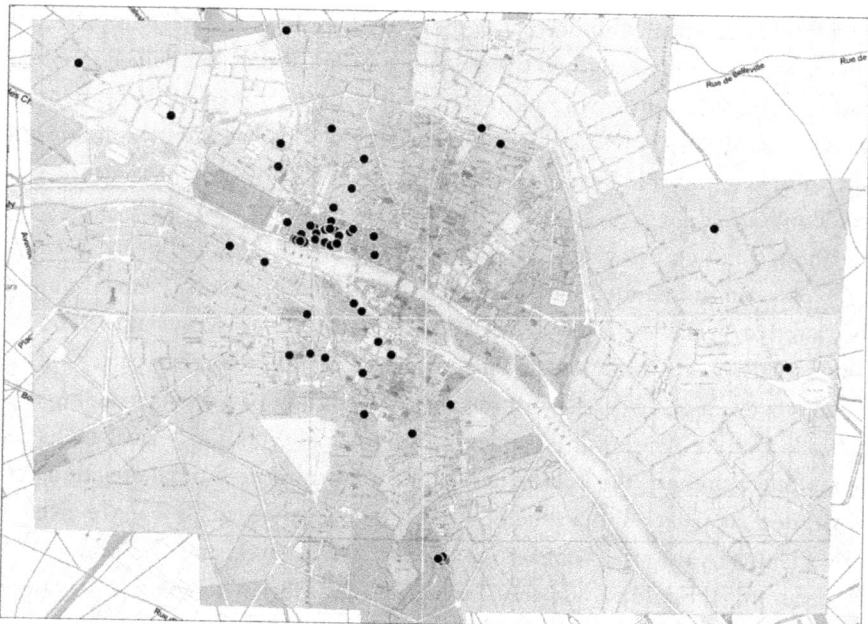

Figure 2.5 Two maps showing the home addresses of the Academy's artists in 1680 and 1780, respectively. Maps courtesy of Hannah Williams and Chris Sparks, *Artists in Paris: Mapping the 18th-Century Art World*, www.artistsinparis.org (accessed January 8, 2018).

Notes

1. For the most recent summary of the Louvre's building phases, see the excellent reconstructions in Guillaume Fonkenell, *Building the Louvre: A Richly Illustrated History* (Paris: Louvre Éditions, 2017).
2. On Colbert's initial resistance to Louis XIV's Versailles project, see Adrian Forty, "Versailles—A Political Theme Park," in *Architecture and the Sites of History: Interpretations of Buildings and Cities*, ed. Iain Borden and David Dunster (New York: Watson Guptill, 1995), 54–5.
3. Jules Guiffrey, "Brevets de logements dans la Galerie du Louvre," in *Nouvelles Archives de l'Art Français* (Paris: Charavay Frères, 1873), 63–4.
4. For artists living in the Louvre's Galerie, see Hannah Williams & Chris Sparks, *Artists in Paris: Mapping the 18th-Century Art World*, www.artistsinparis.org (accessed January 15, 2018).
5. Guiffrey, "Brevets de logements," 63–103. On the Galerie as a space of artistic sociability, see Yvonne Singer-Lecocq, *Quand les artistes logeaient au Louvre 1608–1835* (Paris: Perrin, 1998); and articles in the special issue of *Journal18* on the Louvre, especially David Maskill, "The Neighbor from Hell: André Rouquet's Eviction from the Louvre," *Louvre Local, Journal18* 2 (Fall 2016). Available online: http://www.journal18.org/822
6. For the distribution of the Academies and other residents throughout the Louvre at mid-century, see Jacques-François Blondel, *Architecture Françoise*, 4 vols (Paris: Jombert, 1752–6), 24–39.
7. Blondel, *Architecture Françoise*, vol. 4, 24–39.
8. On the Louvre's transformation into a museum at the end of the century, see Andrew McClellan, *Inventing the Louvre: Art, Politics, and the Origins of the Modern Museum in Eighteenth-Century Paris* (Berkeley: California University Press, 1994).
9. On these curatorial activities, see Esther Bell, "A Curator at the Louvre: Charles Coypel and the Royal Collections," *Louvre Local, Journal18* 2 (2016). Available online: http://www.journal18.org/986
10. For estimations of visitor numbers to the Salons, see Udolpho van de Sandt, "La frequentation des Salons sous l'Ancien Régime, la Révolution et l'Empire," *Revue de l'Art*, 73 (1986): 43–8.
11. Louis-Sébastien Mercier, *Tableau de Paris*, vol. 5 (Amsterdam: n.p., 1782–8), 238.
12. "Vers de M. de Voltaire, sur le Louvre," *Mercure de France* (May 1749), 27–8. With thanks to Gay McAuley for assistance with the translation of this poem.
13. Étienne La Font de Saint Yenne, *L'Ombre du Grand Colbert, le Louvre, et la ville de Paris …, nouvelle édition* (Paris: n.p., 1752), 178.

14 Ibid.
15 Ibid., 2.
16 Ibid., 2–3.
17 Ibid., 6.
18 Ibid., 7.
19 Ibid., 7, 9, 10.
20 "… deshonoré par une multitude de Bâtimens ignobles & indécens qui en ôtent la vûe aux habitants." Ibid., iii–iv.
21 "… le poids de l'insulte & de l'humiliation." Ibid., iv.
22 "… par les soins duquel a été élevé cet incomparable monument." Ibid., iv.
23 Letter from Jean-Baptiste Colbert to Louis XIV, September 28, 1665. *Lettres, instructions et mémoires de Colbert*, ed. Pierre Clément, vol. 5 (Paris: Imprimerie impériale, 1868), 269.
24 Ibid., 270
25 Ibid., 269.
26 Ibid.
27 Discussions regarding the renovation occur throughout the correspondence that year between Marigny and the officers of the *Académie Royale de Peinture et de Sculpture*: *Correspondance de M. de Marigny*, vol. 1, ed. Marc Furcy-Raynaud, *Nouvelles Archives de l'Art Français*, XIX (1903).
28 For a more extended discussion of Demachy's engagement with the Louvre, see Hannah Williams, "Le Louvre de Demachy, le palais et son quartier au XVIIIe siècle," in *Le Témoin méconnu: Pierre-Antoine Demachy, 1723–1807*, exhib. cat. (Versailles: Musée Lambinet, 2014), 28–39.
29 Letter from Marigny to Cochin, March 13, 1769, *Correspondance de M. de Marigny*, vol. 2, ed. Marc Furcy-Raynaud, *Nouvelles Archives de l'Art Français*, XX (1904), 172.
30 Mercier, *Tableau de Paris*, vol. 5, 238.
31 *Inventaire après décès* of Charles-Antoine Coypel, September 25, 1752, Archives nationales: MC LXXVI, 337.
32 Edmé Dumont was the son of Anne-Françoise Coypel, Charles-Antoine Coypel's paternal half aunt.
33 Letter from Pierre to d'Angiviller, September 29, 1775, *Correspondance de M. d'Angiviller*, ed. Marc Furcy-Raynaud, *Nouvelles Archives de l'Art Français*, XXI (1905), 51–2.
34 Letter from Angiviller to Pierre, December 16, 1777, *Correspondance de M. d'Angiviller*, 157.
35 In addition to the works already mentioned throughout this chapter, other recent contributions include Geneviève Bresc-Bautier, Yannick Lintz, Françoise Madrus

and Guillaume Fonkœnell, eds, *Histoire du Louvre*, 3 vols (Paris: Fayard & Louvre Éditions, 2016); David Maskill, "A Good Address: Living at the Louvre in the Eighteenth Century," in *Making Ideas Visible: Essays in Art History from the XVth David Nichol Seminar*, ed. Jennifer Milam (Newark: University of Delaware Press, forthcoming); and Hannah Williams, "Drifting through the Louvre: A Local Guide to the French Academy," in *Eighteenth-Century Art Worlds: Global and Local Geographies of Art*, ed., Stacey Sloboda and Michael Yonan (New York: Bloomsbury, 2019), 171–89.
36 Williams and Sparks, *Artists in Paris* (accessed January 8, 2018).

3

The *Grands Décors* of Charles Le Brun: Between Plan and Serendipity

Bénédicte Gady

This chapter concerns the large-scale painted decorations (*grands décors*) of Versailles by Charles Le Brun.[1] After 1661, Le Brun was almost entirely in the employ of Louis XIV.[2] He was appointed *premier peintre du roi*, director of the Gobelins manufactory, surveyor of the king's drawings and pictures, and he successively held leading roles in the *Académie Royale de Peinture et de Sculpture* as its permanent Chancellor, eventually becoming director in 1683. These positions ensured that Le Brun's hand and style can be found in almost every major royal commission of works of art and furniture for nearly thirty years. So pervasive was this artist's influence that art historian Anthony Blunt went so far as to call Le Brun a "dictator of the arts in France."[3] In the eyes of posterity Le Brun wears two hats: the prolific artist and the efficient project manager, able to successfully direct vast projects and, as Florian Knothe has argued in his chapter for this book, to facilitate collaboration between artists and craftsmen of various expertise.[4] Depending on whether or not they admire his work, art historians have tended to see one or other of these talents—the artistic or the organizational—as the reason that Le Brun came to the attention of Louis XIV and Colbert. The construction of Vaux-le-Vicomte certainly gave him the opportunity to prove his talent in both spheres. But how did the Le Brun the artist and Le Brun the manager interact? If there was tension between these two roles, which one was given priority? I do not propose to spend time on the practical organization of the construction sites, nor on the division of labor among the workers; I would like to focus solely on the evidence of Le Brun's decision-making as an artist before and during the production of the décors, in order to understand how much he had planned and what happened unexpectedly. The famous tapestry representing the king's visit to the Gobelins could well function as an illustration of my inquiry: it depicts the flourishing of the arts under Louis XIV as orchestrated by Le Brun, who used a seemingly random configuration artistically to create an effect of great variety and splendor.[5] The purpose of this chapter is to bring the vast program of decoration of Louis XIV's palace—overwhelmingly complex in sum—back to a more human level, finding the artist's hand in the final alterations and adaptations to the *grands décors*.

Le Brun's creative process appears, at first sight, to have involved careful advance planning, almost to the point of being formulaic. He first thought about the overall organization of his large-scale painted programs, mainly focusing on architectural constraints. The Hall of Mirrors provides a vivid example of this:[6] it demonstrates the primary role of the architectural rhythm of the window bays in determining the overall composition of the ceiling. This was true for two rejected proposals for the ceiling of the Hall of Mirrors—the first a cycle of Apollo, the second Hercules—and for the theme of the king's history that was eventually executed. Once the overall organization had been established, Le Brun moved on to plan each of the individual scenes. A preliminary concept (or overall design) was followed by a study of each figure, first nude and then clothed. Next came a small-scale painted modello (a detailed compositional sketch in paint), which was presumably shown to the patron. Finally, a full-scale cartoon was drawn in order to transpose the scale model onto the support, which would be either the plaster of the vaulted ceilings or a canvas mounted on the wall surface. Before this final transposition, the cartoon might also be positioned in place to confirm that the arrangement of the figures and illusionistic shadows was correct. At that stage, Le Brun would carry out minor retouching, such as in the profile of the allegory of France for the compartment displaying *Order Restored to the National Finances* (Figure 3.1).[7]

This description of the production process follows the interpretation established by art historians who have drawn on an extraordinary archival source: the records stored in Le Brun's workshop and seized by the Crown after his death in 1690. These were found to include 3,000 drawings and cartoons by Le Brun and his assistants, now preserved in the Louvre.[8] But the overall principles governing that process of design and execution did not exclude the possibility of trial and error, or even going back and forth between the different stages of production. The central compartment of the Hall of Mirrors, *The King Governs by Himself*, is a good example of this. Le Brun tried out at least two

Figure 3.1 Charles Le Brun, *Order Restored to the National Finances* (detail), *c*. 1679, black chalk whitened with white chalk, squared with red chalk, outlines incised, on paper, 235 × 208.5 cm, Paris, Musée du Louvre, Département des Arts graphiques, inv. 29950. Image in the public domain.

drawings of the whole scene, followed by a *modello*.[9] The second drawing even includes an area of significant *pentimento* on the figure of the king, extensive enough to have been implemented with a *retombe*, that is to say a piece of paper with the correction overlaid on to the original. Similarly, a close examination of the painted model reveals a pentimento: the trace of a child playing an instrument that disappeared under the royal mantle in the reworking of this design. Some changes in the composition are continuous developments, such as the role assigned to Minerva and Mars in the king's decision to renounce the pleasures of childhood to pursue glory. In another example, the upside-down figure of a soldier appears in the lower middle of the second drawing, then slides to the left in the *modello*, finally being transformed into an allegory of the Seine in the painting, but always with the same formal role of creating space in the composition. By contrast, other changes switch back and forth, such as the representation of children: they are very much present in the first drawing, confined to the right-hand side in the second one, and then expanded again in the paintings. Le Brun made figures appear and disappear, or experimented with moving them around, as in the case of Justice and the Graces. All of his ideas about the composition are expressed in drawings of individual figures. But here again, nothing is rigid: a study of Hercules related to the initial sketch of the composition eventually became the starting-point for a large cartoon of Mars.[10] Planning and experimentation here went hand in hand.

The flexibility evident in Le Brun's thinking is not limited to a few preliminary cases of trial and error; it can take the form of more substantial and unexpected changes. The projects for the Apollo Gallery that Louis XIV had installed in the Louvre palace are a surprising example of this.[11] This was the first great gallery that Le Brun painted for the king, preceding the Hall of Mirrors at Versailles by fifteen years. The project, as Le Brun proposed it to Louis XIV, has long been known about, based on two sheets preserved in the Louvre, which are gradually being extended with the discovery of additional widely scattered fragments—in Darmstadt in Germany, Montpellier in the South of France, and even more recently in a private collection in France.[12]

Between these highly developed drawings made for the patron, which offer a general outline with alternatives at some points, and the final execution, Le Brun amplified the iconographic significance of the décor, adding symbolic value to the ornamental elements and creating relationships between them. In the drawings, for example, the *tondi* are sometimes empty and sometimes decorated with the labors of the months of the year; they are flanked by putti, sphinxes, or griffins and surmounted by false bas-reliefs decorated with scenes of combat in the classical style. In the painted gallery itself, everything refers back to the central theme of Apollo, who is, by turns, the god of Parnassus and of the Sun, regulating time and reigning over space. The transition from one conception of the iconography to another was the result of a partly fortuitous discovery. Evidence for this can be found in a very modest double-sided drawing (Figure 3.2), connected with the Apollo Gallery.[13] It shows twelve arcs flanked by pairs of animals corresponding to the gods whose names are noted within. Some annotations indicating where the light source should appear complete the drawings: thus for Neptune we read "daylight from below," for Jupiter "directly opposite," and Mercury "below." A jotting in Le Brun's own hand notes a problem: "Chercher pour Vulquin [sic] un animal" [find an animal for Vulcan]. The twelve major gods are not arranged in any particular order; they do not relate directly to the months of the year; they do not even represent the gods of Olympus, since Pluto is included in the list. Doubtless it was during his search for an animal to accompany Vulcan that Le Brun learned—perhaps from a book, or a discussion with a scholar—that some writers had established links between deities and signs of the zodiac. As Nicolas Milovanovic brilliantly observed, these "zodiac-guardian relationships" are described in an ancient text, the *Astronomica* of Manilius, and restated by

Figure 3.2 Charles Le Brun, *Study for the Arcs of the Apollo Gallery*, c.1663, black chalk on paper, 42.7 × 56.9 cm, Paris, Musée du Louvre, Département des Arts graphiques, inv. 29484 verso. Image in the public domain.

Francesco Giorgio in his *Harmonia Mundi*, a Latin work translated into French in the sixteenth century.[14] The list of the twelve gods planned in the drawing was modified accordingly. The choice of deities and their order in the Gallery completely match the pairings of gods and signs found in Manilius. There is only one problem—Vulcan, who supposedly watches over Libra and the month of September. In the Gallery, the animal for the month of September is a dog, similar to the one Le Brun associated with Pluto in earlier the drawing. Vulcan's divine attributes, represented in a medallion, relate to fire and things made with fire, which are equally associated with Pluto.

Le Brun's note, in this particular case, suggests that we have here an example of serendipity.[15] In other words, his initial research proved unsuccessful—he did not find an animal for Vulcan—but it leads the attentive researcher to an unexpected and more significant discovery. Le Brun was looking for a specific motif, and he discovered a system of correspondences between the twelve Olympians and the signs of the zodiac. In doing so, he recognized a new opportunity to refine the structure of his design—both iconographically and formally—by creating a link between the vertical ornamental compartments (the gods, their attributes and animals, the labors of the months, flowers of different seasons) and the horizontal motifs positioned on the cornice (the allegory of the months and the signs of the zodiac). The initial problem became a secondary one, solved by sleight-of-hand: unable to find the right animal, Le Brun took the liberty to combine Vulcan and Pluto into one figure.

After the trial and error of the initial design, and significant modifications during the implementation of the project, Le Brun carried out still more last-minute alterations. In the Ambassadors' Staircase at Versailles, the moving of some of the figures and modification of an attribute have had important consequences for our interpretation of the decorative scheme. This staircase was first designed in 1671, and decorated between 1674 and 1679, to provide a grandiose entry to the king's state apartments.[16] It was destroyed in 1752 under Louis XV, and is known today from the engravings and contemporary descriptions, which give an overall sense of it, by a fragment of painting detached from the wall, some *modelli*, and a remarkable set of drawings and cartoons preserved at the Louvre. In 1958 these materials served as the basis for a scale-model reconstruction of the original.[17]

The engravings of the vault show four groups in the center of the arches. In the foreground of each are pairs of Muses. The ones on the long sides of the vault are accompanied by three deities, Minerva, Hercules, and Apollo, and by the ninth Muse (in this case Thalia, the Muse of Comedy). The number of Muses depicted follows tradition—nine, always a problem for ceiling designers—but their attributes do not. We can recognize a Muse of Architecture and another one combining Painting and Sculpture. Above the sculpted bust of the king, on the north side, the motif refers to Louis XIV's military successes. Minerva and Hercules illustrate Wisdom and Strength, and a three-headed monster, according to Félibien's 1705 interpretation, stands for the three enemies of France, Holland, Germany, and Spain. These are being crushed by the king's chariot, adorned with trophies taken from the vanquished. The Muses who acknowledge these victories are Polyhymnia or Eloquence and Clio or History. Opposite them (Figure 3.5), Apollo and Thalia are accompanied by Melpomene or Tragedy and Calliope or Heroic Poetry, evoking the arts and their performance.

The study of a small painted model (Figure 3.3), now in a private collection,[18] and of Le Brun's preparatory cartoons suggests that this elaborate configuration does not match the first design transferred to the vault. The *bozzetto* shows a less coherent group: Minerva is associated with Lyric Poetry, and the monster has five heads. We can deduce from this that Hercules and Apollo were supposed to

Figure 3.3 Charles Le Brun, *Minerva and Three Muses*, c. 1674, oil on canvas, 40.3 × 55.3 cm, Paris, Galerie Éric Coatalem. Photo: Author.

face them, and we recognize here the association of two images of the sovereign rather than a thematic interconnection. The painted model reflects a stage that Le Brun must have judged advanced enough to function as a basis for the development of the cartoons, which conform to it exactly. This is demonstrated by the fact that the cartoons of the two Muses in the foreground, Tragedy and Eloquence, each include one of the monster's serpent heads. The cartoons were thus developed before Le Brun decided to arrange these figures differently. Minerva has retained her original place, but Erato has given way to Hercules. Melpomene has moved to a different arch, being replaced by Polyhymnia (who has thus moved leftward); she in turn is replaced by Clio. All these cartoons bear the marks of the stylus used to trace them onto the vaulting (even the areas left out of the final version, such as Erato's lyre) (Figure 3.4).

This poses a tricky question: What brought about this late change of plan? Why did Le Brun reorganize the pieces of the puzzle formed by the cartoons? Was it the somewhat belated outcome of lengthy reflections on iconography? An idea that germinated during a discussion with the king, Colbert, a scholar, or another artist? A brilliant inspiration resulting from an unplanned rearrangement of the cartoons, either in the studio or on the scaffolding? A formal study that suddenly revealed new thematic possibilities? Pursuing this last hypothesis, we can imagine that Le Brun sought to avoid the unfortunate effect of having the pairs of Muses turning their backs to each other on their shared central motif. We do find him hesitating over the orientation of a figure shown in two different cartoons.[19] By moving the Muses to make them face each other, two of the monster's heads became separated from its body, thus giving rise to the possible symbolism of the monster as the three powers hostile to France; that in turn led to the accentuation of the military character of the north arch, reinforced by the addition of trophies and the introduction of Hercules. The subsequent transfer of Erato to the south side (Figure 3.5), close to Apollo, must have made her look redundant, since the lyre she holds is also the attribute of Apollo. Was it at that point that Thalia was put in Erato's place, and the lyre replaced by two masks, which were apparently painted directly on the wall without the intermediate stage of a new cartoon? Did Le Brun want to position a symbol of the strength of representation facing the representation of Strength? Perhaps it was a subtle reminder of the comedy of power, or at least an echo of the theatrical staging of power accomplished by the staircase, where the fictional ambassadors on the walls admire the vault and the performance of the real

Figure 3.4 Charles Le Brun, *Erato, Muse of Lyric Poetry*, c. 1674, black chalk whitened with white chalk, outlines incised, on paper, 141 x 92.5 cm, Paris, Musée du Louvre, Département des Arts graphiques, inv. 29847/1. Image in the public domain.

Figure 3.5 Étienne Baudet, *Staircase of the Ambassadors* (reversed detail), c. 1679–83, engraving, Versailles, Musée national du Château de Versailles et de Trianon. Photo: RMN.

ambassadors, who go up and down, looking back at them and up at the vaulting, in an endless play of mirror-images.

No doubt this reconstruction of events belongs rather to historical fiction than to history. Nothing is less reliable than the attempt to recapture the intentions, thoughts, and accidents that governed the creation of a work, leaving no written traces. No one will ever really know why these changes were made. We know only the starting-point (the *bozzetto* and the cartoons) and the end-point (through the engravings), which has become more coherent and richer in meaning. The only certain conclusion is that, whatever it was that gave him his insights, here as elsewhere Le Brun knew how to grasp any opportunity to perfect his work, even up to the very last minute.

Notes

1. I am very grateful to Robert Wellington, Mark Ledbury, and Peter Raissis for their trust and their help in preparing this chapter.
2. For Le Brun's career, see Bénédicte Gady, *L'ascension de Charles Le Brun: liens sociaux et production artistique* (Paris: Éditions de la Maison des sciences de l'homme, 2010); Bénédicte Gady and Nicolas Milovanovic, eds, *Charles Le Brun (1619–1690)*, exh. cat. Lens: Louvre-Lens (Paris: Lienart Éditions, 2016); Wolf Burchard, *The Sovereign Artist: Charles Le Brun and the image of Louis XIV* (London: Paul Holberton Publishing, 2016).

3   Anthony Blunt, "The Early Works of Charles Le Brun," *The Burlington Magazine* 85, no. 496 (1944), 165–94.
4   Florian Knothe, "Artisans du roi: Collaboration at the Gobelins, Louvre and the *Académie Royale de Peinture et de Sculpture* under the Influence of the Petite Académie," in *The Versailles Effect*, 45–62.
5   Paris, Mobilier national, GMTT 95/10 (1673–9), see *Charles Le Brun (1619–1690)*, cat. 8, 90–1 (entry by W. Burchard); and Paris, Mobilier national, GMTT 98/10 (1729–34), see *Versailles. Treasures from the Palace*, exh. cat., ed. Béatrix Saule and Lucina Ward (Canberra: National Gallery of Australia, 2016), cat. 17, 70–3 (entry by P.-X. Hans and S. Maxwell).
6   Jennifer Montagu, "Le Brun's Early Designs for the Grande Galerie: Some Comments on the Drawings," *Gazette des Beaux-Arts* 120 (1992): 195–206; *La galerie des Glaces: Charles Le Brun maître d'œuvre*, exh. cat., Alexandre Maral and Nicolas Milovanovic (Versailles: Musée national du Château, 2007); *La Galerie des Glaces. Histoire et restauration* (Dijon: Faton, 2007); Nathalie Volle et Nicolas Milovanovic, eds, *La Galerie des Glaces après sa restauration. Contexte et restitution* (Paris: École du Louvre, 2013); Bénédicte Gady, "From Sketches to Cartoons: Analysis of (and Doubts about) Charles Le Brun's Working Procedures for the Grands Décors," in *The Gallery of Charles XI at the Royal Palace of Stockholm—in Perspective* (Stockholm: Stockholm National Museum; Stockholm University, 2016), 174–84; Bénédicte Gady, "Los cartones de Charles Le Brun, un testimonio único de la fabricación de las grandes decoraciones," and "La Galería de los Espejos, un cambio de escala y de discurso," in *Dibujar Versalles. Bocetos y cartones de Charles Le Brun (1619–1690) para la Escalera de los Embajadores y la Galería de los Espejos*, exh. cat. (Barcelona: Caixa Forum, 2016), 23–39 and 137–43.
7   Paris, Musée du Louvre, Département des Arts graphiques, inv. 29950; *Dibujar Versailles …*, 2015–16, cat. 85, 152.
8   Lydia Beauvais, *Musée du Louvre. Inventaire général des dessins de Charles Le Brun*. I–II (Paris: Éditions RMN, 2000).
9   Paris, Musée du Louvre, Département des Arts graphiques, inv. 27644; inv. 27691 (on permanent loan at Versailles, Musée national du Château de Versailles et de Trianon, MV 7909); Versailles, MV 8975.
10 Paris, Musée du Louvre, Département des Arts graphiques, inv. 29065 et inv. 29847/3.
11 *La galerie d'Apollon au Louvre*, Paris, 2004.
12 *Peupler les cieux. Dessins pour les plafonds parisiens au XVIIe siècle* (Paris: Musée du Louvre, 2014), cat. 64, 230–1 (entry by B. Gady).
13 Paris, Musée du Louvre, Département des Arts graphiques, inv. 29484 recto and verso; Bénédicte Gady, "Le règne du soleil. Conception, mise en œuvre et lectures de la galerie d'Apollon," in *La galerie d'Apollon au Louvre* (Paris: Gallimard/Musée du Louvre Éditions, 2004), 58–68.

14 Nicolas Milovanovic, "Astronomie et astrologie dans les grands décors français du XVIIe siècle: de Vaux-le-Vicomte à Versailles," *Revue de l'art*, no. 140 (2003): 29–40.

15 For this concept, created by Horace Walpole, see Robert K. Merton and Elinor G. Barber, *The Travels and Adventures of Serendipity. A Study in Historical Semantics and the Sociology of Science*, [written in 1958] (Princeton, NJ: Princeton University Press, 2004), and Pek van Andel et Danièle Bourcier, *De la sérendipité dans la science, la technique, l'art et le droit. Leçons de l'inattendu* (Paris: Hermann, 2013).

16 *Charles Le Brun 1619-1690. Le décor de l'escalier des Ambassadeurs à Versailles*, exh. cat., Versailles, musée national du Château (Paris: RMN, 1991); Beauvais, 2000; Alexandre Gady, "La Escalera de los Embajadores, Una obra maestra por adaptación," in *Bocetos y cartones de Charles Le Brun (1619-1690) para la Escalera de los Embajadores y la Galería de los Espejos*, exh. cat. Barcelona: Caixa Forum, 2016), 42–51; Bénédicte Gady, "La escalera es un sueño," ibid., 61–71; Jean-Gérald Castex, "La difusión de la Escalera de los Embajadores," ibid., 124–9; Burchard, *The Sovereign Artist* (chapter 6: "On the Highest Rung—L'Escalier des Ambassadeurs at Versailles," 196–231).

17 Charles Arquinet, Versalles, Musée national du Château de Versailles et de Trianon, V6251-2.

18 Paris, galerie Hahn, 1975; exh. cat. (Versailles, 1990-1), cat. 29; Paris, Galerie Coatalem, 2008.

19 *Woman Holding a Table*, Paris, Musée du Louvre, Département des Arts graphiques, inv. 29982 and inv. 29847/168.

4

Artisans du roi: Collaboration at the Gobelins, Louvre, and the *Académie Royale de Peinture et de Sculpture* under the Influence of the *Petite Académie*

Florian Knothe

Introduction

At the Court of Louis XIV (1643–1715) panegyric, and often allegoric, programs in word and image were carefully devised by the king's image-makers. In 1663, Louis XIV's most capable minister, Jean-Baptiste Colbert, in his new role as *surintendent des bâtiments du roi* [superintendent of the king's works] set about reorganizing the whole system of royal commissions in fine and decorative arts for royal palaces, from design to manufacture. Colbert founded a new *Petite Académie*—a group of writers with a deep knowledge of the ancient Greco-Roman world handpicked from the *Académie française*.[1] The *Petite Académie* was given the task of choosing appropriate subject matter and aiding artists with the research required for complex allegories composed of ancient and modern symbols all to the praise and commemoration of the king. The *Petite Académie* would later claim to have advised in every aspect of the visual program of the palace of Versailles. Colbert made the nascent *Académie Royale de Peinture et de Sculpture* the preeminent institution of its kind, ensuring that its members held an almost exclusive monopoly over royal commissions.[2] In the previous year, 1662, the new *surintendant des bâtiments* founded the *Manufacture royale des Gobelins* in Paris, inducing artists and master craftsmen from within France and without to form a collaborative community to produce tapestries and furniture for the royal palaces of unequaled quality and luxury.[3] The paintings, sculpture, textiles, and furniture of Versailles that have come to define the Sun King's reign were devised by members of the *Petite Académie* and executed in multiple media by master artists from the *Académie Royale de Peinture et de Sculpture*, both at the Gobelins and at the Louvre, as Hannah Williams shows in her chapter in this book.

While the role of the *Petite Académie* in the design for royal medals, Gobelins tapestries, and printed images and texts describing them is well known, their influence on visual art and the employment of artifacts to express royal propaganda expanded far beyond those media.[4] At the palace of Versailles multiple decorative schemes in- and outside the palace show the politically motivated programs of those academicians executed by an extensive group of royal artisans working for the Sun King. Within the context of royal manufacture, the production of all manner of decorative elements for both the interior and the exterior of the Château—and the major task of coordinating and completing both home and gardens—presents an episode that sheds light on the practical methods of employing *artisans du roi* in situ. It also reveals the constant demands from a royal patron, with ever-changing tasks requested from that multitalented community of intellectuals, artists, and artisans.

This chapter concerns the collaboration of royal sculptors who often belonged either to the workshops of the *Manufacture royal des Gobelins* or the Louvre and who were employed for their individual reputation and the services they rendered at the *Académie de Peinture et de Sculpture*. As a case study, this chapter focuses on the first *parterre d'eau*—a particularly public space at Versailles—the collaboration between the *Petite Académie* and artists involved in its making.

Germain Martin stated that "*dans les manufactures royales, ils [the royal artisans] sont logés et nourris et ne peuvent sortir de l'enceinte de l'établissement qu'à des heures fixées*" [in the royal manufactories, the royal artisans lodged, ate, and could not leave the confines of the establishment except at fixed times]. However, it is imperative to the discussion of the *artisans du roi* to acknowledge that royal manufacture can be characterized as collaboration of artists from both the Louvre workshops and the Gobelins manufactory.[5] Strong links between the different individual workshops at the Louvre and the Gobelins developed as they supplied the Crown. There was continual movement between those workshops and royal building sites. These joint ventures exemplify the work patterns of painters, sculptors, and carpenters from both artist colonies who collaborated at various royal châteaux.[6] The account books of the *Bâtiments du roi* list various payments to specialist workers for royal commissions, including Versailles, suggesting that the best specialists were chosen for each task from the Louvre or Gobelins. Such a large number of artists were needed for the timely completion of Louis XIV's large building projects that they had to call up both institutions together.[7]

The lively correspondence of *surintendant des Batîments*, Jean-Baptiste Colbert, and the king indicates that both men took great interest in the ongoing construction work at Versailles, but it omits any indication of their creative input.[8] Colbert's position as *surintendant* bound him to oversee the workers and to push for progress and completion. In his reports, he writes in great detail of sections completed and partial successes achieved, and names further projects ahead. Colbert himself signed contracts with workers, such as Claude Denis who was employed to install the hydraulics for the fountains in the park at Versailles, and appears—at least in retrospect—as commissioner of the statues in an account drawn in 1692.[9] For the king, on the other hand, we cannot assume that he, when writing to Colbert from the seat of war in the Netherlands, would have had a say in artistic matters. No archival source justifies such a statement.

Ascertaining which artists were based at the Louvre or the Gobelins workshops, alongside their status at the *Académie de Peinture et de Sculpture*, helps to reveal their mobility.[10] Among the academicians, painters Adam Frans van der Meulen, François Bonnemer, Sébastien Le Clerc, Baudouin Yvard, Réne-Antoine Houasse, François Jouvenet, Pierre Mignard, Claude-Guy Hallé, Jean-Baptiste Corneille, Baptiste Monoyer, Gilbert de Sève, and François Verdier, sculptors Antoine Coysevox, Jean-Baptiste Tuby, and Jacques Prou, and the engraver Gérard Edelinck worked at the Gobelins.[11] Charles Errard, Jean Lemoine, and Noël Coypel and sculptors Étienne Le Hongre, François Girardon, Jacques Sarrazin, and his sons Pierre Sarrazin, a sculptor, and Bessigne Sarrazin, a painter, and engravers Israël Silvestre and Étienne Baudet— all also members of the *Académie*—had workshops and accommodation at the Louvre.[12] From the early 1660s many of these artists participated in creating the decorative schemes at the Louvre and Versailles. Here, the academy's panegyric theme of the *Quatre Eléments*—the weaving in tapestry of which has been described in much detail before—was executed in three-dimensional sculpture for the gardens of Versailles. Under the supervision of Charles Le Brun, a group of highly skilled sculptors produced three different versions of statues representing the *Elements*.[13]

The Planning and Construction of the *Parterre d'eau*

To date, scholarly discussion around the *grand parterre* at Versailles and attributions of later changes to its original layout center on the individual influence of the most illustrious artists involved in the architectural schemes of the gardens and interiors of the Château, namely, Louis Le Vau (1612–70), André Le Nôtre (1613–1700), Charles Le Brun (1619–90), and Jules Hardouin-Mansart (1646–1708).[14] Le Brun is the most likely designer of the second version of the *parterre* under Louis XIV—the first *parterre d'eau*—constructed between 1672 and 1674.[15] Although it has always been taken for granted that all of the gardens at Versailles are Le Nôtre's design, there is no evidence that connects him to that particular parterre. The account books of the *Bâtiments du roi* list no payment in his favor for that project.[16] His influence upon the creation of French formal gardens in general, however, cannot be denied, and his involvement in redesigning the park for which he was employed and acted as general supervisor is certain.[17]

With regard to the water basins of the *Parterre d'eau*, Le Brun's artistic authority stands out and his influence in the program of sculpture made in collaboration with fellow *artisans du roi* is central to this examination. Within the large collection of drawings left by the painter after his death and confiscated from his widow by Louvois, who saw these as property of the *Bâtiments du roi*, there are two drawings related to the ground-plan of the parterre (Figures 4.1 and 4.2). These plans are evidence of Le Brun's interest in the basins, and not only as a space for the display of his sculptures.

In her extensive study of this early panegyric project, Ann Friedman attributed the parterre to Le Brun, without, however, examining the influence of the *Petite Académie*.[18] However, the thematic program and the complex allegorical theme of the *parterre d'eau* suggest the authorship of the literary scholars of the *Petite Académie*. They, in turn, relied on Le Brun, at this date rector of the *Académie Royale de Peinture et de Sculpture* and director of the Gobelins manufactory, to choose from the community of royal artists and academicians those who were best suited for the execution of each project. Where Colbert acted as inspector of buildings and mediator between the Crown and its servants, Le Brun organized all artistic collaboration.[19] This enormous project necessitated commissions from not one but many leading sculptors chosen to work on the *Parterre d'eau*, including François Girardon, Jean-Baptiste Tuby, and Martin Desjardins. Due to the enormous scale of projects such as this, most of the members of the academy

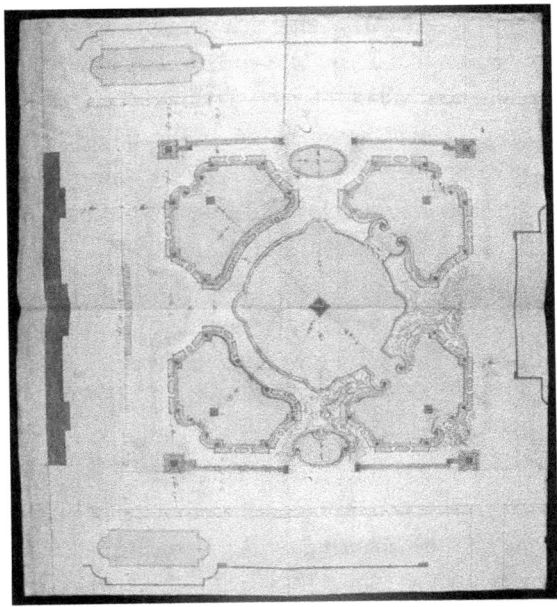

Figure 4.1 Workshop of Charles Le Brun (1619–90), Plan du premier parterre d'eau de Versailles, black chalk, black ink, pen, wash with gray and watercolor on paper, 63 × 72 cm, c. 1674, Paris: Musée du Louvre, Cabinet des Dessins, INV30326-recto. Photo: RMN.

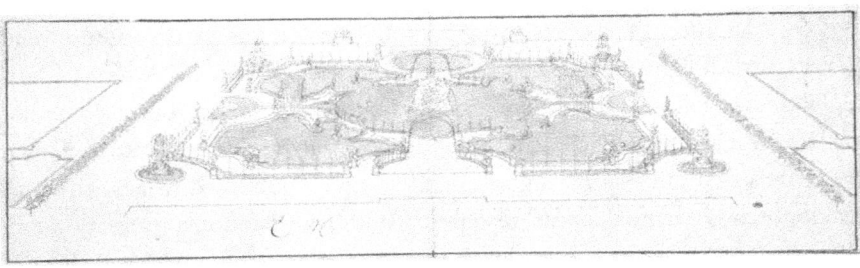

Figure 4.2 Workshop of Charles Le Brun (1619–90), Vue en perspective du premier parterre d'Eau de Versailles, black chalk, brown ink, pen and watercolor on paper, 15.3 × 52.7 cm, c. 1674, Paris: Musée du Louvre, Cabinet des Dessins, INV30321-recto. Image in the public domain.

were commissioned to contribute to the decoration of Versailles. Le Brun favored each of them for their artistic skill. Having those artists work on projects as central to the representational concerns of the king's *Grand Commande* was an acknowledgment of their status.[20]

In his history of the *Pétite Académie* that appears at the start of the official records of their meetings that began only in 1696, Abbé Tallemant claimed that the company had a hand in all of the representation program in the palace and gardens at Versailles from its inception in 1663.[21] The statute for the establishment of the company as *Académie Royale des Médailles et Inscriptions* in 1701 states the academicians' task was to develop and spread royal propaganda by means of visual display.[22] As with the royal orders upon which the organization of the *Manufacture des Gobelins* or the workshops at the Louvre were based, the statutes of the academy describe its professional scope as much as ongoing or already completed projects.[23] Since the *Petite Académie*'s involvement had been initiated by Colbert in 1663, these statutes covered the preceding thirty-eight years. Judging by the number of monuments built and texts published, the *Petite Académie* held their greatest influence during their first twenty years under Colbert.[24] Indeed, there is much surviving correspondence between members of the *Petite Académie* and the *surintendant des bâtiments* discussing the projects with which they were involved.[25]

Much of the secondary literature on the quarrel over the planning of the *parterre* is devoted to the importance of Le Brun as the sole genius responsible for the initial designs of the sculptures commissioned for the *Grande Commande* and whether, therefore, all pieces executed show a perfect unity of Le Brun's style.[26] As the original preliminary drawings for the statues have been preserved and the sculptures themselves survive, similarities between the sculptures and the original designs have been found and models attributed.[27] Artemis Klidis highlights the painter's dependence on Cesare Ripa's *Iconologia*, but she does not explain the reasons for his choice.[28] Ripa's text was widely known in Europe, having been translated into many languages and regularly published in new editions, making it an influential artists' resource.[29] With Jean Baudoin's translation and reprint of 1644 it became accessible to French scholars and popularized allegory at a time when Le Brun himself completed his education by producing copies after the allegoric paintings by Raphael and antique statuary in Rome.[30]

Le Brun produced the overall design for the *Parterre d'eau* and offered suggestions for single sculptures therein. Ripa's *Iconologia* influenced the design of the iconographic theme and artistic execution. As some of the figures after existing drawings attributed to Le Brun seem to show the personal style of their sculptors, the lack of perfect unity can be explained as the merit of collaborating with highly skilled artists who were known for their own particular style.[31] The surviving drawings show different stages of completion and do not always represent the final designs for his subordinate sculptors to work from. They seem to include early ideas for designs that were refined at a later stage. This refinement might include the work of the executing sculptors, who by transferring two-dimensional designs into three-dimensional sculptures would have had the liberty to correct and modify (Figures 4.3 and 4.4).³²

On one occasion, Le Brun exclusively addressed his colleagues of the royal manufactory as a team when he asked Guillaume Anguire (1628–1708), Domenico Cucci (c. 1635–1705), Philippe Caffièri (c. 1633–1716), and Jean-Baptiste Tuby (1635–1700) for a model of the *Parterre d'eau*—a commission that suggests the call for rapid production after the director's design.³³ This three-dimensional model (sadly no longer extant) guided the initial construction and might have indicated the exact positioning of individual sculptures, of which several pieces had not been completed by the time the *parterre* was remodeled a third time from 1683. Friedman refers to a payment of 800 *livres* to the sculptor Georges Sibrayque (or Siebrecht, active at Versailles between 1672 and 1682) for a second model, and argues that it offered an alternative design for the king to choose from.³⁴ However, it seems more plausible that Sibrayque, who was largely

Figure 4.3 Charles Le Brun, *Les Quatre Complexions de l'Homme*, black chalk, gray wash on cream paper: c. 1674, Paris: Musée du Louvre, Cabinet des Dessins. Dépôt Versailles, Châteaux de Versailles et de Trianon. Photo: RMN.

Figure 4.4 Matthieu Lespagnandelle (1616–89), *Le Flegmatique* (*Les Quatre Complexions de l'Homme*), marble, c. 1674, Versailles, Châteaux de Versailles et de Trianon. Image in the public domain. Photo: Myrabella/Wikimedia Commons.

employed for basic preparatory and building work before he began his statue of *l'Afrique* (one of the pieces commissioned for the parterre), never supplied a model, but was, instead, paid for physically remodeling the original parterre and for digging the cavity for the large water basin.[35] If so, he would no doubt have worked from the model produced by sculptors at the Gobelins after Le Brun's design and transferred the dimensions and lay-out from drawn designs and the small-scale model in order to reshape the full-scale parterre. The large sum to him from the royal account supports this hypothesis.

It is noteworthy that the final design presented a highly developed space that because of its extensive sculpture program resembled a theatrical stage or a *cour versaillaise* rather than a garden. Allen S. Weiss commented on this development of the formal garden in seventeenth-century France saying that it was constructed against nature and that "the use of the garden as a social, political and theatrical setting only exacerbated the anti-naturalist sentiments in this regard. Nature was transformed into sign, symbol, and stage."[36] This phenomenon was well understood at the time. Contemporary texts describing this new form of landscape architecture show little interest in nature itself and omit all mention of the little that was left. Such apparent ignorance, only further indicates the subordination of the elements and human mastery to the "shape" of nature.[37] The park of Versailles and its iconographic program were designed to glorify Louis XIV by celebrating his political strength, his power over nature (park), animals (*Ménagerie*), the domestic (*Parterre d'eau*), and exotic (*Trianon de Porcelaine*) spheres.[38]

The Impact of Sculpture in the *Parterre d'eau*

The parterre displayed representations of the elements, times of the day, and seasons positioned around a central marble globe. Together they represented a "universe" that, when seen from a higher position at the Château, lay at the feet of Louis XIV. Much like the imagery of the tapestries and other works of art commissioned by the Crown, and in multiple descriptions of the royal body, its acts, and representation in the *Mercure Galant*, the Sun King's preeminence at the *Parterre d'eau* was part of the multifaceted propaganda of the Bourbon reign.[39]

The accessibility of the gardens at Versailles and regular receptions at the Château guaranteed public knowledge of the parterre's sculptures and led to numerous texts describing its allegorical themes—most notably the King's own *Manière de montrer les jardins de Versailles* of 1689.[40] Unlike the *Elements* and *Seasons* tapestries, which were accompanied by a detailed explanation and engravings describing them in terms of the king's glorification, the *Petite Académie* did not publish a text on the gardens and its sculptures.[41] The extant manuscripts of the *Manière de montrer les jardins* purport to be a personal invitation from the king for how his guests should view the panegyric themes of the gardens, and the marvels of engineering they contain, such as the hydraulic pumps feeding water to the fountains, and the insulated caves of the ice houses. Members of the *Petite Académie* supervised the reporting of several "private" visits to the Château and its gardens by Mlle. de Scudéry, La Fontaine, and Félibien, which provided the interested public with first-hand observations promoting the *"plus grand beautez"* of the new royal residence.[42] However, unlike the *Manière de montrer* that led visitors on a political *parcours*, none of those three descriptive tales draw parallels to the political events of the time, as noted by Stefan Germer in his analysis of Félibien's *Description du Château*.[43]

The multiple angles from which the gardens (and Château) are approached—both physically and literary—exemplify the multifaceted thinking behind the representational program of the *Petite Académie*. The landscaping of the gardens took place in parallel to the *Mercure Galant*'s weekly reporting of the king's political and military accomplishments, episodes that were produced in tapestries woven to commemorate the *Histoire du roi*.[44] The form of glorification found in the parterre is detached from current events and expresses Louis' *gloire* in a way that reminds us of the *Petite Académie*'s production of the *Elements* and *Seasons* tapestries. It also developed in parallel with other programs, notably the *Histoire métallique*, which concentrate on preserving an image of universal dominance, testifying to complexity of the multilayered visual themes of the academicians.[45]

The original *Parterre d'eau* was destroyed shortly after Colbert's death in 1683, testifying to both the short-lived nature of some expensive building projects, the representational value connected to it, and the individual power and personal interest of succeeding superintendents.[46] The reason cited for the remodeling of the parterre was that it blocked access to the lower parts of the gardens. Changes to the first floor of the palace, with the construction of the Hall of Mirrors and the loss of the terrace from where the parterre and its iconographic scheme was best seen and most enjoyed, are another reason for rebuilding the basin. At the same time, Hardouin-Mansart was extending the existing Château by building two enormous wings that changed the original ground plan of the palace and its relationship with the surrounding gardens.

The construction and decoration of the new Hall of Mirrors (begun in 1679), which occupied the central passage space of the terrace, changed the view outside from within the palace and concentrated the focus inside the new gallery.[47] Instead of functioning as an intermediate zone between the park and palace, the gallery offered a semi-public space for the reception of guests and presentation of the collaborative work of the artisans of the royal manufactories and artists of the royal academies.[48] This was not the first royal gallery designed to this end. Before the Hall of Mirrors at Versailles, the Apollo Gallery at the Louvre (1663–77) marked the unparalleled ambition of the young king to represent his power and influence through the collaborative work of many highly reputed royal painters and sculptors to create a display of political representation.[49] It must also be remembered what, while they were somewhat separate from the public spaces of the king's gardens and galleries, the execution of the royal families' private apartments received no lesser care.[50]

The artistic program of Versailles during the second half of the seventeenth century was the product of collaboration of the *artisans du roi* from the Gobelins, the Louvre, and the *Académie Royale de Peinture et de Sculpture*. Artists, freed from the guild restrictions, worked flexibly within their professional specialization (sculptors worked in wood, stone, and bronze) and in the places of employment as they worked in individual royal workshops and collectively under the guidance of Le Brun and the *Petite Académie*. The case study presented calls for a networked approach to the study of royal commissions in the arts. The vast artistic program of the palace of Versailles was the product of collective artistic expression where individual artists and craftsmen were able to demonstrate their particular talents, under the careful management of the king's ministers, a committee of advisors and his *premier peintre*.

Notes

1 On the *Petite Académie*, see Robert Wellington, *Antiquarianism and the Visual Histories of Louis XIV: Artifacts for a Future Past* (Aldershot; Burlington: Ashgate, 2014); Marin Mersenne, *Correspondance du P. Marin Mersenne, religieux minime (1617–1648)*, ed. Mme Paul Tannery and Cornélis de Waard, 17 vols (Paris: G. Beauchesne, 1932–88); Jacques Vanuxem, "Emblèmes et devises vers 1660–1680," *Bulletin de la Société de l'Histoire de l'Art français* (1954): 60–70; Peter Burke, *The Fabrication of Louis XIV* (New Haven, CT and London: Yale University Press, 1992).

2 On Colbert's role in the reorganization of the *Académie des peintures et des sculptures*, see Christian Michel, *The Académie Royale de Peinture et de Sculpture: The Birth of the French School, 1648–1793*, trans. Chris Miller (Los Angeles, CA: Getty Publications, 2018), ch. 2; Ludovic Vitet, *L'Académie Royale de Peinture et de Sculpture* (Paris: Michel Lévy frères, 1861); Alexandra Bettag, *Die Kunstpolitik Jean Baptiste Colberts unter besonderer Berücksichtigung der Académie Royale de Peinture et de Sculpture* (Weimar: VDG, 1998); Bénédicte Gady, *L'ascension de Charles Le Brun: Liens sociaux et production artistique* (Paris: Édition de la Maison des sciences de l'homme, 2010).

3 On the Gobelins Manufactory, see Florian Knothe, *The Manufacture des meubles de la couronne aux Gobelins under Louis XIV: A Social, Political and Cultural History* (Brussels: Brepols, 2016).

4 See Fabian Stein, *Charles Le Brun, la tenture de l'Histoire du Roy* (Worms: Werner, 1985); Wellington, *Antiquarianism and the Visual Histories of Louis XIV*; and Knothe, *The Manufacture des meubles de la couronne aux Gobelins under Louis XIV*.

5   Germain Martin, *La grande industrie sous le règne de Louis XIV (plus particulièrement de 1660 à 1715)* (Paris: Rousseau, 1899), 85.
6   The tapestry weavers, although they undoubtedly formed the core of the Gobelins, worked in a less flexible field, as the nature of their work and the organization of their production limited their activity to a single workshop or even an individual weaving loom.
7   See the entries for Versailles and Marly in Jules Guiffrey, *Comptes des bâtiments du roy, sous le règne de Louis XIV*, 5 vols (Paris: Imprimerie nationale, 1881–1901).
8   Pierre Clément, *Lettres, instructions et mémoires de Colbert*, 8 vols (Paris, 1861–82), vol. 5, letters ("*Beaux-arts et bâtiments*") 49–51, 82, 85, 105, 111–12, 121, 123–5, 135–7, 140, pp. 296–300, 324–6, 328–331, 348–9, 354–7, 363–7, 378–380, 381–3.
9   For the contract with Claude Denis (October 10, 1670), see A.N. O^1 1854$^{1/8}$. For Colbert's involvement with the statuary see "Estimation faits le 15e aoust 1692 pour seruir aux parfaits payemens de partie des Groupes, Figures, Termes, et vases à Versailles," in A.N. O^1 1964^2, that includes the sculptures made for the *Grande Commande* of which most (but not all) are marked as "*figures faites par ordres de M. Colbert.*"
10 For both establishments the Archives nationales in Paris holds *brevêts de logement* and, although one day's listing of names might not be considered appropriate to judge a generation of craftsmen, a comparison to ongoing payments of the *Comptes des bâtiments* as well as to contemporary literature such as Germain Brice's *Description nouvelle de ce qu'il y a de plus remarquable dans la ville de Paris* (Paris: Chez Le Gras, 1684); Michel de Marolles's *Livre des peintres et graveurs* (Paris: n.p., 1677); and an article in the *Mercure Galant* of 1673, provides further grounding. Extracts of these sources have been reproduced in, Knote, (2016), Appendices II, 1–4.
11 Antoine Coysevox moved to the Louvre on April 27, 1698, where he took over Étienne Baudet's lodgings and worked there until his death on October 10, 1720. For the Gobelins workers, see Knothe 2016, appendix IV.
12 For the Louvre workers, see the "*Brevets de logements sous la grande galerie du Louvre accordés à des artistes et à des artisans*," Paris, n.d. (A.N. O^1 1672).
13 For the discussion of the tapestry series depicting the *Quatre Eléments*, see Knothe 2016, pp. 87–99. Further programs originally woven in tapestry were repeated inside the castle where, among other projects, group of painters, also working under Le Brun, painted the vaulted ceiling of the Galerie des Glaces with the extensive History of the King.
14 See the monographs by André Pératé, *Le parterre d'eau du parc de Versailles sous Louis XIV* (Versailles: L Bernard, 1899), 15–35; and Ann Friedman, "The Evolution of the Parterre d'eau," *Journal of Garden History* 8, no. 1 (1988): 1–30; as well as the more comprehensive text by Gerold Weber, *Brunnen und Wasserkünste in*

Frankreich im Zeitalter von Louis XIV. Mit einem typengeschichtlichen Überblick über die französischen Brunnen ab 1500 (Worms: Werner'sche Verlagsgesellschaft, 1985), 155–66.

15 Hardouin-Mansart only became a driving force in royal commissions after the death of Colbert in 1683, and Le Nôtre's involvement cannot be claimed with certainty. Le Vau's professional activity focused on domestic architecture and the rebuilding of the Château—the so-called *envelope*. Jules Hardouin Mansart succeeded his teacher Le Vau in becoming the king's favorite architect. Under Jules Hardouin-Mansart (1649-1708, *architecte des bâtiments du roi* since 1675) the "Aile du Midi" (1678-82), "Aile du Nord" (1685-9), and the "Grand Commun" (at the angle of the "Aile du Sud des Ministres" and the "Aile du Midi") (1682–4) were built. See Yves Bottineau, *Versailles, miroir des princes* (Paris: Arthaud, 1989), 64.

16 For the payments of the 1670s, see the first volume of Guiffrey 1881–1901.

17 Artemis Klidis, *François Girardon, Bildhauer in königlichen Diensten 1663–1700* (Weimar: VDG, 2001), 28–9.

18 Friedman, 1988.

19 This process of selecting artistic talent provided the superintendence with sculptors working in various areas of the Châteaux and gardens. In the cabinet des dessins at the Louvre one drawing by Charles Le Brun from the early 1660s depicts a vase the center frieze of which depicts a scene from the *Histoire du Roi*. This design was later executed in bronze by Claude Ballin (1615–78), a metalsmith at the Louvre workshops, as one of twenty-six vases for the marble balustrade separating the parterre Nord and parterre du Midi from the center terrasse du palais at Versailles in 1665–6 (see Musée du Louvre, Département des arts graphiques, Inventaire de Reiset no. 29833r). Another study by Le Brun depicts a figure representing *Diana* or *Night* that Balthazard Marsy (1628–74), an independent sculptor made for one of the octagonal cartouches decorating the ceiling in the Galerie d'Apollon at the Louvre. The same kind of faceted ceiling decoration was later repeated at the Galerie des Glaces at Versailles (see Musée du Louvre, Département des arts graphiques, Inventaire de Reiset no. 29543r).

20 For the Grande Commande, see Alexandre Maral, "La sculpture en son jardin," in *Versailles*, ed. Pierre Arizzoli-Clementel (Paris: Citadelles & Mazenod, 2009).

21 See Wellington, 2014, 39ff.

22 The *Reglement ordonné par le Roi Louis XIV pour l'Académie des Inscriptions & Médailles*, published originally on July 16, 1701, when the academy was renamed as *Académie des Inscriptions & Médailles*, has been reprinted in Claude Gros de Boze, *Histoire de l'académie royale des inscriptions et belles-lettres depuis son etablissement, avec les eloges des academiciens morts depuis son renouvellement*, 3 vols (Paris, 1740), I, 23–46.

23 See *Idem*, especially articles XIX and XX, 29-31.
24 Josèphe Jacquiot, *Médailles et jetons de Louis XIV, d'après le manuscrit de Londres (ADD 31908)*, 4 vols (Paris: Académie des Inscriptions et Belles Lettres, 1968), 1: 1-22.
25 See Clément, *Lettres, instructions et mémoires de Colbert*, vol. 5, especially letters (1662-73) by Jean Chapelain (1595-1674) to Colbert, 587-650; Philippe Tamizey de Larroque, ed., *Lettres de Jean Chapelain, de l'Académie Française*, 2 vols (Paris: Imprimerie Nationale, 1880-3); Charles Perrault, *Mémoires de ma vie (et Voyage à Bordeaux [1669])* (Paris: Paul Bonnefon, 1909).
26 Zimmermann argues that Le Brun chose all the sculptors working for the *Bâtiments du roi* at Versailles. See Hans-Joachim Zimmermann, *Der Triumph der Akademie: Eine allegorische Komposition von Charles Le Brun und ihr historisches Umfeld (Sitzungsberichte der Heidelberger Akademie der Wissenschaften, Philosophisch-Historische Klasse)* (Heidelberg: Winter, 1988), 29.
27 Garden sculpture was included in the Garde-meuble's account of the "*Meubles de la couronne*" in which also furniture and textiles made and delivered by Gobelins artists is registered but only to a lesser extend sculptures executed for the Grand Commande and other projects at Versailles. See Jules Guiffrey, *Inventaire général du mobilier de la couronne sous Louis XIV (1663-1715)*, 2 vols (Paris: J Rouam, 1885-6).
28 Klidis, 2001, 52. Milanovic also describes the painted ceilings at Versailles and the influence of the *Petite Académie* and, in particular, of Perrault. Further he supports the argument that, in the allegoric program of the Grands Apartements at Versailles, he discusses, individual scenes, relate to Ripa's *Iconologia*. See Nicolas Milovanovic, "Les plafonds des Grands Appartements du Château de Versailles: un traité du bon gouvernement," in *Monuments et mémoires de la Fondation Eugène Piot* 78 (2000): 85-139, especially 101.
29 Cesare Ripa, *Iconologia overo descrittione dell'imagini universali cavate all antichita et da altri luonghi* (Rome, 1603).
30 Cesare Ripa and Jean Baudoin, *Iconologie ou explication nouvelle de plusieurs images…tiréer des recherches et des figures de Cesare Ripa, moralisées par I. Baudoin*, 2 vols (Paris, 1644).
31 Where no drawings exist, the attribution of artworks to individual hands remains difficult for the fact that no perfect unity in style characterizes the statues.
32 For the "*Quatre Tempéraments de l'homme*" of the famous Grande Commande Jacques Houzeau executed *Le Colérique*, Noel V Jouvenet *Le Sanguin*, Michel de La Perdrix *Le Mélancolique*, and Mathieu Lespagnandelle *Le Flegmatique*. Lespagnandelle basically followed Le Brun's drawing, but he depicted an older, "colder"-looking man with a mature beard and a hat, and a more serious—or phlegmatic—facial expression.

33 "Année 1672—Versailles (Sculpture): 14 avril: à Anguier, Tuby, Cuccy et Caffiers, pour le modelle qu'ils ont fait du parterre d'eau...550 L." See Guiffrey, 1881–1901, vol. I, col. 615.
34 Guiffrey, 1881–1901, vol. I, col. 618; Friedman, 1988. Neither André Pératé's nor Weber's earlier texts make any mention of this form of competition.
35 Sibrayque had family connections to Gaspard Marsy (1624–81) and might have guided by the more experienced and established sculptor and presented to Le Brun by him. See Marquis Léon de Laborde, *Répertoire alphabétique manuscrit de noms d'artistes et artisans des XVIe, XVIIe et XVIIIe siècles relevés dans les anciens registres de l'état civil parisien (XVIIe-XVIIIe siècle), dit Fichier Laborde*, Nouvelles Acquisitions Françaises, NF, NAF 12186 and NAF 606973-6, the first reference of which is quoted in Souchal, 1977–93, vol. 3, 271.
36 Allen S. Weiss, *Mirrors of Infinity. The French Formal Garden and 17th-Century Metaphysics* (New York: Princeton Architectural Press, 1995), 29. For the representational value of the gardens of Versailles see also Lars Olaf Larsson, "Versailles als Schauplatz. Die bildende Kunst im Dienste der Repräsentation im Schloss und Garten von Versailles," in *Die Inszenierung des Absolutismus. Politische Begründung und künstlerische Gestaltung höfischer Feste im Frankreich Ludwigs XIV*, ed. Fritz Reckow. (Erlangen: Universitätsbund Erlangen-Nürnberg, 1992), 51–69.
37 Compare René Descartes, "Meditations on First Philosophy," in vol. I of *The Philosophical Works* (Cambridge: Cambridge University Press, 1975–6), 175.
38 See Edouard Pommier, "Versailles, l'image du souverain," in *Les lieux de mémoire*, vol. 2, ed. Pierre Nora (Paris: Gallimard, 1984–6), 2: 193–234, especially 202.
39 In the *Mercure Galant*, several articles describe the interiors as settings for festivities or diplomatic affairs, but do not mention individual artifacts. See "Arrivé, Séjour & Départ des Ambassadeurs de Moscovie," in *Mercure Galant* (September, 1687): 329–37.
40 Louis XIV, *Manière de montrer les jardins de Versailles par Louis XIV* [Versailles 1689], edited and reprinted (Paris: Simone Hoog, 1982); Madeleine de Scudéry, *La promenade de Versailles* (Paris: Claude Barbin, 1669); and "Voyage des Ambassadeurs de Siam," in *Mercure Galant* (September, 1686): II, 339–75, and ibid. (November, 1686): 272–308.
41 The *escalier des Ambassadeur and the Gallerie des Glaces*, however, was popularized by publications. See "Description de l'escalier de Versailles," in *Mercure Galant*, September 1680, part II, 276–320; LB, Escalier des ambassadeurs (Paris, 1725); and "Explication de la Galerie de Versailles," in *Mercure Galant* (December, 1684): 3–85; "Description des deux salons peints par Le Brun qui sont aux deux bouts de la Grande Galerie du Château de Versailles," *Mercure Galant* (April, 1687): 14–57.

42 Scudery, 1669; Jean de La Fontaine, *Recueil des poesies chrestiennes et diverses* (Paris, 1671); André Félibien, *Description sommaire du Château de Versailles* (Paris, 1674).

43 Stefan Germer, *Kunst, Macht, Diskurs. Die intellektuelle Karriere des André Félibien im Frankreich von Louis XIV* (Munich: Wilhelm Fink, 1997), 256.

44 In addition, Jean Edelinck *le jeune* (1643–80) was commissioned to produce engravings after the marble sculptures in the Grotto of Thesis and the *Parterre d'eau* suggesting that individual plates and sets of images where produced to remember and disseminate knowledge of this scheme. See Guiffrey 1881–1901, I, cols. 1207 (600 *livres*), 1346 (250 *livres*), 1347 (1150 *livres*). Edelinck did at least four figures including *Winter*.

45 *Académie des inscription et belles-lettres, Médailles sur les principaux évènements du règne entier de Louis le Grand, avec des explication historiques* (Paris: Imprimerie royale, 1723).

46 Colbert was followed by François-Michel Le Tellier, marquis de Louvois (1641–91) who held that office until his own death in 1691.

47 The employment of allegory and the depiction of the myth of Hercules, as firstly shown by Le Brun in the gallery of the Hôtel Lambert in Paris in the early 1650s and as originally planned for the Galerie des Glaces "offered a better mythological pretext for glorifying the sovereign than that of Apollo" (see Bajou, 1998, 176). When the ceiling was painted from 1681 to 1684 both former themes were abandoned and, following the success of Le Brun and Adam Franz Van der Meulen's (1632–90) paintings describing the *Histoire du roi*, the vaulted space was similarly decorated with large illustrations of Louis XIV's own political achievements rather than the iconography of the Apollo theme that stuck to the Louvre where it had firstly be shown at the *Petit Galerie*. As with the programs previously discussed in the discussion of the tapestries, history painting succeeded earlier mythological and allegorical themes also in this composition. See Gérard Sabatier, *Versailles ou le figure du roi* (Paris: A Michel, 1999), 192 ff.

48 See Robert W. Berger, *Versailles: The Château of Louis XIV* (University Park, Pa: Penn State Press, 1985), 51; and Gérard Mabille, "La galerie d'Apollon dans l'histoire des galeries royales française," in *Le galerie d'Apollon au palais du Louvre*, ed. Genevieve Bresc-Bautier and Étienne Revault (Paris: Gallimard, 2004), 14–15.

49 Le Brun had been asked for new decoration of the interior of the Galerie d'Apollon in 1663 and collaborated with the painters Jacques Gervaise, Jean-Baptiste Monnoyer, as well as the sculptors Gaspard and Balthazard Marsy, Francois Girardon, Thomas Regnaudin, and Antoine Coysevox. Originally thirteen large Savonnerie carpets had been woven after designs Le Brun and delivered by Lourdet for the Galerie d'Apollon in 1667. See Verlet, 1945, 4 and 15. See also, Gérard

Sabatier, *Le prince et les arts: stratégies figuratives de la monarchie française, de la Renaissance aux Lumières* (Paris: Champ Vallon, 2010).

50 Detailed descriptions of many of the royal interiors were published and widely circulated among interested contemporary connoisseurs and domestic as well as foreign visitors to the Château. See, among other texts, "Description de l'escalier de Versailles," in *Mercure Galant* (September, 1680): part II, 276–320; "Description de la Galerie, du Sallon, & du grand Apartement de Versailles, & tout ce qui s'y passe les jours de Jeu," in ibid. (December, 1682): 1–73 ("C'est icy [in the gallery] ou les bontez & les manieres du Roy doivent paroistre toutes engageantes" (48); "Explication de la Galerie de Versailles," in ibid. (December, 1684), 3–85; Scudéry, 1684; "Description des deux salons peints par Le Brun qui sont aux deux bouts de la Grande Galerie du Château de Versailles," in *Mercure Galant* (April, 1687): 14–57.

5

Rough Surfaces: Etching Louis XIV's Grotto at Versailles

Louis Marchesano

By the middle of the 1660s, the demand for water at Versailles prompted the construction of an above grade reservoir on the northern flank of the old Château (Figure 5.1). The reservoir, behind the attic of this structure, lay atop vaults supported by thick walls and pillars, which inspired artists and Louis XIV's advisors in the *Petite Académie* to transform the interior of this functional structure into an artificial grotto, one that vied in craftsmanship and iconographic ingenuity with those found in the gardens of Italian and French notables.[1] This site was obviously suited to such a decorative purpose given that water and hydraulics for waterworks were principal requirements for a successful grotto.[2]

Grottoes also required ornamentation of a very special kind, the effects of which were imagined within the mythological world where decorated caves served as the homes of nymphs, the minor divinities of nature. In book XI of Ovid's *Metamorphoses*, the narrator pauses from the drama of Peleus chasing his future wife the sea nymph Thetis and draws attention to her cave. This narrator is puzzled. He wonders if the cave of Thetis is the product of nature or art; or, is it a combination of nature and art? He concludes by supposing that what he sees is entirely art.[3] This delightful confusion, rooted in the dialectic between nature and artifice, was a familiar trope that buttressed the idea of grottoes and challenged designers in the early modern period to "out-nature nature," or to outperform nature, by transforming this garden feature into a site of wonder.

Artisans and artists devised an astonishing array of ingenious methods by which to decorate walls, floors, and ceilings with shells, tufa, pumice, colored stones, marble, coral, and mother of pearl. When at Versailles the grotto and its décor were completed in 1676, the extraordinary effect of the richly encrusted

Figure 5.1 Jean Lepautre, View of the interior of the Grotto of Versailles (plate 2). Etching, 1676. Image Courtesy of the Getty Research Institute.

surfaces was amplified into infinity by a set of awe-inspiring mirrors, all of which provided a backdrop to the prominent marble sculpture groups nestled within their protective niches (Figure 5.2). This mise-en-scene was enchanted by dazzling water works, as well as pleasant sounds of music and nature from a concealed hydraulically powered organ.

In the official publication *Description de la Grotte de Versailles*, the reader is told how nature has succumbed to the king's creative impulse. Louis as a rational creator bestows harmony and balance upon irrational nature. He reshapes her raw materials into a grotto whose form, decoration, and function were perfectly unified to express the king's repose as an allegory of the setting sun.[4] In the central marble panel on the exterior entablature appears the mythological alter ego of Louis, the Sun God Apollo, who after the day's arduous task of illuminating the world in his chariot descends with his horses toward the oceanic palace of Thetis.[5] Before guests enter the structure through the central portal, they see suspended in the arch above the gate the radiant face of the Sun. Decorated with gold leaf, the symbolic face of Apollo-Louis XIV greeted visitors by reflecting the actual light of the setting sun. Upon entering the grotto's splendorous interior, a visitor would have been confronted by François Girardon's marble sculpture comprised of Thetis's nymph-courtesans attending Apollo at his bath. Flanking the Apollo group were the god's horses and their caretakers, marble groups executed by the sculptors Gilles Guerin and the Marsy brothers. Here then is an allegorical inflection of the sun that has already set; this resting Apollo in the confines of the palace of Thetis, the reader is informed, is Louis XIV accepting comfort at Versailles after facing the daily burdens of governing the French Empire.

One of the most frequently visited features of Versailles, the grotto was conceived in 1664 only to be destroyed in 1684 to make way for the expansion of the Château, which is the reason scholars rightly ascribe a kind of documentary value to the Crown's illustrated publication. While the text first appeared as a simple guidebook in 1672, the first illustrated edition appeared 1676, followed by a second edition in 1679. The text of Andre Félibien (1619–95), the chronicler of the arts during the first decades of Louis XIV's governance (1661–1715), has been labeled as one of the richest descriptions devoted to a single grotto of the early modern period. The same can be said of the twenty large images systematically recording the grotto's façade and interior features. The first three intaglios provide general views of the interior and exterior and the remainder offer separate illustrations of the grotto's most important features.

The images were made during a five-year period, from 1672 through 1676. The illustrations begin with a ground plan and general views of the exterior and interior (Figures 5.1 and 5.2). The ground plan shows six bays separated by two massive pillars in the center of the room. These central pillars, however, have been "removed" from the print in order to provide an unobstructed view of the niches. The three arches of the façade, the only source of natural light, correspond to the three niches in which sit the marble sculptures at the opposite end of the building. After four sheets of illustrations dedicated to each of the façade's fourteen bas reliefs and roundels come views of the grotto's interior pillars encrusted with *coquillage* (shell-work), *rocaillage* (stone-work), and other materials in the form of tritons, cornucopia, grotesques, conch-shaped basins, and Louis's double-L insignia (Figure 5.3). The suite of prints concludes with large illustrations devoted to each sculptural group, which document Versailles's first significant commission of marble works[6] (Figure 5.5).

Published by the French Crown, this album contains 20 of the 956 prints comprising the so-called *Cabinet du roi*, the huge multi-volume collection of etchings and engravings by which the king's treasures were disseminated

Figure 5.2 Jean Lepautre, View of the interior of the Grotto of Versailles (plate 7). Etching, 1676. Image Courtesy of the Getty Research Institute.

Figure 5.3 Jean Lepautre, Pillar ornamented with seashells and rocks (plate 9). Etching, engraving, and drypoint, 1673. Image Courtesy of the Getty Research Institute.

throughout Europe.⁷ Aside from acting as visual ambassadors on behalf of the king's collections and events, the quality and scale of the prints were to demonstrate that Paris had become the new printmaking center of Europe. Given that this royal printing enterprise fell under the auspices of the *surintendant des bâtiments*, that is, the superintendent of the king's works who oversaw architectural commissions, it is not too difficult to imagine a coordinated effort between architects, designers, and printmakers.

Within the tradition of grotto representations, few match the scale of *Description de la Grotte de Versailles*. In addition to scale, one must also consider scope for no other grotto was illustrated in the manner of the Versailles example.⁸ If scope and scale are distinguishing characteristics of the Versailles publication, so too is technique. None of the other published works align specific printmaking techniques with the variety of materials and surfaces that might be found in a grotto—precisely those materials that visitors to these sites were expected to admire. The twenty images in the Versailles publication come from the hands of two etchers and three engravers, a collaborative effort in and of itself distinguishing this volume from works such as Dominique Barriére's *Villa Aldobrandina Tusculana: siue, uarij illius hortorum et fontium prospectus* (1647) and Stefano della Bella's *Vues de la villa de Pratolino* (c. 1653).

Etching refers to the method of making prints from a copperplate, into which the design has been incised by a mordant (or acid). The copperplate is first coated with a ground, a hard wax-like coating through which the design is drawn with an etching needle. The ground is resistant to acid. The plate is then carefully treated with acid, which bites or eats away at those exposed areas. The longer the exposure to acid, the deeper the troughs that hold the ink. The plate is inked, wiped clean of excess ink, and then placed through a press by which the ink is transferred to paper. The depth and width of the troughs can be adjusted to hold more ink, while the roughness and sharpness of the lines can also be manipulated, affording the printmaker remarkable variations in tone and effect (Figure 5.4). Engraving requires a tool called a burin, a metal shaft with a beveled end, which is used to manually incise crisp lines into the plate. The hand holding the burin is somewhat stationary, while the other hand turns the copperplate. This technique requires highly specialized skills, knowledge of complex linear patterns, and patience. With engraving, tone, shading, and form are suggested by precise parallel lines, crosshatching, and the so-called dot-and-lozenge technique all of which results in a polished effect suitable for the reproduction of paintings and carved marble (Figures 5.5 and 5.6). The horse's face in Figure 5.6

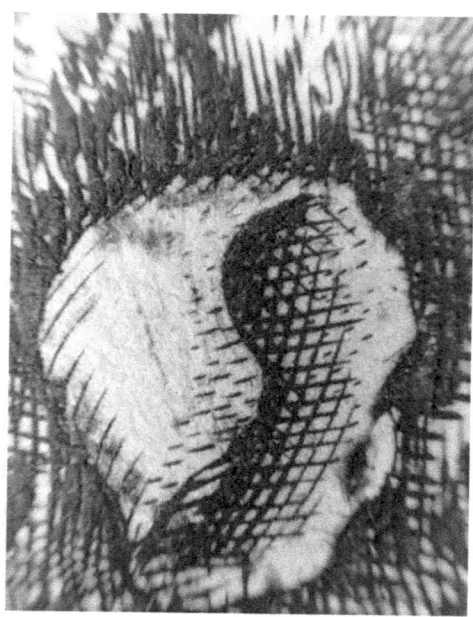

Figure 5.4 Conch Shell, detail of Figure 5.3.

Figure 5.5 Étienne Picart after G. Marsy and B. Marsy, *Horses of Apollo Tended by Tritons* (plate 17). Engraving and etching, 1675. Image Courtesy of the Getty Research Institute.

Figure 5.6 Horse and Niche, detail of Figure 5.5.

is comprised of dot-and-lozenge patterns, while the wall behind the horse has been loosely etched in order to suggest the grotto's irregular surfaces.

Etching was especially suited to produce the picturesque effects of landscapes, gardens, and of course grottoes. The label *brut pittoresque* (rough picturesque) referred to the spirited, less polished effects that were the hallmarks of these views.[9] Of the twenty images in the Versailles volume, twelve are by Jean Lepautre (1618–82) and in scale, size, and quality they match the prints he made for other royal commissions. He was a prolific printmaker praised for his facility as a draughtsman and for the fecundity of his inventiveness. His corpus of predominantly original etchings with some engravings comprises ornaments, decorative arts, and architecture.

The challenge for Lepautre was to "simulate" in graphic terms the effects of complex surfaces. These effects were from the very stuff, the shells and coral, that made the grotto's interior extraordinary in the eyes of French and foreign visitors alike. According to the mythological propaganda of the Crown itself, the hand of Louis has reshaped nature. So how does a printmaker react to this potent propaganda and a commission of this importance?

While the remarkable variety of mark-making distinguishes Lepautre from predecessors such as Stefano della Bella and Dominique Barriére, he is indebted to their tradition of etching, which also appears in the background of Étienne Picart's illustration of Apollo's engraved horses (Figures 5.5 and 5.6). The typical quavering marks in the niche behind the horses were called *grignotis* (referring to a tremulous line) and associated with the representation of natural or irregular surfaces such as bark or roughly hewn stones.[10] In the eyes of French critics, this was a straightforward convention. Less straightforward, in the eyes of those same critics, was the way in which Lepautre apparently abused the copperplate to create tonal effects (Figure 5.4). A highly magnified detail of a conch shell reveals lines of varying plumpness and shape emerging as a thick impasto of ink in combination with precise hatching and cross-hatching, for example, inside the shell itself. In addition to this linear work, the tonal effects in this miniscule area were also produced by what appear to be pools or smudges of ink, products of the so-called drypoint technique. In targeted areas, the printmaker scratched his design directly into the copperplate with a drypoint needle, displacing small bits of metal, that is burrs, around which the ink pools in ways that are less precise than with etching and engraving. French critics and printmakers such as Bernard Picart (the son of Étienne), Florent le Comte, Pierre-Jean Mariette, Edme-François Gersaint, and Claude-Henri Watelet read these inky pools as signs of "lack of control and finish." Although many of them admired Lepautre, they described the faults in his etchings with negative terms such as *creusant* and *rongeant*, digging and gnawing, and thereby implied that Lepautre lacked judgment and care. In short, the manufacture of those tonal marks was ascribed more to the detritus of the copperplate, the burr, and the overly enthusiastic use of acid than to the controlled, deliberative hand of the artist.[11] Despite the objections of some critics, Lepautre had obviously mastered the chance effects of the burr in order to do justice to the grotto's surfaces and in general the structure, which the French Crown treated, at least for a few years, as one of the most important commissions of the period.

When a seventeenth-century reader of the *Description* happened upon Lepautre's illustration of the pillars, the combination of the precisely defined form and the picturesque surface details would have appeared striking and unusual. There was nothing in Lepautre's oeuvre, or that of any other French printmaker, that comprised these combined techniques in quite this manner. And there were few instances of French printmakers who relied on drypoint as extensively as Lepautre during the reign of Louis XIV. More typical of the French school was the work of Étienne Picart, an engraver who specialized in translating original works of art into their graphic equivalents. Picart employs the burin to conjure solid forms by means of *gravure rangée*, referring to the complex linear vocabulary of precisely arranged engraved lines with which to suggest form, texture, and chiaroscuro. The visual effect of the *gravure rangée* was described as polish (*poli*), firmness (*fermeté*), and sharpness (*netteté*), terms which denoted a calculated, rationalized approach directed by the artist's judgment and knowledge. These terms were borrowed from academic discourse by engravers and their defenders who established a hierarchy of printmaking techniques and genres: engraved narratives (*Histoires*) ranked above etched landscapes, ornaments, and views. As usual in this genre of print, etching of a sketchy sort plays a supporting role in a number of ways; for example, Picart relies on etching to define the setting of the composition, namely, the ornamented niche. The encrusted surface of the niche wall is convincingly distinguished from the smooth surface of the horse carved from white marble. It may have been Picart's equal facility with the engraving burin and etching needle that convinced Lepautre to combine printmaking techniques in a new way and thereby distinguish the surfaces of his prints from the encrusted surfaces in the prints of Étienne, for whom etching served a mere secondary role.

The choice to commission an engraver, rather than an etcher, to reproduce the sculptural monuments distinguishes the *Description* from suites of prints such as Dominique Barriére's nineteen plates devoted to the Aldobrandini gardens and grotto in Frascati (*Villa Aldobrandina Tusculana* ...) in which a uniform, sketchy etching style characterizes every view and kind of natural and fabricated object regardless of the object's surface characteristics. Published in Rome in 1647, Barriére's work was known in France not only because he was Frenchman working in Rome but also because he had dedicated the volume to the then nine-year old Louis XIV. Perhaps the mastermind behind the Versailles volume had decided to surpass the quality of Barriére's efforts by carefully considering how a variety of printmaking techniques could best express the particular characteristics of each section of Louis XIV's magnificent grotto? The most likely candidate overseeing the production of the *Description* is Charles Le Brun (1619–90), Louis XIV's first painter, head of the royal manufactory, right hand man of the superintendent of the king's works, Jean-Baptiste Colbert, and designer of the grotto's main sculpture groups.[12] Le Brun was also a print publisher of the first order who understood more than most the intricacies of printmaking and the potential visual effects of each technique.

Notes

1. On the *Petite Académie*, see Florian Knothe's chapter in this book. See also Robert Wellington, *Antiquarianism and the Visual Histories of Louis XIV: Artifacts for a Future Past* (Aldershot; Burlington: Ashgate, 2015), chapter 2.
2. Liliane Lange, "La grotte de Thétis et le premier Versailles de Louis XIV," *Art de France*, no. 1 (1961): 133–48. Robert W. Berger, "André Félibien: Description de la grotte de Versailles (description of the Grotto of Versailles). The original French text with facing English translation, introduction and notes," *History of Gardens and Designed Landscapes* 36, no. 2 (2015): 89–133. Hervé Brunon and Monique Mosser, *L'Imaginaire des Grottes dans les Jardins Européens* (Paris: Editions Hazan, 2014).
3. *Les Métamorphoses d'Ovide divisées en deux parties, traduites en françois par P. Du Ryer* (Paris: A. Sommaville, 1666), 453.
4. André Félibien, *Description de la Grotte de Versailles* (Paris: Imprimerie royale, 1676).
5. In the seventeenth century, the sea nymph Thetis was conflated with the ocean goddess Tethys. Although it was Tethys who Apollo visited, I am maintaining the early modern French practice, repeated by Félibien, and refer to the goddess as Thetis.
6. Thomas Hedin, *The Sculpture of Gaspard and Balthazard Marsy: Art and Patronage in the Early Reign of Louis XIV, with a Catalogue Raisonné* (Columbia: University of Missouri, 1983), 133–9.
7. *A Kingdom of Images: French Prints in the Age of Louis XIV* (Los Angeles, CA: Getty Research Institute, 2015), 11 and 262–4.
8. Dominique Barriére, *Villa Aldobrandina Tusculana* (Rome: n.p., 1647).
9. Louis Marchesano, "The Impostures Innocentes: Bernard Picart's Defense of the Professional Engraver," in *Bernard Picart and the First Global Vision of Religion*, ed. Lynn Hunt, Margaret Jacob, and Wijnand Mijnhardt (Los Angeles, CA: Getty Research Institute, 2010), 105–35.

10 Antoine-Joseph Pernety, *Dictionnaire portatif de peinture, sculpture et gravure: avec un traité pratique des differentes manieres de peindre, dont la théorie est développée dans les articles qui en sont susceptibles: ouvrage utile aux artistes, aux eleves & aux amateurs* (Paris: Bauche, 1757), 353.

11 Florent le Comte, *Cabinet des singularitez d'architecture, peinture, sculpture et graveure ...* (Paris: Étienne Picart and Nicolas Le Clerc, 1699–1700), vol. 3, 159–60; Watelet Claude-Henri, *Dictionnaire des arts de peinture, sculpture et gravure* (Paris: L.F. Prault 1792), 543–4.

12 Louis Marchesano and Christian Michel, *Printing the Grand Manner: Monumental Prints in the Age of Louis XIV* (Los Angeles, CA: Getty Research Institute, 2010).

Part Two

Versailles Life

6

Porcelain and Power: The Meaning of Sèvres Porcelain in Ancien-Régime France

Matthew J. Martin

The products of the Manufacture Royale de Sèvres are some of the most admired artistic creations associated with the world of the ancien-régime French Court (Figure 6.1). Their refined artistry and technical sophistication made them objects of connoisseurship and collecting from the moment of their creation in the eighteenth century. But far more than being beautiful examples of the extraordinary achievements of eighteenth-century French ceramic art, the Sèvres porcelain services created for the French Court, both for use by the king and other high-ranking courtiers and to serve as diplomatic gifts, point to the intimate connection that existed between the porcelain medium and royal power in ancien-régime France.

The ubiquity of porcelain in our lives today—we eat off it daily, it is essential to our hygiene practices, it is found in engineering and electronic components, it can even be found in our bodies in the guise of dental fillings and artificial hips—leads us to take this substance somewhat for granted. But European porcelain was far more than a utilitarian material in the eighteenth century. The medium was symbolically charged and functioned as a metaphor for power in the context of the absolutist state. After the discovery of the secret of a hard-paste porcelain at Dresden in Saxony in 1708, the newly mastered material immediately assumed a vital representational role at the Saxon Court. Augustus the Strong, Elector of Saxony and King of Poland, dispatched diplomatic gifts of porcelain produced at his factory established in the town of Meissen in 1710 to Courts across Europe. These gifts served as demonstration of Saxon cultural and material accomplishment, and as proof of the glory of the House of Wettin.[1]

Figure 6.1 Sèvres Porcelain Manufactory. Part of the Cameo service, 1778–9, State Hermitage, St Petersburg. Image in the public domain.

Other princes quickly sought to emulate the Saxon achievement, often taking advantage of the fruits of industrial espionage to achieve this end—the arcanum, or mystery, of porcelain production was a closely guarded state secret protected by the death penalty in Saxony.² But the race to establish porcelain manufactories by the ruling houses of Europe cannot be satisfactorily explained solely in mercantilist economic terms. Although one of Augustus the Strong's cabinet ministers and field marshals, Jacob Heinrich Graf von Flemming, was famously reported to have quipped that the Chinese were Saxony's "porcelain cupping glasses"³ so profligate was Augustus the Strong's spending on imported Asian porcelains, the extraordinary expenses involved in European porcelain production meant that it was generally only with extensive state subventions that these manufactories could continue to function. In other words, none of the great eighteenth-century continental porcelain factories were truly commercially viable enterprises in the modern sense. They were instead, first and foremost, Court institutions—departments of state—and they served the interests of the ruling prince; eighteenth-century European porcelain was a part of statecraft. The proliferation of princely sponsored porcelain manufactories across the German states and the rest of continental Europe should be seen, not primarily as an example of economic competition between states, but instead as evidence of the rapid apprehension of porcelain production as a new and essential element in the symbolic arsenal of absolutism. The key to understanding this symbolic function of European porcelain lies in its origins in the enterprise of alchemy, the field of natural philosophy concerned with understanding the nature of matter and learning the secrets of its manipulation.[4] It is surely no coincidence that it was at the Saxon Court, where there was a long history of interest in, and support for, alchemical enterprises, that the secret of porcelain production was achieved.[5] Two figures were crucial to the Saxon success: Ehrenfried Walther von Tschirnhaus and Johann Friedrich Böttger. If von Tschirnhaus is remembered as a mathematician, physicist, physician, philosopher, *Académicien*, and correspondent of Leibniz and Spinoza,[6] Böttger, his fellow investigator, was an apothecary, metallurgist, and professional alchemist who was being held under house arrest in Dresden after coming to the attention of Augustus the Strong for purported success in transforming base metals into gold.[7] Although there is dispute over which of this pair, von Tschirnhaus or Böttger, was ultimately responsible for the breakthrough, it is clear that Böttger—an acquaintance of Johann Kunckel von Löwenstern, an alchemist and founding figure of modern chemistry—and his technical laboratory skills, together with his commitment to the *possibility* of material transmutation, were critical to the success of the enterprise.[8] Together, the natural philosophers von Tschirnhaus and Böttger succeeded where so many others had failed.[9]

Meissen porcelain was not merely symbolic of Saxon technical and cultural achievement—it was physical proof of the Saxon Elector-Kings' status as anointed princes and their God-given mastery over created matter, able to command the perfection of base earth and its transformation into a marvelous, translucent, white material. The secrets of successful alchemical transformation had long been regarded as *donum dei*, so success in creating porcelain was naturally deemed to reflect divine favour.[10] Porcelain's alchemical origins imbued the material with a sacral quality. The continuing currency of this notion in absolutist Court circles in the eighteenth century is evidenced in the famous 1758 founding decree of the Ludwigsburg porcelain manufactory where the enterprise's patron, Carl Eugen von Württemberg, offered the telling observation that for a prince of his rank, a porcelain factory was "ein notwendiges Attribut des Glanzes und der Würde" [an essential attribute of splendour and dignity].[11]

I will argue here that the same symbolic understanding of European porcelain was at work in eighteenth-century France and that this often-overlooked aspect of the material's signification can cast light on certain of the more puzzling aspects of the Royal Sèvres Manufactory, considered by many the preeminent eighteenth-century European porcelain manufacturer. How do we explain the presence of an *appartement du roi* in the purpose-built factory complex at Sèvres? And why, during the Revolution and the years of the constitutional monarchy, did Louis XVI dedicate a not insignificant part of his limited financial resources to supporting the Sèvres factory? An appreciation of eighteenth-century European porcelain's sacral quality allows us to move beyond simplistic economic explanations for these phenomena to consider the role of porcelain and the Sèvres porcelain factory in eighteenth-century French royal ideology.

The *Grands Services*

It is often difficult today to appreciate the full impact of Sèvres tableware in their original contexts of display and use. In a museum exhibition, we are often invited to admire the beauties of individual items of porcelain, cosseted in secure display cases, with carefully contrived lighting highlighting the details of the richly executed decoration. But we must bear in mind that what we are viewing are but a handful of individual components from what were conceived of as extensive table services. The *Rubans bleu céleste* service of 1769–70 for Madame du Barry, the last *maîtresse-en-titre* of Louis XV, consisted of 270 components, the *Perles et Barbeaux*, service of 1781 for Marie-Antoinette, comprised 283 components and the 1784 *Riche en couleurs variées* service, again for Marie-Antoinette had over 300 components.[12]

The *grands services* were the most ambitious and celebrated of Sèvres's productions and a major contributor to the factory's reputation. They were also the most expensive: writing in 1781 factory director Jean-Jacques Bachelier protested "En general, la porcelaine de Sèvres est trop chère; elle ne doit pas être seulement à l'usage des rois et des grands; le debit en seroit trop borné" [Sèvres porcelain is too expensive; it should not be only for the use of kings and grandees; the turnover will be too small].[13] The scope of such services, with a huge range of specialized vessel types produced in large series, every piece bearing identical forms of decoration, presented enormous technical challenges for the manufactory and contributed to their equally enormous cost. Mimi Hellmann has acutely observed that the serial nature of much of the Sèvres factory's production—the labor-intensive creation of sets of identical objects, whether garnitures of vases or components of a dinner service—functioned as a statement of calculated excess, evidencing the ability to command a range of resources and production techniques to create these extraordinarily refined and beautiful objects intended for elite delectation and, perhaps occasionally, use.[14]

And when they were put to use, the components of a table service combined to create spectacle as pointedly theatrical as any other form of courtly display. A table set with elements of the Cameo service commissioned for Catherine the Great of Russia—at 744 pieces one of the grandest and most expensive Sèvres services ever created—gives a sense of the calculated visual impact of a *grand service* arrayed for use. The disposition of such a service upon the table top was executed according to carefully drawn up principles of display, with dishes laid out symmetrically along both axes of the table, similar to the arrangement seen in a diagram from a 1742 manual on the etiquette of grand banquets, *Le cuisinier moderne* by Vincent La Chapelle, principal chef to the Prince of Orange (Figure 6.2). The repetition of uniformly decorated porcelain forms, expanding across the surface of a monumentally scaled tabletop, brings to mind the diagrams for battlefield troop dispositions found in contemporaneous military manuals, or the plans of the park of Versailles itself, where order is established and control asserted through imposition of a visual discipline over the field of display—be

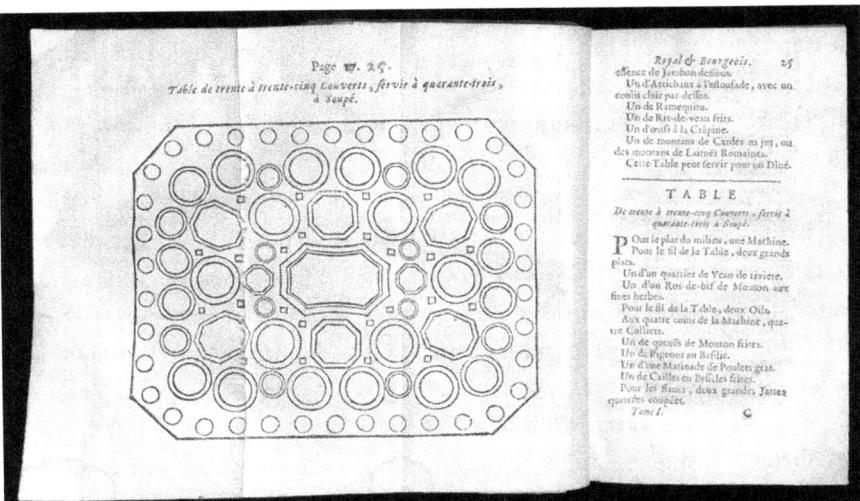

Figure 6.2 Vincent Chapelle, *Le nouveau cuisinier royal et bourgeois…* in François Massialot (1660–1733). Paris: La Veuve Prudhomme, 1742: Image courtesy of the University of Utah Libraries.

it the tabletop, the field of war, or the landscape—all according to the will of the prince.

In other words, the *grands services*—their manufacture, their disposition on the tabletop, their display and use—functioned at multiple levels as statements of princely power. But I wish to go one step further than this and suggest that the very material itself here, porcelain, brought to these objects and the ways in which they were used, further symbolic expressions of absolute power; that porcelain was understood in absolutist Court culture of the eighteenth century, including that of the French Court, as a material manifestation of princely dignity, signifying the anointed prince's divinely legitimized authority over the created world.

Trianon de Porcelaine

The association between porcelain and royal authority in France was long-standing and predated the foundation of Sèvres in 1756. At Versailles during the reign of Louis XIV, we find the first important instance of the power of the king and his political ambitions being expressed through the idea of porcelain. In 1670-1 Louis XIV had a *maison de plaisance* erected on the site of the village of Trianon, recently annexed to the park of Versailles at the northern end of the transverse arm of the Grand Canal. Designed by Louis Le Vau and François d'Orbay this small pleasure palace was situated in extensive flower gardens which gave the complex its original name, the *Pavillon de Flore*. But very quickly, the pavilion acquired an alternative title, the *Trianon de porcelaine*[15] (Figure 6.3). This name derived from the predominantly blue and white color scheme which dominated the decoration of the interiors and parts of the exteriors of the building, "in the manner of wares from China" (à la manière des ouvrages qui viennent de la Chine).[16] Contrary to reports in older literature, the exteriors and roofs of the pavilions were not tiled in blue and white ceramics; instead both the gambrel roofs and the numerous large vases on the roof balustrade, as well as the gables were covered with blue-and-white painted lead sheets and copper vase forms.[17] Inside the building the blue-and-white continued in faience tiled floors, mirror frames, furniture, fabrics, and stucco ornaments: even the window frames were painted with blue-and-white patterns.[18] Interestingly, there is no mention of any Asian porcelain in connection with the building's decoration and the ceramic tiles employed in its adornment were largely produced by

Figure 6.3 Pierre Aveline, l'ancien, (c. 1656–1722) *Entrée du Trianon de Porcelaine*, Etching/Engraving, in *Recueil de 58 planches vues de Trianon et de Versailles*- c. 1690 GR104. Photo: Château de Versailles, Dist. RMN-Grand Palais/Christophe Fouin.

French manufacturers.[19] It was instead the color scheme, intimately associated in the seventeenth century with imported Asian porcelain, that lent the pavilion its name.[20]

This evocation of the idea of porcelain was no mere decorative whim on Louis XIV's part. Rather, it was a pointed statement of political ambitions. If blue and white evoked the idea of porcelain, porcelain itself was intimately associated with the idea of the Chinese Empire whose emperor was construed in Europe at the time as a model absolute ruler, a role in which Louis no doubt saw himself. But the politics of porcelain also resonated in a far more immediate fashion in the French king's jealous rivalry with the Dutch Republic. The architectural use of porcelain to adorn interior spaces had been pioneered in seventeenth-century Europe by the women of the Dutch House of Orange. The Republic of the United Netherlands enjoyed a virtual monopoly on the importation of Asian commodities, including porcelain, into Europe for much of the seventeenth century and Asian porcelain was adopted by the Orange Court as a means of visually representing the mercantile supremacy of the Dutch global trading empire. The porcelain cabinet created in 1654 by Amalia von Solms-Braunfels at Huis Ten Bosch, adorned with imported lacquer and her collection of 398 pieces of porcelain, is considered the first "porcelain room" in Europe.[21]

The architectural use of porcelain thus came to be emblematic of the power of the Dutch Republic, a power which, by the 1670s, the French king eyed enviously and plotted to usurp. The extensive flower gardens of the Trianon, too, reflected the king's political ambitions, containing as they did numerous exotic plants imported from across the globe by Dutch merchants—chestnut trees from India, limes from the West Indies, tuberoses from Mexico, and narcissi from Turkey.[22] There were no fewer than 96,000 flowering plants and hundreds of thousands of plants in pots employed in the Trianon's gardens, many of them forced in hot houses which, when circulated, allowed the gardens to remain full of flowers all through the year, even in the heart of winter.[23] The flower gardens thus not only represented the king's claims to global authority, but also reflected his power over the very laws of nature themselves.

In the *Trianon de porcelaine*, despite the absence of real porcelain, Louis XIV nevertheless invoked the *idea* of porcelain as an expression of his claim to universal dominion and his aspirations to eclipse the Dutch Republic and lay claim to the trade which brought porcelain to Europe, aspirations which he would begin to pursue in earnest in 1672, a year after the pavilion's completion, with the opening of his Dutch War.[24]

Sèvres

If, in the seventeenth century, porcelain symbolized the French king's metaphorical claim to the riches of the East and his aspirations to control global trade, this symbolism shifted in the eighteenth century as the foundation of first the Vincennes and then the Sèvres manufactories delivered to Louis XV the power to command porcelain production. The Vincennes factory was founded in 1740 in the Château de Vincennes east of Paris under the direction of Jean-Louis Orry de Fulvy, intendant of finance and director of the French East India Company. Funded by private shareholders, the factory's starting capital also included a personal loan of 10,000 livres from Louis XV's privy purse, indicating the king's personal interest in the enterprise from its very outset.[25] Louis continued to grant the company valuable privileges throughout its early years, confirming on it the exclusive right to produce porcelain in "the Saxon style" in 1745, referring to the products of the Meissen factory that dominated European porcelain at the time.[26] A crisis in 1751 saw the king, in 1752, subscribe to a quarter of the factory's financial stock, becoming the single largest stockholder, and in 1753 the factory was granted the title *Manufacture Royale de Porcelaine de France*.[27]

In 1756 the factory was moved, at great expense, to imposing purpose-built premises on the site of the village of Sèvres on the road to Versailles from Paris. In 1759 the onset of further financial difficulties for the factory saw the king acquire the entire capital stock of the manufactory for the impressive sum of 1,937,509 livres.[28]

The string of financial difficulties that dogged the early history of the French Royal Porcelain Manufactory illustrate the enterprise's lack of sustained commercial viability. Such financial problems would remain perennial; by the end of the first decade of the factory's operations as a state enterprise in 1769, the Crown had to make up a cumulative deficit of almost 750,000 livres.[29] And we should recall that the construction of the factory premises at Sèvres and the king's purchase of the venture outright coincide with the period of the Seven Years Wars (1756–63), making royal intervention seem quite extravagant.

How do we explain the seemingly peculiar priorities on the part of the French monarch? First, we need to take account of the mercantilist model which dominated eighteenth-century economic thought. This taught that there was only a finite amount of wealth in the world for which individual states competed, so that discouraging the purchase of Asian or Saxon porcelain in place of a French product served to preserve France's share of this limited wealth pool. Conversely, selling French porcelain to the rest of the world served to simultaneously enrich France and impoverish foreign states.

But beyond this economic imperative, there was, as we have suggested, a more profound significance to being able to command the fabrication of porcelain. In eighteenth-century Europe porcelain production continued to be widely framed as part of alchemy. Alchemy encompassed a broad range of laboratory-based procedures but is best known for its pursuit of chrysopoeia, the transmutation of base metals into gold. This alchemical idea of perfecting baser matter had informed the pursuit of the secret of porcelain from its beginnings in Europe. The earliest European production of an artificial soft-paste porcelain took place in Florence in 1575 in the context of Grand Duke Francesco I de Medici's program of alchemical experimentation conducted at the Casino di San Marco.[30]

Following its heyday in the seventeenth century, the eighteenth century is often characterized as the era that saw the categorical demise of alchemy as a legitimate intellectual pursuit. From the 1720s onwards Europe's scientific academies conducted a public campaign to discredit the alchemical enterprise as fraudulent. But work by historians of science like Lawrence Principe has demonstrated that a gap existed between the public denouncement of alchemy and the actual practices of leading chemists of the period.[31] Just as the alchemist Böttger had played a key role in the formulation of a true hard-paste porcelain in Dresden in 1708, in France too, alchemy played an important role in the pursuit of porcelain. Jean Hellot, noted chemist and member of the *Académie Royale des Sciences*, was from 1751 until his death in 1766, the chief technician at the royal porcelain factory, appointed to formulate pastes, glazes, and enamel colours.[32] Hellot had also held a position at the Gobelins since 1739 as administrator of the department of dyes, a realm that still very much framed its endeavors in terms of arcana.[33] As Principe has demonstrated, Hellot, the so-called father of French industrial chemistry, actively pursued alchemical, and in particular, chrysopoeiac knowledge in privacy throughout his career in the royal manufactories. Hellot's library contained a large number of important sixteenth and seventeenth-century alchemical treatises—we know this through the records of his estate sale where, interestingly enough, some of these texts were purchased by Antoine Lavoisier.[34]

That persons generally remembered as founding figures of scientific chemistry should have had truck with "irrational" pursuits like alchemy alerts us to the fact that the separation of modern science from natural philosophy was a less clear-cut process than has sometimes been described, and that the realms of chemistry and alchemy remained continuous for much of the eighteenth century. The pursuit of material transmutation, associated with alchemical knowledge, was fully compatible with the laboratory-based artisanal practices associated with the eighteenth-century royal manufactories that sought to master the creation of porcelain or the manufacture of dye-stuffs. Indeed, the transformation of raw earth into hard, translucent, white porcelain could be understood by natural philosophers as a resounding affirmation of the transmutational goals pursued by alchemy. An interest in alchemy did not merely derive from the potential for generating material wealth. The alchemical transmutation of matter, achieved through the patronage, and at the command, of a prince, testified to that prince's authority. We should not be surprised then to learn that Louis XV entertained a personal interest in chemistry, engaging in chemical experimentation.[35] His mistress, Madame de Pompadour, shared these interests, being reported to have conducted thermal-shock experiments upon different porcelain bodies in the salon of her apartments before an audience that included the king.[36] Louis XVI, too, maintained workshops devoted to applied sciences including physics and chemistry in close proximity to his private apartments at Versailles. Rather than evidence of simple intellectual curiosity, these activities instantiate the rehearsal of scientific phenomena in order to demonstrate inherent personal qualities, providing proof, as historian of science William Eamon has suggested, that "nature's occult forces existed for the use and delight of the prince."[37]

The creation of porcelain, then, was proof that the alchemical enterprise could produce the types of material transformation that its practitioners had vigorously pursued for so long, while serving as a physical demonstration of a prince's worldly dominion. A royal porcelain factory enabled Louis XV to command the transformation of French earth into a miraculous, beautiful material that was at once art and nature. The nature of the Sèvres manufactory as a self-contained society emphasized the enterprise's unique status in France. Workers were legally prevented from leaving the manufactory's employ without the king's consent, to protect the factory's secrets, but by way of compensation, many workers lived rent-free in the manufactory grounds, worshipping in the factory chapel, while children borne of marriages between factory workers frequently entered the factory rolls as apprentices in the workshop of their father or mother.[38] The extraordinary presence of an *appartement du roi* in the Sèvres factory complex indicates clearly the relationship between porcelain production and royal power.[39] Propriety dictated that the king, or any other noble for that matter, could not involve themselves in a commercial enterprise or manual labor without derogation of status.[40] But at the Sèvres factory, the royal presence and the process of porcelain creation were intimately linked architecturally and spatially (Figure 6.4). The main approach to the factory building provided the appearance of a royal residence, with its own entrance giving access to the king's apartment. Beyond lay the factory proper. The different parts of the porcelain production process were housed across four floors, discretely separating the various teams of artists and artisans who were collectively responsible for the final product.[41] The staircase from the main entrance allowed customers access to the library in the royal apartment, where recent creations were set aside for the monarch's inspection and where, in 1758, the king established a permanent sales outlet. The doors to this room were surmounted by a portrait medallion of Louis XV and the coat of arms of France, framed by garlands, emphasizing the

Figure 6.4 *Manufacture royale de Sèvres. Façade de la cour royale.* Archives de la Manufacture. 2012.1.1637. Photo: RMN-Grand Palais (Sèvres, Cité de la céramique)/ Martine Beck-Coppola.

intimate relationship between French porcelain and the French king.[42] A second staircase, accessible only from the king's salon, allowed the monarch private access to all of the workshops and studios in the factory, giving him alone a panoptic oversight of the entire porcelain production process.[43] The only other person to have regular access to this staircase was the chemist Hellot, the factory's chief technician, who vicariously represented the king and his command of porcelain creation in the monarch's absence. The *appartement du roi* guaranteed the king's perpetual presence where French earth was transformed into French porcelain.

Augustus the Strong's establishment of the royal porcelain manufactory at Meissen in 1710 provided the Saxon ruler with a new medium for the projection of prestige on the European political stage; from the outset, the factory produced porcelain objects intended as diplomatic gifts, the material serving to represent the power of the Saxon monarch to foreign Courts and princes.[44] Significant gifts of Saxon porcelain made to the French Court provided a precedent for the use of the material for diplomatic gifts that was emulated by Louis XV and his grandson in the second half of the eighteenth century. From 1758 until the Revolution, French porcelain produced at the Royal Manufactory was gifted to foreign princes and ambassadors, simultaneously marking the favor of the monarch, and demonstrating French artistic supremacy in the medium, firmly established in Europe after the sacking of Meissen by Prussian troops during the Seven Years War saw that manufactory descend into disarray that lasted for years.[45] The products of the king's factory at Sèvres functioned as an extension of the *gloire* of the monarch, advertising royal power and the prestige of the French state, physically projecting the king's will into foreign lands.

If porcelain production served as a demonstration of the actuality of the anointed monarch's power, then a number of other aspects of the history of French porcelain production which are usually explained in economic terms take on new significance. The various legal restrictions placed upon the manufacturing and decorating of porcelain outside the royal enterprise did not simply serve to protect Sèvres position in the market—they also emphasize the intimate and exclusive connection between French porcelain and royal power.[46] The curtailing of the types of decoration which might be employed by other French porcelain makers reduced their wares' marketability, effectively creating a royal monopoly on the production of sophisticated "regal" porcelain wares. The two longest established and most successful of the porcelain factories predating the royal manufactory, Saint Cloud (established in around 1693) and Chantilly (established around 1726), both enjoyed early princely patronage, that of the regent Philippe II duc d'Orléans, and Louis Henri de Bourbon, prince de Condé, respectively.[47] The progressive reduction of the privileges enjoyed by these factories not only damaged their market competitiveness but simultaneously pressed the exclusive claim of the monarch to the mystery of porcelain creation over factories who had enjoyed the sponsorship of princes of the blood.

The final chapter in the story of French porcelain's role in royal ideology was played out during the Revolution. On September 11, 1789, the National Assembly voted to deny Louis XVI access to tax revenues. Instead he was granted an annual civil list to the value of 25 million livres, in addition to the costs involved in the upkeep of his parks, domains, and forests. The fate of the royal manufactories was also under discussion by the revolutionary government when in August 1790 the king intervened, making the oft-cited declaration, added by the king himself to a report of the comte d'Angiviller, director of the Bâtiments du Roi, to the *comité des pensions*: "Je garde la Manufacture de Sèvres à mes frais" [I keep the Sèvres Manufactory at my expense].[48] Louis dedicated 100,000 écus (600,000 livres) per annum from the civil list to the upkeep of the Sèvres manufactory, effectively ensuring that the factory remained property of the king.

Given the gravity of the political situation and the numerous demands on the king's resources, this support for the royal porcelain manufactory might seem puzzling. Arguments were made at the time by d'Angiviller that the economic advantages of maintaining production of a renowned French luxury export, as well as keeping 200–300 people in employment during a period of considerable economic disruption, was paramount. In addition to this, D'Angiviller argued, was the reality that, if sold at that point in time, the factory would not realize its true value and an enormous loss would be suffered.[49]

But any real economic benefits from maintaining an enterprise which, in addition to having lost the majority of its client base, had never been able to survive without royal financial support were arguably negligible. The benefits, certainly in the mind of the king, must have been other than economic. Far more compelling I would suggest is the notion that, so significant, was the Sèvres factory in his conception of monarchy that Louis XVI could not countenance his role as king without the manufactory at his command. At a moment when the National Assembly denied him any opportunity to conduct independent foreign policy, the ability to continue to command the production of Sèvres porcelain gave the king, through the established practice of diplomatic gifts of porcelain, a possible means to project royal authority both domestically and abroad.[50] For the king, the factory so instantiated royal authority that its loss would have left him without the ability to materialize his status as an anointed ruler and thereby command, quite literally, not just the French, but the soil of France itself. Here the reaction of the manufactory's staff to the fall of the monarchy on August 10, 1792, is interesting. On August 14, with financial support for the manufactory having vanished, all the papers containing the secrets pertaining to the fabrication of porcelain were sealed by the manufacturers, locked in a cupboard and then guarded around the clock. These actions were curious since, by the 1790s, everyone *knew* the technical practicalities of making porcelain—as the proliferation of Paris-based porcelain enterprises demonstrates. Yet immediately afterwards, the manufactory employees summoned a representative of the new regime, the procurer of Sèvres, in order that their arrangements be made legal by a repeat performance in the presence of a *Juge de la Paix*.[51] What the manufacturers were guarding was a secret. What Sèvres had always done was guard a secret; therein had always lain part of its special status. But that secret, that *Arcanum*, was not a mundane material recipe for the manufacture of ceramics. Rather, it was the claim to authority that was manifest in the manipulation of natural forces. With the king gone, there was no one to wield that authority. It needed to be set aside until a new claimant—the French Republic—stepped forward to take up the mantle.

Notes

1. See Maureen Cassidy-Geiger, ed., *Fragile Diplomacy: Meissen Porcelain for European Courts ca. 1710–63* (New Haven, CT and London: Yale University Press, 2007).
2. The *Special privilegium* granted on May 27, 1718, to the Flemish Claudius Innocentius du Paquier, founder (with the help of a deserter from Meissen, the kilnmaster Samuel Stözel) of a porcelain factory in the imperial capital of Vienna speaks of porcelain production being "no ordinary craft, but a secret and most excellent art." See Meredith Chilton, ed., *Fired by Passion: Vienna Baroque Porcelain of Claudius Innocentius du Paquier*, vol. 1 (Stuttgart: Arnoldsche Art Publishers, 2009), 550.
3. Ulrich Pietsch, "Meissen Porcelain: Making a Brilliant Entrance, 1710 to 1763," in *Triumph of the Blue Swords; Meissen Porcelain for Aristocracy and Bourgeoisie, 1710–1815*, ed. Ulrich Pietsch and Claudia Banz (Leipzig: Seeman Verlag, 2010), 14.
4. On the history of alchemy in European thought, see Lawrence Principe, *The Secrets of Alchemy* (Chicago, IL and London: Chicago University Press, 2013).
5. Helen Watanabe O'Kelly, *Court Culture in Dresden from Renaissance to Baroque* (Basingstoke: Palgrave Macmillan, 2002), 100–29, esp. 115ff.
6. Martin Schönfeld, "Was There a Western Inventor of Porcelain?" *Technology and Culture* 39, no. 4 (1998): 716–27.
7. For an overview of the discovery of the Arcanum in Dresden, see Christina Nelson and Letitia Roberts, *History of Eighteenth-Century German Porcelain: The Warda Stevens Stout Collection* (New York: Hudson Hills Press, 2013), 117–83. Examples of gold and silver attributed to experiments conducted by Böttger in 1713 for Augustus the Strong survive today in the Porzellansammlung in Dresden. See Dirk Syndram and Ulrike Weinhold, eds, *Böttger Stoneware: Johann Friedrich Böttger and Treasury Art* (Berlin: Deutscher Kunstverlag, 2009), 27–8.
8. Klaus Hoffmann, "Johann Friedrich Böttger—Stationen seines Lebens," in *Johann Friedrich Böttger: Die Erfindung des europäischen Porzellans*, ed. Willi Goder, Klaus Hoffmann, Rolf Sonnemann and Eberhard Wächtler (Leipzig: Staatliche Kunstsammlungen Dresden, 1982), 71–80.
9. Roald Hoffmann, "Meissen Chymistry," *American Scientist* 92, no. 4 (2004): 312–15.
10. Principe, *Secrets of Alchemy*, 192ff; Pamela H. Smith, *The Business of Alchemy: Science and Culture in the Holy Roman Empire* (Princeton, NJ: Princeton University Press, 1994), 182.
11. April 5, 1758, Hauptstaatsarchiv Stuttgart A 248 Bü 2430. The Württemberg Court at Stuttgart had a long-standing association with alchemical research.

Tara Nummedal, *Alchemy and Authority in the Holy Roman Empire* (Chicago, IL: University of Chicago Press, 2007), 32, 122–40.

12 David Peters, *Sèvres Plates and Services of the 18th Century*, 7 vols (London: The French Porcelain Society, 2005).

13 Jean-Jacques Bachelier, *Memoire Historique sur la Manufacture Nationale de Porcelaine de France*, ed. Gustave Gouellain (Paris: R. Simon, 1878), 26.

14 Mimi Hellman, "The Joy of Sets: The Uses of Seriality in the French Interior," in *Furnishing the Eighteenth Century: What Furniture Can Tell Us about the European and American Past*, ed. Dena Goodman and Kathryn Norberg (New York and London: Routledge, 2006), 129–53.

15 For a description of the *Trianon de porcelain* and its interiors, see André Félibien, *Description sommaire du chasteau de Versailles* (Paris: Charles Savreaux, 1674), 104–11.

16 Félibien, *Description sommaire*, 110.

17 Andrew Zega and Bernd H. Dams, *Palaces of the Sun King. Versailles, Trianon, Marly: The châteaux of Louis XIV* (London: Laurence King Publishing, 2002), 99, 198 n.3.

18 Félibien, *Description sommaire*, 111. There exists a painted fan leaf in the collections of the V&A which, presents an imaginative interpretation of the Trianon's interior, highlighting the predominant blue and white colour scheme. See Pamela Cowan, *A Fanfare for the Sun King: Unfolding Fans for Louis XIV* (London: Third Millennium Publishing, 2003), 84–91.

19 Georg Kaufmann, *Bemalte Wandfliesen. Bunte Welt auf kleinen Platten. Kulturgeschichte, Technik und Dekoration der Fliesen in Mitteleuropa* (Leipzig: Duncker und Humblot, 1880), 27; J-M. de Montoclos and Robert Polidori, *Versailles* (Cologne: Könneman, 1996), 160.

20 The Trianon's interiors in turn instigated a new mode of elite decoration: *façon de pourceline*, employing a blue and white palette. See Cordula Bischoff, "Women Collectors and the Rise of the Porcelain Cabinet," in *Chinese and Japanese Porcelain for the Dutch Golden Age*, ed. Jan van Campen and Titus Eliëens (Zwolle: Waanders, 2014), 171–89.

21 Bischoff, *Women Collectors*, 175.

22 Zega and Dams, *Palaces of the Sun King*, 103.

23 Bischoff, *Women Collectors*, 175.

24 This political dimension of the *Trianon de porcelain*'s representational function is emphasized by the fact that the pavilion was shown to foreign dignitaries on diplomatic tours through the gardens of Versailles. See Robert Berger and Thomas Hedin, *Diplomatic Tours in the Gardens of Versailles under Louis XIV* (Philadelphia: University of Pennsylvania Press, 2008).

25 See Sven Eriksen and Geoffrey de Bellaigue, *Sèvres Porcelain: Vincennes and Sèvres 1740–1800* (London and Boston, MA: Faber and Faber, 1987), 25.
26 In 1745 the company's shareholders applied to the *conseil d'Etat* for the exclusive right to produce "porcelaine façon de Saxe," and this application was accepted in July of that year with the grant of a patent "de fabriques en France, des porcelaines de la même qualité que celles qui se font en Saxe, pour dispenser les consommateurs de ce royaume de faire passer leurs fonds dans les pays étrangeres." Arch. Nat., 01 2059, Arrest du Conseil d'Etat du Roi qui accorde a Charles Adam le privilege pour l'établissement de la Manufacture de Porcelaine façon de Saxe, au Château de Vincennes du 24 Juillet 1745.
27 Eriksen and de Bellaigue, *Sèvres Porcelain*, 35, 102–3.
28 Charles Coulston Gillespie, *Science and Polity in France at the end of the Old Regime* (Princeton, NJ: Princeton University Press, 1980), 394.
29 Gillespie, *Science and Polity*, 395.
30 Marco Beretta, "Material and Temporal Powers at the Casino Di San Marco (1574–1621)," in *Laboratories of Art: Alchemy and Art Technology from Antiquity to the Eighteenth Century*, ed. Sven Dupré (New York: Springer, 2014), 129–56.
31 Lawrence M. Principe, "The End of Alchemy? The Repudiation and Persistence of Chrysopoeia at the Académie Royale des Sciences in the Eighteenth Century," *Osiris* 29, no. 1 (2014): 96–116.
32 Gillespie, *Science and Polity*, 399.
33 Gillespie, *Science and Polity*, 408.
34 Principe, *The End of Alchemy*, 112; Marco Beretta, "Transmutations and Frauds in Enlightened Paris: Lavoisier and Alchemy," in *Fakes!? Hoaxes, Counterfeits and Deception in Early Modern Science*, ed. Marco Beretta and Maria Conforti (Sagamore Beach: Science History Publications, 2014), 69–108.
35 Donald Posner, "Mme. de Pompadour as a Patron of the Visual Arts," *Art Bulletin* 72, no. 1 (1990): 87.
36 Millot, *Origin de la Manufacture des Porcelaines du Roi en 1740*, M.N.S. Arch Y-53—Y-59, fol. 5, recounted in Gillispie, *Science and Polity*, 402.
37 William Eamon, *Science and the Secrets of Nature: Books of Secrets in Medieval and Early Modern Culture* (Princeton, NJ: Princeton University Press, 1994), 271.
38 Derek Ostergard, ed., *The Sèvres Porcelain Manufactory: Alexandre Brongniart and the Triumph of Art and Industry, 1800–1847* (New Haven, CT: Yale University Press, 1997), 17.
39 Bachelier comments in his *memoire* that the king took interest in all of the manufactory's operations: Bachelier, *Memoire Historique*, 9. The royal apartment is already present in the plans for the new buildings drawn up in 1752.
40 Leora Auslander, *Taste and Power: Furnishing Modern France* (Los Angeles: University of California Press, 1996), 96.

41 John Whitehead, *Sèvres at the time of Louis XV: Birth of the Legend* (Paris: Editions Courtes et Longues, 2010), 96.
42 Whitehead, *Sèvres at the time of Louis XV*, 96.
43 The directive defining Jean Hellot's responsibilities at the royal porcelain manufactory issued on June 25, 1751, by the controller-general of finances, Jean-Baptiste de Machault, speaks of the fact that the king reserved for himself "the secret of the said [porcelain] compositions." Gillespie, *Science and Polity*, 399.
44 For a comprehensive examination of the role of Meissen porcelain in eighteenth-century Saxon diplomacy, see Geiger, *Fragile Diplomacy*.
45 Marie-Laure de Rochbrune, "La porcelain de Vincennes-Sèvres: une arme diplomatique au 18e siècle," *The French Porcelain Society Journal* 3 (2007): 20–34.
46 The restrictions imposed on the production of porcelain by other manufactories are detailed in Arrest du Conseil d'Etat du Roi of August 19, 1753, see Arch. Nat., 01 2059.
47 On Saint Cloud, see Bertrand Rondot, ed., *Discovering the Secrets of Soft-Paste Porcelain at the Saint Cloud Manufactory ca. 1690–1766* (New Haven, CT and London: Yale University Press, 1999). On Chantilly see Geneviève Le Duc, *Porcelaine tendre de Chantilly au XVIIIe siècle* (Paris: Hazan, 1996). The duc d'Orléans had an intense interest in alchemy and pursued transmutational experiments in a magnificent laboratory he maintained in the Palais Royal (Principe, *The End of Alchemy*, 99).
48 Arch. Nat., 0^1 2061, *Memoire*, August 1790.
49 D'Angiviller's response to questions put to him about the manufactory by Armand-Gaston Camus's *Comite des Pensions*, Arch. Nat., 0^1 2061, *Memoire*, August 1790.
50 I thank the reviewer of the draft of this chapter for suggesting the connection between the king's continued control of Sèvres and the ability to conduct diplomacy independent of the National Assembly.
51 Arch. M.N.S., B^4, "Procès-verbal des Scellés apposés sur les papiers de la manufacture des porcelaines de Sèvres."

7

Hair, Politics, and Power at the Court of Versailles

Kimberly Chrisman-Campbell

From the improbably lush, dark curls of the elderly King Louis the Fourteenth to the gravity-defying whitened hair of the young Queen Marie-Antoinette almost a century later, one of the characteristic features of the Court of Versailles was elaborately artificial hair, sometimes in the form of a neatly cropped and curled wig, sometimes worn tumbling to the waist or towering to the chandelier.

Scholarly studies of hair have focused on its natural, anthropological, and corporeal properties. As historian Angela Rosenthal has written, "Emerging from the flesh and thus both of, and without the body .... hair occupies an extraordinary position between the natural and the cultural."[1] But hair at Versailles was never "natural"; often it wasn't human hair at all, or at least not the wearer's own hair. And it was frequently obscured by wigs, powder, flowers, feathers, and other trimmings. Culture was everything, and hair was as laden with meaning as it was with ornamentation, reflecting the era's social, political, and aesthetic revolutions.

As a young man, Louis XIV was blessed with naturally thick, curly dark blond hair. Long hair was not considered a feminine ornament in the seventeenth century, but a sign of virility (Figure 7.1). (Women had long hair, too, of course, but only young, unmarried girls wore it loose and uncovered.) But what happened when a man began to go gray or lose his hair, as Louis did, probably in his late teens? Prior to the seventeenth century, wigs were worn only in exceptional circumstances, to disguise baldness, not as an everyday accoutrement for men of all ages. Louis XIII was said to have worn a wig or a small toupee, but it did not become a general fashion; that changed with his successor.

Figure 7.1 Nicolas Bonnart, *Habit d'Espée en Esté,* hand-colored engraving on paper, c. 1678, Los Angeles, Los Angeles County Museum of Art (M.2002.57.34). Image in the public domain.

From natural hair, Louis XIV progressed to natural-looking wigs. As he grew older, however, he adopted much larger, sculpted, and obviously artificial wigs, suggesting that wigs were no longer considered cosmetic devices but important status symbols and fashion statements (Figure 7.2). Indeed, the king continued to wear brown wigs even as younger and more fashion-conscious men somewhat perversely began powdering their wigs white, in deference to the king's (presumably) graying hair. (Louis shaved off his moustache in around 1683, possibly signaling that he was going gray.) Wigs were not supposed to fool anyone, instead functioning almost as garments; men threw them over their shoulders when bowing, tied them in knots, accidentally set them on fire, and appreciated their warmth in the winter but not in the summer.

By 1673, wigs had become so ubiquitous that Louis incorporated the Parisian guild of barbers and wigmakers—two professions that went hand-in-hand and often shared the same workspace (Figure 7.3). In 1678, the *Mercure galant* noted that "the wigs we wear now are very informal. They are half frizzed and half

Hair, Politics, and Power at the Court of Versailles 97

Figure 7.2 Charles Simonneau after Antoine Benoist, *Portraits de Louis le Grand gravés suivant ses differents âges MDCCIV* [1704]. Text by the poet Étienne Pavillon. Engraving, 1704, Princeton University, Graphic Arts Collection. Image in the public domain.

Figure 7.3 *Le Perruquier Barbier* engraving by R. Bénard after J.R. Lucotte, 1762. London, Wellcome Collection. Photo: Creative Commons license CC-BY.

curled .... They are not worn quite as long as last year's."[2] Indeed, fashions in wigs changed quickly, from season to season, and required constant updating. As a result, they are a very reliable method of dating portraits.

The concept of a professional hairdresser, male or female, was a novelty in the seventeenth century. Women's maids had traditionally styled their hair, while men relied on male barbers, who also performed services such as shaving, bloodletting, and amputations—anything requiring a razor. In 1659, however, the barbers' guild was split into two new guilds, one for medical men, or barber-surgeons, and one for *barbier-perruquiers*, who dressed hair, shaved beards, and made and maintained wigs or *perruques*.

From their early natural look, wigs began to fill out from the bottom up; once they could get no fuller, they grew vertically. By 1700, they had separated into two distinctive peaks. Men began to carry their tricorn hats under one arm because they could not sit comfortably on the peaked wigs of the period, earning them the name *chapeaux bras* or "arm hats." The back of the wig, rarely visible in portraits, changed as dramatically as the front.

Considering how often the French were at war under Louis XIV, it is not surprising that fashions—including fashions in hair—frequently took inspiration from military dress. The campaign wig, for example, was sectioned off and either tied or knotted, to keep it out of the way during battle. In Antoine Dieu's tapestry cartoon depicting the wedding of Louis XIV's grandson the duc de Bourgogne, the royal guard in the left foreground wears ceremonial uniform based on medieval dress and centuries out of date, but his hairstyle is the most modern in the group.[3] Soldiers had begun to tie their hair back, for convenience and hygiene in camp and on the battlefield. Within a few decades, the cumbersome long wig had virtually disappeared, and all men wore queues, either curled or covered by a black silk bag. The bag wig (*perruque à bourse*) was the height of fashion by the 1720s and remained an essential element of formal dress until the French Revolution. Even as shorter styles replaced long wigs, endless variety was possible through different arrangements of curls and ribbons.

The decision to wear a wig was a momentous one for any man, because it meant shaving his head; it was the only way to wear a wig comfortably, and it also eliminated the persistent problem of lice. At home, a man would take off his wig and put on a soft cap or turban for warmth. Hair powder, like the wig itself, had multiple practical and symbolic functions. Essentially a powdered perfume heavily diluted with inexpensive starch, it was sold by perfumers, not hairdressers or wigmakers. It functioned much as dry shampoo does today, but with an added aesthetic component; it absorbed oils from natural hair while giving both hair and wigs a fresh, uniform appearance. It acted as a deodorant, as well—an important consideration in an age when bathing was considered eccentric and even dangerous. Ironically, by imitating gray hair, it masked one's true age.

Perfumer's accounts indicate that hair powder was almost always purchased with pomade, an ointment made from apples—or *pommes*, in French—mixed with rendered fat, among other ingredients, which scented, conditioned, thickened, and set hair and wigs. It was sold in pots and later sticks, which were better suited to the more complex hairstyles that came into vogue in the 1770s. Without powder, the pomade would have been sticky and wet-looking, and without pomade, powder would not adhere well.[4]

Powder was applied daily, using large swansdown powder puffs. A mask kept powder off the face and out of the lungs, while a cloth or *peignoir* (from the verb *peigner*, meaning "to comb") protected the clothes. But traces of powder might be visible along the hairline, or dusting a man's shoulders; stray powder is sometimes visible in portraits, suggesting that it was not a sartorial faux pas but a desirable proof of one's fashionability and youth. In the second half of the eighteenth century, powder bellows permitted a more uniform and less wasteful method of application. Even after white powder finally went out of fashion, men (and women) continued to use hair-colored powder, for hygienic reasons.

Mens' wigs continued to shrink in the 1760s, mirroring the new fashion for slim-fitting, streamlined suits. More and more young men began to forego them altogether, to the mutual horror of wigmakers and balding and graying men. But they remained an essential part of formal dress, and it was considered sensational when Benjamin Franklin paid a diplomatic visit to Versailles in 1778 wearing his own thinning, gray hair. On a previous visit in 1764, Franklin had allowed a French tailor and *perruquier* to "[transform him] into a Frenchman," as he put it.[5] But when he returned to solicit France's support for the American Revolution, his dressed-down appearance reinforced the newly United States of America's reputation as a nation of unpretentious, freedom-loving farmers. Marie-Antoinette's lady-in-waiting Madame Campan, among others, noted how "his straight, unpowdered hair, his round hat, [and] his suit of brown wool" contrasted "with the sequined and embroidered suits, the powdered and perfumed coiffures of the courtiers of Versailles." But far from offending his hosts, Campan testified, "this novelty charmed all … the French women."[6]

Contrary to popular belief, women did not wear wigs in the seventeenth and eighteenth centuries, except in rare cases to conceal severe hair loss. While fashions in men's wigs changed frequently, female hairstyles evolved comparatively slowly, while following the broad contours of the male silhouette. The *fontages* headdress, a tower of lace supported by a wire frame with lace lappets trailing down the back, was named for the duchesse de Fontages, who became Louis XIV's mistress in 1679. By the 1690s, these edifices had grown high, narrow, and pointed, mirroring the rising peaks of the male wig.

By the middle of the eighteenth century, women wore their hair close to the head, tightly curled and sometimes powdered, mirroring the more restrained men's wigs. This so-called *tête de mouton* or sheep's head was usually adorned with small hair ornaments called *pompoms*, named for another royal mistress, Madame de Pompadour. Pompadour was famous for the quantity of business and intrigue conducted at her morning *toilette*, and just as French women of all classes imitated the fashions and hair ornaments she wore, they used her multitasking *toilette* as a model for their own ambitious social goals. It was not unusual for a woman to receive visitors and tradesmen, read books, or write letters while her hairdresser worked. "One went to women's *toilettes* as if to the theatre, and gallants, chambermaids, dogs, and clergymen made up the decoration."[7]

Women's hair grew steadily higher and more volatile beginning in the 1760s. On April 26, 1774, the *Mémoires secrets* noted the appearance of a curious new fashion, dubbed the *pouf*. As the baronne d'Oberkirch explained: "It was a *coiffure* in which one introduced the persons or things one loved. Thus, the portrait of one's daughter, one's mother, a picture of one's canary, one's dog, etc., the whole thing trimmed with the hair of your father or a bosom friend. It was an unbelievable extravagance."[8] The stylish and immensely wealthy duchesse de Chartres, a cousin of the king's, launched the trend with a pouf depicting her infant son and his nurse, her pet parrot, and her Black servant boy, trimmed with the hair of her husband, her father, and her father-in-law, all nestled in a mountain of powder and pomade. The *Mémoires secrets* declared: "All the women are mad about Poufs and want to have one."[9]

Intensely personal "sentimental poufs," like the one devised for the duchesse de Chartres, quickly gave way to so-called "circumstantial poufs" inspired by current events. The *Correspondance litteraire* described coiffures depicting "sometimes naturally, sometimes allegorically the most important items in the newspapers. We see on one bonnet the opening of Parlement, on another the peace between the Russians and the Turks … or even an English garden, and in short all the great events ancient and modern."[10] To create these non-wigs, a professional hairdresser—usually male—augmented his client's own hair with false curls, wire supports, and cushions stuffed with horsehair or wool, before adding flowers, feathers, and other ornaments. A final layer of powder camouflaged the complex understructure and gave the head a smooth, uniform, and ageless appearance.

Hairdressing schools were opened and hairdressing manuals published to teach professional *coiffeurs* and ladies' maids how to achieve the crucial height. "Women could no longer find carriages high enough to sit in," Madame Campan observed. "One often saw them tilting their heads or holding them out the window. Others chose to kneel down in order to manage the ridiculous edifices with which they were burdened in a safer manner."[11] (As if in response to the encroaching *pouf*, men's wigs experienced a resurgence in size and popularity; though they were never quite as outsized as they appear in macaroni caricatures, there was a distinct increase in height, hard to achieve with natural hair.) New, high-tech inventions like the powder bellows and the swivel chair eased the arduous, messy, and time-consuming process of hairdressing (Figure 7.4).

Figure 7.4 Georges Jacob and J-B.S Rode, *Chaise de toilette*, c. 1787, carved beech; caning; modern silk Velvet upholstery J. Paul Getty Museum, inv. 72.DA.51. Image in the public domain.

Fueled by the rise of fashion magazines, fashions in hair changed even faster than fashions in clothes, and never more rapidly or radically than between the 1760s and the 1780s. These hairstyles encouraged the perceived correlation between high hair and high status. As the painter Elisabeth Vigée-Lebrun remembered of the Court of Louis XVI, "Women reigned then."[12] The *poufs* of the 1770s and the lower but wider hairstyles and broad-brimmed hats of the 1780s took up physical and visual space, enhancing women's prominence. In addition, they were expensive. Men's wigs were available at a variety of price points depending on their size and complexity, and the type of hair used; furthermore, they could be worn over and over again, while a woman's coiffure had to be changed and maintained frequently.

When she became queen in 1774, Marie-Antoinette insisted on hiring the most fashionable *coiffeur* in Paris, Monsieur Léonard, though this decision flouted centuries of royal etiquette. In the past, Court appointees had dressed the queen—and the queen alone. According to Campan, this custom "was … intended to cut off all communication between the royal family's household and society, which was always curious for the least details of their private life." But Marie-Antoinette feared that Léonard's taste would suffer if he was "cut off" from the inspiration of Paris, and allowed him to continue to service other clients, which, Campan remarked, "multiplied the opportunities of learning private details and often of distorting them."[13] As Campan feared, Léonard was a terrible gossip. He kept Marie-Antoinette informed of the latest scandals in Paris while at the same time spreading tales about the Court to his clients in the city. In 1800, a former courtier would describe his shoemaker as being "as chatty as Léonard."[14] Léonard's royal appointment (together with that of Marie-Jeanne "Rose" Bertin, who became the queen's *marchande de modes*) marks an important turning point in Court fashion in the late eighteenth century, demonstrating a decisive move from Versailles to Paris as wellspring of fashion. However, the shift was not unilateral; Bertin and other fashion merchants would open premises in the town of Versailles, lending reflected urban glamour to the Court.

Marie-Antoinette's hair was unusually high maintenance. She had a large Hapsburg forehead, which *poufs* helped to minimize.[15] Her mother, the Austrian Empress Maria Theresa, complained in a letter of March 1775: "They say your hair is 36 inches high from the roots, and with so many feathers and ribbons that it rises even higher! … A pretty young queen, full of attractions, has no need of all these follies."[16] When her hair fell out after the birth of her daughter in December 1779, the towering sculptures of hair, feathers, and flowers that Marie-Antoinette had popularized (and that probably contributed to her hair loss) were no longer possible. Léonard quickly devised a new, less voluminous hairstyle, the so-called *coiffure à l'enfant*, which was instantly adopted at Court and in Paris.[17]

Léonard made the most of his royal connections. He would arrive at Versailles in a coach drawn by six horses, and it was widely known that he had secured thirty lucrative positions at Court for his friends and family members, and "became quite rich" himself.[18] Lady Elizabeth Foster, who visited France in 1783, remembered that "Léonard ... dress'd me once, & put on the feathers & chiffon but he was very slow & conceited .... He was so pleas'd with his work that when done he said, 'when you go, tell them that it was Léonard who did your hair.'"[19]

Léonard—whose full name was Léonard-Alexis Autié—had two brothers, Pierre and Jean-François, who were also hairdressers and also went by the name of Monsieur Léonard professionally; thus, his clientèle may have seemed larger than it actually was. Both Léonard and Jean-François worked for Marie-Antoinette; Jean-François specialized in cutting hair while Léonard styled it. The king's brother, the comte de Provence, nicknamed them "le marquis Léonard" and "le chevalier Léonard" to tell them apart, suggesting their self-importance and their privileged status at Court.[20] By 1787, the original Léonard had retired and only dressed the queen's hair on special occasions, leaving the everyday duties to Jean-François. Their cousin, Villanou, was a hairdresser in the queen's household, as well; Pierre Autié is the Monsieur Léonard who worked for Louis XVI's sister, Madame Élisabeth.

No known portraits of any of the three Léonards have survived, but Gautier-Dagoty's scene depicting Marie-Antoinette at her *toilette* in her apartment at Versailles may include Léonard and Jean-François (Figure 7.5). Two men in plain coats wearing combs in their bag wigs can be seen in the background; one holds a powderpuff with a black handle. While the queen's hair has been combed into order and powdered, she is not yet wearing any of the ornaments that decorate the heads of the other ladies in the room. A basket of ostrich feathers and ribbons waits on her *toilette* table, presented by a woman in a low hairstyle and a cap, probably Rose Bertin, who was famously admitted to the royal bedchamber. Like other French *toilette* scenes of the eighteenth century, this captures the chaotic and collaborative nature of elite dressing and hairdressing, where the lines between spectator and participant, servant and tradesman were not always clear.

Figure 7.5 Jean-Baptiste Gautier-Dagoty, *Marie-Antoinette Playing the Harp in Her Room at Versailles*, gouache, c. 1777, Versailles, Châteaux de Versailles et de Trianon. Photo: Art Resource.

A series of poor harvests beginning in 1775 spelled disaster for a trade that used large quantities of hair powder, a starch derived from wheat. As the journalist Louis-Sebastien Mercier reflected, "When one considers that the powder with which 200,000 individuals whiten their hair is taken from the food of the poor; that the flour that enters into the ample wig of the fool, the clothes-brush of the fashion victim, the officer's military wig … could nourish ten thousand unfortunates … one laments this custom."[21] While barbers were considered necessary and useful, *coiffeurs*—and, to a lesser extent, *perruquiers*— were increasingly seen as luxurious and wasteful.[22] The resulting trend toward simpler, more natural, unpowdered hairstyles in the 1780s made the hairdressers' expensive services unnecessary; the painter Elisabeth Vigee-Lebrun boasted that "my coiffure cost me nothing. I arranged my hair myself."[23]

Big hair for both sexes finally went out of fashion with the French Revolution; along with other elite fashions, powder, *poufs*, and *perruques* were deemed unnatural and even deceitful, as well as inappropriately luxurious.[24] Some Parisian hairdressers followed their clients to the guillotine, including Charles Platre, known as Bellecour, *coiffeur* to Marie-Antoinette's daughter, Marie-Thérèse. Others made abrupt career changes; Louis Hippolyte Leroy, *marchand de modes* to Empress Joséphine, had worked as a hairdresser before the Revolution.[25] Still more emigrated, flooding the streets of Europe's capitals. Léonard himself was spotted in London and St. Petersburg in the aftermath of the Revolution.

The widely publicized excavations of the ancient cities of Pompeii and Herculaneum in the second half of the eighteenth century had generated interest in the art, interiors, fashions, and politics of the ancient Greeks and Romans; supporters of the Revolution promoted the comparative freedom and simplicity of classical dress and ornamentation as an antidote to immoral modern fripperies. Art and fashion began to mimic the austere aesthetics of these ancient, democratic civilizations. In November 1790, the *Journal de la Mode et du Goût* reported that young men dressed with "the greatest simplicity," and wore their hair "cut and curled like that of an antique bust."[26] The style was dubbed *à la Titus* the following spring when the celebrated actor Talma adopted it—along with historically accurate toga and sandals—to portray the Roman Emperor Titus in a production of Voltaire's historical tragedy *Brutus*; he would go on to play Nero, Cinna, and other heroes of antiquity in the same hairstyle.[27] Hair had always been an important vehicle for political expression, but it now became an instantly recognizable badge of royalist or republican sympathies.

Women, too, cropped their hair—a rare and daring example of a unisex fashion, symptomatic of the country's anarchic mood. Of course, short hair could have another, more sinister meaning; victims of the guillotine had their hair cut before they went to the scaffold. Short hairstyles and thin red ribbons "à la victime" worn at the neck or the bodice—imitating the cut of a blade—enjoyed a brief, macabre vogue.[28] David poignantly sketched Marie-Antoinette with her famous hair shorn, covered by a simple bonnet, on her way to her death on October 16, 1793. The woman who had been notorious for her elaborate hairstyles and extravagant dress was virtually unrecognizable without them, a female Sampson stripped of not just her strength but her very identity.

Notes

1 Angela Rosenthal, "Raising Hair," *Eighteenth-Century Studies* 38, no. 1 (2004), 1–2. For a history of wigs see Michael Kwass, "Big Hair: A Wig History of Consumption

in Eighteenth-Century France," *The American Historical Review* 11, no. 3 (2003): 631–59, and Daniel Roche, *The Culture of Clothing: Dress and Fashion in the Ancien Regime*, trans. Jean Birrell (Cambridge: Cambridge University Press, 1994).

2   "On porte présentement les perruques fort dégagées. Elles sont travillées moitié crêpé, et moitié boucles…. On ne les porte pas tout à fait si longues que l'année passée." *Mercure Galant, Extraordinaire de Janvier 1678.*

3   Antoine Dieu, *Mariage de Louis de France, duc de Bourgogne et de Marie-Adélaïde de Savoie, 7 décembre 1697*, n.d, Châteaux de Versailles et de Trianon, MV9177.

4   See Kimberly Chrisman-Campbell, "Dressing to Impress: The Morning Toilette and the Fabrication of Femininity," in *Paris: Life & Luxury in the Eighteenth Century*, ed. Charissa Bremer-David (Los Angeles, CA: J. Paul Getty Museum, 2011), 52–73.

5   Ronald W. Clark, *Benjamin Franklin: A Biography* (New York: Random House, 1983), 209.

6   "Ses cheveux plats sans poudre, son chapeau rond, son habit de drap brun contrastaient avec les habits pailletés, brodés, les coiffures poudrées et embaumantes des courtisans de Versailles. Cette nouveauté charma toutes les… femmes françaises." Madame Campan, *Mémoires de Madame Campan, première femme de chambre de Marie-Antoinette*, ed. Jean Chalon (Paris: Mercure de France, 1988), 193.

7   "On courut à la toilette de femmes comme au théâtre, & des petit-maîtres, des filles de chambre, des chiens & un abbé en firent la décoration," in *Le papillotage, ouvrage comique et moral* (Rotterdam: E. D. V. W et Cie, 1769), 110.

8   "C'était une coiffure dans laquelle on introduisait les personnes ou les choses qu'on préférait. Ainsi le portrait de sa fille, de sa mère, l'image de son serin, de son chien, etc., tout cela garni des cheveux de son père ou d'un ami de cœur. C'était incroyable d'extravagance." Baronne d'Oberkirch, *Mémoires de la baronne d'Oberkirch*, ed. Suzanne Burkard (Paris: Mercure de France, 1989), 74.

9   "Toutes les femmes veulent avoir un Pouff & en raffolent." Louis Petit de Bachaumont et al., *Mémoires secrets pour servir à l'histoire de la république des lettres en France*, avril 26, 1774 (London: John Adamson, 1780), 7, 165.

10 "… soit au naturel, soit allégoriquement, les articles les plus importants des Gazettes. On voit sur un bonnet la rentrée du Parlement, sur un autre la paix des Russes et des Turcs, sur un autre la bataille d'Ivry et Henri IV, ou bien un jardin anglais, et enfin tous les événements anciens et modernes." Denis Diderot, Friedrich Melchior Grimm, Jakob Heinrich Meister, and Guillaume-Thomas Raynal, *Correspondance littéraire, philosophique et critique*, Novembre 1774, ed. Maurice Tourneux, 16 vols (Reprint, Lichtenstein: Kraus Reprint, 1968 [1813]), 10, 511.

11 "Les femmes ne trouvaient plus de voitures assez élevées pour s'y placer et qu'on leur voyait souvent pencher la tête ou la placer à la portière. D'autres prirent le parti de s'agenouiller pour ménager, d'une manière encore plus sûre, le ridicule édifice dont elles étaient surchargées." Campan, *Mémoires*, 89.

12 "Les femmes régnaient alors." Elisabeth Vigée-Lebrun, *Souvenirs*, ed. Claudine Herrmann, 2 vols (Paris: Des femmes, 1986), 1, 122.

13 "L'usage…. avait sans doute pour base de couper toute communication entre l'intérieur des princes et la société toujours curieuse des moindres details de leur vie privée. La reine, craignant que le goût du coiffeur ne se perdît en cessant de practiquer son état, voulut qu'il continuât à servir plusieurs femmes de la cour et de Paris; ce qui multiplia les occasions de connaître les détails de l'intérieur et souvent de les dénaturer." Campan, *Mémoires*, 92. Unfortunately, the hair-raising memoir *Souvenirs de Léonard* (Paris: Alfonse Levavasseur et cie, 1838) is apocryphal.

14 "…aussi bavard que Léonard." Lucien Perey, *Histoire d'une grande dame au XVIIIe siècle: La Comtesse Hélène Potocka* (Paris: Calmann-Lévy, 1890), 194.

15 Comte de Saint-Priest, *Mémoires: La Revolution et l'Émigration*, ed. baron de Barante (Paris: Calmann-Lévy, 1929), 71.

16 "On la dit depuis de la racine des cheveux 36 pouces de haut, et avec tant de plumes et rubans qui relèvent tout cela!… Une jeune, jolie reine, pleine d'agrément, n'a pas besoin de toutes ces folies." Alfred d'Arneth and A. Geoffroy, eds, *Correspondance secrète entre Marie-Thérèse et le comte de Mercy-Argenteau*, 3 vols (Paris: Firmin-Didot Frères, 1875), 2, 306.

17 *Mémoires secrets*, juin 26, 1780, 15, 204; Oberkirch, 175.

18 "Il était devenu fort riche." Saint-Priest 71.

19 Transcript of Dormer archives at Chatsworth, Lady Elizabeth Foster's Journals, December 30, 1782, 19.

20 Victoire Renée Caroline de Froulay, Marquise de Créquy, *Souvenirs de la Marquise de Créquy, 1710 à 1803* (Paris: Michel Lévy, 1867), 3, 392.

21 "Lorsqu'on songe que la poudre dont deux cents mille individus blanchissent leurs cheveux, est prise sur l'aliment du pauvre; que la farine qui entre dans l'ample perruque du robin, la vergette du petit-maître, la boucle miliatire de l'officier… nourriraient dix mille infortunés… on gémit sur cet usage." Louis-Sébastien Mercier, *Tableau de Paris* 97 (Amsterdam: n.p., 1783), "Perruquiers."

22 Fayçal Falaky, "From Barber to Coiffeur: Art and Economic Liberalisation in Eighteenth-Century France," *Journal for Eighteenth-Century Studies* 36, no. 1 (March 2013): 35–48, 46.

23 "Ma coiffure ne me coûtait rien, j'arrangeais mes cheveux moi-même." Vigée-Lebrun, 1.93.

24 Morag Martin, *Selling Beauty: Cosmetics, Commerce, and French Society, 1750–1830* (Baltimore, MD: Johns Hopkins University Press, 2009), 158.

25 Fiona Foulkes, "'Quality Always Distinguishes Itself': Louis Hippolyte LeRoy and the Luxury Clothing Industry in Early Nineteenth-Century Paris,'" in *Consumers and Luxury: Consumer Culture in Europe, 1650–1850*, ed. Maxine Berg and Helen Clifford (Manchester: Manchester University Press, 1999), 186.

26 "La plus grand simplicité le caractérise ... Les cheveux coupés et frisés comme ceux d'une tête antique." *Journal de la mode et du goût*, no. 27 (novembre 15, 1790), 1.
27 Aileen Ribeiro, *The Art of Dress* (London: Yale University Press, 1995), 84.
28 See, for example, *Journal des dames et des modes*, "Chignon à la Grecque.... Ceinture à la Victime," pl. 9, 1797; "Coiffure néligée en fichu.... Croisures à la Victime," pl. 37, 1797; and "Chevelure en porc-épic," pl. 25, 1798.

8

The Politics of Attachment: Visualizing Young Louis XV and His Governess

Mimi Hellman

On February 15, 1717, the seventh birthday of Louis XV, a wardrobe adjustment marked a turning point in his life. He was dressed without his *lisières*—the leading strings affixed to children's garments so that adults could control their movement and encourage proper deportment. The boy was accustomed to being guided by his governess, Charlotte-Eléonore-Madeleine de La Motte-Houdancourt, duchesse de Ventadour, as he learned to navigate the spaces and protocols of Court life. But on this day, in a ceremony supervised by the regent, the duc d'Orléans, the governess separated herself from her charge both physically and structurally. She relinquished her role as the king's constant companion so that his formal education could begin under the guidance of men.[1]

A description of the ceremony in a widely read Court gazette presented the relationship between Madame de Ventadour and Louis XV in terms of her devotion, his gratitude, and strong mutual attachment.[2] The governess announced to the regent, "Here is the trust that the late king [Louis XIV] consigned to me … I have taken every possible care and deliver him in perfect health." The regent replied that both Louis and the state he embodied were "infinitely obliged" to her for "safeguarding such a precious time from any accident," and urged the boy "to conserve the memory of her important services" and "spare nothing in granting her tangible marks of his gratitude." The governess declared "my ministry is finished," tenderly kissed Louis's hand, and "could not contain her tears." Louis embraced her tightly and also began to cry. He remained inconsolable for hours until she returned briefly and urged him to take satisfaction in being under the tutelage of men. During the following weeks, the king gave his "dear Mother" gifts of jewelry and silverware, and gradually learned to remain composed during their visits.[3]

The emotional tenor of this account might seem surprising. Why publicize the mutual attachment of the boy and his governess rather than using the occasion to celebrate masculine authority and credit the child with regal self-control in a major step toward political autonomy? Leading strings and teary eyes may have been part of the actual events, but that hardly guaranteed them a place in the realm of representation. This chapter explores how the relationship between young Louis XV and his governess, especially as constructed through images, became integral to the official rhetoric of his early reign and continued to resonate for decades thereafter. It also suggests how Madame de Ventadour exercised a distinctive mode of female agency in Court society that shaped her own status and that of her extended family. The topic reaches beyond the dynamics of Versailles itself in order to trace affective formations that first emerged at the monarchy's iconic headquarters, accompanied the Court to Paris during the Regency, and continued to shape its social performances after Louis XV reclaimed the domain in 1722.

A Uniquely Positioned Woman

Service to the monarch was an important way for members of the nobility to demonstrate loyalty and garner privilege. Among a wide range of positions, the most prestigious ones involved close proximity to royal bodies. The *gouvernante des enfants de France* swore an oath to foster the physical and moral well-being of the king's children. Supported by assistants and a sizeable budget, she supervised their living quarters and daily routines, escorted them wherever they went, and guided their first lessons in normative values and conduct.[4] She cared for boys until they turned seven, and for girls until they married, moved to a convent, or became old enough to manage their own affairs.

Women from Madame de Ventadour's family served as royal governesses from the 1640s until the 1780s. She began in 1704 as her mother's officially designated successor and held the position officially from 1709 until 1732. She helped her mother to care for two great-grandsons of Louis XIV and took primary responsibility for seven royal children, including three more boys.[5] Kingship in France was patrilineal and considered divinely ordained, so responsibility for male children, especially the official heir (dauphin), entailed particular privilege and high political stakes.

Madame de Ventadour's early career unfolded amid a succession crisis that factionalized the Court, unsettled the public, and threatened France's international standing. Three dauphins from three different generations died between spring of 1711 and spring of 1712, leaving a two-year-old orphan called the duc d'Anjou as the only direct successor of his great-grandfather Louis XIV.[6] Madame de Ventadour served as the boy's governess through his succession in 1715 and the first two years of a regency destabilized by (among other things) the competing interests of the regent, the Bourbon king of Spain, and Louis XIV's two legitimized sons by one of his mistresses.[7] The future of the throne remained uncertain even after the duc d'Anjou became Louis XV, was crowned in 1722 (at age 12), and produced a male heir in 1729.

The role of Madame de Ventadour in Louis XV's early life should be understood in relation to the duc d'Orléans's role as regent. Past regencies under French queens had been shaped by anxieties about their gender and links to foreign dynasties. However, a proscription against female succession and essentialist ideas about maternal nurturing made it possible to imagine that a female regent would not interfere with her son's destiny. In contrast, a male regent was thought to harbor a natural drive to further his own dynastic and political ambitions, with no inherent protective impulse toward the young king he was supposed to represent. In the case of Philippe II d'Orléans, these assumptions were compounded by concerns about his spiritual and moral compass. Although official rhetoric praised him as a virtuous father-figure, many doubted not only his capacity for self-control and wise policies, but also his investment in Louis XV's survival.[8]

Madame de Ventadour was uniquely positioned to help counter these problems. She could embody selfless maternal love without the threatening potential power of queen regents. Besides being descended from two previous royal governesses, she was separated from husband, had no sons, had married off her only daughter, and was approaching her sixtieth year when the duc d'Anjou was born. She therefore could be considered free from family pressures or sexual intrigues that might compromise her duty to France.[9]

Origin Stories

During the period of imperiled royal lives and uncertain political fortunes that constituted the final years of Louis XIV's reign, the identities of young Louis and his governess became entwined in a narrative of mutual attachment. It stemmed from two incidents that became part of the Court's collective memory and circulated in written form through the mid-eighteenth century and beyond.

The first involved Madame de Ventadour saving the duc d'Anjou's life after the deaths of his grandfather, parents, and older brother. She reportedly prevented doctors from subjecting him to their standard regimen of bleeding and purging, then assumed sole control of his care at the behest of a desperate Louis XIV. Some courtiers suspected a poison plot and believed that she gave the child an antidote; many credited her for preserving the principal Bourbon bloodline.[10]

The second incident took place at the bedside of the dying Louis XIV. In what one witness called a "tender spectacle [that] drew tears from us all," the king thanked Madame de Ventadour for her care and affection in raising his great-grandson, exhorted her to continue, and instructed the boy to profit from her guidance and "to grant her every possible mark of his esteem."[11] It was a tremendous honor for the governess be acknowledged and instructed under such circumstances, just as eternal kingship was about to be transmitted from one royal body to another.

The account of Louis XV's official separation from his governess in 1717 thus built on established ideas about their relationship. All three stories thematize vulnerable royal bodies, tender emotions, and a reciprocal bond of devotion and gratitude. All involve liminal events at the boundary between life and death or childhood and maturity—events in which the future of France was at stake. A dedication to Madame de Ventadour preceding one of Louis XIV's published eulogies distills the essence of her role. It stresses the honor of caring for the "royal trust," praising her ability to unite "the sanctity of Religion with the politeness of the Court." It calls upon her "to fashion his mind, prepare his heart, and imbue his spirit with the first fundamentals of all that forms Heroes, Monarchs, and Saints."[12] This implicitly acknowledges a paradox of absolutist ideology: although the boy-king was considered innately princely in spirit, his mortal and social body needed protection and formation. Madame de Ventadour would not be allowed to participate in his formal education, but was expected to prepare him for that process by shaping exceptional, god-given qualities into properly embodied kingship.

Anchoring the Monarchy

Images of Louis XV with his governess, especially prints, expressed and shaped perceptions of his early reign at least as pervasively, if not more so, as ideas circulating in texts or through the social networks of courtiers. Representations of their relationship should not be seen as merely documenting protocols for guiding a child through elaborate state rituals. Rather, they articulated political desires and anxieties—probably both purposefully and unconsciously—during a fraught transitional period in French political culture. Three prints exemplify some pictorial trends that carried important implications.

The first (Figure 8.1) commemorates the start of the Regency by adapting another print made the previous year to mark the end of the War of Spanish Succession.[13] The composition retains the original print's architectural setting and semicircle of European rulers holding laurel branches. But instead of the original allegory of Peace beneath the dais, this zone of power contains the regent, Madame de Ventadour, and Louis XV. The governess holds the child, seated on a throne-like chair matching those of the assembled princes. Her hand steadies his grasp on a scepter, rhyming with the gesture of Louis XIV who sits to her left. Her pose suggests not only the iconography of the Virgin Mary, but also—despite an inscription identifying the regent—the status of a queen or even a regent.[14]

Figure 8.1 *Seuccession [sic] du Roy Louis XV à la couronne de France et de Navarre le 1er Septembre 1715 sous la Regence de Monseigneur le Duc d'Orléans*. 1715. Paris, Bibliothèque Nationale de France. Photo: BNF.

Madame de Ventadour also frames Louis's diminutive body in a scene of him receiving the archbishop of Paris on the day of his succession (Figure 8.2). Again, her role as governess justifies a privileged location in a male ritual; she claims as much spatial prominence as the duc d'Orléans. Although she gestures less boldly than the regent, who points authoritatively toward the king, she stands closer to the royal body and seems to gently nudge him toward his deferential visitor.

A more overt sign of the governess's guidance appears in an image of Louis XV arriving at his first *lit de justice*, a traditional demonstration of royal legislative authority at a session of the *parlement* of Paris (Figures 8.3). Joining the king at the center of the composition, Madame de Ventadour holds his leading strings with both hands. Her figure forms a pendant to that of a priest, her grasp of the *lisières* mirroring his grasp of a holy water wand. Both gestures

Figure 8.2 *Les premiers hommages rendus à sa majesté Louis XV par son eminence Monseigneur le cardinal de Noailles, présenté par Monseigneur le duc d'Orléans, regent du royaume, à Versailles le 1er Septembre 1715.* 1715. Paris, Bibliothèque Nationale de France. Photo: BNF.

Figure 8.3 *Le roi Louis XV allant au parlement tenir son lit de justice le XII Septembre 1715* (detail). 1715. Paris, Bibliothèque Nationale de France. Photo: BNF.

resonate with that of an allegory of Renown holding a crown above the vertically aligned heads of regent and king. Despite his axial location, the duc d'Orléans is much less prominent than the governess—overlapped by other figures, dressed and coiffed like several other men.[15] As in the other two prints, the governess exercises pictorial agency because she protects and forms the embodiment of the state.

These images (and others from the same period) present Louis XV as sturdy yet small, regally composed yet in need of guidance, exalted as a king yet clearly a child. Such tensions encouraged a subject position for viewers that turned on both concern and confidence. The prints simultaneously invited reflection on the fragility of succession and offered reassurance that the "royal trust" was in good hands. This message was crucial for the duc d'Orléans, whose regency emerged from contentious debates about succession and the structure of governance under a minor king, and whose positions on certain issues diverged from those of Louis XIV.[16] To secure the power celebrated in Figure 8.1, he renegotiated the terms of Louis XIV's will, which had granted him only a circumscribed role in a regency council.[17] He signaled a major shift in religious policy by extending favor to the archbishop of Paris (Figure 8.2), a leader of opposition to a papal bull endorsed by Louis XIV.[18] And he enhanced the *parlement*'s authority to challenge royal decrees, thereby tempering the monarchical authority represented by the *lit de justice* (Figure 8.3).[19]

Amid this instability, Madame de Ventadour's presence in official images signaled continuity with the past and unambiguous commitment to the destiny of an orphaned king. Her vigilant, maternal care tempered uneasiness about the regent's character and motives without threatening his authority. While alluding to queenship, her role was both more limited and more empowered. Queens were defined by desirable fertility and suspicious foreignness. They played no official role in raising their children unless they became regents or claimed untraditional prerogatives—in which case their agency became problematic.[20] Madame de Ventadour provided an accepted kind of royal service, limited in duration and centered on a child who could not yet govern for himself. In other words, her body was both strategic and safe, signifying in ways that no one else's ever could.

Devotion as Strategy

The discussion so far begs questions about Madame de Ventadour's own social strategies. Although her representational efficacy depended on the idea of altruistic devotion, there is strong evidence of keen self-awareness and active engagement with the rhetoric of kingship. For example, during the final years of Louis XIV's reign she often addressed the dauphin's progress in letters to Madame de Maintenon, the king's morganatic wife and an influential mediator for those who sought his favor.[21] Her reports shift from assurances about the child's health to details about his illnesses, from references to her exhaustion to declarations of total commitment. She often alludes to a sense of political urgency. These moves lead Madame de Maintenon—and, by implication, the king—to express appreciation for her efforts.

In an exchange of 1714, the governess describes the dauphin's recovery after an alarming seizure and notes how his strength depends on hers: "My pains are undertaken willingly ... my vigor is surprising for my age ... I cannot reproach myself for the least little care or precaution, and hope they will bear good results—this Prince promises all that can be desired in body and mind." In response, Madame de Maintenon urges her to stay well and affirms the high-stakes attachment: "I am persuaded that you do everything for him with a good heart, and cannot prevent yourself from doing so, loving him as much as you do and knowing full well his importance."[22] In these passages, and others like them, the governess employed an astute sense of how politics and affect were entwined, fashioning her identity along with that of the dauphin.

Madame de Ventadour's long history with both Louis XV and his great-grandfather enhanced the status of the Rohan-Soubise, a highly placed noble dynasty with whom she became closely allied through her daughter's second marriage. For example, when Louis XIV granted a coveted duchy-peerage to her son-in-law in 1714, he expressed regard for "the zeal and dedication with which she devoted herself entirely to raising the Dauphin of France ... the most precious trust that we could have consigned to her care."[23] During the 1720s, she secured royal approval for the transmission of her role to a granddaughter-in-law and then (after the young woman's death) to a granddaughter; the position remained with her descendants long after her death.[24]

Perhaps the most compelling evidence of Madame de Ventadour's prestige is a group portrait that incorporates her into a survey of the Bourbon lineage (Figure 8.4). No evidence has surfaced regarding the painting's commission and

Figure 8.4 French School. *Madame de Ventadour with Louis XIV and His Heirs.* 1715–22. London, The Wallace Collection, P122. Image in the public domain.

its authorship remains uncertain, but it probably was made for the governess between Louis XV's succession in 1715 and his coronation in 1722. It depicts an imaginary gathering of Bourbons whose live spans intersected for little more than a year and whose heads were copied from earlier portraits.[25] The composition revolves around Louis XIV flanked by the grand dauphin and the duc de Bourgogne, the son and grandson whose deaths in 1711–12 precipitated the succession crisis. The Sun King points to his sole surviving heir, not yet wearing breeches and attached by *lisières* to Madame de Ventadour. Two busts extend the genealogy back to the first Bourbon king Henri IV and his son Louis XIII, respectively the grandfather and father of Louis XIV.

Most obviously, the picture proclaims the glory and continuity of the monarchy. The heads and gestures of the three Louis who lived to occupy the throne (XIII, XIV, and XV) align along a diagonal axis. Several hands draw attention to the space where Louis XIV's gesture almost meets the tiny fingers of his successor. The room's decoration teems with royal symbolism, including the solar chariot of Apollo (on the wall) and the complementary attributes of eloquent Mercury and forceful Hercules (a cadeucis and a club on plinths beneath the busts). Even a basket of fruit, conventional in many non-royal portraits, here suggests what a Court poet would call a happy harvest: dynastic fertility and the abundance assured by beneficent rule.[26]

More subtly, the picture also celebrates Madame de Ventadour's role in the transmission of kingship. The governess's extended arms and the angle of her head mirror the right arm and head of Louis XIV, whose gesture implicitly designates her as well as his heir. The child appears to be the age at which she supposedly saved his life. The line of the leading strings flows into the blue sash of his Order of Saint-Esprit, a device for guidance becoming an emblem of honor. The gold, tasseled cords valorize not just him, but also the bond between them. Indeed, this accessory played a more prominent role in the iconography of Louis XV and his governess than in that of any other royal children.[27]

The painting resonates with the origin stories and prints discussed above: a life saved, a dying king's charge, a bond of devotion and gratitude, the cords of attachment. Furthermore, the governess's own lineage hovers behind this assembly of kings. Henri IV chose her great-great grandfather as governor of the royal children, and Louis XIII appointed her great-grandmother to care for his sons. One of those boys became Louis XIV and made Madame de Ventadour's mother responsible for his own offspring, as well as those of the son and grandson depicted here. The painting thus celebrates the symbiosis of royal trust and devoted service that braided the governess and her family into the destiny of France.[28]

The composition also links her with two other pictorial presences. She stands directly below Apollo, her grasp of leading strings echoing the sun god's hold on the reins that govern an eternal cosmic cycle. Her gender and placement also resonate with a depiction of Minerva, goddess of wisdom, armed and seated on a throne. Despite the understated presence of this element as a sketchily rendered bas relief on the dado between Louis XIV and the duc de Bourgogne, the gestures of those two men point toward it. The motif may be the version of Minerva's iconography known as "force of body and mind," crucial qualities of kings that a royal governess pledged to instill.[29] A similar conception of Madame de Ventadour's formative role shapes an epitaph published upon her death in 1744: "Her devoted days have passed in illustrious governments. They will mark her wisdom, her zeal and attachment, which find august monuments in the pupils she leaves behind."[30] The circular logic of these lines captures the intertwined identities of a governess and her charges: her dedication produces a legacy which then constitutes her reward.

The accumulation of visual cues and associations in the group portrait makes a bolder claim than prints showing Louis XV and his governess sharing the ritual stage with the duc d'Orléans. Here, her presence more strongly invokes the idea of a queen regent. Indeed, two of the depicted kings, Louis XIII and Louis XIV, began their reigns with mothers serving as regents. A dedication to Madame de Ventadour preceding one of the published funeral orations for Louis XIV affirms the possibility of associating her with those women. It tells her that the late king's exhortation to protect and form his heir "places you, so to speak, at the rank of Catherine and Marie de Médicis and Anne of Austria."[31] Thirty years later, her obituary noted that the necessity of holding Louis XV on ritual occasions granted her "a place where only the Queen Mother had been able to sit before her."[32]

The Politics of Attachment

Royal rhetoric throughout Louis XV's reign attempted to frame his authority as what the historian Thomas Kaiser calls a "love contract," a myth of mutual devotion between a benevolent ruler and his adoring subjects that culminated in the 1740s in efforts to fashion him as "Louis the beloved."[33] Visual and verbal images of the king's childhood relationship with his governess seem to anticipate this project. Madame de Ventadour modeled not merely duty but rather unconditional love, and thus exemplified the affective position of an ideal French subject. This, in turn, enabled the king to demonstrate the resilient body, sound mind, and generous heart that defined an ideal sovereign. It seems likely that these two people shared a sincere emotional bond that cannot be fully explained in terms of ideology. But in the realm of representation, imagining their feelings was a means of imagining the state.

A few final examples suggest how their personas remained mutually defining long after she consigned him to the care of men. In 1721, when the eleven-year-old king became ill, popular songs praised the governess's ongoing concern for his well-being. One calls her "mama-duchess," echoing his ongoing habit of addressing her as "mother." Another casts her and the king's governor, the duc de Villeroy, as parents who "revived this young and charming monarch/despite the jaws of Fate."[34] In another tribute, a personification of Religion reveals that she handled the health crisis by sending France an incarnation of Devotion in the form of Madame de Ventadour. The poem credits the governess with emotions that surpass maternal instincts: "In her vigil she felt in turn/Fear and hope, joy and love;/A mother for her son would not feel such tenderness."[35] At a time when the specter of a succession crisis still loomed, this woman's image continued to reassure.

Social protocols at Court also marked the governess as a recipient of royal esteem and fostered collective memory of her role in sustaining the monarchy. After the return to Versailles in 1722, she belonged to the exclusive group allowed to enter the king's bedchamber when he first awoke and just before he went to sleep.[36] Such access to the royal body repeatedly affirmed their distinctive bond. When the governess began raising a new generation of children in 1727, including a dauphin born in 1729, she became an even more visible embodiment of vigilant care. Her sedan chair could traverse areas of the palace where most others were required to walk, especially when she carried one of her charges on her lap.[37] Privileges continued after retirement. When she became seriously ill, an official rifle salute took place outside her private residence in the town of Versailles, the king and queen visited, and their daughters attended a prayer service in her honor.[38] And when she died in 1744, an obituary recirculated the origin story of Louis XIV's deathbed charge, calling it "an eternal monument to the lively zeal and tender, respectful attachment with which she always applied herself."[39]

Indeed, Madame de Ventadour's contribution to the perpetuation of royal lineage remained resonant a decade later, when Charles-Nicolas Cochin created a print series celebrating Louis XV early life.⁴⁰ Between scenes of his birth and coronation is the moment at Versailles in which the Sun King personally enjoined the governess to safeguard the state's most precious trust (Figure 8.5). The rhyming bodies of the woman and child align with the central axis of the composition, her figure much more substantial and active than that of the recumbent king. The gestures of the three figures form a close circuit, making a moment of international—and, indeed, cosmic—import seem like an intimate, familial exchange. By the 1750s, both Louis XV's reputation and the very concept of absolute monarchy were becoming increasingly problematic.⁴¹ Yet the image attempted to sustain a politics of attachment, a claim of affectively charged interdependence between rulership and subjecthood.

The role of *gouvernantes des enfants de France* has been overlooked in scholarship on the conception and enactment of kingship, perhaps in part because it was so effectively naturalized within royal culture and its representations. Studies of women in eighteenth-century French Court society have focused on how some of its most visible members negotiated, and often

Figure 8.5 Charles-Nicolas Cochin, *Death of Louis XIV*. From *L'Histoire de Louis XV par les Medailles* 1753. Etching (cropped to image), Châteaux de Versailles et de Trianon. Photo: RMN.

overtly challenged, assumptions about how gender roles, ritual protocols, and political authority were supposed to operate.[42] Yet the fascination with contested identities can prevent recognition of those who exercised agency precisely because they managed not to threaten patriarchal authority. A focus on contentious relationships also discourages questions about the sociopolitical significance of emotional attachment. The story of Louis XV and Madame de Ventadour challenges us to consider how images and social performances could encode affective bonds that were crucial to the construction of royal and noble identities.

Notes

1. Philippe II d'Orléans governed on behalf of Louis XV from the death of Louis XIV in 1715 until his own death in 1723. One of Louis XIV's legitimated sons, Louis-Auguste, duc du Maine, served as superintendent of the young king's household. François de Neufville, duc and maréchal de Villeroy, was the boy's governor; André-Hercule de Fleury, bishop of Fréjus and abbé de Fleury (later cardinal de Fleury and minister of state) was his tutor.
2. "Voilà le Dépôt que le feu Roy m'a confié…j'en ai pris tous les soins possibles, & je le rend en parfait santé." "avoient une obligation infinite…préserver des jours si précieux de tout accident…conserver la memoire de ses services si importans… n'oublieroit rien pour lui donner des marques sensibles de sa renconnoissance." "voilà mon ministere fini;" "qu'il ne lui fut pas possible de retenir ses larmes;" "chère Mère." *Le Nouveau Mercure* (February 1717), 153–66; quotations 157–8, 160. Translations are mine unless otherwise indicated.
3. An unattributed portrait of Madame de Ventadour made around this time (Château de Versailles inv. V.2015.29) depicts jewels that closely match those described in the 1717 gazette. They not only commemorate the king's gesture of gratitude, but also suggest an analogy between carefully stored gems and responsibility for a child regarded as a treasure of the state.
4. For royal service as social strategy, Leonhard Horowski, "'Such a Great Advantage for My Son': Office-Holding and Career Mechanisms at the Court of France, 1661 to 1789," *The Court Historian* 8 (2003): 125–75. For the governess's oath of office, Lucien Bély, *La société des princes, XVIe-XVIIIe siècle* (Paris: Fayard 1999), 48–9.
5. Madame de Ventadour assisted her mother with first two sons of duc de Bourgogne (the first and second ducs de Bretagne, 1704–5 and 1707–9). She assumed sole charge of the duc d'Anjou (born 1710), who became Louis XV and had six children between 1727 and 1732 (twin girls, another girl, the dauphin, a boy who died, and

another girl). She also cared for a young Spanish princess who lived at the French Court in 1721–5 in (unfulfilled) anticipation of marriage to Louis XV. Even after her official retirement in 1732 and succession by her granddaughter, Madame de Ventadour continued to participate in the care of the dauphin and his siblings, who were joined by four more girls born in 1733–7.

6   The three deceased dauphins were the Grand Dauphin (1661–1711), his son the duc de Bourgogne (1682–1712), and the duc de Bourgogne's second son (1707–12). Another son of the duc de Bourgogne had already died (1704–5); his wife died a few days before him (1685–1712); his brother, the duc de Berry, died two years later (1686–1714).

7   Katherine Crawford, *Perilous Performances: Gender and Regency in Early Modern France* (Cambridge, MA and London: Harvard University Press, 2004), 137–76; Harold A. Ellis, *Boulainvilliers and the French Monarchy: Aristocratic Politics in Early Eighteenth-Century France* (Ithaca, NY and London: Cornell University Press, 1988), 169–206. For a broad political history of this period, Colin Jones, *The Great Nation: France from Louis XV to Napoleon* (London: Penguin Books, 2003), 1–81.

8   Crawford, *Perilous Performances*, 137–76.

9   Madame de Ventadour separated from her husband, Louis-Charles de Lévis, long before his death in 1717. Her daughter married in 1691, remarried in 1694, and died in 1727. According to the duc de Saint-Simon, Louis-Charles led a dissolute life; see Louis de Rouvroy, *Mémoires*, 7 vols (Paris: Gallimard, 1986), 6:435.

10 The regent's mother, the duchesse d'Orléans, was certain that medical treatments killed the duc de Bourgogne only months after he became dauphin, and that his younger brother (the future Louis XV) survived only because Madame de Ventadour and her assistants insisted upon a less drastic form of care. Elisabeth Charlotte Orléans, *Lettres de madame duchesse d'Orléans, née princesse Palatine*, ed. Olivier Amiel (Paris: Mercure de France, 1985), 317–18. The duc de Luynes suspected poisoning: Charles-Philippe d'Albert de Luynes, *Mémoires*, ed. Louis Dussieux and Eudore Soulié, 17 vols (Paris: Firmin Didot, 1860–5), 6:185–6.

11 "ce tendre spectacle nous à tiré des larmes à tous;" "toutes les marques possibles de sa reconnaissance." Philippe de Courcillon, *Journal du marquis de Dangeau*, ed. Eudore Soulié, 19 vols (Paris: Firmin Didot, 1854–60), 17:127.

12 "Dépôt royal;" "la sainteté de la Religion avec la politesse de la Cour;" "façonner son esprit, dresser son coeur & jetter dans son ame les premiers fondemens de tout ce qui fait les Heros, les Monarques, & les Saints." André-François de Tournon, "Oraison funèbre de Louis XIV roy de France et de Navarre," in *Recueil de plusieurs oraisons funèbres de Louis XIV*, 2 vols (Paris: n.p., 1716), 1:353, 356.

13 Bibliothèque Nationale de France online catalogue IFN-55002303. The War of Spanish Succession (1700–14) ended with the Holy Roman Emperor relinquishing his claim on Spanish throne in favor of the Bourbon prince Philip V, uncle of Louis

XV. Katherine Crawford's study of the Regency briefly considers some of prints analyzed here (*Perilous Performances*, 139–40, 171–4), but my interpretation differs from hers.

14 It is not clear whether the governess ever actually held Louis XV while sitting on his throne, but the idea had become part of her narrative by the time she died in 1744. On that occasion, the duc de Luynes noted that she was the only non-royal woman since the beginning of the monarchy to "sit on the fleurs de lis." Luynes, *Mémoires*, 6: 186.

15 Madame de Ventadour's vigilance also was articulated through the spatial dynamics of the *lit de justice* ceremony itself. She and the king's governor, the duc de Villeroy, sat at the foot of his throne, an unprecedented place for a woman who was not a queen regent.

16 Crawford, *Perilous Performances*, 137–76.

17 Ibid., 141–8.

18 The archbishop, Cardinal Louis-Antoine de Noailles, led opposition to the 1713 papal bull *Unigenitus*, a condemnation of Jansenism. Olivier Andurand, "Fluctuat nec mergiture, les hésitations du cardinal de Noailles," *Cahiers de recherches médiévales et humanistes* 24 (2012): 267–98.

19 To secure the *parlement*'s support for his regency, the duc d'Orléans countered a long-standing position of Louis XIV by granting magistrates the power of formal objection to royal decrees (remonstrance) before registering them as law. Sarah Hanley, *The Lit de Justice of the Kings of France: Constitutional Ideology in Legend, Ritual, and Discourse* (Princeton, NJ: Princeton University Press, 1983), 329–44.

20 For the conception of queenship, Jennifer G. Germann, *Picturing Marie Leszczinska (1703–1768): Representing Queenship in Eighteenth-Century France* (London and New York: Routledge, 2015), 21–52. For a queen encroaching on a governess's role, Thomas E. Kaiser, "Scandal in the Royal Nursery: Marie-Antoinette and the 'Gouvernantes des Enfants de France,'" *Historical Reflections* 32 (Summer 2006): 403–20.

21 A letter of 1715 indicates that Madame de Maintenon read at least some of Madame de Ventadour's letters to the king. Françoise d'Aubigné, *Lettres de Madame de Maintenon*, nouvelle edition, 9 vols (n.p., 1758), 7:37.

22 Ventadour: "mes peines se prennent volontiers; mais les nuits sont longues à passer: j'ai une force qui me surprend pour mon âge …le bon Dieu me secourt, & je n'en desire la continuation, que pour ce qui me reste de tems à demeurer auprès de mon petit Maitre…j'ose dire que je n'ai pas le moindre petit soin ni la moindre précaution à me reprocher; j'espère aussi qu'elles auront une bonne issue: car ce Prince-là promet & de corps & d'esprit tout ce qu'on peut desirer." Maintenon: "je suis bien persuadée que vous faites de bon Coeur ce que vous faites auprès de lui, &

que vous ne pourriez pas même vous empêcher de le faire, l'aimant autant que vous l'aimez, & connoissant aussi-bien l'importance dont il est." D'Aubigné, *Lettres de Madame de Maintenon*, 7:32–3. This mid-eighteenth-century edition of the letters may have contributed to the reputations of the authors and those they discussed.

23 "du zèle et de l'application avec laquelle elle s'est donnée tout entière à élever le Dauphin de France…dépôt le plus précieux que nous puissions confier à ses soins." Luynes, *Mémoires*, 6:186–7.

24 Officially sanctioned transmission (*survivance*) was granted in 1721 to Anne-Julie-Adélaïde de Melun, princesse de Soubise, and in 1729 to Marie-Isabelle-Gabrielle-Angélique de Rohan-Soubise, duchesse de Tallard. The next two generations of recipients after Madame de Ventadour's death in 1744 were Marie-Louise-Geneviève de Rohan-Soubise, comtesse Marsan (as of 1754) and Victoire-Armande-Josèphe de Rohan-Soubise, princesse de Guéméné (as of 1775).

25 The most useful discussion, including attribution issues and pictorial sources, is John Ingamells, *The Wallace Collection: Catalogue of Pictures* (London: The Trustees of the Wallace Collection, 1989), 3:170–5. For alternative perspectives see Jean Cailleux, "Some Family and Group Portraits by François de Troy (1645–1730)," *The Burlington Magazine* 113, no. 817 (1971): 1–18; Georges de Lastic, "Nicolas de Largillière: heurs et malheurs d'un chef-d'oeuvre," *L'Oeil* 365 (December 1985): 36–45. The lifespans of everyone in the painting overlapped for only fourteen months between the birth of the duc d'Anjou in mid-February 1710 and the death of the Grand Dauphin in mid-April 1711.

26 Similar symbolism appeared in a triumphal "Arch of Minerva" at Louis XV's coronation in 1722, including Hercules' club, Mercury's cadeucis, fruit, and a scene of Louis entering a Temple of Glory adorned with busts of Bourbon predecessors. *Journal du voyage du roi à Rheims contenant ce qui s'est passé de plus remarquable à la cérémonie de son sacre*, 2 vols (La Haye: Rutgert Alberts, 1723), 1:82–6. Madame de Ventadour herself mobilized the harvest trope in a 1732 ceremony organized for Louis XV's three-year-old son: the child cut grapevines hung in a salon at Versailles and distributed them to courtiers. *Mercure de France* (October, 1732), 2279.

27 *Lisières* were probably used for other royal children, but to the best of my knowledge they only figure prominently in the iconography of the young Louis XV. They appear in at least two prints of Louis XV's father and uncle made in the 1680s, but the women who hold them are unidentified walkers (*promeneuses*), a position less prestigious than that of governess. As Enlightenment conceptions of childrearing took hold during the second half of the eighteenth century, leading strings came to be seen as an unnatural restraint.

28 The lineage of governesses was overtly commemorated in a series of portraits commissioned by Madame de Ventadour's sister, the duchesse de La Ferté, only

29 "force de corps et d'esprit." Cesar Ripa, *Iconologie ou la science des emblems devises &c*, 2 vols (Amsterdam: n.p., 1698), 2:354. A number of images made during Louis XV's youth invoked Minerva as a formative guide.

30 "Dans les Gouvernemens illustres,/Ses pieux jours se sont passés./Ils signalerent sa sagesse,/Son zèle & son attachement,/Et les Eleves qu'elle laisse,/En sont l'auguste monument." *Mercure de France* (December, 1744), 212.

31 "occuper un Place, où il n'y avoit que la Reine Mere qui eut été assise avant elle;" "vous a mis en quelque sorte au rang des Catherine & Marie de Medicis, & des Anne d'Autriche." Tournon, "Oraison funèbre de Louis XIV," 356. Catherine de Médicis was regent for Charles IX, Marie de Médicis for Louis XIII, and Anne of Austria for Louis XIV.

32 "un Place, où il n'y avoit que la Reine Mere qui eut été assise avant elle." *Mercure de France* (December, 1744), 212.

33 Thomas E. Kaiser, "Louis le Bien-Aimé and the Rhetoric of the Royal Body," in *From the Royal to the Republican Body: Incorporating the Political in Seventeenth- and Eighteenth-Century France*, ed. Sara E. Melzer and Kathryn Norberg (Berkeley: University of California Press, 1998), 131–61.

34 "ils ont ressuscité/Ce jeune et charmant monarque/Malgré les dents de la Parque." Emile Raunié, ed., *Chansonnier historique du XVIIIe siècle*, 10 vols (Paris: A. Quantin, 1879–84), 4:55–6:60.

35 "Occupée à sa garde, elle sent tout à tour,/Et la crainte, & l'espoir, & la joye, & l'amour./La mere pour son fils, a bien moins de tendresse." The French term for the personification is "Piété." Raunié, *Chansonnier historique*, 4:73–4.

36 Levels of access (*entrées*) were formalized upon the king's majority in 1723. The "family" category to which Madame de Ventadour belonged also included the regent and his chief minister, royal princes, and the king's tutor and doctors. Luynes, *Mémoires*, 1, 262–3.

37 Luynes, *Mémoires*, 1, 191. In this entry, the duc de Luynes reports seeing the governess, by then in her eighties, carried in an armchair through the Hall of Mirrors.

38 Ibid., 1, 124.

39 "un monument éternel du zèle vif & de l'attachement tendre & respectueux avec lequel elle s'est toujours acquittée." *Mercure de France* (December, 1744), 212.

40 Christian Michel, *Charles-Nicolas Cochin et l'art des Lumières* (Rome: Ecole française de Rome, 1993), 94–8. The prints were designed in conjunction with a series of medals.

41 For the ideological context Dale Van Kley, *The Damiens Affair and the Unraveling of the Ancien Régime, 1750–1770* (Princeton, NJ: Princeton University Press, 1984); Jeffrey W. Merrick, *The Desacralization of the French Monarchy in the Eighteenth Century* (Baton Rouge and London: Louisiana University Press, 1990); Jeffrey Merrick, "Fathers and Kings: Patriarchalism and Absolutism in Eighteenth-Century French Politics," *SVEC* 308 (1993): 281–303.

42 To cite just a few examples: Thomas E. Kaiser, "Madame de Pompadour and the Theatres of Power," *French Historical Studies* 19, no. 4 (1996): 1025–44; Chantal Thomas, *The Wicked Queen: The Origins of the Myth of Marie-Antionette*, trans. Julie Rose (New York: Zone Books, 1999); Dena Goodman, ed., *Marie-Antoinette: Writings on the Body of a Queen* (New York: Routledge, 2003); Humphrey Wine, "Madame de Pompadour," in *The Saint-Aubin* Livre de caricatures: *Drawing Satire in Eighteenth-Century Paris*, ed. Colin Jones (Oxford: Voltaire Foundation, 2012), 179–90. Germann, *Picturing Marie Leszczinska* explores female agency within a more normative persona.

9

Courting Favor: The Apartments of the Princesse de Lamballe at Versailles, 1767–89

Sarah Grant

Introduction

The Italian-born Marie Thérèse Louise de Savoie-Carignan, princesse de Lamballe (1749–92), rose to the highest levels of French Court society becoming Marie-Antoinette's longest-serving and most devoted confidante (Figure 9.1). As a mark of their friendship, the queen appointed Lamballe, *Surintendante de la Maison de la Reine* (Superintendent of the Queen's Household), in 1775. The office of *Surintendante* was the highest position a female courtier could aspire to obtain and conferred on the princess immense privileges, a much-coveted access to the royal family, and considerable scope for personal enrichment. Lamballe presided over all other courtiers, including the *Gouvernante des enfants de France*—the role her rival, the duchesse de Polignac, was to occupy—and answered only to the royal family. This seniority gave Lamballe the power to "admonish" her peers for their faults, to present candidates for vacant positions within the queen's household, meaning there was the potential for her to

---

I thank Olivier Delahaye for allowing me access to the princess's former apartments and his very generous assistance. I am also indebted to Pierre Jugie for his help with the plans in the Archives Nationales. I am grateful to The Art Fund for the Jonathan Ruffer Curatorial Grant that enabled me to participate in the conference from which this chapter derives. NB. The allocation of lodgings at Versailles was notoriously complicated and with the passage of time it has become still more opaque. Because the princesse de Lamballe occupied two apartments with identical footprints, which also underwent successive alterations, but only one of the relevant floorplans is dated, it is not always clear which apartment is recorded in which plan. The matter is confused by plans being updated to reflect changes made by a different occupant and conflicting dates of residence. Where ambiguities remain I have indicated them. Portions of this text were published in the monograph Sarah Grant, *Female Portraiture and Patronage in Marie-Antoinette's Court: The Princesse de Lamballe* (New York and Abingdon: Routledge, 2019).

Figure 9.1 Karl Anton Hickel, Portrait of the princesse de Lamballe, 1788, oil on canvas, Vienna, Liechtenstein, The Princely Collections. © 2018 Liechtenstein, The Princely Collections, Vaduz-Vienna/SCALA, Florence. Photo: SCALA, Florence.

surround herself with her own intimates, and it was on her authority that the treasurer would pay the wages of the other office-holders.[1] The princess was responsible for maintaining the list of persons who were granted an audience with the queen, thus increasing her control of her fellow courtiers' contact with the royal consort. The superintendency was a highly visible role and its holders had all been forceful personalities of previous reigns, but it had originally been dissolved precisely because of the discord it created amongst courtiers who feared the superintendent's almost limitless authority over them. Despite her evident power, the resentment Lamballe incurred in the execution of her duties made her position at Court vulnerable and the queen's intermittent inconstancy toward her, coupled with a very public rivalry with the duchesse de Polignac, made her position more precarious still.[2] Nevertheless, she had been groomed from an early age for Court life and was well-versed in princely etiquette and her place within the entrenched systems and protocol of Versailles. In her attempts to navigate these difficulties she was encouraged by her ambitious father-in-law, the duc de Penthièvre (1725–93), who likely cherished his family's long association with this post—both his cousin and grandmother had served as *surintendante*—and, following the death of his sole male heir, hoped to use Lamballe's office to expand and consolidate his house's influence at Court.

While Lamballe had a large suite of rooms at Fontainebleau and apartments in other royal palaces, Versailles was her most critical sphere.[3] In addition to her administrative and ceremonial duties, the princess was expected to entertain the queen and their circle in her official palace apartment. Her official salary was intended to provide her with "the means to maintain herself in this important role with the dignity appropriate to a princess of the blood."[4] There was a competitive character to these entertainments and the number and frequency of the queen's visits were assiduously tabulated and remarked on by courtiers. Madame de Staël, for instance, reported Marie-Antoinette's oscillation between the two salons of Lamballe and Polignac during a stay at Fontainebleau: "On soupe trois fois par semaine chez Mme De Polignac, trois fois chez Mme de Lamballe" [We dine three times a week at Madame De Polignac's, and three times at Madame de Lamballe's].[5]

A survey of Lamballe's successive apartments at Versailles, the setting for these activities, is therefore instructive, not only shedding light on late-eighteenth-century female courtly taste and the way these spaces were inhabited but also providing a fascinating perspective on the complex politics that attended the furnishing and maintenance of the lodging of a prominent senior courtier, one of the great palace's final royal inhabitants. For courtiers at Versailles, the prestige of an official apartment was such that they were prepared to endure significant incommodity as only their physical presence in the Château could protect a status that was constantly under threat.[6]

First Apartment: First Floor, *Pavillon de la Surintendance, Aile du Midi*, 1767–80

Courtiers at Versailles were housed according to a complex scale of gradation based on rank, professional role, and their relationship to the monarch. During the reign of Louis XVI, space became ever more constricted as the expanding Royal Family appropriated lodgings previously reserved for their courtiers.[7] Lamballe's peregrinations between three apartments reveal the extent to which accommodation had become a perpetual game of musical chairs.

At Versailles, the princess's first apartment was one she shared with her father-in-law, the duc de Penthièvre, and her late husband, the prince de Lamballe (1747–68), which the duke had first been allocated in 1756.[8] The apartment was prestigiously located in the extreme corner of the *aile du Midi*, a section of the wing known as the *pavillon de la Surintendance* (Figure 9.2).[9] The *pavillon* was easily accessible from the *cour des Princes*, yet far enough away from the main bustle of the palace to retain a certain privacy. The rooms here were spacious and those in the central enfilade were flooded with light. The corner location meant that there were windows on three sides, giving on to an internal courtyard—the *cour de l'Apothicaiererie*[sic][10], an external courtyard—the *cour de la Bouche de Mesdames*[11] and the road that ran parallel to the *aile du Midi*, the *rue de la Surintendance* (now the *rue de l'Indépendance Américaine*). The duke's apartment was on the first floor and situated across the road from the *Hôtel des Affaires Étrangères et de la Marine* (now the *Bibliothèque de Versailles*), which the duke frequented as *Grand Admiral de France*.

Figure 9.2 The *Pavillon de la Surintendance* on the *rue de l'indépendance Américaine*, with the marked sections numbered 1 and 2 indicating the location of the princesse de Lamballe's first and second apartments, respectively. Photo: Author.

From the *cour des Princes*, where carriages drew up, the princess would walk the length of the *Galerie de Pierre* and pass through a door at the end on the left to gain access to the stairwell leading to her apartment.[12] The apartment comprised twelve rooms, its high ceilings allowing for eleven *entresols* (mezzanine rooms). Once appointed to *Surintendante* in September 1775, with the enlarged retinue of ladies-in-waiting this role brought, it became clear that this suite of rooms could no longer practically accommodate both the princesse de Lamballe, the duke and their respective attendants. And so, in 1776, Louis XVI agreed that the duke would move to the late prince de Conti's former suite, leaving the princesse de Lamballe to occupy the apartment in its entirety.[13] The *aile du Midi* was extensively altered in the nineteenth century, first under Louis-Philippe, then again in the 1870s. This first apartment occupied by the princesse de Lamballe was remodeled and is today used by the French Government as part of their *salles du sénat* which, like the rest of the *pavillon*, are closed to the public; her rooms now form the *appartement du président de l'Assemblée nationale*. However, surviving plans show the apartment's original distribution during Lamballe's occupation (Figure 9.3).[14] From the stairwell, two doors gave

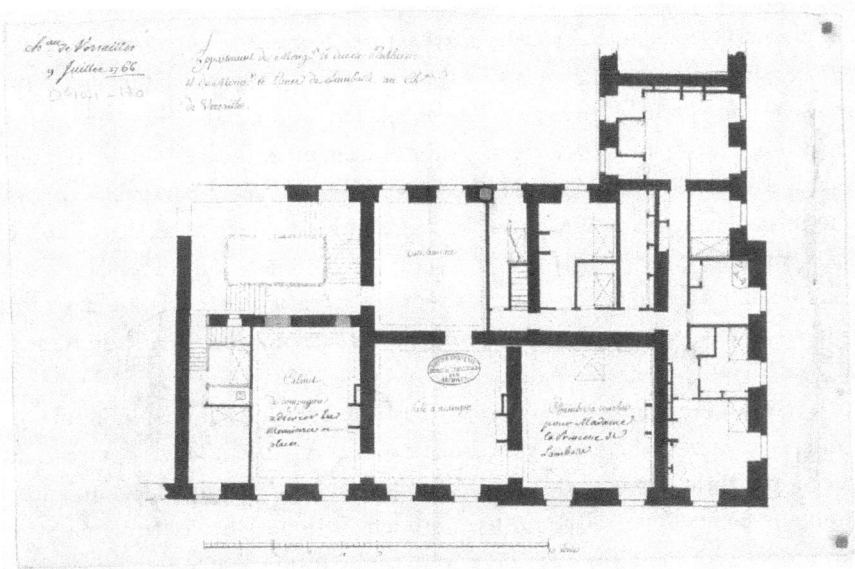

Figure 9.3 Floorplan of the princesse de Lamballe's first apartment at Versailles in 1766, with the *entresols* flaps lifted. Paris, Archives Nationales. Image in the public domain.

access to the apartment, one a service entrance used by the princess's staff, and the second, the principal door through which one entered the *antichambre*, a reception room where guests were received. This was a large space with two windows overlooking the internal courtyard. In the corner of the *antichambre*, a staircase led up to the *entresols* where the princess's ladies and attendants were housed. A door at the other end led to a corridor connecting with the princess's expansive *garderobe*, almost equal in size to the reception room, doubtless serving as both wardrobe and dressing room. Another door in the antechamber led to the dining room, the central room of the enfilade, from which one accessed the large *cabinet de compagnie*, the principal reception room, decorated with mirrored panelling, and the princess's bedroom. These rooms all overlooked the *cour de la bouche de Mesdames* and were bright and sunlit. The bedroom, dining room, antechamber, and *cabinet* had the highest ceilings of the apartment as they did not have any *entresols* above them. The *entresols* comprised three for the *service* (*garçons de chambre*, etc.), the separate rooms and bathrooms of her senior ladies-in-waiting and the remaining rooms for female attendants. The princess therefore shared her apartment with her entourage: her two *dames d'honneur*—Madame de Guébriant and Madame de la Caze— and two *dames de compagnie*: the comtesse de Lâge de Volude and Madame de Ginestous. Overseeing her wardrobe were three *femmes de chambre*, a *femme de garderobbe*[sic] and a *fille de garderobbe*[sic]. Further attendants included two *valets de chambre* and three *valets de pied*.[15] Later floorplans of either the first or second apartment show a room off the antechamber for the "Suisse" or Swiss guard, essentially a bodyguard, who was in the princess's personal employ.[16] The princess's ladies' rooms were far more modestly furnished than those of their mistress, containing a bed, a screen, silk curtains and a fireplace, while the *femmes de chambre* had portable beds and occasionally a writing desk. The *entresol* rooms at the palace did not have *boiseries* and were usually hung with decorative wallpaper.[17]

It was not the princess who bore the costs of furnishing and maintaining her Court apartments where she was required to accompany and give service to the queen, but the *Bâtiments du Roi* and *Garde-Meuble de la Couronne* and, apart from any personal items the princess brought with her, the contents remained the property of the Crown.[18] There were limits to the structural changes and furnishings a courtier could demand and requests were occasionally denied and frequently modified. Courtiers were expected to pay themselves for any work deemed unnecessary and for "luxury" items.[19]

After the Revolution, virtually every piece of furniture and work of art in every room at Versailles and all the other royal palaces was disposed of in the notoriously devastating revolutionary sales held between August 25, 1793 and October 1795.[20] Traces of Lamballe's residence at countless royal palaces vanished with the disposal of these treasures and the palaces' rooms have undergone many alterations since the period of her residence. The situation is further complicated by the fact that French royal furniture was regarded as a moveable chattel.[21] In a constant cycle of acquisition, modification, and disposal, the furniture and furnishings in French royal palaces drifted from one room to another, from occupant to occupant and palace to palace, descending down through the ranks as they grew gradually outmoded until finally stripped for valuable materials and destroyed.

Here and there, pieces of Lamballe's furniture from royal palaces have surfaced, but it is difficult to appreciate which of these and their corresponding interiors were indisputably evidence of the princess's own taste, as many arose from the Garde-Meuble's policy of recycling. For example, in 1777, identical orders of benches and matching stools were filled for the comte d'Artois and Lamballe, to be used in their billiard rooms at Fontainebleau.[22] By 1786, two of these had found their way to the duchesse de Polignac's apartment.[23] A lyre-backed chair from Lamballe's second and third apartments at Versailles later reappeared in her rooms at the Tuileries.[24] Similarly, a suite of furniture commissioned by Madame du Barry in 1771 for the Château de Saint-Hubert was reemployed for the princesse de Lamballe in her rooms at Fontainebleau.[25]

Many famous *menuisiers* and *ébénistes* attached to the *Garde-Meuble* are known to have worked for the princess though often the commissions themselves are yet to resurface. It is the Château inventories that provide the most information about the furnishing of her apartments.

A 1776 inventory of Lamballe's first apartment, made not long after she had assumed sole occupation, reveals that the *antichambre* was lit by a six-branch chandelier and contained a marquetry table, twelve chairs upholstered in blue and white striped fabric and a crimson silk folding screen.[26] The walls were hung with five panels of gilded leather, these were an earlier fashion and, despite their enormous expense and association with royal interiors, would have seemed rather dated by 1776. The dining room had a silk damask-covered screen, a six-branch rock crystal chandelier and twenty chairs upholstered in crimson silk.[27] The *Salle de compagnie* appeared rather sparsely furnished, with crimson Gros de Tours silk curtains and a screen and six folding stools covered in crimson silk damask. It is possible the princess supplemented with her own furniture in this room but more likely this reflects the fact that, up until this point, the princess had had no official role at Court and not much call to entertain. The *cabinet* was furnished with an armchair and two folding stools upholstered in crimson silk and velvet, respectively, and a "lit de repos." A crimson silk damask armchair and a foot stool are visible in the princess's 1788 portrait by Anton Hickel (Figure 9.1). The room contained two relics from a previous reign that were clear evidence of the Garde-Meuble's recycling policy: one, a marble-topped marquetry commode "à la Régence," and the second, a large Boulle *bureau plat* with gilt-bronze mounts of female masks and smiling espagnolettes, which was later sent to the Tuileries in 1791, and is now in the Hôtel de Soubise (Figure 9.4).[28] In 1776 the princess tried, with some difficulty, to obtain wall-lights and console tables from either the *Garde-Meuble* or the *Bâtiments* and wrestled with the latter over her desire to modernize the water

Figure 9.4 André-Charles Boulle, *bureau plat* from the princesse de Lamballe's *cabinet de compagnie* in her first apartment at Versailles, *c.* 1710, rosewood (palissandre), gilt-bronze, and black morocco leather. Paris, Archives Nationales. Photo: Author.

heating arrangement in her bathroom.[29] Such improvements coincided with the queen's social visits. Throughout 1775–6, Maria-Theresa's ambassador, the comte de Mercy-Argenteau, reported that Marie-Antoinette frequently went to the princesse de Lamballe's apartment to gamble or pass the time.[30] It was undoubtedly a desire to assert her new status and to provide a setting fit for a queen that prompted Lamballe in 1780 to request new panelling with gilded borders for her *salon*. Gilded *boiserie* was an extravagance reserved solely for members of the royal family and ultimately the princess had to accept substitute wallpaper instead.[31] She requested two mirrors to illuminate her library[32] and later asked for a marble-topped gilded console table, a mirror and two pairs of two-branched wall-lights.[33] Further bids were successful: on March 21, 1780, it was recorded in the *Journal du Garde-Meuble* that the *Garçons du Garde-meuble* had delivered to the princess's apartment, a suite of crimson silk damask furniture with white painted moldings: an *ottomane*, twelve little chairs and six *voyeuses en prie Dieu*.[34] Thus we can see that incrementally the princess was able to bring about change in her surroundings, in a clear campaign to upgrade the social spaces of her apartment.

Second Apartment: Ground Floor, *Pavillon de la Surintendance, Aile du Midi*, July 23, 1780–December 1786

In July 1780, the princess was forced to relinquish her choice terrain to the duc d'Angoulême, the comte d'Artois's eldest son.[35] Such displacements, by now thoroughly routine at Court,[36] were always made to accommodate a courtier of a superior status, which in Lamballe's case could only be a member of the royal family. She was moved to an apartment directly beneath it on the ground floor, composed of an antichamber, dining room, *salon de compagnie*, billiard room, bedroom, boudoir, *garderobe*, library and again *entresol* rooms for her staff (Figure 9.2).[37] This was the very same apartment that had once been occupied by the duc de Penthièvre's cousin and Lamballe's illustrious predecessor as *Surintendante*, Mlle de Clermont.[38] Today, once again, the space is vastly altered, with walls having been both removed and inserted. The apartment is used by the museum as a conservation studio, but it retains some of the original chimneypieces and in addition, part of the *boiserie* and *volets* from the time of the comte and comtesse de Provence, who occupied the apartment immediately after the princess.[39]

The benefits of this apartment were much the same as the one above: light, and spacious quarters. A 1785 inventory shows different furniture and furnishings in the central enfilade from those Lamballe had had in her previous apartment—a greater variety of more sumptuous objects reflecting her elevation in status.[40] The dining room was decorated with a crimson and gold scheme and now contained twenty chairs and several screens covered in crimson silk, a Bohemian crystal chandelier, the same Regency marquetry commode from her first apartment, a three-branch wall-light "à Rocaille" and crimson Gros de Tours silk curtains bordered by gold thread trim. The principal entertaining room, the *salon de compagnie*, was decorated in green and white with a wide array of social types of furniture, including sofas and *voyeuses* and twenty-four lyre-backed mahogany chairs covered in green morocco. Today, two of these understated neoclassical chairs with their little sun moldings, by Sené and bearing his stamp, one still pasted with the label "Pour … la princesse de Lamballe a Versailles. N° 93," are in the Hôtel de Soubise.[41] A third was sold at auction in 2017 (Figure 9.5).[42] The

Figure 9.5 Jean-Baptiste Sené, lyre-backed chair from the princesse de Lamballe's *salon de compagnie* in her second and third apartments at Versailles, 1787, mahogany and velvet. Private collection. Photo: Daguerre, Paris.

focal point of this room was a 16-foot Savonnerie carpet depicting a royal coat of arms and insignia: a sceptre and the Hand of Justice surmounted by a crown. At either end was a crowned sun surrounded by horns of plenty. A Savonnerie carpet with a similar design, originally displayed in the Royal Chapel at Versailles, was acquired by the Château in 2009.[43] Also present in the *salon* were two pairs of two-branch wall-lights with rams' heads, interlacing laurel garlands and a garlanded vase surmounted by a pinecone finial. A pair almost exactly matching this description was sold recently by a French dealer, identified as being after a design by Jean-Charles Delafosse.[44] The green décor of the *salon* continued in the billiard room with green silk hangings and curtains, and green Utrecht velvet and green Gros de Tours silk-covered white benches, and again in the library where green curtains protected the books. A crimson silk curtain can be seen covering part of the princess's library in her portrait by Hickel (Figure 9.1).

In the bedroom the princess had a large floral and ribbon-patterned white ground carpet and another pair of ram's-head wall-lights. Her boudoir contained a niche bed swathed in drapery and elaborate white silk *passementerie* and an assortment of carved and gilded furniture all upholstered in the same floral white-ground Gros de Tours silk. Like the Boulle *bureau plat* from the princess's first apartment, a number of pieces in the second apartment—the commodes and wall-lights, for instance—dated from a previous generation and suggest something of the impersonal touch of the Garde-Meuble's furnishing policy.

In January 1782 the princess asked for a communicating door to be introduced to a partition wall between two *entresol* rooms, one of which was destined for her lady-in-waiting, the comtesse de Lâge de Voludé, who was also requesting an overmantel mirror.[45] By now, the princess had grown significantly in importance and influence and she had more ambitious plans for this apartment. In January 1783, she made a request to extend her quarters by adding a gallery that would run the length of the external courtyard and connect with the *hôtel de la Surintendance des bâtiments* on the other side.[46] Several plans were drawn up, but ultimately her proposal was denied (Figure 9.6).[47] The *Directeur Général des Bâtiments du Roi*, the comte d'Angiviller, wrote to the king advising against the construction on the grounds that it would do away with three windows in the apartments of the duchesse de FitzJames and duchesse de Fresnes, among others.[48] His trump card was the estimate that construction would cost at least 40,000 *livres*. Grandiose extension and refurbishment plans were frequently turned down but it is significant that the princess's request was denied at a time when she was comparatively out of favor with the queen, while, in contrast, her

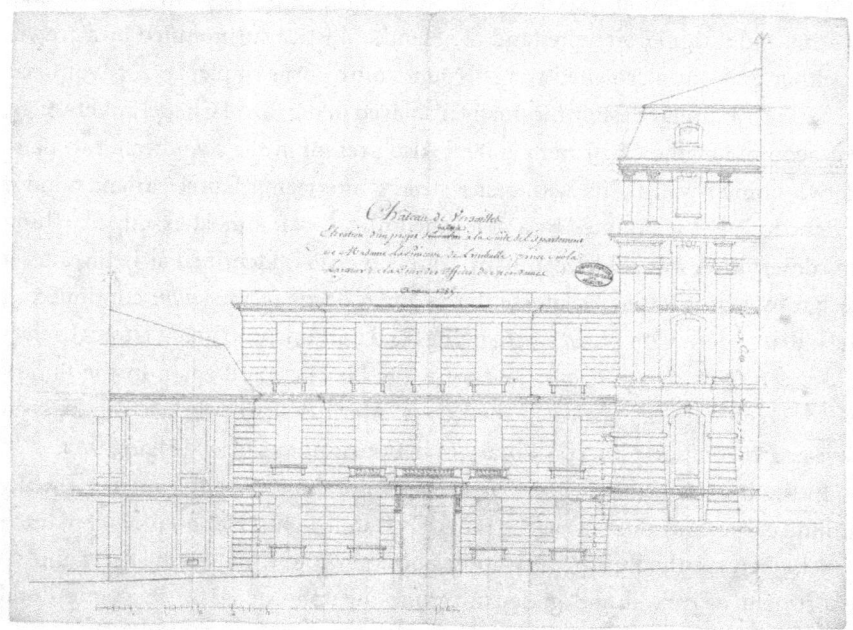

Figure 9.6 *Elévation d'un projet de galerie à la suite de Madame la Princesse de Lamballe*, 1785, Paris, Archives Nationales. Image in the public domain.

rival, the duchesse de Polignac, who was at that time in ascendancy, had been allowed to make extensive costly alterations to her suite of rooms.[49] It is important to state that while the princess experienced a decline in the queen's affections which peaked in 1778, she continued to execute her duties as *Surintendante* and hostess, attend key social and ceremonial events and maintain her apartments. To have behaved otherwise would have meant risking her position.

Contemporaries spoke of the princess frequently entertaining in this apartment and her unsuccessful attempt to build a gallery extension was no doubt motivated by social ends. One of Gustav III's favorites, Baron Taube, on a visit to Versailles in April 1780, wrote of the little parties and parlor games that the princess and the duchesse de Polignac often hosted in their apartments, which the queen always attended and often Louis XVI as well.[50] The following year the marquise de Bombelles described a late summer supper hosted by the princesse de Lamballe in her apartment, which the queen and Mme Élisabeth attended; the marquise only retiring to bed at one o'clock in the morning.[51] Catherine the Great's son, Paul Grand Duke of Russia (the future emperor) and his wife, Maria Feodorovna, visited the princesse de Lamballe a number of times during their visit to Versailles in May–June 1782, attending a supper and two balls the princess hosted, where the queen, the comtes and comtesses de Provence and d'Artois, and Madame Élisabeth were present.[52] One such ball finished at 3 o'clock in the morning with the queen staying right to the end (but then, she had arrived at midnight). Similarly, Gustav III attended Lamballe's suppers at Versailles, including one event in June 1784.[53] The baronne d'Oberkirch recalled attending a *souper* hosted by the princess at Versailles where together with members of the royal family they played at *loto* "fort à la mode en ce temps-là et où l'on perdait beaucoup d'argent" [highly fashionable at that time and where one lost much money].[54]

It seems likely that the princess would have decorated her apartment interiors with some of her own possessions, primarily porcelain garnitures and framed prints, which were found in abundance at her other residences. Throughout this period, the princess also had an alternative entertainment space (as did some members of the royal family and other senior courtiers)—the townhouse she had purchased from her father-in-law in November 1775, the Hôtel d'Eu, situated a stone's throw away from the palace. Here the princess had more freedom to arrange the interiors to suit her whims and inventories reveal her fashionably current neoclassical tastes—a wide array of portraits, sentimental prints of antique subjects, and a forest of Sèvres biscuit porcelain figures.[55] A quantity of social types of furniture and games reinforce the residence's function. Although she was there in an official capacity, the princess also covered the maintenance costs—in 1789, for example, when she arranged for the house to be connected to a water supply, a very expensive exercise, the Bâtiments expected her to pay for this herself.[56]

Third Apartment: Ground Floor, *Parterre du Midi façade*, *Aile du Midi*, October 28, 1786–9

In October of 1786,[57] Lamballe was asked to move for a third and final time, ceding her apartment to the comtesse de Provence. The new apartment was on the ground floor of the garden-façade of the *Aile du Midi*, level with and overlooking the *parterre du Midi* (Figure 9.7).[58] This location was less private and the layout less commodious than in the *pavillon de la Surintendance*. As with her first two apartments, these rooms have changed beyond all recognition,

Figure 9.7 The garden façade of the *Aile du Midi* overlooking the *Parterre du Midi*, with the marked section indicating the location of the princesse de Lamballe's third apartment. Photo: Author.

undergoing substantial changes in the nineteenth century and are now the *Salles Empire*. A plan shows the original distribution and also reveals that the duchesse de Polignac occupied the opposing corner and a good number of rooms in between, and thus was far more splendidly housed than Lamballe, although this was probably because, in addition to herself, the duchess's apartment was required to accommodate the royal children and the *sous-gouvernante* (Figure 9.8).[59] Nevertheless, her rooms were considered among the palace's most desirable.[60] Lamballe's apartment was composed of four large rooms, two with chimneypieces, and four *entresols*. The plans show that one of these large rooms and the entresols above all of them had been subdivided several times, with partition walls erected to create a complex network of multiple smaller rooms. In all, the apartment comprised an antichamber and adjoining room; a dining room; a *salon de compagnie*; a billiard room; bedroom; boudoir; a library; *garderobe* and several rooms for her staff. Billiard rooms were a fashionable addition to the apartments at the time; in 1786 Madame de Staël recorded Marie-Antoinette

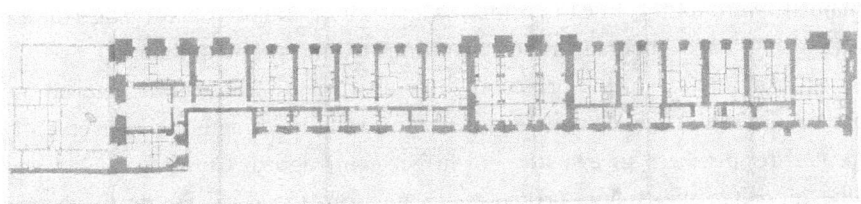

Figure 9.8 Plan of the Apartment of the princesse de Lamballe in the *Aile du Midi*, Paris, Archives Nationales. Photo: Image in the public domain.

visiting the princesse de Lamballe's apartment at Fontainebleau to play billiards: "Cet amuseument est devenu fort à la mode, et les femmes y réussissent bien" [This amusement became very fashionable, and the women played well].[61]

The 1788 and 1789 inventories show that the princess had brought with her the furniture from her previous apartment.[62] The secondary rooms contained the same furnishings she had had since 1776 and the principal enfilade contained the furniture and furnishings from the second apartment.

On November 22nd, 1786 Marie-Antoinette herself came to see the princess's new apartment.[63] Lamballe had requested a number of changes including the removal of a partition to enlarge her dining room; the demolition of a staircase to create more space for a *garde-robe*; repairs to the panelling and replacement of the parquet floors in the *salon* and dining room; and the installation of three mirrors. With the insistence of the princess and the queen, it was agreed that these changes were essential and that they be made with "the greatest speed" possible.[64] In March the following year, the princess requested the construction of a boiler and a little reservoir to supply hot water for her bath and finally, in 1788, she asked for the construction of three large *armoires* to create a library in her *cabinet*.[65]

Conclusion

After the Revolution and the dissolution of the Court at Versailles, chaos reigned at the palace. Lamballe attempted to rent out her residence in the town[66] and the contents of her palace apartment were inventoried, this time more perfunctorily. Notes made in 1790, in the margins of the 1785 inventory, refer to the condition of some of the pieces in her rooms and indicate where some were put into store, couldn't be located, or, occasionally, were destroyed.[67] Ultimately, the majority were sold. While the princess's apartments are no more, vestiges of the furnishings have emerged, and may continue to emerge, on the market.

An examination of the princess's three apartments tells us much about the career of a senior female courtier. Generous, well-appointed, and conveniently located rooms were an essential aid in her campaign to Court favor and win allies and her apartments hosted everyone from the royal family to visiting dignitaries. The princess's constant attempts to improve her lodgings, the site of and backdrop to lavish entertainments, are revealing of her ambitions. The diminished size of her final apartment and the resistance to her plans to extend her second apartment lay bare her temporary decline in the queen's affections. The contents of the apartments themselves chart the princess's increase in status after her nomination to *surintendante* and provide intimate insights into how these spaces were used and the day-to-day co-habitation of the princess and her household—sufficient space was needed to accommodate the extensive entourage befitting one of her station. The queen herself took an interest in her *surintendante*'s quarters. And yet, as we have seen, even a princess of the blood and royal favorite was at the mercy of the *Bâtiments* and *Garde-Meuble*, the latter largely determining the appearance of the princess's interiors. The inventories show that, unlike the royal family, the princess did not have summer and winter furnishings—her interiors remained the same year-round. Some adornments were out of reach—the gilded *boiseries* the princess enjoyed in her own residences, for instance, were not permitted her at Versailles. She was allocated an, at times, eclectic combination of furniture—specially commissioned suites and articles of the greatest luxury took their place alongside recycled pieces taken out of storage or transferred from other palaces. However, it is important to stress that the princess had richly decorated interiors furnished to her exact tastes in her private townhouse located mere minutes away from the palace. And the whole Court was fully cognizant of the palace's limitations—the inconveniences Lamballe encountered were experienced with increasing severity by her colleagues further down the chain of hierarchy.

Perhaps most vividly, this case study illustrates the precarious state of the residential areas of the palace at the end of the ancien régime when the strain of over a century of countless residents had begun to show. The constant reshuffling of lodgings necessitated interminable refurbishments, remodeling, and general "refreshing." Repairs to both the fabric and contents of the apartments were a frequent occurrence.[68] It is telling that when Benjamin Franklin visited Versailles in 1767, the diplomat was shocked by the shabbiness and disrepair he encountered remarking, "There is, in short, both at Versailles and Paris, a prodigious Mixture of Magnificence and Negligence, with every kind of Elegance except that of Cleanliness, and what we call *Tidyness*."[69]

Notes

1 The office of *Surintendante* is described in detail in Joseph-Nicolas Guyot, *Traité des Droits, Fonctions, Franchises, Exemptions, Prérogatives et Privilèges Annexés en France à chaque Dignité, à chaque Office & à chaque État, soit Civil, soit Militaire, soit Ecclésiastique*, 4 vols (Paris: Visse, 1787), 2, 245. For more on Lamballe's execution of this role see Grant, *Female Portraiture*, 36–40. On early modern European ladies-in-waiting generally see Nadine Akkerman, and Birgit Houben, eds, *The Politics of Female Households: Ladies-in-Waiting across Early Modern Europe* (Leiden: Brill, 2013).
2 The rivalry was observed and remarked on by the comte de Mercy-Argenteau, among other contemporary sources, and is mentioned in most published biographies of Marie-Antoinette. For a detailed discussion see Grant, *Female Portraiture*, 64–75. On the duchesse de Polignac see Diane, comtesse de Polignac, *Mémoires sur la vie et le caractere de Mme. La duchesse de Polignac …* (London: Chez J. Debrett, 1796); H. Schlesinger, *La Duchesse de Polignac et son temps* (Paris: Auguste Ghio, 1889), and more recently, Nathalie Colas des Francs, *Madame de Polignac Intime de Marie-Antoinette*, 2nd edn. (Paris: Tallandier, 2013).
3 AN O¹ 3395.
4 "En facilitant à la D.te dame Princesse de Lamballe les moyens de se soutenir dans Cette Charge importante avec la dignite Convenable á[*sic*] une Princesse de Son Sang," *Brevet de Traitement* signed by Louis XVI at Fontainebleau, October 20, 1775, Archivio di Stato, Turin, Categ 107, Mazzo 3.
5 Letter dated November 11, 1786, Staël, Anne-Louise-Germaine, Madame de, "Lettres de Jeunesse, 1789," in Madame de Staël (Anne-Louise-Germaine), *Correspondance Générale*, ed. Béatrice W. Jasinski (Paris: Hachette, 1962), 136.
6 On the character, composition, and function of the Court at Versailles, see the comprehensive studies of William Ritchey Newton: *Vivre à Versailles: Derrière la façade, la vie quotidienne au Château*, 2nd edn. (Paris: Flammarion, 2014); *La Petite Cour: Services et serviteurs à la Cour de Versailles au XVIII siècle* (Paris: Fayard, 2006) and most especially, *L'espace du roi: La Cour de France au Château de Versailles, 1682–1789* (Paris: Le Grand livre du mois, 2000). See also Jeroen F. J. Duindam, *Vienna and Versailles: The Courts of Europe's Dynastic Rivals, 1550–1780* (Cambridge: Cambridge University Press, 2007) and for early modern European

Courts, and their courtiers, see John Adamson, ed., *The Princely Courts of Europe* (London: Weidenfeld and Nicholson, 1998).

7   Newton, *L'espace du roi*, 24.
8   AN O^1 1076 444 cited by Newton, *L'espace du roi*, 254.
9   The *aile du Midi* was also called the *aile des Princes* as the princes and princesses of the blood, senior ranking courtiers and the queen's favorites were lodged there.
10 Blondel's *Plan du rez-de-chaussée de l'aile du Midi et du parterre du Midi dans le Château de Versailles*, shows the *cour Apothicaiererie* divided in two, with a separate *petit cour*. Jacques-François Blondel, *Architecture Françoise ou recueil des plans, élévations, coupes et profils*, 4 vols (Paris: Jombert, 1756), 4, plate 480. The *cour Apothicaiererie* was later renamed the *cour de Monsieur* for the comte de Provence.
11 The *cour de la Bouche de Mesdames* was also called the *cour des Offices de Mesdames* and is not to be confused with the large internal courtyard at the other end of the wing, the *cour de la Bouche*. In Blondel's plan it is called the *cour basse*, ibid. The courtyard is now used as a car park.
12 Today the gallery is called the *Galerie des bustes*. The elegant existing *escalier de Provence* was remodeled in 1788–9 at Louis XVI's request, and therefore dates from after Lamballe's period of residence.
13 AN O^1 1799 636 cited in Newton, *L'espace du roi*, 109; 255.
14 Appartement de Mons.r le duc de Penthievre et de Mons.r le Prince de Lamballe au Ch.au de Versailles. 9 Juillet 1766 [with later amendments from the time of the princess de Lamballe's residence] AN, O^1 1071 n° 170.
15 The princess employed large numbers of staff across her multiple residences. It is not clear how many accompanied her to Versailles. A room for the *valet de chambre* is indicated on the floorplan, located off the *cabinet de compagnie*.
16 O^1 1781^8 n° 5. Lamballe's Swiss guard is listed in her staff accounts where he is named as "Gauchat." Archivio di Stato, Turin, Categ 107, Mazzo 1, No. 29.
17 As was the case with the rooms of Mme Victoire's female attendants. Jean-Claude Le Guillou, "L'appartement de Madame Sophie Au Château de Versailles. Formation et Métamorphoses, 1774–1790," *Gazette des Beaux-Arts* 97 (1981): 201–18.
18 On the history of the Garde-Meuble during the reign of Louis XVI, see Stéphane Castelluccio, *Le Garde-Meuble de la Couronne et ses intendants du XVIe au XVIIIe siècle* (Paris, 2004).
19 Newton, *L'espace du roi*, 69.
20 Pierre Verlet, *French Royal Furniture* (London: Barrie and Rockliff, 1963), 52.
21 Ibid., 42.
22 Pierre Verlet, *Le Mobilier Royal Français*, 4 vols, Rev. edn. (Paris: Picard, 1990), 1:68.
23 Ibid.

24 Ibid., 2:150.
25 Inv. V5756 and Inv. V5749 (1/2), *Château de Versailles: Les Collections*. Available online: http://collections.chateauversailles.fr/#b88603f5-c81c-4503-bfc0-e5128b98b282 (accessed August 18, 2015).
26 Inventaire des meubles du gardemeuble de la couronne Existans a Versailles en 1776 Tome P.er Château et Grand Commun, AN O¹ 3457.
27 "20 chaises de panne cramoisie," *Panne* had a weave similar to velvet and could be woven from silk, wool, or cotton but in this case would most likely have been silk. Jean-François Féraud, "Panne," in *Dictionnaire Critique de La Langue Française*, ed. Féraud Jean-François (Marseille: Chez Jean Mossy Père et Fils, 1787–8), 3.
28 Inventory number: AN, AE/VIa/4. I am grateful to Stéphanie Maillet-Marqué for her kind assistance. The association with Lamballe was identified by Pierre Verlet and this information comes from his notes on the object file.
29 Newton, *L'espace du roi*, 255–6.
30 Alfred Von Arneth and M. A. Geffroy, eds, *Correspondance secrète entre Marie-Thérèse et le comte de Mercy-Argenteau*, 3 vols (Paris: Firmin-Didot, 1874), 2:398; 521–2.
31 AN, O¹ 1800 513 & 514 cited in Newton, *L'espace du roi*, 256.
32 AN O¹ 1800 319 cited in ibid.
33 AN, O¹ 1800 513 & 514 cited in ibid.
34 The maker was not recorded. AN O¹ 3320.
35 AN O¹ 1800 593 cited in in Newton, *L'espace du roi*, 257.
36 Like a row of dominos, each displacement triggered further moves down the chain. See Newton on these "cascades": *Vivre à Versailles*, 30.
37 Inventaire General des Meubles du Château et dehors de Versailles. 2.e. Volume [1785]. AN O¹ 3462. Plans differing from those of her first apartment are AN, O¹ 1781³ n° 56 *bis*—59 and O¹ 1781⁸ n° 2 & 5, but these are undated and could still be the first apartment following the changes that were made. Newton describes this apartment as composed of four rooms, two with chimneypieces, and four *entresols*, this however does not match the floor plans and the date of this archival reference is given as 1787 which is from the time Lamballe had moved to her third apartment. The number of rooms and chimneypieces matches that of her third apartment. Newton, *L'espace du roi*, 204. See also Pierre de Nolhac, *Histoire du Château de Versailles au XVIIIe siècle* (Paris: Emile-Paul, 1918), 130.
38 "Mlle de Clermont Surintendante de la Maison de la Reine" is indicated as the occupant on Blondel's *c*. 1735 plan.
39 On the *boiseries*, see Frédéric Didier, "Les appartements de Monsieur et de Madame à l'extrémité de l'aile du Midi en 1787," *Versalia* 21 (2018): 59–80.
40 Inventaire General des Meubles du Château et dehors de Versailles. 2.e. Volume [1785]. AN O¹ 3462.

41 Inventory number: AN, AE/VIa/187. I am grateful to Stéphanie Maillet-Marqué for her kind assistance. This information comes from notes on the object file made by Verlet—who identified the chairs from their entry in the Journal du Garde-Meuble (O^1 3641): *Le Mobilier royal français* (1992), 2, plate 35.
42 Daguerre, Paris, November 11, 2017, lot n° 265.
43 Inventory number: V 6273. This can be viewed on the palace's database available online: http://collections.chateauversailles.fr/#ed39f590-703c-4eeb-a7bf-ffc4b7e15cc3 (accessed August 8, 2018).
44 "Paire d'appliques d'époque Louis XVI, modèle de Jean-Charles Delafosse," Antiquités Rigot et Fils, Ref. 54761. These have flames instead of the pinecone finial but it is possible that the clerk mistook them for a more conventional pinecone. The two-branch model is unusual and therefore considerably rare.
45 AN O^1 1801 236 cited by Newton, *L'espace du roi*, 225.
46 1783 is the date given by Newton citing AN. O^1 1801 419: Newton, *L'espace du roi*, 225. The plans themselves, however, are dated 1785.
47 "Élévation d'un projet de galerie à la suite de l'appartement de la princesse de Lamballe." AN O^1 1781^3 n° 27–35.
48 AN O^1 1801 419 cited by Newton, *L'espace du roi*, 225.
49 Pierre Verlet, *Versailles* (Paris: Fayard, 1961), 720.
50 Letter from Evert Vilhelm Taube, Baron Taube to Gustav III, King of Sweden, dated Versailles, Thursday April 20, 1780. *Electronic Enlightenment*.
51 Letter from the marquise de Bombelles to the marquis de Bombelles, Versailles, August 13, 1781, in Évelyne Lever, *"Que je suis heureuse d'être ta femme": lettres intimes, 1778–1782* (Paris: Tallandier, 2009), 364.
52 Anonymous, "Journal de ce qui s'est passé à Versailles depuis l'instant de l'arrivée de Monsieur le comte et de Madame la comtesse du Nord, jusqu'à celui de leur départ" *Bulletin du Centre de recherche du Château de Versailles* [En ligne], 2014. Available online: http://journals.openedition.org/crcv/12396 (accessed septembre 13, 2018); and "Nottes sur le voyage de M. le comte et de Mme la comtesse du Nord en France au mois de may 1782," *Bulletin du Centre de recherche du Château de Versailles* [En ligne], 2014. Available online: http://journals.openedition.org/crcv/12398 (accessed septembre 13, 2018).
53 Letter from Gustav III, King of Sweden to Greve Gustaf Filip Creutz, Paris, Sunday, June 20,1784. *Electronic Enlightenment*.
54 Oberkirch, Henriette-Louise de Waldner de Freundstein and Léonce Bernard de Montbrison, *Mémoires de la baronne d'Oberkirch*, 2 vols (Paris: Charpentier, 1869), 1:267
55 See Grant, *Female Portraiture*, 146–57.
56 Fernand Évrard, *Versailles, ville du roi* (Paris: Leroux, 1935), 233.

57 AN O¹ 1802 242 & 243 cited by Newton, L'espace du roi, 216.
58 AN O¹ 1780⁴ n° 5, 6, 6 bis & 7. See also Verlet, Versailles, 717–21 and de Nolhac, Histoire du Château de Versailles, 130.
59 AN O¹ 1780⁴ n° 5, 6, 6 bis & 7.
60 Newton, L'espace du roi, 192.
61 Letter dated November 11, 1786, Staël, Anne-Louise-Germaine, Madame de, "Lettres de Jeunesse, 1789," 136.
62 Inventaire Général des Meubles du Château et dehors de Versailles. Second Volume [1788], AN O¹ 3464. Estimation des meubles des Logemens de Seigneurs, Oficiers et de la Suite du Château et dehors de Versailles [1789], AN O¹ 3466.
63 AN O¹ 1802 264 & 265 cited in Newton, L'espace du roi, 216.
64 Ibid.
65 AN O¹ 1802 439 cited in ibid.
66 In fact, two adjoining houses. See Grant, Female Portraiture, 146.
67 AN O¹ 3462.
68 In addition to the multiple works requested by the princess, she occasionally had to send some of her furniture back to Paris to be repaired, as was the case with two commodes, *inter alia*, which she sent to the Garde-Meuble from Fontainebleau in 1785. AN O¹ 3287.
69 Letter from Benjamin Franklin to Mary Stevenson, Paris, September 14, 1767, *Benjamin Franklin Papers*, 14.250a.

Part Three

Outsiders

10

Enslaved Muslims at the Sun King's Court

Meredith Martin and Gillian Weiss

During carnival season 1683, Louis, duc de Bourbon, future prince de Condé, staged a masked ball at Versailles. One of several spectacular parties thrown by royal family members in the months after the palace's official inauguration, it received a detailed write-up in the *Mercure galant*. Courtiers in elaborate costumes spent the first part of the evening in two *salles de bal*. Then the host led the king and his retinue to a third, hidden ballroom decorated with crimson velvet fabrics and gilded columns. On one side, Court designers had set up risers for guests and, on the opposite wall, a *tableau vivant* starring Louis XIV's oldest legitimized daughter, Marie Anne de Bourbon, princesse de Conti. As she sat on a throne dressed as the "Queen of Egypt," two enslaved Moors (*esclaves maures*) in "thick silver chains" adopted a "posture marking respect and submission" at her feet.[1]

An engraving by Jacques Le Pautre, made after a drawing by Jean Bérain and published in the same issue, depicts these dark-skinned, bare-chested men, whose serpentine chains appear as ornamental extensions of the garlands and arabesques adorning the walls (Figure 10.1). It includes additional members of the princesse de Conti's "Court" and the royal violin band conducted by Jean-Baptiste Lully all clad "as Egyptians." On the dance floor, members of the king's guard in blackface and "dressed as Moors" passed out refreshments. These "counterfeit *Maures*," emphasized the *Mercure*'s author, drew a striking and "diverting" contrast with the "real" slaves, a sight "capable of making even the most serious man laugh."[2] Wearing turbans and classical garb and carrying trays piled high with treats, they also bore an uncanny resemblance to a Jean Le Pautre-designed *guéridon*, one of several furnishings decorated with heads and bodies of *Maures* owned by Versailles courtiers and royal family members, among them Louis XIV's mother.[3]

Figure 10.1 Jacques Le Pautre (after Jean Bérain), Ballroom at Court during Carnival, 1683, published in *Mercure galant*, March 1683, p. 242, etching and engraving. Paris, Bibliothèque Nationale de France, Hennin 5282. Photo: BNF.

In late-seventeenth-century France, ballets with an "Egyptian" theme were nothing new. Referring more often than not to "gypsies" (i.e., Roma) associated with Bohemia rather than natives of Egypt proper, such Court entertainments played up the exotic attire and alluring danger of nomads known for fortune-telling and thievery.[4] A program enacting a world turned upside down may have resonated with noblemen and women newly corralled at Versailles to become the opposite of wanderers. Ironically, a recent law had threatened "*Bohémiens* or *Egyptiens*, their wives, children and followers" who lived as vagabonds with draconian punishments: perpetual servitude on the galleys for men; and shaved heads, enclosure and, ultimately, banishment for unreformed women.[5] Equally common as aristocrats masquerading as gypsies were courtiers incarnating Moors. As a young man, Louis XIV himself had danced "sous l'habit Africain," and both "galant" and subjugated *Maures* took part in later seventeenth-century equestrian *carrousels* and theatrical performances. In a reversal of her carnival role at Versailles, the princesse de Conti appeared as one of several obsequious

"Afriquaines" in an opera-ballet staged at Fontainebleau, singing and dancing submission to her father's imperial rule.[6]

What *was* unusual about the duc de Bourbon's masked ball was the inclusion of actual *esclaves maures*, likely drawn from a group of "fifty-four Moors, true Africans" (*cinquante-quatre Maures, véritables Afriquains*) purchased by the monarchy three years earlier to row a model galley and other craft on the palace's Grand Canal. There, chief minister Jean-Baptiste Colbert had assembled a miniature flotilla as a way of impressing visitors, stimulating royal interest in naval affairs and assessing shipbuilding innovations. According to a 1680 entry in the *Mercure galant*, when the enslaved Moors were lined up in a courtyard at Versailles wearing nothing but yellow shorts to await inspection by the king, they had skin "of a black so gleaming that it seemed like varnish."[7] The description suggests sub-Saharan origins and, indeed, Colbert had recently contracted with the *Compagnie de Sénégal* to deliver an initial shipment of "noirs de Guinée" or "nègres" for the royal galleys in Marseille.[8] However, in some contexts the French term "Maure," variably spelled "More," simply denoted Muslims in general or Iberian Muslims or Moriscos (Catholic converts), or else natives of Mauritania in particular.[9] In others, it referred to enslaved people indigenous to North Africa (rather than the descendants of Ottoman occupiers) or acquired in Morocco (which could or could not imply a degree of West African ancestry).[10] Men, women, and children from Madagascar and Ethiopia were also brought to Court during the reign of Louis XIV.[11] Whatever their provenance, the incorporation of actual enslaved Moors into pageants at Versailles, coupled with their impersonation by the Sun King's courtiers, signified subjugation, and mastery on multiple levels.

Esclaves maures conscripted to row on the Grand Canal, for instance, celebrated the Crown's real-life naval victories over Ottoman and Moroccan opponents in the Mediterranean. Indeed, an explicit rationale for building up the royal galley fleet in Marseille from the 1660s had been to fight so-called "Barbary pirates." These intrepid corsairs had plagued France's maritime commerce for over a century until a series of massive bombardments launched against North African targets in the 1680s eradicated their threat to French interests.[12] When, in the wake of one such assault, a diplomatic embassy from Algiers was summoned to Versailles to perform ritual humiliation before Louis XIV, the envoys' garden tour included a cruise on the Canal in a flat-bottomed rowboat (*chaloupe*), possibly powered by some of the same "true Africans" purchased for the model flotilla. Allegedly already convinced by the sight of the majestic

French fleet at Toulon that their *dey* had been reckless in waging war against "the most powerful prince of the sea," the Algerians were cowed even further by this nautical spectacle. At the joking suggestion that the lead ambassador abduct the beautiful princesse de Conti from a passing boat, he demurred, lest he bring on "the complete destruction" of Algiers. "The sea of Versailles [is] the sea of the Emperor of the world," his fellow emissary reportedly observed, and out of respect we "make no prizes there."[13]

Perhaps more than proclaiming French sea power, galleys amplified Louis XIV's image as "The Most Christian King." Although largely superseded by warships and other vessels like bomb ketches that had done most of the damage during the North African naval campaigns, galleys retained significant symbolic value for the crown.[14] Not only did they conjure classical conquerors like Caesar, who had used them to wage war against the "barbarians" of his day; they also conjured medieval crusaders like Saint Louis, an important archetype for Louis XIV. The labor of non-Catholic oarsmen added verisimilitude to the monarchy's display of Catholic conquest. Thus during the second half of the seventeenth century, despite a tradition of "free soil" requiring that any person who set foot on French territory be liberated, royal agents captured or purchased thousands of presumed Muslims in Mediterranean ports and along the Ottoman-Habsburg front.[15] Formally categorized as *esclaves turcs* (or *Turcs*), even though some were acknowledged to be "Maures," they hailed from Eastern and Southern Europe as well as Morocco, Ottoman North Africa, and the Levant (and for a brief period rowed alongside a handful of Iroquois chiefs transported from Quebec). Despite concern about the unsuitability of West Africans to the oar, the king's *chiourme* (rowing force) also incorporated a small percentage of "noirs," either sourced in groups directly from the coast of "Guinée" or bought individually at European markets.[16] Following the 1685 Revocation of the Edict of Nantes, Protestants caught fleeing France and sentenced to the galleys further enhanced the crusading connotations of the royal fleet. In addition, Muslims at the oar helped deflect attacks against Louis XIV stemming from the commercial agreements France had signed with the Ottoman Empire. These "Capitulations" angered European rivals who branded the king a "slave" to the sultan and a friend of Islam.[17]

Yet not all *esclaves turcs* or *esclaves maures* in France rowed on royal galleys to boost the reputation of the king. A significant number arrived at Court as diplomatic gifts or war booty and worked for courtiers as fashionably exotic domestic servants. As such, they took part in the continuum of coercion that was Versailles, far below noble lords and ladies in waiting but at least one rung above the flotilla's enslaved oarsmen. "Turkish" and "Moorish" lackeys were also coopted into palace entertainments and, it seems, obliged to pose for artworks bearing their likeness. Their employers tended to be female: royal women who flaunted them in both life and art, whether to curry favor with the king or to highlight piety, political utility, and social capital. This chapter focuses on representations and relations at Versailles between enslaved *Turcs* and *Maures* and Court ladies such as Maria Anna Victoria, dauphine of France (1660–90); Elisabeth Charlotte, princesse Palatine (1652–1722); and the princesse de Conti.

There is a substantial literature on portraits of early modern Europeans accompanied by black servants or slaves. However, much of it focuses on the eighteenth rather than the seventeenth century and on Britain rather than continental Europe.[18] And even though the majority of such images feature women, the majority of sustained, in-depth analysis seems to concern those representing men. Dark-skinned figures in female portraits are often read one-dimensionally as flattering the whiteness, gentility, and wealth of the women they serve. Such perspectives accept at face value the inscription on a 1677 French fashion print (see Figure 10.5) about "beauties whose only object/in showing off a bright complexion/is to be adored by all/use a Moor like I do."[19] For example, scholarship on Pierre Mignard's painting of Louise de Kérouaille, duchess of Portsmouth, made during her visit to Versailles in 1682 follows these interpretive lines, failing to consider that the child may have been a girl named Zoula receptive to Catholic conversion who accompanied her mistress back to France a few years later.[20] This chapter departs from convention by arguing that images of French royal women with *Turcs* and *Maures* were about more than picturing female desirability or fashion trends. Instead, they conveyed serious, culturally specific meanings and raised probing questions about the very nature and function of portraiture, power, and the self.

As for the examples discussed here, several of the women portrayed, like the *Turcs* and *Maures* they exploited, had themselves come to the French Court as war prizes or pawns exchanged among European heads of state. One way they resisted their subaltern position was by demonstrating authority over subordinates of a different race, rank, or religion. The historian Jennifer Palmer has convincingly argued that portraits of French princesses with black attendants from the late seventeenth and early eighteenth centuries helped shape emerging discourses about race by accentuating the power of a pale complexion over the weakness of the female sex.[21] Yet another unacknowledged aspect of these images, particularly those made around the Revocation of the Edict of Nantes, is their interest in touting a special feminine ability to evangelize. Textual evidence corroborates that at Louis XIV's Court high-ranking women regularly stood as godmothers or spiritual guardians to non-Christians. By displaying Catholic sponsorship in a period of Franco-North African conflict and rising intolerance for Huguenots, these women declared allegiance to the French Crown. By broadcasting their part in converting Muslims or even pagans, they affirmed religious influence, while also forging bonds with female relatives throughout France and across Europe, as well as female missionaries in France's expanding empire. In so doing, they transcended their own subordinate status at Court as objects of display or shining jewels in the Sun King's crown.

Performing Conversion at the French Court

As in other parts of Europe, enslaved Turks and Moors became fixtures at the French Court long before Louis XIV assumed the throne.[22] One Moorish and two Turkish girls accompanied Catherine de' Medici when she moved from Tuscany to France in 1533. Seized during raids against North African corsairs, the young captives were said to have "add[ed] to the Oriental splendour" of her wedding to Henri II.[23] After Catherine became queen, the king's cousin François de Lorraine, a French galley captain who also served as grand prior of the crusading Knights of Malta, presented her with Ayche and Fatma from Istanbul. Although conversion to Catholicism brought the girls some perks at Court (including the use of a servant) and allowed them to contract prestigious marriages, it caused diplomatic tensions over two decades as their mother Huma repeatedly entreated the sultan to have her daughters repatriated.[24]

In preparation for her 1600 marriage to Henri IV, Catherine's relative Marie de' Médici engaged several *esclaves turcs* to row her ceremonial galley to Marseille, and later wrote to her uncle, Ferdinand de' Médici, asking him to send additional enslaved Turks for another galley she maintained at the Provençal port.[25] Throughout her reign and regency, Marie personally devoted herself to converting Muslims to Catholicism. One catechumen was her own servant, christened "Madeleine Vernacini, dite Médicis" in 1602 and known as "The Queen's Moor." As queen, Marie supported missionary activity throughout the Mediterranean in addition to founding religious orders intent on proselytizing to heretics and infidels.[26] In encouraging maritime crusades against North African corsairs and adopting the moniker "The Most Christian Queen," she anticipated many of the self-aggrandizing activities of her grandson, Louis XIV.

The Sun King's mother, Anne of Austria, also sponsored Muslim baptisms, a practice embraced by queens and noblewomen at other European Courts during the seventeenth and eighteenth centuries.[27] In 1642, she paid for the religious education of three *Turcs* from the same family whose public conversion ceremony, as reported in the *Gazette de France*, was held in the Parisian convent of the Carmelites on the rue Saint-Jacques, attracting throngs of spectators.[28] In Paris less than two months after his 1654 coronation, a teenage Louis XIV and his mother delegated the duc and duchesse de Mercœur to hold the baptismal font for a "Turc de nation et de profession"—here indicating an Ottoman subject of Muslim faith from North Africa. Their son later became the chief commander of the royal galleys.[29] Later in the century, as the Crown stepped up efforts to increase its number of oared vessels and to procure *esclaves turcs* and other infidel rowers for the *chiourme*, high-profile baptisms became even more prevalent, especially in Marseille and Paris, with converts in white tunics processing solemnly before "persons of quality" who had volunteered as godparents.[30] One prominent godmother was Anne Geneviève de Bourbon, duchesse de Longueville. Educated by the Carmelites in Paris, she had fought against the king during the Fronde and later achieved recognition as an active Jansenist. Her pension in 1663 for a *Turc* neophyte known as "Charles, dit Sainte-Marie," a bodyguard of her late husband, along with her patronage in 1670 of "Joseph Charles," a captive *Turc* the Venetians presented to her brother-in-law for his assistance battling the Ottomans at Candia (Crete), may have been part of an effort to get back into the good graces of Louis XIV.[31]

During the intensifying religiosity of the 1680s, Louis XIV intervened in the Catholic-Protestant competition for Muslim souls with an edict requiring that all "Mahometans and idolators who would like to convert" receive instruction only in the apostolic faith.[32] Meanwhile, royal success in luring Turks and Moors into the Gallican Church, advertised in Court gazettes, functioned as anti-Protestant propaganda. Several publicized conversion ceremonies took place in and around Versailles and other royal palaces. Both Louis XIV and his Spanish queen Marie-Thérèse, for example, signed the parish register in September 1681 when a "Turc de nation," brought to France by famed French general Anne Jules de Noailles, was baptized near Fontainebleau.[33] In February 1686, a "petit Turc"—in fact an eighteen- to twenty-year-old man—previously known as Huceïn or "Houssi" accepted baptism along with the name "Louis" at the royal chapel of Versailles.

He had been sent as a gift from Max Emanuel, elector of Bavaria, victor in several battles against Ottoman forces, to his sister Maria Anna, dauphine of France.³⁴ She had arrived at Versailles in 1680 to marry Louis XIV's heir, an arrangement that cemented an earlier diplomatic alliance between their two countries. Despite producing three male successors, the king and his courtiers ridiculed the dauphine for her plain appearance and chronic health problems, which led to her increasing isolation, piety, and close friendship with another German-born foreigner, the princesse Palatine.³⁵

Maria Anna's presence at Court, however, became politically expedient in 1686, when her brother allied with the Holy Roman Emperor and heads of other European states to form an anti-French coalition known as the League of Augsburg. Its members resented Louis XIV's expansionist policies and reluctance to join the pan-European Holy League to fight the Ottomans in Central and Eastern Europe. Partly constrained by long-standing commercial agreements with the Sublime Porte, Versailles also hoped that European battles against the Turk might weaken rival armies to France's benefit.³⁶ Such inaction led to scores of pamphlets, prints, and satirical medals—produced mainly in Protestant Germany, England, and the Netherlands, though some in France by the king's own courtiers—branding the king a power-hungry despot just like the sultan with whom he was accused of colluding. Some of them, like the anonymous 1690 British tract entitled "The Most Christian Turk: or, a view of the life and bloody reign of Lewis XIV," further labeled him a charlatan, whose puffed-up performance as a crusader merely masked his imperial maneuvering.³⁷

To counter such criticisms, the Crown launched a media campaign intimating that France did in fact belong to the Holy League and was spearheading efforts to drive the Ottomans out of Europe. One of its primary vehicles were almanac prints—large (approximately 3' x 2'), inexpensive broadsides sold at the end of each year to be used as a calendar over the following months.³⁸ Like other visual productions, they aimed to burnish Louis XIV's Catholic credentials by amalgamating maritime and territorial conflicts with Muslims, and by conflating the persecution of heretics with the crusade against infidels. "The Glorious Actions of the Duc of Bavaria Presented to His Sister Madame La Dauphine" from 1688, for example, shows the Bavarian elector and his fellow League commander, the duc of Lorraine, collecting spoils outside the grand vizier's tent after their combined victory over Ottoman forces at Essek in Hungary (Figure 10.2). A small roundel near the top right corner portrays Turkish captives like Huceïn bowing down before Max Emanuel. Immediately above it, the dauphine shares with Louis XIV a letter from her brother heralding news of the triumph. No calendar appears in the blank white rectangle at the bottom, suggesting that the image, which advertises itself for sale at the Paris print shop of Henri Bonnart, may have only been a proof. However, several other prints implying Louis XIV's collaboration with the League and his supposed role in procuring continental "peace" did circulate by the thousands throughout France and abroad.[39]

Muslims dispatched to European Courts to serve as galley slaves, sedan bearers, domestics, or even quasi-familial dependents embodied another form of propaganda for promoting Christianity's triumph over Islam.[40] Expressly charged with the conversion and guardianship of young Turks and Moors, royal and elite women contributed to the war effort by winning souls at home while their male relatives made territorial conquests on the battlefield. They especially prized pre-adolescent boys, considered both easy targets of religious and social integration and well suited for positions as juvenile retainers. Long popular among the European aristocracy, exotic valets became particularly voguish in

Figure 10.2 Henri Bonnart (publisher), *The Glorious Actions of the Duc of Bavaria Presented to His Sister Madame La Dauphine*, almanac print for 1688, etching and engraving. Paris, Bibliothèque Nationale de France, Hennin 5602. Photo: BNF.

France during the last quarter of the seventeenth century, coinciding with their appearance in portraiture.[41]

Portraying Royals and Retainers

A painting of Louis XIV and his heir, the dauphin, riding past the Thetis grotto at Versailles appears to show the dauphine descending a flight of stairs with assistance from a young black man (Figure 10.3).[42] It was most likely created

Figure 10.3 Anonymous, *Louis XIV Followed by the Grand Dauphin Passing on Horseback in Front of the Thetis Grotto at Versailles*, oil on canvas, *c*. 1680–4. Versailles, Châteaux de Versailles et de Trianon. Photo: RMN/Art Resource, NY.

between 1680, the year she arrived at Court, and 1684, when the grotto was razed to make room for the palace's expanding north wing. The enslaved figure wears a fancy costume of orange silk livery styled with frogging, a pearl earring and a gleaming metal collar around his neck. His outfit and features resemble those in other images of noblewomen with dark-skinned retainers made in France around the same time, including François de Troy's 1680 portrait of the dauphine's confidante, the princesse Palatine (Figure 10.4), which according to one source might be the earliest of its kind in France[43]; Claude Vignon's late-seventeenth-century double portrait of Louis XIV's legitimized daughters, Mademoiselle de Blois and Mademoiselle de Nantes; and several fashion prints engraved and published by Bonnart and his brothers as well as by Nicolas Arnoult, including the 1677 print cited above (Figure 10.5) and c. 1695 print of the princesse de Conti with a turbaned black attendant (Figure 10.6).[44]

Figure 10.4 François de Troy, *Charlotte-Elisabeth de Bavière, princesse Palatine, Duchesse d'Orléans*, 1680, oil on canvas, Versailles, Châteaux de Versailles et de Trianon. Photo: RMN/Art Resource, NY.

Figure 10.5 Henri Bonnart, *Dame*, from *Recueil des modes de la cour de France*, 1677, hand-colored engraving. Los Angeles, Los Angeles County Museum of Art. Image in the public domain.

Figure 10.6 Nicolas Arnoult, *Madame la Princesse de Conty douarière* [c. 1695], reprinted in *Recueil des modes*, 4 vol. (Paris: Menus-Plaisirs du roi, c. 1750). Engraving. Paris, Bibliothèque Nationale de France, Cabinet des estampes, RES-926 (8). Photo: BNF.

Like the distribution of Ottoman war prizes, the portrayal of elite women with dark-skinned valets was a pan-European phenomenon with roots going back at least as early as Titian's *c.* 1520–5 portrait of Laura Dianti, lover of Alfonso d'Este.[45] Not all of the enslaved figures depicted in these portraits, which became conventionalized into a type by the late seventeenth century, had real-life referents; in some cases, they did serve merely as vehicles for artists, sitters, and patrons to indicate beauty, civility, exoticism, and wealth. And yet their frequent appearance in representations of Louis XIV-era Court ladies, combined with the distinctive facial features some of them display, suggests that a few may have been inspired by or painted from life, a fact that art historians focused on the pictorial role of black attendants have mostly overlooked (see Figure 10.4).[46] If so, who were these servile individuals? Should they encourage us to reconsider these images not as single but as double portraits? No scholar seems to have tackled this question, at least not for this specific set of French female portraits from the late seventeenth century. Yet the general assumption is that they evoke enslaved West Africans derived from France's growing role in trans-Atlantic trade and New World bondage.

For instance, historian Sue Peabody's seminal study *There Are No Slaves in France* reproduces the 1677 Bonnart fashion print on its cover (Figure 10.5), making it the defining image for a book almost exclusively concerned with the arrival of enslaved West Africans via the Caribbean during the eighteenth century. However, even though France's Atlantic trade was robust enough by 1685 to necessitate the passage of the *Code Noir* (a royal decree regulating relations between masters and slaves in the colonies), relatively few enslaved persons entered France from this part of the world until the final years of the seventeenth century.[47] If the black figures in the portraits of French princesses refer to actual people, therefore, it is more likely that most are "Turks" or "Moors" acquired through the Mediterranean slave trade, or through military conflicts with Morocco or the Ottoman Empire and its North African affiliates, than through Atlantic trafficking, a form of commerce that was prevalent in Britain (and in British slave portraits) by this period but that only began to transform French art, society, and culture around 1700.

In fact, the Bonnart print's inscription expressly identifies the collared figure as a "More," suggesting that he came from North Africa rather than West Africa via the Caribbean colonies. In hand-colored versions of the image, his skin is slightly lighter and his features stereotypically less sub-Saharan than those of black retainers who accompany fashion mavens in other prints by the Bonnarts and Arnoult.⁴⁸ However, as Paul Kaplan explains, even Moorish and Turkish subjects who were not sub-Saharan or dark-skinned were often depicted as such in early modern European art. As Kaplan suggests, this tradition of "black Turks" (*turchi mori*) derived in part from a long-standing link in the European imagination between the religion of Muhammad and people with dark skin, and it sometimes served as "a crude marker of the alien nature of Islam and the otherness of Ottoman society."⁴⁹ It is thus possible that other fashion prints from the same period also allude to enslaved "Turcs" or "Mores," with blackness augmented in part to set off the white skin of their mistresses.

Late-seventeenth-century paintings of four princesses at Versailles (the dauphine, the princesse Palatine, Mademoiselle de Blois, and Mademoiselle de Nantes) may well show "black Turks"—or, as the French would call them, either *esclaves turcs* or *esclaves maures*. The dark-skinned valet holding up the dauphine's train in the painting of the Thetis grotto could even be a reference to Huceïn, whose conversion she later sponsored. Or maybe it depicts one of the fifty-four *esclaves maures* who arrived at Versailles in 1680 to row on the nearby Canal, and who also served the princesse de Conti. The crudely rendered enslaved figure in Vignon's portrait of the Mademoiselles does not appear to be modeled from life, but he could nonetheless refer to a real-life person: in 1664, the girls' mother, Madame de Montespan, reportedly stood as godmother for a converted "More." Perhaps her daughters later followed in her footsteps.⁵⁰

One of the Canal's enslaved oarsmen could have also posed for the youthful boy with African features in de Troy's 1680 portrait of the princesse Palatine (Figure 10.4), as well as for the lifelike sculpted figure of a "Maure" that adorned the model galley on the Grand Canal.⁵¹ De Troy's canvas follows precedent in using a black figure to highlight his female sitter's beauty and sexuality and contains an erotic *frisson* in the figures' poses, sumptuous fabrics, and other motifs. Yet his work also plays with Christian symbolism, in the Marian blue and gold that the princess wears and in the adoring gaze of her attendant, a modern-day Magi offering a basket filled with exotic blooms.⁵² She lifts up a delicate double anemone, a flower treasured among Louis XIV's courtiers that required careful tending and signified a "tranquil and moderate soul."⁵³ Perhaps its presence alludes to the dual ability of the foreign princess and her acolyte to "acclimate" to Versailles and to embrace Catholicism, a religion she herself had been forced to adopt a decade earlier during a public conversion ceremony in Metz.⁵⁴ Indeed, the princesse Palatine's own status as a former "heretic" shaped her promotion of religious tolerance at Court, particularly around the time of the Revocation of the Edict of Nantes. Many years later, it also led her to beseech her son, by then appointed regent, to release Huguenots from the royal galleys.[55] Though most of her efforts seem directed at her former Reformed Christian brethren, she preached acceptance of all religions, and may on some level have identified with Muslim or pagan converts at Court. (How significant is it that her retainer does not wear a metal collar?) Presumably whatever sympathy she felt would not have precluded her from appropriating enslaved figures to stage her Catholic piety, in de Troy's portrait and elsewhere.

Some images of French noblewomen with servants or slaves from the late seventeenth and early eighteenth centuries may show them with Ottoman war orphans whose religious education they supervised. A handful of such children joined the households of their noble godparents or the families of the military commanders who had brought them to France. In 1686, for instance, a two-year-old Hungarian "Turque de nation" renamed "Marie-Julie Julistanne" and taken in by the Comtesse Beautru de Nogent, sister of the soldier who "saved her," was baptized in the Paris church of Saint-Nicolas-des-Champs. At the age of twenty-four, she was raped and impregnated by her stepbrother who initially denied paternity of the child she bore—a reminder of the brutal treatments other captives and converts likely suffered, whatever the plush outfits and palatial surroundings shown in any images might suggest.[56] Meanwhile, in 1690 the future prince de Condé, host of the Egyptian carnival masquerade at Versailles, sponsored the baptism of his own servant from Belgrade, "Louis Elisabeth Ally."[57] A 1694 military portrait of the prince (by then known as the duc de Bourbon) from the workshop of Hyacinthe Rigaud shows him accompanied by a dark-skinned man who wears the same orange livery, pearl earring, and metal collar as several of the valets in the previous images, including Vignon's portrait, which depicts the duke's wife, Mademoiselle de Nantes.[58] While underscoring how enslaved figures had by this time become recurring stock characters in portraits of French royal family members, it also reminds us how "noble" aristocrats were perpetually shadowed by real-life subordinates whose identities have been both preserved and obscured by art.

Conclusion

At the end of the seventeenth century, the masquerading "Egyptian" princesse de Conti became famous for rejecting the hand of Moulay Isma'il, sultan of

Morocco.⁵⁹ Widowed without children at age nineteen and a dowager until her death, she must have had considerable practice spurning suitors, even ones deemed more suitable than a Muslim ruler for a daughter of "The Most Christian King." Rather than become a wife and bear children, or cloister herself inside a convent like her mother, Louise de la Vallière, this "legitimized daughter of France" seems to have embraced the role of Court luminary and caretaker. She took under her wing not only the infanta of Spain, betrothed to the future Louis XV, but also two "filles turques" named Fatima and Yasmine and one "petit more" known as Emmanuel, who might be evoked in her fashion print by Arnoult (Figure 10.6).⁶⁰ Whereas the young man in the engraving, dressed in a feathered turban and a metal collar, is clearly represented as inferior, the possible connection to a real-life individual in the princess's orbit raises doubts about whether such servile figures functioned only as exotic props for their mistresses, "who acquired them as playthings and who discarded them when they reached adolescence."⁶¹

The princesse de Conti, in fact, maintained a relationship with Emmanuel, paying for his upkeep and medical care during a year-long stint at the Maison de Saint-Lazare, Parisian home to Vincent de Paul's *Congrégation de la Mission*, known for ministering to galley slaves and evangelizing Muslims.⁶² In the tradition of French queens Catherine and Marie de' Medici, she also oversaw the upbringing of her Turkish wards. In 1686 and 1687, she made sure that the young women (presumably baptized years earlier) were taught to read and were properly attired and transported before taking first communion at Notre Dame and making a visit to Versailles. It appears that both entered convents. Yasmine took her Carmelite vows in 1688, wearing a black nun's habit, while in 1693 the *Gazette de France* reported that "the Dowager Princesse de Conti gave the veil to one of her Turkish daughters, who made profession at the Abbey of Saint Genevieve."⁶³ Although the princess's stewardship does not in any way expiate her exploitation of enslaved Turks and Moors, it does imply that there is more to these slave portraits than meets the eye, and it may prompt us to reassess whether the subjectivity they represent applies only to their white sitters—however circumscribed or contingent that subjectivity may have been.

As for the princesse de Conti herself, she remained at Court until 1725, when her charge, the infanta, was sent back to Spain. Her display, sponsorship, and conversion of Muslims, notably at the height of Louis XIV's troubles with Protestant dissidents and the Catholic Holy League, likely abetted her privileged status as the king's favorite daughter, while also enabling her to contribute to the royal cause without producing heirs. Ironically her enslaved attendants helped safeguard her freedom and made her more than a mere "prize" whose fate was determined by men.

Notes

1. *Mercure galant* (March 1683): 322–3.
2. Ibid., 326–7.
3. Jean Le Pautre, Large *guéridon* decorated with a "Maure," n.d. Etching. Los Angeles, Getty Research Institute, Digital Collection. See Adrienne L. Childs, "A *Blackamoor's Progress:* The Ornamental Black Body in European Furniture," in *ReSignifications: European Blackamoors, Africana Readings*, ed. Ellyn Toscano and Awam Amkpa (Rome: Postcart, 2017), 117–26.
4. On French representations of "gypsies," see François de Vaux de Foletier, *Les Tsiganes dans l'ancienne France* (Paris: Connaissance du Monde, 1961); François Moreau, "Égyptiens et égyptiennes à la cour et à la ville: la trace gitane sous Louis XIV," in *Le Théâtre des voyages: une scénographie de l'âge classique*, ed. François Moreau (Paris: Presses de l'Université Paris-Sorbonne, 2005), 445–52; and Henriette Asséo, "Travestissement et divertissement: bohémiens et égyptiens à l'époque moderne," *Les Dossiers du Grihl* 2 (2009). Available online: https://doi.org/10.4000/dossiersgrihl.3680 (accessed October 10, 2018).
5. "Déclaration du roy contre les Bohémiens ou Egyptiens," *Versailles*, July 11, 1682, reprinted in Isambert, François André, and Alphonse Taillandier, eds, *Recueil général des anciennes lois françaises*, 29 vols (Paris: Belin-Leprieur, 1821–33), 19: 393–4.
6. On the aristocratic adoption of black African personae during a reception for Christina of Sweden (1656), the *Ballet des muses* (1666–7), the *Carrousel des galans maures* (1685) and *Le Temple de la paix* (1685), see Ellen R. Welch, *A Theater of Diplomacy: International Relations and the Performing Arts in Early Modern France* (Philadelphia: University of Pennsylvania Press, 2017), 140, 145–8, 154–5; and Jérôme de La Gorce, "Le Premier grand spectacle équestre donné à Versailles: le carrousel des galants maures," in *Les Ecuries royales du XVIe au XVIIe siècle*, ed. Daniel Roche (Versailles: Association pour l'académie d'art équestre de Versailles, 1998), 276–85. There do seem to have been a few instances of actual Africans dancing or acting in French Court spectacles during Louis XIV's reign—for example in Philippe Quinault's *Thésée*, first staged at the palace of Saint-Germain-en-Laye in 1675—but it was far more common for French performers to appear in blackface. See, for example, the costume design by Jean Bérain for *Thésée* in David

Bindman, Bruce Boucher and Helen Weston, "The Theater of Court and Church: Blacks as Figures of Fantasy," in *The Image of the Black in Western Art*, ed. Bindman and Henry Louis Gates, Jr., 10 vols (Cambridge, MA: Harvard University Press, 2011), 3: part 3, 57.

7 *Mercure galant* (September 1680): 296.

8 Colbert had expressed interest in procuring West Africans for the royal galleys from the 1660s (Bibliothèque nationale [hereafter BnF], Nouvelles acquisitions françaises 21307) but only did so for a brief period starting in 1678 (see, for instance, *Gazette de France* [1679]: 41).

9 For example, Jean Nicot, *Thresor de la langue francoyse tant ancienne que moderne...* (Paris: D. Douceur, 1606), 418; Antoine Furetière, *Dictionnaire universel, contenant généralement tous les mots françois, tant vieux que modernes...*, 3 vols. (The Hague: Arnout et Reinier Leers, 1690), 2:583; as well as discussions in François Lebrun, "Turcs, barbaresques, musulmans, vus par les français du XVIIe siècles, d'après le 'Dictionnaire' de Furetière," *Cahiers de Tunisie* 44, no. 3-4 (1991): 69-74; and Sonia Gadhoum, "Presence réelle et mythique dans le Dictionnaire universel d'Antoine Furetière," in *L'Afrique au XVIIe siècle, mythes et réalités...*, ed. Alia Baccar Bornaz (Tübingen: Gunter Narr Verlag, 2003), 23-30.

10 On slave trading routes from sub-Saharan Africa into the Ottoman Empire and Morocco during the seventeenth century and the black slave army of Sultan Mulay Isma'il, see John Hunwick Powell and Eve Trout, eds, *The African Diaspora in the Mediterranean Lands of Islam* (Princeton, NJ: Markus Wiener, 2002); and Chouki El Hamel, *Black Morocco: A History of Slavery, Race, and Islam* (Cambridge: Cambridge University Press, 2013).

11 Jules Mathorez, *Les Étrangers en France sous l'ancien régime: histoire de la formation de la population française*, 2 vols (Paris: Edouard Champion, 1919), 1: 392-4; Anne Lombard-Jourdan, "Des Malgaches à Paris sous Louis XIV: exotisme et mentalités en France au XVIIe siècle," *Archipel* 9, no. 1 (1975): 79-90.

12 See Meredith Martin and Gillian Weiss, "A Tale of Two Guns: Maritime Weapons between France and Algiers," in *The Mobility of People and Things in the Early Modern Mediterranean: The Art of Travel*, ed. Elisabeth A. Fraser (New York: Routledge, 2019), 27-48; and Martin and Weiss, *The Sun King at Sea: Maritime Art and Galley Slavery in Louis XIV's France* (Los Angeles, CA: The Getty Research Institute, Forthcoming 2021), esp. chap 2.

13 *Mercure galant* (August 1684): 240-2.

14 On bomb ketches, whose early prototypes were tested on the Grand Canal, see Larrie D. Ferreiro, "Bernard Renau d'Elissagary," *Neptunia* 225 (2009): 22.

15 On France's "free soil principle," see Sue Peabody, *"There Are No Slaves in France": The Political Culture of Race and Slavery in the Ancien Régime* (New York: Oxford University Press, 1996). On its suspension in French ports, see Weiss, "Infidels at

the Oar: A Mediterranean Exception to France's Free Soil Principle," *Slavery & Abolition* 32, no. 3 (2011): 397–412.

16 On the origins of convict and slave oarsmen on Louis XIV's royal galleys, see Paul Bamford, *Fighting Ships and Prisons: The Mediterranean Galleys of France in the Age of Louis XIV* (Minneapolis: University of Minnesota Press, 1973); and André Zysberg, *Les Galériens: vies et destins de 60,000 forçats sur les galères de France, 1680–1748* (Paris: Éditions du Seuil, 1987). In his 1757 account of the years 1701–13, the Huguenot galley slave Jean Marteilhe noted the geographical diversity in unusually stark (and racist) terms, distinguishing between "les Turcs de l'Afrique, nommément ceux des royaumes de *Maroc, Alger, Tripoli*, etc., qui sont en général des gens de sac & de corde, fripons, cruels, parjûres, traitres et scelerats" and "les Turcs d'Asie & de l'Europe, nommément ceux de la *Bosnie*, & autres Frontieres de la *Hongrie*, & de *Transylvanie*, ceux de *Constantinople*, etc…ces derniers, dis-je, sont en général très-bien fait de corps, blancs & blonds de visage, sages dans leur conduite, zelès à l'observation de leur Religion, gens de parole & d'honneur, & surtout charitables": *Mémoire d'un Protestant condamné aux galères de France pour cause de religion…* (Rotterdam: J.D. Beman & fils, 1757), 265–6.

17 On the commercial agreements or Capitulations between France and the Ottoman Empire, which dated to the sixteenth century but were renewed in 1674, see Gilles Veinstein, "Les Capitulations franco-ottomanes de 1536: sont-elles encore controversables," in *Living in the Ottoman Ecumenical Community: Essays in Honour of Suraiya Faroqhi*, ed. Vera Costantini and Markus Koller (Leiden: Brill, 2008), 71–88; and Christine Isom-Verhaaren, *Allies with the Infidel: The Ottoman and French Alliance in the Sixteenth Century* (London: Tauris Academic Studies, 2011). On attacks against Louis XIV see Martin and Weiss, "'Turks' on Display at Versailles during the Reign of Louis XIV," *L'Ésprit Créateur* 53, no. 4 (2013): 98–112; and Martin and Weiss, *The Sun King at Sea*, chap. 2.

18 These portraits are discussed extensively in Bindman and Gates, ed., *The Image of the Black in Western Art*, which does analyze numerous examples beyond Britain. See especially the chapter by Bindman, Boucher, and Weston, "Between Court and City: Fantasies in Transition," vol. 3, part 3, chap. 2. Also see, among other key works, Elizabeth McGrath, "Caryatids, Page Boys, and African Fetters: Themes of Slavery in European Art," in *The Slave in European Art: From Renaissance Trophy to Abolitionist Emblem*, ed. McGrath and Jean Michel Massig (London: Warburg Institute, 2012), 3–38; David Dabydeen, *Hogarth's Blacks: Images of Blacks in Eighteenth-Century English Art* (Athens: University of Georgia Press, 1987); Beth Fowkes Tobin, *Picturing Imperial Power: Colonial Subjects in Eighteenth-Century British Painting* (Durham, NC: Duke University Press, 1999); Agnes Lugo-Ortiz and Angela Rosenthal, eds, *Slave Portraiture in the Atlantic World* (New York:

Cambridge University Press, 2013), especially Bindman's "Subjectivity and Slavery in Portraiture: From Courtly to Commercial Societies," 71–87; and Catherine Molineux, *Faces of Perfect Ebony: Encountering Atlantic Slavery in Imperial Britain* (Cambridge, MA: Harvard University Press, 2012).

19 "Belles dont l'unique dessein/Est que partout on vous adore/Pour relever l'Esclat du tein/Comme moy servez vous d'un More": quoted and translated in Bindman et al., "Between Court and City," 152.

20 The *Mercure galant* (June 1686): 119–20 refers to her as "la petite Zoula qui est presentement avec Madame la Duchesse de Portmouth, & qui est celle là mesme que Dieu avoit preservée de la fureur d'un Soldat qui avoit le Cimeterre levé pour la fendre en deux. Cette petite Fille receut volontiers la proposition qui luy fut faite d'embrasser le Christianisme." The painting is in the collection of London's National Portrait Gallery (NPG 497), and its description on the museum's website is representative: "The enslaved African child's identity is unknown and she may have been a fictitious character included in the composition only to further elevate the status of the duchess. The black child is shown presenting precious coral and pearls in a shell to the duchess to emphasise her wealth and position. Pearls have always been objects of desire due to their rarity and beauty, they may have been used here as a symbolic reference to sitter's beauty or her desire to be portrayed as beautiful. The child's dark skin marks a stark contrast from the fairness of the duchess, serving to further emphasise the whiteness of the duchess's complexion. Ideas on beauty and class prevalent in Europe at the time would have considered the palest complexions to be the most beautiful and an indicating factor of the person's class also. In the 17th and 18th Centuries both men and women resorted to artifice to make their complexions even whiter as a result." See https://www.npg.org.uk/collections/search/portrait/mw05102/Louise-de-Kroualle-Duchess-of-Portsmouth (accessed July 3, 2018).

21 Jennifer L. Palmer, "The Princess Served by Slaves: Making Race Visible through Portraiture in Eighteenth-Century France," *Gender & History* 26, no. 2 (2014), 242–62.

22 For numerous early examples, see Mathorez, *Les Étrangers en France*.

23 Susan A. Skilliter, "Catherine de' Medici's Turkish Ladies-in-Waiting," *Turcica* 7 (1975): 194 and citing Edith Helen Sichel, *Catherine de' Medici and the French Reformation* (New York: E. P. Dutton, 1905), 34–5, which refers to the girls to as "Marie the Moor" and "Agnes and Margaret the Turks."

24 Ibid. See also Frédéric Hitzel, "Turcs et turqueries à la cour de Catherine de Médicis," in *Les Musulmans dans l'histoire de l'Europe: Tome 1. Une intégration invisible*, ed. Jocelyne Dakhlia and Bernard Vincent (Paris: Albin Michel, 2011), 33–54.

25 Archivio di Stato di Firenze, Mediceo del Principato, f. 4729, c. 156.

26 Brian Sandberg, "'The Recovering of God's Heritage': Marie de' Medici and French Religious Politics in the Eastern Mediterranean," in *The Medici and the Levant*, ed. Marta Caroscio and Maurizio Arfaioli (Turnhout: Brepols, 2016), 47.

27 For instance, during the late seventeenth century Sophia Charlotte of Hanover co-sponsored several baptisms of Muslim Turks with her husband Frederick, elector of Brandenburg and later King in Prussia; meanwhile Maria Amalia, queen consort of Naples and Sicily, "proudly" converted Muslim galley slaves at the royal palace of Caserta around the mid-eighteenth century. See Stefan Gehlen, "'Portée en chaise par ses Turcs': Turquerie und 'Kammertürken am Hof Sophie Charlottes,'" in *Sophie Charlotte und ihr Schloss: Ein Musenhof des Barock in Brandenburg-Preussen* (Munich: Prestel, 1999) 106–12; and Robin L. Thomas, "Slavery and Construction at the Royal Palace of Caserta," *Journal of the Society of Architectural Historians* 78, no. 2 (2019): 167–86.

28 *Gazette de France* 138 (1642): 1016.

29 Cited in Augustin Jal, *Dictionnaire critique de biographie et d'histoire: errata and supplement pour tous les dictionnaires historiques d'après des documents authentiques inédits*, 2nd edn. (Paris: Henri Plon, 1872), 804. Louis-Joseph de Vendôme served as *général des galères* in 1659–94.

30 We describe several of these ceremonies in *The Sun King at Sea*.

31 Châtelet de Paris, Insinuations, Notice 1393, July 7, 1663, AN, Y 203, f. 310; *Gazette de France* 53 (1670): 432. For a biography of the duchesse de Longueville, see Arlette Lebigre, *La Duchesse de Longueville* (Paris: Perrin, 2004).

32 "Déclaration portant que les Mahométans et idolâtres qui voudront se convertir ne pourront être instruits que dans la religion catholique," *Versailles*, January 25, 1683, reproduced in Isambert, *Recueil général*, 19: 414r.–415r.

33 Partial facsimile from the Registres paroissiaux d'Avon, September 13, 1681, in Roseline Grimaldi-Hierholtz, *Les Trinitaires de Fontainebleau et d'Avon* (Fontainebleau: Centre d'études culturelles civiques et sociales de Seine-et-Marne, 1990), 63–4. Two days later, the queen stood as godmother for "Louis-François Dangola (*nègre*) de parents inconnus, âgé de neuf ou dix ans"; the godfather was Grand Squire of France, Henri de Brionne (Baptismal registers of the Saint-Louis, GG 8, f. 21).

34 *Gazette de France* 9 (1686), 108, and cited in Philippe de Courcillon de Dangeau, *Journal du Marquis de Dangeau, avec les additions du duc de Saint-Simon*, ed. Eudore Soulié, 19 vols (Paris: Firmin Didot, 1854–60), 1, 300–1. For the original baptismal record from Notre Dame de Versailles dated February 23, 1686, see Archives départementales des Yvelines (online).

35 Émile Collas, *La Belle-fille de Louis XIV* (Paris: Emile Paul frères, 1920).

36 Richard Place, "The Self-Deception of the Strong: France on the Eve of the War of the League of Augsburg," *French Historical Studies* 6, no. 4 (1970): 459–73.

37 Anonymous, *The Most Christian Turk: Or a View of the Life and Bloody Reign of Lewis XIV...* (London: Henry Rhodes, 1690), esp. 113–14. See also Damien Tricoire, "Attacking the Monarchy's Sacrality in Late Seventeenth-Century France: The Underground Literature against Louis XIV, Jansenism and the Dauphin's Court Faction," *French History* 31, no. 2 (2017): 152–73.

38 Maxime Préaud, *Les Effets du soleil: almanachs du règne de Louis XIV* (Paris: Réunion des musées nationaux, 1995).

39 See, for example, a 1688 almanac print engraved by Pierre Le Pautre entitled "The Triumph of Religion by the Zeal of Christian Princes," discussed in Martin and Weiss, *The Sun King at Sea*, chap. 2.

40 For Muslim captives at German Courts, including an image of two "Turks" serving as sedan bearers, see Stefan Jakob Wimmer, *München und der Orient* (Munich: Kunstverlag Josef Fink, 2012).

41 Dakhlia, "Musulmans en France et en Grand-Bretagne à l'époque moderne: exemplaires et invisibles," in *Les Musulmans*, esp. 1:315–16.

42 Both the Réunion des musées nationaux and Château de Versailles websites identify this woman as the dauphine.

43 Bindman et al., "Between Court and City," 153.

44 Palmer illustrates and discusses the de Troy and Vignon portraits in "The Princess Served by Slaves." On prints by Arnoult and Bonnart see Kathryn Norberg and Sandra Rosenbaum, eds, *Fashion Prints in the Age of Louis XIV: Interpreting the Art of Elegance* (Lubbock: Texas Tech University Press, 2014). The *c.* 1695 print of the princesse de Conti (BnF, Estampes, OA-5O-PET-FOL, vol. 3. Fol. 37) is noted in Bindman et al., "Between Court and City," 152. We have reproduced a *c.* 1750 reprinting, which depicts the princess and her slave on an outdoor terrace overlooking a garden landscape. In the original print the background is blank.

45 Paul H. D. Kaplan, "Titian's 'Laura Dianti' and the Origins of the Motif of the Black Page in Portraiture," *Antichità viva* 21 (1982): 10–18; Joaneath A. Spicer, ed., *Revealing the African Presence in Renaissance Europe* (Baltimore, MD: Walters Art Museum, 2012). See also Tom Earle and Kate J. P. Lowe, *Black Africans in Renaissance Europe* (Cambridge: Cambridge University Press, 2005).

46 Susan Dwyer Amussen, *Caribbean Exchanges: Slavery and the Transformation of English Society, 1640–1700* (Chapel Hill: University of North Carolina Press, 2007), 192, 216–17.

47 Peabody, *"There Are No Slaves in France,"* 12.

48 See, for example, Nicolas Bonnart, "Dame de la Cour," 1679–93, Los Angeles County Museum of Art, M.2002.57.19; and Nicolas Arnoult, "Femme de qualité habillé en sultane," 1688, BnF, OA-51-PET-FOL.

49 Kaplan, "Black Turks: Venetian Artists and Perceptions of Ottoman Ethnicity," in *The Turk and Islam in the Western Eye, 1450–1750: Visual Imagery before Orientalism*, ed. James G. Harper (Aldershot, UK: Ashgate, 2011), 41–66.
50 Jacques-Bénigne Bossuet purportedly preached at the baptism, held on April 28, 1664, at the Church of Saint-Sulpice in Paris. In his *Muse historique* (May 3, 1664): 66-7, Jean Loret wrote, "La Marraine, fut cette Belle/qui contient tant d'apas en elle/La Marquize de Montespan."
51 See Martin and Weiss, *The Sun King at Sea*, chap. 2.
52 Dabydeen describes such female slave portraits as "degenerate version[s] of the religious iconography of the Madonna and Magi" in *Hogarth's Blacks*, 36. We agree with the connection without necessarily viewing it as degenerate.
53 Elizabeth Hyde, *Cultivated Power: Flowers, Culture, and Politics in the Reign of Louis XIV* (Philadelphia: University of Pennsylvania Press, 2005), 118–19.
54 The princesse Palatine's official act of abjuration may be found at Archives nationales [hereafter AN], K 542, n. 15. For her description of the ceremony and her father's punishing response see Arvède Barine, *Madame, Mother of the Regent: 1652–1722*, trans. Jeanne Mairet (New York: G.P. Putnam's Sons, 1909), 78–9.
55 Katherine Prescott Wormeley, *The Correspondence of Madame, Princess Palatine, Mother of the Regent; of Marie-Adélaïde de Savoie, Duchesse de Bourgogne; and of Madame de Maintenton, in Relation to Saint-Cyr* (Boston, MA: Hardy, Pratt & Company, 1902), 9.
56 On Marie-Julie Julistanne, see AN, O¹ 220, f. 214; 0/1/22 1, f. 112; PP 151, cited in Peter Sahlins, "Fictions of a Catholic France: The Naturalization of Foreigners, 1685–1787," *Representations* 47 (1994): 91; and Matthew Gerber, *Bastards: Politics, Family, and Law in Early Modern France* (New York: Oxford University Press, 2012), 115–16. Also see Louis de Rouvroy, duc de Saint-Simon, *Mémoires de Saint-Simon*, ed., Arthur de Boislisle, 45 vols (Paris: Hachette, 1896), 12: 568.
57 See AN, O¹ 220, f. 19, cited in Sahlins, "Fictions of a Catholic France," 91.
58 Workshop of Hyacinthe Rigaud, *Louis III de Bourbon, 6ème prince de Condé en 1709*, Châteaux de Versailles et de Trianon, MV4327.
59 The Princesse de Conti's rejection of sultan Moulay Isma'il was depicted in at least one painting and many poems. See French School, seventeenth century, "The Dowager Princess of Conti (Marie Anne de Bourbon) refusing the marriage proposal on behalf of Moulay Ismaïl, King of Morocco," auctioned by Bonhams in 2012; and Eugène Plantet, *Mouley Ismaël, empereur du Maroc et la Princesse de Conti* (Paris: E. Jamin, 1893).
60 On the Princesse de Conti's "filles turques" Fatima (spelled Fatement) and Yasmine (spelled Ismiane, Ysmane); and "petit Emmanuel More," see AN, R3 145, ff. 121–48.
61 Bindman et al., "Between Court and City," 123.

62 Bill and receipt for 471 *livres* payment "tant pour une année et quinze jours de la pension de petit Emmanuel More que pour Les fournitures qu'on a faites pour luy pendant qu'il a esté a St. Lazare pour la seconde fois," March 12, 1689, AN, R3 145, ff. 121, 122.

63 Expense reports for 1688, including a salary for a "mestrese a lire" and for paper, ink, and plume; items for "ysmianne pour entrer dans les Carmelites" and shoes for Fatima and a "voiture" to take her to "la veture dismiane." AN, R 3 145, ff. 125, 126; *Gazette de France* 34 (1693): 435: "Le 22, la Princesse de Conty Doüairiere a donné le voile à une de ses filles Turques, qui a fait profession en l'Abbaye de Sainte Geneviéve de Chaillot."

11

A Turk in the Hall of Mirrors

David Maskill

Diplomatic embassies in the Court society ran the risk of misunderstandings and perceived or intended slights to one side or the other. The risk was even greater when the embassy involved different cultures. The history of diplomatic exchanges between European and "Oriental" Courts is replete with incidences of misinterpretation and miscommunication. However, more recent studies have argued for the degree to which one side or the other sought to minimize potential gaffs (and to manipulate a favorable outcome) through informed attention to different cultural practices. For example, as Ronald Love was the first to point out and more recently Meredith Martin has reiterated, the reception of the ambassadors of Siam by Louis XIV at Versailles in 1686 deliberately echoed, both in reality and in imagery, the ceremony of the Thai Court.[1] Another such instance is considered here. When the Ottoman Sultan Mahmud I sent his ambassador to the Sun King's successor, Louis XV in 1742, he chose a man who was familiar with French Court ceremonial and who was fluent in the French language. Crucially, his ambassador understood the role of art in creating a favorable public image.

At a little after two o'clock on the afternoon of January 11, 1742, Yirmisekizzade Mehmed Saïd Pasha (c. 1697–1761),[2] ambassador extraordinary from the Ottoman Sultan Mahmud I (1696–1754), turned left from the Salon of War and into the Hall of Mirrors at Versailles. The sight that greeted him must have been enough to make his heart skip a beat. For the scene that confronted him we have remarkably accurate evidence both in an image and in text. There is the highly finished drawing, intended to be reproduced as a print (Figure 11.1) by Charles-Nicolas Cochin (1715–90) and a detailed account by the Court diarist, Charles Philippe d'Albert, duc de Luynes (1695–1758)—both of whom were eyewitnesses to the event.

Figure 11.1 Charles Nicolas Cochin, *The Reception by Louis XV of Saïd Méhémet Pacha in the Grand Gallery at Versailles*, c. 1744–5, pencil and wash on vellum. Paris, Louvre, Cabinet des dessins. Reversed horizontally. Image in the public domain.

This was the only occasion during Louis XV's reign that the Hall of Mirrors was used for an ambassadorial audience. These normally took place in the Apollo Salon or in the king's state bedchamber. The official reason for this embassy was to thank King Louis XV for his government's role in brokering the recent peace treaty between the Ottomans, Austria, and Russia.[3] The embassy also acknowledged the long-standing trade treaty between France and the Ottoman Empire, which had been recently ratified by Sultan Mahmud I and which gave France a favorable position over the other European powers.[4] Just as importantly, the ceremonial purpose of the visit was intended to send a clear message to both Austria and Russia of the strong Franco-Ottoman alliance. As a result, no expense was spared in the reception of the ambassador.

According to the duc de Luynes, such was the public interest in the ambassador's first public audience that tickets were issued indicating which room in suite of the state apartments the ticket-holder could occupy.[5] All ticket holders were required to be in place by 10:30 a.m. The most sought-after space was the Hall of Mirrors (Figure 11.2). Courtiers and the fortunate public who had tickets stood on tiered steps all along the gallery's seventy-three-meter length.

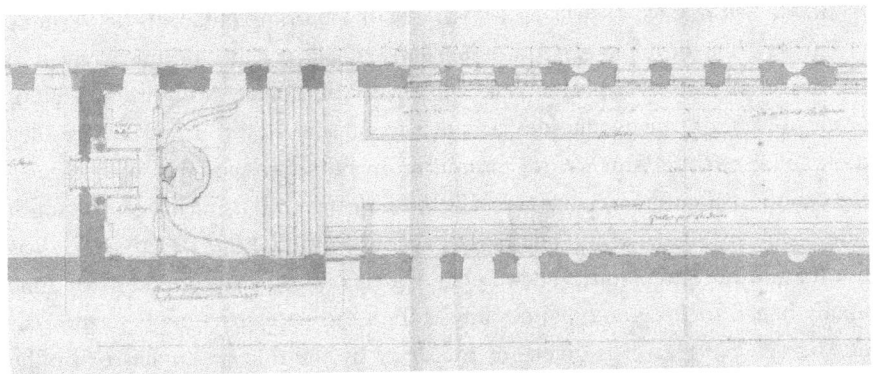

Figure 11.2 Unknown draughtsman, *Plan of the Hall of Mirrors, the Salons of Peace and War for the Audience of the Turkish Ambassador in 1742*, detail showing the new arrangement for the 1742 audience overlaying the earlier plan for the audience of the ambassador of the Shah of Persia in 1715, pen, ink, and wash on paper. Paris: Archives Nationales (CP/O/1/1772 dossier 2, no. 4). Image in the public domain.

On the window side stood an estimated eight hundred gentlemen. The front row nearest the throne was reserved for ambassadors with permanent embassies in Paris. Opposite them, on the mirror side of the gallery, closest to the throne some eighty ladies of the Court sat on tiered benches in full Court dress. The king's throne was placed at the far end of the gallery on a raised dais under a high canopy. To the right of the throne stood the king's son, the dauphin, the princes of the blood and high Court officials. On either side of the throne were two low tribunes, behind one of which sat Queen Marie Leszczyńska (1703–68) surrounded by her ladies-in-waiting.

The audience was carefully planned according to well-established protocols. The ceremony followed the same format as that of the audiences accorded by the king's predecessor, Louis XIV, to the ambassadors of the king of Siam in 1686 and the ambassador of the shah of Persia in 1715, both of which took place in the Hall of Mirrors. For each of these audiences, a temporary canopied dais was erected at the south end of the gallery where it connected with the queen's state apartment. A design drawing survives showing the proposed arrangement for the audience. The drawing has in fact been recycled from an earlier project with the new details of the 1742 audience drawn onto a separate sheet of paper which is hinged on one side and laid over the earlier drawing.

On the day of his audience at Versailles, the ambassador was driven from Paris in one of the king's own carriages accompanied by Louis de Lorraine, comte de Brionne (1725–61), and Eusèbe Félix Chaspoux, marquis de Verneüil (1720–91), the *Introducteur des ambassadeurs*. He and his retinue arrived at the house of the *premier valet de chambre du Roi,* Louis Alexandre Bontemps (1669–1742), on the avenue de Paris at Versailles at eleven o'clock where they took some refreshments before mounting on horseback for the final stage of the ceremonial entry, arriving at last at the *salle des ambassadeurs* on the south side of the courtyard of the palace. But according to the duc de Luynes, it was not for another three hours, at two o'clock, that the ambassador and his retinue finally began their ceremonial circuit through the state apartments to the Hall of Mirrors. No reason is given for the delay by the duc de Luynes or by the official account in the *Mercure de France.* Only the diary of Pierre Narbonne (d. 1746), a commissioner of police at Versailles, hints at the reason. According to Narbonne, an unfortunate accident befell the ambassador, which necessitated a change of clothing, hence the delay.[6]

The ambassador's ceremonial progress through the palace began at the bottom of the Ambassadors' Staircase. There, as was his privilege as an ambassador extraordinary, he was met by the *Grand maître des cérémonies,* Michel, marquis de Dreux-Brézé (1700–1754). At the top of the staircase in the first of the state rooms, the Salon of Venus, he was met by Adrien Maurice, duc de Noailles (1678–1766), Marshall of France and Captain of the First Company of the King's Guard. He, the comte de Brionne and M. de Verneuil then conducted the ambassador and his retinue the length of the state apartment through the Salons of Venus, Diana, Mars, Mercury, Apollo, and War to the Hall of Mirrors all of which were lined with onlookers. Just as he crossed the threshold of the Salon of War into the Hall the Mirrors, the ambassador made the first of three low bows to the king who acknowledged them by removing and immediately replacing his hat. Everyone else was bareheaded as a sign of respect both for the king and for the emissary from the sultan who, as the ambassador of a sovereign prince, was treated as if the sultan himself were present.

Ambassador Mehmed Saïd was no stranger to such ceremonial audiences. He was a career diplomat, having already represented the sultan on embassies to Poland and Sweden in the 1730s. Nor was he unfamiliar with the French Court. In 1721, he had served as secretary to his father Yirmisekiz Mehmed Çelebi Efendi (1670–1732) as ambassador extraordinary to Paris. His father's embassy aroused as much if not more interest among the French public, evidenced by the large number of popular images produced at the time. One of them (Figure 11.3) shows the moment when the ambassador presented his letters of credential

A Turk in the Hall of Mirrors 181

Figure 11.3 Anon., *Audience Given by King Louis XV to Mehmed Çelebi Efendi, Ambassador of Sultan Achmet III, March 16, 1721, at the Tuileries Palace*. Etching and engraving. Paris, Bibliothèque Nationale de France. Photo: BNF.

to the eleven-year old Louis XV. Mehmed Saïd Pasha reenacted this precise moment twenty-one years later with the same king, but at Versailles rather than the Tuileries Palace in Paris. He can be seen in the print prostrating directly behind his father and identified in the legend by the letter M.

By the time of his return, this time as ambassador extraordinary in his own right, Mehmed Saïd was fluent in the French language. Now aged about forty-five, he was an accomplished and cosmopolitan diplomat and during his six-month embassy he endeared himself to all who met him. The audience itself was exclusively ceremonial. No actual business was conducted. Despite his linguistic skills, Mehmed Saïd spoke in Ottoman Turkish, following a prescribed script relying on the services of a French interpreter. The climax of the ceremony was the handing over the ambassador's credentials contained in a letter from the sultan to the king. According to the duc de Luynes's account, the letter was carried by the ambassador's secretary on a basin covered with crimson satin, as shown in this detail from Cochin's drawing (Figure 11.4). At the appointed time, the secretary advanced with the letter, which was then presented to the king by the ambassador, who in turn passed it Jean Jacques Amelot de Chaillou (1689–1749), the Secretary of State for Foreign Affairs. With the letter delivered, the ambassador introduced his son and son-in-law who were present in his retinue to the king. Then, retracing his steps though the state apartment to the *salle des ambassadeurs*, the ambassador and his retinue dined for two hours. Then, the ambassador made a ceremonial visit to the king's heir, the thirteen-year-old dauphin in his apartment on the ground floor of the palace. There was then a viewing of the gifts sent from the sultan to the king which were displayed in the *petite galerie du Roi*, in the king's interior apartment during which time the king and the ambassador conversed at some length. The king was well pleased with the magnificent gifts from the sultan which included a tent made of fine fabric, an enameled and jewel-studded horse's harness, a bejeweled quiver, several finely decorated ceremonial guns, and a crescent-shaped powder flask encrusted with precious stones.[7] Finally, the ambassador returned to the first floor of the palace overlooking the great courtyard to pay a visit to Cardinal Fleury (1653–

Figure 11.4 Detail of Figure 11.1.

1743), the king's chief minister to whom the ambassador delivered a letter from his counterpart in Istanbul, the grand vizier. Members of the Court looked on while these visits took place observing that the proper etiquette was followed. As evening fell, the ambassador returned to Paris in the king's carriage, well pleased no doubt with the events of the day.

We now turn to the remarkable portrait of Mehmed Saïd by Jacques-André-Joseph Aved (1702–66) that is now in the collections of Versailles (Figure 11.5). The painting was exhibited in public in August 1742 in the Salon exhibition of the Royal Academy in the Louvre within weeks of the departure of the ambassador. It entered the royal collection soon after its exhibition and was placed in the guardroom of the king's country retreat at Choisy.[8] However, it was never paid for, much to the painter's annoyance. It is still unclear who commissioned the portrait. Current thinking is that it was a speculative venture by the painter in the hope that it would be bought by the king. At over two meters in height, the portrait belongs to the most prestigious type of portraiture—the *portrait*

Figure 11.5 Jacques André Joseph Aved, *Portrait of Mehmed Saïd Efendi*, 1742, oil on canvas. Versailles: Musée national des Châteaux de Versailles et de Trianon, MV 3716. Photo: RMN.

d'apparat—or state portrait. The ambassador is depicted life-size and full-length. He is dressed in the robes he wore on the day of his official entry into Paris, which event is depicted in the detail in the background of the portrait. He stands on a huge Turkish carpet that fills the fictive ground plan of the space of the portrait.

The ambassador is surrounded by symbols of his learning and cosmopolitanism. In the left foreground, a globe and a telescope allude to his travels and knowledge. The open book is a copy of the first printed Ottoman atlas, which was produced at the printing house established under his aegis in Istanbul on his return from Paris in 1721. On the desk in the background are books that allude to his expertise in international diplomacy. In his left hand, he holds a sealed letter tied with a blue ribbon that he appears to be tucking into the pocket of his robe.

Mehmed Saïd is shown pointing with his right hand to a document, which has been unfolded from a silver-gilt casket and covered with crimson cloth. Two contemporary descriptions agree that it represents the ambassador's letters of credential. According to the exhibition catalogue, or *livret*, the portrait is described thus:

By M. *Aved,* academician

> 98. The full-length portrait of His Excellency Said Pacha, Lord of Lords of Romelie, Ambassador Extraordinary of the Sultan, surrounded by all the attributes which indicate his particular knowledge and an Atlas, the first book printed in Constantinople under his aegis. In the foreground of the picture are his letters of credential, surmounted by the Seal of the Empire under a plaque of silver gilt. The background depicts a view of Paris and the beginning of his public entry.[9]

And, according to the anonymous author of a pamphlet on the painting published at the time of the exhibition:

> His Excellency is depicted full-length in his cabinet, standing in front of a desk on which are his letters of credential and books such as the *Grotius* and the *Peace Treaties,* by which the painter has characterised his subject.[10]

But in more recent scholarship, there has been a degree of confusion over the precise nature of the document.[11]

The document is, indeed, a representation of his diplomatic credentials. It is written in the elite form of Ottoman Court language reserved for official decrees and other diplomatic documents. This was a written rather than spoken language and combined words and phrases from both Arabic and Persian. Though not legible in its entirety—consistent with its being painted by an artist who was unfamiliar with the language—certain key words and phrases in the document can be identified[12] (Figure 11.6). The first line refers to the sultan as "Glorious Majesty … the King of Kings." The second line introduces his emissary by name. He is described as, "chosen by God, the veiler of sins, the Honourable Saïd." In the third line, he is described as "righteous" or "ethical" and "of pure lineage."

These references to the ambassador's rank accorded with both French and Ottoman expectations of emissaries. According to François de Callières's (1645–1717) book on the correct manner of conducting diplomacy, the *lettres de créance* should indicate the precise rank of the emissary. Indeed, Callières states that the first questions asked of a visiting diplomat to the Ottoman Court were to ascertain his rank.

> When a new French ambassador arrives in Constantinople, the Turks first ask via the interpreter if he is an *Ichoglan* or a *Cadi*. If they are told he is an *Ichoglan*,

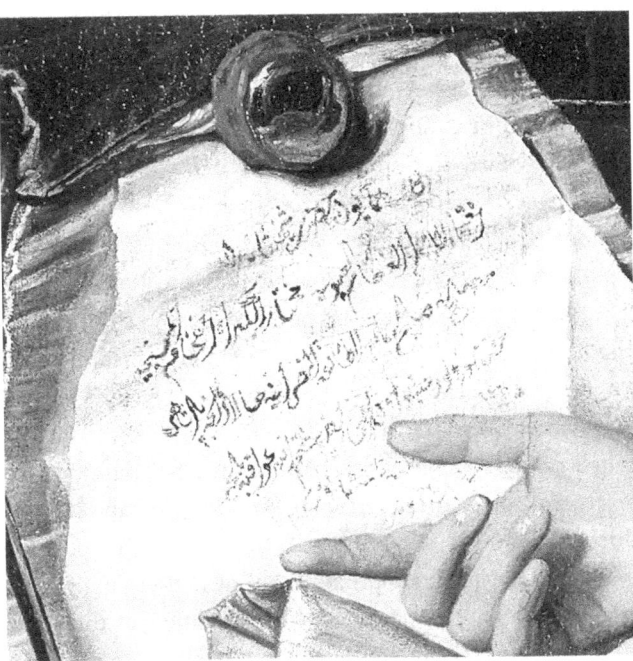

Figure 11.6 Detail of Figure 11.5

they are well pleased, but if he is a *Cadi*, they are much less so. They understand by the term *Ichoglan*, a courtier, the *Ichoglans* being men raised in the palace as pages to the sultan, and who often attain the highest offices; and by a *Cadi*, they understand a churchman or a bureaucrat, a *Cadi* being among them a judge who decides on matters of law and religion.[13]

Returning to the painted document, how could the French painter, Aved, have known how to transcribe this text? Could he have copied this inscription from an actual document? Aved's powers of painterly realism were certainly capable of such a task. A comparison of the simulated writing in the printed atlas in the foreground with the document on the desk shows that former only suggests the written text, while the latter is carefully rendered with a view to legibility. Why would the painter have bothered to take such trouble when the intended viewers, firstly the Salon audience and secondly the king, could never have been expected to read it? Surely, this degree of accuracy was of greater importance to the subject of the portrait than to any European viewer?

The ambassador's interest in French painting is well recorded in the contemporary sources, which tell us that he visited the studios of a number of painters including the miniaturist and engraver Jean-Baptiste Massé (1687–1767) and the painter Jean-Siméon Chardin (1699–1779). The pastellist Maurice-Quentin de La Tour (1704–88) and the miniaturist Jean-Adam Mathieu (*c.* 1698–1753) are recorded as having done his portrait.[14]

Given the ambassador's willingness to be depicted, it is likely that he would have been closely involved in the production of such a grand and detailed image. He surely must have lent his winter wardrobe to the painter to work from, presumably modeled by a mannequin or lay figure. But, when it comes to the ambassador's letters of credential, this involvement must have been more direct. The accuracy of the Ottoman script can only have been achieved with the active agency of the ambassador himself. Did the painter transcribe the unfamiliar calligraphy under the supervision of the ambassador or one of his retinue? Is this in fact a collaborative work?

Viewing the work as a whole, what strikes one is the abundance of text in the image. There are the books, the letter being pocketed and above all the Ottoman script to which the ambassador points. In the case of this document, we are dealing with more than just an approximation of written text (as in the case of the open Atlas), but a carefully rendered transcription of the subject's official identity that only he and the elite members of his retinue (and of course the all-seeing Allāh) could understand.

Mehmed Saïd had long demonstrated his interest in promoting the Ottoman language and making use of foreign technology to do so. On his return from the first Ottoman embassy in 1721, he had established the first publishing house in the empire. When he returned to France in 1742, he brought with him copies of some of these publications which he presented to the royal librarian, abbé Bignon (1662–1743). They included a Turkish and Arabic dictionary, a geographical treatise illustrated with maps and a two-volume history of the Ottoman Empire. He also visited the library at the Abbey of Sainte-Geneviève, where he was surprised to be shown two letters written in Turkish by Köprülüzade Fazıl Mustafa Pasha (1637–91), the grand vizier of Sultan Suleiman II (1642–91).[15]

From the ambassador's point of view, then, this juxtaposition of image and text in Aved's portrait would have been particularly meaningful. To him, which was the more "truthful"? Or, perhaps more correctly, would he not have viewed them as equally truthful but different modes of representation? As a cosmopolitan diplomat, Mehmed Said was equally conversant and familiar with both. Surely the accuracy of the document to which Mehmed Saïd gestures, though superfluous to the French viewer, was deemed necessary in order to complement the veracity of the painted image, at least from the point of view of its distinguished subject.

Postscript

After nearly ten months in France, Ambassador Mehmed Saïd and his retinue departed Paris on June 30, 1742, and arrived in Istanbul in early October. He had taken with him a horde of splendid gifts valued at over 200,000 *livres* from the king to the sultan and members of his Court. These included eight free-standing silver candelabra in the shape of palm and laurel trees and two silver tables by the royal silversmith Claude Ballin the Younger (*c.* 1660–1754); Savonnerie carpets, Saint-Gobain mirrors in gilt-bronze frames, marquetry furniture, a Japanese lacquer tea service, several pieces of furniture in the Turkish style; a portable organ and various optical instruments including a microscope.[16] The ambassador personally received a large diamond, two Savonnerie carpets, a rock crystal chandelier, a pair of braziers in semilor (a copper-zinc alloy) by Jean-Claude Duplessis (1699–1774) and no less than four gold snuffboxes.[17]

Yirmisekizzade Mehmed Saïd Pasha continued to feature in the political landscape of the Ottoman Empire. From October 25, 1755, to April 1, 1756, he reached the pinnacle of his career by serving as grand vizier to Sultan Osman III (1699–1757). His embassy to France was officially commemorated years after the event by the striking of a medal for the medallic history of Louis XV. An inscription on the drawn design for the medal by Edme Bouchardon (1698–1762) indicates that it was not sent to medalist Benjamin Duvivier (1730–1819) for casting until April 1760.[18] The reverse of the medal depicts a diminutive ambassador handing over the sultan's letter to a seated Louis XV (Figure 11.7). He cuts a poor figure compared to his commanding presence in the portrait by Aved—perhaps the earliest image of the "Sick Man of Europe." The medallic image of the ambassador conforms to the somewhat formulaic nature of the medium. It conveys none of the immediacy and élan of the portrait by which Mehmed Saïd is now justly remembered.

Figure 11.7 Benjamin Duvivier after Edme Bouchardon, reverse of a bronze medal commemorating the Turkish embassy of 1742, *c.* 1760, bronze. Private collection. Photo: Author.

Notes

1 See Ronald S. Love, "Rituals of Majesty: France, Siam, and Court Spectacle in Royal Image-Building at Versailles in 1685 and 1686," *Canadian Journal of History* 31 (August 1996), 171–98; and Meredith Martin, "Mirror Reflections: Louis XIV, Phra Narai, and the Material Culture of Kingship," *Art History* 38, no. 4 (September 2015), 652–67.

2 In the *Mercure de France*, juin, 1742, part 2: 849, he is described as about forty-five years old.

3 The Treaty of Belgrade. 1739, ibid.

4 For the significance of the ratification of the Franco-Ottoman trade concessions by Sultan Mahmud I, see Robert Olson, "The Ottoman-French Treaty of 1740: A Year to Be Remembered?" *Turkish Studies Association Bulletin*, 15, no. 2 (September 1991), 347–55.

5 Charles Philippe d'Albert, duc de Luynes, *Mémoires du duc de Luynes sur la cour de Louis XV (1735–1758)*, ed. Louis Dussieux and Eudore Soulié, 17 vols (Paris: Firmin Didot Frères, 1860–5), 4:70ff. See also Stéphane Castellucio, "La Galerie des Glaces: les réceptions d'ambassadeurs," *Versalia*, 9 (2006), 24–52 and especially 45–50.

6 Pierre Narbonne, *Journal des règnes de Louis XIV et Louis XV: de l'année 1701 à l'année 1744*, ed. Joseph-Adrien Le Roi (Paris: Durand, 1866), 501–4. According to Narbonne, the ambassador, who had been indisposed for several days, soiled himself upon arrival at the *salle des ambassadeurs*, requiring a fresh shirt and under garments to be sent for. The reliability of Narbonne's account is somewhat questionable. He states, for example, that the ambassador slept at Bontemps' house the night preceding his audience.

7 See Marie-Laure Buku Pongo, "La seconde ambassade Ottomane, 1742," in *Visiteurs de Versailles, voyageurs, princes, ambassadeurs 1682–1789*, ed. Daniëlle Kisluk-Grosheide and Bertrand Rondot (Paris and Versailles: Gallimard, 2017), 186–91. Several of these gifts from the sultan are now in the Musée de l'Armée in Paris.

8 Georges Wildenstein, *Le peintre Aved: sa vie et son oeuvre, 1702–1766*, 2 vols (Paris: Les Beaux-Arts, 1922), 1: 60–3, 102–3.

9 *Explication des peintures, sculptures et autres ouvrages de Messieurs de l'Académie royale* … (Paris: Jacques Collombat, 1742): 23–4. "Par M. *Aved*, Académicien 98. Le Portrait en pied de Son Excellence Said Pacha Beglierbey de Roumely, Ambassadeur Extraordinaire du Grand Siegneur, entouré de tous les attributs, qui désignent particulierement ses connaissances, & d'un Athlas, premier Livre imprimé par ses soins à Constantinople. On voit sur le devant du Tableau les Lettres de Croyance, surmontées du Sceau de l'Empire, renfermé sous une Plaque

de vermeil. Le fond représente une vue de Paris, & le commencement de son Entrée."

10 *Lettre au sujet du portrait de son excellence, Saïd-Pacha, ambassadeur extraordinaire du Grand-Seigneur à la cour de France, en 1742, exposé au Salon du Louvre, le 25 août de la même année* (Paris: Prault, 1742), 14. "S.E. est peinte en pied dans son Cabinet, debout devant un Bureau, sur lequel sont ses Lettres de Créance & et des Livres tells que le *Grotius*, & des *Traités de Paix*, par lesquels le Peintre a characterisé son sujet."

11 In Perrin Stein, "Exoticism as Metaphor: *Turquerie* in Eighteenth-Century French Art" (PhD diss., Institute of Fine Arts, New York University, 1997), 147, the document is described as a signed peace treaty and the letter in his hand is identified as the official letter from the sultan to the king. Following Stein, in Julia Landweber's PhD dissertation of 2001, the document has become a copy of the renewed trade concessions between France and Turkey and the letter in his other hand has become his letter of credential. See Julia Landweber, "French Delight in Turkey: The Impact of Turkey on the Construction of French Identity, 1660–1789" (PhD diss., Rutgers, The State University of New Jersey, 2001), 100. And in the Metropolitan Museum of Art's catalogue for the "Visitors to Versailles" exhibition, through a slight misreading of the anonymous pamphlet of 1742, Meredith Martin identifies the document as a trade agreement. See Meredith Martin, "Special Embassies and Overseas Visitors," in *Visitors to Versailles. From Louis XIV to the French Revolution*, ed. Daniëlle Kisluk-Grosheide and Bertrand Rondot (New York: Metropolitan Museum of Art and Yale University Press, 2018), 318, note 43.

12 I am especially grateful to Negar Partow and Fahim Afarainasadi for their assistance with the translation of the text in the document.

13 François de Callières [1716], *De la manière de négoicier avec les souverains*, 2 vols, new edition (London: Jean Nourse, 1750), 1:278–9. "Lorsqu'il arrive un nouvel Ambassadeur de France à Constantinople, les Turcs demandent d'abord à l'interprete, si c'est un *Ichoglan* ou un *Cadi*, s'il leur dit que c'est un *Ichoglan*, ils en sont fort contens, mais si c'est un *Cadi*, ils en sont beaucoup moins d'état. Ils entendent par le terme d'*Ichoglan*, un homme de la Cour, les *Ichoglans* étant des hommes élevés dans le serail comme des especes de Pages du Grand Seigneur, & qui parviennent souvent aux premiers emplois; & par un *Cadi* ils entendent un homme d'Eglise ou de Robe, un *Cadi* étant chez eux un Juge qui decide les points de droit & ceux de leur religion."

14 *Mercure de France* (June 1742), part 2: 986; *Lettre au sujet du portrait de son excellence, Saïd-Pacha*, 12–13. Neither portrait appears to have survived. However, an enamel portrait of Mehmed Saïd by Mathieu was included in a sale in Paris on November 27, 1752. See *Annonces, affiches, et avis divers*, novembre 15, 1752: 114.

15 *Mercure de France* (June 1742), part 2: 986–8.
16 Ibid., 1023–32.
17 Marie-Laure Buku Pongo as in note 6 above, esp., 192–3. On the gifts given to the departing ambassador, see John Whitehead, "Royal Riches and Parisian Trinkets: The Embassy of Saïd Mehmet Pasha to France in 1741–42 and Its Exchange of Gifts," *Court Historian* 14, no. 2 (December 2009), 161–75. The royal gifts were reportedly well received at the Ottoman Court. See *Mercure de France* (December 1743), 2:2778–84.
18 Winslow Ames, "Bouchardon and Company," *Master Drawings* 13, no. 2 (Winter 1975), 397, cat. no. 48.

12

Cornelis Hop (1685–1762), Dutch Ambassador to the Court of Louis XV

Daniëlle Kisluk-Grosheide

Cornelis Hop was a scion of a prominent Amsterdam family of wealthy merchants who by the early eighteenth century were part of the ruling elite of the Dutch Republic.[1] The future diplomat grew up in a majestic canal house on the Herengracht which was built between 1685 and 1687 for his father Jacob Hop (1654–1725), a leading town official (pensionary) in Amsterdam, who undertook a number of diplomatic missions and subsequently served as the treasurer general of the Republic (Figure 12.1).[2] After his law studies the younger Hop occupied various positions. He was an alderman in Amsterdam, an administrator in an important trading enterprise, the West India Company, and later as a director of the Society of Suriname, a private company chartered to manage and defend the Dutch colony. In March 1718, at the age of thirty-three, Hop was named resident ambassador to France.[3] As such, Hop was expected, exactly like the diplomats from other countries, to advance the interests of his state, negotiate on its behalf, gather political and military information as well as news about daily life at the French Court, all of which he sent in dispatches to The Hague. The only difference between Hop and his Dutch predecessors was his status as full ambassador. France and the Republic had been enemies for nearly five decades starting with the Franco-Dutch War of 1672–8. Charles Le Brun glorified Louis XIV's victories won during this conflict on the vault of the Hall of Mirrors.[4] The States General, representatives of the seven provinces who constituted the de facto federal government of the Republic, had long insisted that the Dutch representative to the French Court should be received with the same honors as the diplomats from other European monarchies and the Venetian Republic. France consented to this request only in 1717 when

Figure 12.1 House built for Jacob Hop at Herengracht 605, Amsterdam (façade altered in 1739; now the Willet-Holthuysen Museum). Photo: Author.

the Dutch Republic joined her and Great Britain in a military alliance against Spain.[5]

With instructions from the Dutch government, Hop left The Hague on October 7, 1718. He traveled incognito in an attempt to speed up his journey and reached Paris twelve days later.[6] The young diplomat established himself and his household in a rented *hôtel particulier* in the Faubourg St. Germain, the district where other ambassadors resided as well.[7] As was customary for arriving foreign representatives, Hop immediately announced his presence to Nicolas Sixte de Sainctot (1683–1753), who served as the *introducteur des ambassadeurs*, the Court official responsible for arranging private and public audiences with the king, the regent, Philippe II, duke of Orléans (1674–1723), and other members of the royal family.[8] Hop first met with Louis XV (1710–74) in a private audience on Friday, November 11, 1718. The audience took place at the Tuileries Palace where the eight-year-old king resided when the Court returned from Versailles in 1715 after the death of the Sun King.[9] Sainctot and Monsieur Merlin, secretary to the *introducteurs*, conducted Hop from the reception room, the *Salle des*

Ambassadeurs, to the monarch's cabinet. The two officials walked ahead in order to clear the way for the Dutch diplomat in the crowd of courtiers. Hop found the king standing, his head bare, in the company of the royal governor, François de Neufville, duke of Villeroy, marshal of France (1644–1730), his tutor, André-Hercule de Fleury, bishop of Fréjus (later Cardinal) (1653–1743), and the secretary of state for foreign affairs, Abbé (later Cardinal) Guillaume Dubois (1656–1723). As per established diplomatic protocol, Hop bowed three times before addressing Louis XV with a short speech in French. The king responded (with words whispered into his ears by his governor) stating that he desired nothing more than for France to live in harmony and peace with the Dutch Republic.[10]

As a full resident minister Hop was entitled to a formal entry into Paris which would be followed two days later by a public audience with the king. Both were magnificent occasions, demanding a display of coaches, horses, and liveried servants. Most ambassadors ordered suitable parade carriages in Paris to manifest the wealth and power of their respective states, such as the magnificent coach commissioned by the Portuguese diplomat Luís Manuel da Câmara, third count of Ribeira Grande (1685–1723) for his official audience in 1715 (Figure 12.2).[11] It is likely that Hop's ceremonial coach was made in Paris as well. According to a contemporary description, it was richly decorated with "artful carving" and painted on the backside with a likeness of Amphitrite, Goddess of the sea, wearing a coral crown and holding an olive branch in her hand, while riding a shell-shaped carriage pulled by Tritons. Various Naiads presented her with the riches from the sea. Flanking Hop's coat of arms on the front of the carriage, the personifications of Unity and Peace were depicted. Commerce and Sincerity embellished the back, while the carriage doors portrayed Faithfulness and Fortitude on one side, and Prudence and Liberty, on the other.[12] The corners of the carriage showed additional water nymphs holding cornucopias. Hop studied descriptions of past ceremonies to make sure that the respect paid to him (and therefore to the Republic) was identical to what was accorded to the Venetian ambassador Lorenzo Tiepolo in 1704.[13] On July 14, 1719, after months of preparations, Hop sent word to Sainctot that everything was ready and his formal entry from Rambouillet into Paris was scheduled for July 23, 1719.[14] A severe thunderstorm threatened the event but abated just in time so that the procession could take place in full splendor and was witnessed by many spectators lining the route. Judging from the descriptions Hop gave of the event and those which were published in the *Europische Mercurius*, Adolf van der

Figure 12.2 Carriage ordered by the Count of Ribeira Grande for his official audience at Versailles, 1715, painted and gilded wood, metal, velvet, tortoiseshell, and brass. 240 × 370 × 740 cm. Museu Nacional dos Coches, Lisbon V0007. Photo: DGCP/ADF.

Laan's drawing, a rare rendition of such an ambassadorial entry, is an accurate depiction[15] (Figure 12.3). Preceded by two equestrians, Hop's own coach, pulled by eight black Friesian horses, is illustrated in the lower right. It remained empty since the ambassador himself was riding in the third or royal carriage with the *introducteur* and Pierre de Montesquiou, marshal of France (1640–1725).[16] The undated "*Mémoire de l'argent que M. l'Ambassadeur des Provinces unies donne en present le jour d'entrée*" (Memorandum of the Money That the Ambassador of the United Provinces Is to Give as Presents on the Day of His Entry), among Hop's papers, was most likely provided by the *introducteur* specifying how much to tip the different coachmen and valets.[17]

Figure 12.3 Adolf van der Laan (1684–1755), *The Formal Entry of Cornelis Hop into Paris*, c. 1719–20, ink on paper, 13.7 × 18.6 cm. Amsterdam, Rijksmuseum, RP-T-00-1741. Image in the public domain.

Two days later the Dutch ambassador's public audience took place at the Louvre where Louis XV temporarily resided while the Tuileries palace was being cleaned.[18] The ceremony went on as scheduled despite the death of the regent's daughter, Marie Louise Élisabeth of Orléans, duchesse de Berry (1695–1719). Arranged according to the protocol appropriate for a diplomat of his rank, the audience was the subject of a painting by Louis Michel Dumesnil (Figure 12.4).[19] Similar to the day of Hop's entry into Paris, the diplomat was escorted by the *introducteur*, this time together with Charles Louis de Lorraine, prince of Pons (1696–1755), in a royal carriage and accompanied by a large retinue of footmen, pages, and grooms dressed in colorful liveries. At the Louvre Hop was greeted with the roll of drums while the royal guards presented their arms, before being brought to the king.[20] Both leaves of the double doors he passed through were opened for him, a distinction reserved for a diplomat of Hop's standing in contrast to just a single door panel for lower ranking envoys.[21] Although an ambassador was usually received in the king's bedchamber, Hop's public audience took place in the grand cabinet of the late Anne of Austria (1601–66),

Figure 12.4 Louis Michel Dumesnil (1663?–1739), *The Formal Audience of Cornelis Hop at the Court of Louis XV*, c. 1720–29, oil on canvas. 104.5 × 163 cm. Amsterdam, Rijksmuseum, on loan from the Koninklijk Oudheidkundig Genootschap SK-C-512. Image in the public domain.

Louis XV's great-great-grandmother.[22] After the three obligatory bows, Hop is shown delivering his harangue (speech) following which he would present the king with his credentials, now still in his hand.[23] According to Hop's account, the monarch had listened to him with full attention and passed his letter, unopened, immediately on to Abbé Dubois. Louis XV then spoke the following words furnished to him by his governor:

> Sir, please assure the States General that I have always the best intentions to give them true expressions of my goodwill and that I will seek every opportunity to meet their expectations; that their friendship is always very dear to me and marked by the new honors I have bestowed on you today. Your person, Sir, is very pleasant to me, and at any time that I can demonstrate to you that I have the satisfaction of seeing you I shall happily do so.[24]

The legend in Simon Fokke's etching after the Dumesnil painting identifies the officials surrounding the king, marshal of Villeroy, to the left of the king's armchair, bishop of Fréjus, and Louis Henri, duke of Bourbon (1692–1740) to the right of the ruler. Directly behind the Dutch diplomat, stand Sainctot, Hop's secretary Ruijsch, and Abbé Dubois[25] (Figure 12.5). The gentleman dressed in

Figure 12.5 Simon Fokke (1712–84), *The Formal Audience of Cornelis Hop at the Court of Louis XV*, c. 1747–59, etching. 18.5 × 28.5 cm. Private collection. Photo: Author.

a light blue coat taking notes may be the artist himself who, given his accurate representation of the audience, is likely to have been present. Hop noted that following the ceremony the king "incognito" took a peek at his carriage.[26]

Many of Hop's dispatches provide information about Louis XV whom he literally watched grow up. In 1720 he reported on a number of the king's new experiences, such as participating in a ballet while the entire Court and the foreign ambassadors were in attendance, something the ten-year-old monarch apparently did very gracefully and to everyone's admiration.[27] Later that same year Louis XV went hawking for the first time in the forest at Vincennes, and horseback riding in the park at La Muette, a hunting castle near the Bois de Bologne.[28] Hop also informed the leaders of the Republic about some of the ruler's mishaps as when he fell down the stairs at La Muette and ended up with a bump above his right eye.[29] The following year Louis XV caused concern when, while working on a mosaic, he accidently swallowed one of the tesserae. Fortunately, the Dutch diplomat communicated in the same account that the small stone passed through the king's system three days later ending the anxiety at the Court.[30]

On September 15, 1719, Hop visited Versailles for the first time by special invitation of the regent. All he reported was that the fountains, which were turned on in his honor, did not function as well as those at the nearby Château de Marly due to that summer's extreme drought.[31] In respect to Versailles, it becomes very clear from Hop's dispatches that the Court moved back there in 1722 at the insistence of the king who was impatient to leave Paris. In April of that year, much to everyone's surprise, it was announced that Louis XV wanted to spend four or five weeks at Versailles.[32] At first, it was unclear if this would just be for the summer or for a longer period of time. In the meantime various preparations were made and the palace was cleaned which delayed the king's departure.[33] Not wanting to return to Versailles and not so secretly hoping that the journey would not happen, the courtiers nevertheless jockeyed for apartments at the palace which were allocated by the regent, leaving many of them disappointed.[34] Hop reported on a quarrel erupting between the duke of Bourbon and Louis Alexandre, count of Toulouse (1678–1737) because the duke desired the rooms of the count which the latter refused to give up.[35] Multiple delays occurred before the Court actually left Paris, partly because of an outbreak of smallpox in Versailles and partly because it was considered unhealthy for the king to stay in a residence where so much plastering was recently done.[36] The regent himself went to check on the Château's condition on May 22 and finally the journey took place on June 15.[37] Immediately after his arrival, the king inspected the palace and the gardens. According to Hop it was due "to the amusements of the location, the magnificence of his apartment and the newness of it all for a prince of his age" that Louis XV preferred to remain at Versailles.[38] The lords and ladies of the Court, however, found very little pleasure there and only hoped that the sovereign's enthusiasm would lessen over time. Even though the Tuileries palace was being prepared in case of the king's return during the winter, he didn't leave Versailles where, the Dutch ambassador observed, he had become "less reserved and more talkative in public." Hop himself had the distinct honor that the ruler addressed him several times during his *soupé* which the diplomat believed "had never happened to any foreign representative before."[39]

During the seven years Hop spent in France he sent more than 2,000 dispatches home often writing four times a week, sometimes several times a day. The reports were addressed to either the "Heeren" or lords of the States General or to the "griffier," the secretary of this body, a function capably performed for many years by François Fagel (1659–1746). Generally the mail reached The Hague in four days. Hop's diplomatic correspondence offers an excellent account of the daily life at the

French Court and of contemporary events such as the total solar eclipse on May 22, 1724, which the king and his Court observed at the Trianon.[40] The ambassador's descriptions also detail certain social practices. Explaining, for instance, why Louis XV's fourteenth birthday was not celebrated, the diplomat wrote: "It is not customary here to remind someone of getting older and therefore closer to the end [of his life]."[41] The reports also inform us about Hop's ambassadorial responsibilities while serving as the official observer for his government.

Every Tuesday the foreign ministers, as Hop referred to them, were received at Court, to pay their respects to the king and to meet with the secretary of state for foreign affairs who hosted that day a luncheon for the ambassadors. This was an excellent opportunity to represent the interests of the Republic, discuss political matters, catch up on the latest news, and exchange gossip, all of which were dutifully passed on to the States General. As it becomes very clear from his correspondence, the Court was an outstanding source of information. Conveying the news that the duke of Orléans had died, he wrote in December 1723: "I'm leaving for Versailles shortly to find out further circumstances and what consequences this sudden and important death may have."[42] Various audiences, visits of congratulations or condolences, kept the diplomat occupied and his letters filled.[43] In March 1724, for instance, Hop announced the recent death of Madame Royale. Since she was the great-grandmother of Louis XV, the Court would adopt the *grand deuil* (deep mourning) for a period of four and a half months.[44] He asked for (and received) permission from the States General to drape his carriages and horses in black cloth, an unexpected expense, and reported on the respects that he and the other foreign ministers paid the king on April 11, 1724, dressed in long black trailing robes with formal neckwear or bands.[45] According to Hop this solemn reverence did not displease the young king who received it with dignity although he was still shy and unable to answer the compliments addressed to him.

Early during his tenure, Hop was amazed to learn that the contents of the dispatches he had written were known to the other ambassadors. He was then plainly told that it was very easy and inexpensive to obtain copies of anything that was sent by mail.[46] The diplomat learned his lesson and was more careful in what he sent by post, occasionally writing in code and only sharing his frank opinions about the French Court in hand-delivered reports.[47]

Matters of protocol and nuances of etiquette occupy considerable space in the ambassador's correspondence. Any real or perceived breaches in precedence which could be considered as a diplomatic slight were described in great detail. In December 1721, for instance, Hop paid a ceremonial visit to José Maria

Téllez-Girón, seventh duke of Osuna (1685–1733), ambassador extraordinary of Spain. The Dutch representative noted that "this gentleman was either not informed of the appropriate ceremonial or didn't think it necessary to submit himself to it and received me on the sixth step of the stairs instead of at the door of my carriage; he accompanied me into his cabinet instead of below the canopy; and when I was leaving he escorted me to the bottom of the stairs instead of into the courtyard to see me off."[48] Hop concluded that he would treat the duke of Osuna in exactly the same manner when the Spanish diplomat paid him a return visit, which is indeed what happened later that same month.[49]

According to Hop's dispatches, Louis XV began to hunt on a regular basis in 1723, an activity he remained passionate about for the rest of his life. Hop reported: "Everything at the Court is completely tranquil. The king is very healthy and amuses himself daily with the hunt … He even went deer hunting last Wednesday despite the foul weather."[50] To practice his favorite pastime, Louis XV also spent time at the palaces of Meudon and Chantilly where the ruler stayed during the summer of 1724. Hop related that as soon as the king was back at Versailles, a messenger was sent to Paris to the duke of Bourbon. This caused much concern until it became clear that the monarch had enjoyed himself so much at Chantilly that he felt terribly bored at Versailles and desired the immediate return of the duke to amuse him.[51] That may not have been enough so a prolonged stay at the Château de Fontainebleau was undertaken shortly thereafter.[52] The foreign diplomats followed the Court to Fontainebleau and Hop notified the States General of his intention to go there a day or two ahead of time in order to avoid the traffic of the king's retinue on the road.[53] When Louis XV stayed at one of the smaller residences, Cardinal Dubois would travel to Paris once a week for the regular Tuesday meetings with the ambassadors.[54]

For several years Hop devoted a great deal of attention to a disastrous 1720 outbreak of the bubonic plague in the south of France which killed over 100,000 people in Marseille and the surrounding region. He kept the States General well-informed including regular updates, forwarding broadsheets with instructions on the preventive measures that were to be observed in the affected areas and, in October 1723, a notification for a *Te Deum* to be sung in the cathedral of the Nôtre Dame, Paris, out of gratitude that the epidemic had ended.[55] Illnesses in general are a frequent subject in the diplomat's reports reflecting the pervading fear at Court of contagious diseases, especially smallpox. The ambassador recorded in detail when the king, regent, or another member of the royal family were indisposed, often on the verge of sharing what we today would consider too much information, but was then considered crucial for measuring the vitality of the king, issues of succession, and the stability of the dynasty.[56] On February 9, 1723, for instance, Hop described that the king fainted in church and that the regent hurried back to Versailles suspecting (incorrectly as it turned out) that the young ruler had contracted smallpox.[57] From Fontainebleau it was reported that "the king had been two or three days inconvenienced by diarrhea but apparently it did not prevent him from going hunting."[58] At another time, Louis XV suffered from fever and headaches. As a result, he was bled twice and given laxatives which, fortunately, perked him up again. It was thought that the monarch's ailment was caused by eating too much chocolate.[59] Hop experienced a personal tragedy in 1719 when his cousin, who lived with him in Paris, died of smallpox which had erupted at the time in the city. The Dutch diplomat stayed away from Court in a self-imposed exile for six weeks and noted that the king would not dine in public. Once Hop returned to Court he observed that the sovereign had become noticeably more robust.[60] If a member of the royal family came down with the measles or another infectious sickness, preparations were made to transport the monarch quickly to either the Trianon, Marly or Meudon, to prevent contagion.[61] Despite such precautions, Louis XV would die of smallpox in May of 1774.

Hop was an eyewitness to several important milestones in Louis XV's life. In September 1722, he wrote to the States General that there were few *nouvelles* to be shared other than the preparations for Louis XV's coronation which was to take place in Rheims on October 25.[62] When Cardinal Dubois conveyed the king's wish that all the ambassadors should be present, Hop asked the States General for permission to attend this solemn occasion, noting that he would incur additional expenses for his equipage, carriage, and liveries.[63] For his presence at the coronation he received a commemorative gold medal.[64] After Louis XV's safe return from Rheims, a decree went out that the entire city of Paris should be illuminated for which Hop requested approval for the extra cost of candles.[65]

In 1721 the Dutch diplomat reported on the engagement of the eleven-year-old Louis XV with the three-year-old Mariana Victoria, infanta of Spain (1718–81). As a daughter of Philip V, Mariana was a full cousin of the French king. Arranged by the regent, this engagement was as much an expression of the latter's dynastic ambitions as of his desire to improve the strained relationship between France and Spain. At the same time, the duke of Orléans married off his own daughter, Louise Élisabeth (1709–42) to Louis, the crown prince of Spain (1707–24). Not surprisingly, this attempt by the Orléans family to improve their fortunes met with resistance from the Bourbons, reflecting the rivalry between the two branches of the royal family. Following the death of the duke of Orléans in December of 1723, the duke of Bourbon staged what could be called a palace coup by offering the king his services as first minister which were accepted.[66] Hop reported that the members of the late regent's household were asked to vacate their lodgings at Versailles and to return the keys.[67] From a long conversation Hop had with the regent's widow, it became very clear to Hop that there was no love lost between the two branches of the royal family, since the new duke of Orléans, although next in line to the throne, felt slighted by the duke of Bourbon.[68]

Being "too delicate to trust to the mail," a candid account of the French Court was hand delivered to the grand pensionary of the Republic in April of 1724.[69] According to Hop, Louis XV—then fourteen years old—was timid and did not communicate with those who were unfamiliar to him and never responded to any speeches or compliments. Furthermore, he had an aversion to the female sex in general and to the infanta in particular. The king did not meddle with the affairs of state leaving them largely to the duke of Bourbon and bishop of Fréjus. Hop observed that of the king's council, Fréjus was the most influential member noting also that he yielded too much to the Jesuits and was intolerant of other religious persuasions.[70] He described Charles Jean-Baptiste Fleuriau, count of Morville (1686–1732), the new secretary of state for foreign affairs, as paying less attention to important matters than to insignificant ones and as having little energy to fulfill the duties of his position. Hop concluded scathingly that the council had not consisted of people with so little knowledge or experience for a long time. The king's ministers did not fare any better in his view. François Victor Le Tonnelier de Breteuil (1686–1743), minister of War, for instance, had, according to Hop, never seen any troops except for the king's guards nor had Jean-Frédéric Phélypeaux, count of Maurepas (1701–81), minister of the Navy, ever seen ships other than those depicted in paintings. Both went on, however, to have long and successful careers at the Court.

Charming and witty as she was for a child of her age, the infanta was still very young and it would take years until the marriage could be consummated. If the king died without an heir, the Crown would pass to the Orléans line which was an undesirable prospect for the duke of Bourbon who now made it a priority to marry Louis XV to an older princess. In March of 1725, Hop first reported about rumors that the infanta would be sent back to Spain under a false pretext.[71] Having received from the king a "magnificent present of a golden dressing table set as well as various parcels of clothes," the infanta left Versailles in early April.[72] Even before she reached the Spanish border the engagement of Louis XV with Maria Leszczyńska (1703–68), daughter of the former king of Poland, was announced.⁷³ Although she was not the first choice and considered too poor, the Polish princess at least was a Roman Catholic and of child-bearing age.⁷⁴ After the wedding which took place at Fontainebleau on September 5, 1725, Hop went to Court to compliment the queen on her marriage and described her as "very slender but not beautiful .... but [with] good teeth which gets much attention here. She is very polite and pleasant and tries to please everyone." More than anything else she was extremely pious. The day Hop met her she had taken Communion, been to Mass four times, and also participated in Vespers.⁷⁵ Several days later, in a private audience, Hop congratulated the king on behalf of the States General, a tribute which the monarch received in silence.⁷⁶

Hop also reported on other contemporary events such as the financial activities of John Law (1671-1729), controller general of finances and founder of the Banque Générale which was given the authority to issue banknotes. Law's Compagnie d'Occident (later Compagnie des Indes) enjoyed the privilege of developing French territories in Mississippi and as well as a monopoly on colonial trade with a great potential for profit. Demand for shares in his company triggered a speculative frenzy and ultimately resulted in a stock market crash with disastrous consequences. Hop gave a vivid description of this so-called Mississippi Bubble including an account of how on July 17, 1720, such a large crowd went to the bank to exchange their banknotes for coin that four people were trampled to death. Since the duke of Orléans was meeting with Law at the Palais Royal, the bodies were transported there in the hope of forcing the regent to make more coin available. Enraged by the casualties, the mob destroyed Law's carriage and shattered the windows of his house.⁷⁷

Just like diplomats today, Hop also looked after the interests of his countrymen and regularly intervened on behalf of Dutch merchants who experienced problems in France.⁷⁸ Some interventions concerned less important matters. In 1720 he described how he assisted Barbara Grave, a Dutch rope dancer who performed at fairs. In order to prevent a misalliance between the entertainer and her lover, the marquess of Fiennes, his family had her arrested in Valenciennes. Hop was able to get her released from prison under the condition that she would leave France immediately.⁷⁹

As one of the few Protestant diplomats in France, Hop regularly consulted with the British ambassador, John Dalrymple, second Earl of Stair (1673-1747), about sensitive religious issues. Both embassies housed chapels where Protestant services were held on a weekly basis and at regular intervals people who had worshiped in Hop's chapel were arrested. The diplomat would intervene on their behalf, and usually managed to get them released after a few days.⁸⁰ Another issue was the public celebration of important Catholic holidays. Corpus Christi, for instance, included a procession of the holy sacraments with the display of tapestries on the walls of houses along the processional route. As a representative of a Protestant state, Hop could not agree to the use of his residence for this purpose. However, a compromise was found by attaching the tapestries to poles placed in the street in front of Hop's house.[81]

Having served the Republic in France for seven years, Hop returned home in November of 1725.[82] He took leave of the king in a private audience at Fontainebleau during which the monarch, as usual, didn't speak a word, while the queen, in a separate meeting, very graciously answered Hop's compliments.[83] As parting gifts he received a collection of ninety gold medals of the kings of France and the history of the life of Louis XIV valued at 12,000 livres. He was also presented with a gold and diamond-mounted snuffbox with the portraits of Louis XV and Marie Leszczyńska inside the lid (Figure 12.6).[84]

Figure 12.6 Snuffbox with Miniature Portraits of Louis XV and Marie Leszczyńska, Box by Daniel Govaers (active 1717–c. 54); Miniature portraits: Attributed to Jean-Baptiste Massé (1687–1767). 1725-6, gold, diamonds, enamel, and tortoiseshell. 3 × 8.5 × 6.5 cm. Paris, Musée du Louvre, Département des Objets d'Art OA 10670. Image in the public domain.

In turn, Hop gave generous contra gifts to the *introducteur* and the secretary of the *introducteurs*.[85] Although his diplomatic dispatches came to an end, Hop continued to serve the Republic in various functions as a deputy from the province of Holland to the States General, as administrator of the Dutch East India Company, as well as four terms as mayor of Amsterdam.[86] It is very likely, however, that Hop considered his years as an ambassador to France as the highlight of his public life.

Notes

1   P. J. Blok and P. C. Molhuysen, eds, *Nieuw Nederlandsch Biografisch Woordenboek*, vol. 2 (Leiden: n.p., 1912), column 601, entry by Nicolaas Japikse about Cornelis Hop (1620–1704), grandfather of Ambassador Cornelis Hop.
2   Ibid., vol. 3 (1914), column 614, entry by C. H. Th. Bussemaker about Jacob Hop (1654–1725).
3   Ibid., vol. 2 (1912), column 602, entry by C. H.Th. Bussemaker about Cornelis Hop.
4   See Lydia Beauvais, "The Thirty Paintings Explained: An Allegorised History of the First Eighteen Years of Louis XIV's Reign," in Christine Albanel, Pierre Arizzoli-Clémentel, and Pierre Coppey, *The Hall of Mirrors History and Restoration*, trans. Ann Sautier-Greening (Dijon: Faton, 2007), 220–42.
5   The intention of the alliance between France, Great Britain, and The Netherlands was to check the ambitions of King Philip V of Spain, who wanted to claim the French throne in the event his young nephew, Louis XV would die childless. Remmet van Luttervelt, "De ontvangst van Cornelis Hop als Nederlandsch ambassadeur te Parijs," *Jaarverslag van het Koninklijk Oudheidkundig Genootschap*, 90–1 (1950), 80–104, 80–5.
6   By traveling incognito, Hop tried to avoid official receptions and marks of honor in the towns he traveled through. Reports of October 16 and 21, 1718. National Archives, The Hague, 1.10.97 (Familie Archief Hop), 1282, 64. See also 1.10.97, 1282, 57 [undated report] where Hop describes his farewell from the States General. Unless otherwise noted, all the cited documents are in the National Archives [NA] in The Hague.
7   In 1725, Hop declared 600 livres for presumably half a year of rent. The list of his semi-annual expenses was received in The Hague on July 4, 1725. NA 1.01.02 (Staten Generaal), 6797.
8   See Jean Rousset [de Missy], *Le ceremonial diplomatique des cours de l'Europe, ou collection des actes, memoires et relations* (Amsterdam: Zacharie Chatelain; The Hague: Pieter de Hondt, 1739), 63–4.

9 Ibid., 65. The fact that Hop was received on a Friday, rather than a Tuesday, the day normally reserved for the reception of foreign ambassadors, was considered a special mark of distinction. See also Hop's report of November 11, 1718. NA 1.10.97, 1282, 64.
10 Report of November 14, 1718. NA 1.10.97, 1282, 64.
11 Now in the collection of the Museu Nacional dos Coches, Lisbon (V0007). See also the report of July 10, 1722, from Otto Bosch, Hop's deputy, addressed to François Fagel regarding the carriages ordered for the public entry of the Venetian Ambassadors. Bosch noted that "everyone is hard at work here preparing the equipages of the Venetian ambassadors and, among other things, six exquisite carriages are being made for their formal entry." NA 1.01.02, 11295, Incoming letters, 1722.
12 *Europische Mercurius* (July 1719), 10.
13 Abbé Dubois sent Hop on March 10, 1719, a detailed description of the ceremony of both the public entry into Paris and the public audience of Lorenzo Tiepolo, ambassador of the Venetian Republic which took place on November 16 and 18, 1704, respectively. NA1.01.02, Staten Generaal, 6798. See also Hop's report of March 17, 1719. NA 1.10.97, 1282, 64.
14 Reports of July 14 and 17, 1719. NA 1.10.97, 1282, 64.
15 *Europische Mercurius* (July 1719), 9–11. For Hop's description see report of July 28, 1719. NA 1.10.97, 1282, 64. See also Daniëlle Kisluk-Grosheide and Bertrand Rondot, eds, *Visitors to Versailles. From Louis XIV to the French Revolution*, exh. cat., The Metropolitan Museum of Art, New York (New York: The Metropolitan Museum of Art, 2018), 146–7, cat. no. 52.
16 In his report of October 8, 1719, Hop included his declaration, noting especially the cost of the horses needed for his ceremonial entry and audience. NA 1.10.97, 1282, 64.
17 Undated memo. NA 1.10.110 (ambassadors), 1287.
18 Report of July 14, 1719. NA 1.10.97, 1282, 64.
19 See Kisluk-Grosheide and Rondot, *Visitors to Versailles*, 2018, 146–7, cat. no. 53.
20 Hop noted in his report that neither the French nor the Swiss Guards carried their standards nor that the Cent Suisses wore their gala uniforms as was customary for a public audience which he pointed out to the introducteur. Report of July 28, 1719. NA 1.10.97, 1282, 64.
21 See the report of August 27, 1723, envoy Count Conrad von Dehn wrote to the duke of Braunschweig Wolfenbüttel about his public audience at Versailles. Niedersächsisches Landesarchiv, Staatsarchiv Wolfenbüttel, 2 Alt no. 3642, fols. 47r–v.
22 Christiane Aulanier, *Histoire du Palais et du Musée du Louvre*, vol. 5, *La petite galerie: Appartement d'Anne d'Autriche; salles romaines* (Paris: Musées Nationaux, 1955), 45–7.

23 For the complete text of Hop's credentials, see NA 1.01.02, 12006, letter from the States General addressed Au Roy très Chrestien, September 15, 1718. The letters of introduction intended for the Regent and other members of the Royal Family were all slightly different.
24 "Monsieur, Vous assurerez les Etats Generaux que je suis toujours bien intentioné à leur donner des marques certains de ma bien viellance, et que je chercherai touttes les occasions à repondre à leur attente, que leur amitié m'est toujours très chère, j'en donne des marques certaines par les nouv[e]aux honneurs que je vous ay fait rendre aujourd'huy. Votre personne Monsieur m'est très agreable et en tout où je pourrai vous temoigner la satisfaction que j'ay de vous voir je le feray avec plaisir." Report of July 28, 1719. NA 1.10.97, 1282, 64.
25 A copy of this etching is also in the Collection of the Rijksmuseum. Available online: http://hdl.handle.net/10934/RM0001.COLLECT.477165
26 Report of July 28, 1719. NA 1.10.97, 1282, 64.
27 Ibid. Report of February 9, 1720.
28 Ibid. Reports of April 8 and May 10, 1720.
29 Ibid. Reports of November 18 and 22, 1720.
30 Ibid. Report of April 7, 1721.
31 Ibid. Report of September 15, 1719.
32 Report of April 10, 1722. NA 1.10.97, 1282, 65.
33 Ibid. Reports of April 13 and 20, and May 4, 1722.
34 Ibid. Reports of April 13 and May 4, 1722.
35 Ibid. Report of July 3, 1722.
36 Ibid. Report of May 22, 1722.
37 Ibid. Reports of May 25, June 8 and 15, 1722.
38 Ibid. Reports of June 19 and 22, 1722.
39 Ibid. Report of July 31, 1722.
40 Ibid. Report of May 26, 1724.
41 Ibid. The only festivity consisted of music played during the king's meal. Report of February 18, 1724.
42 Ibid. Report of December 3, 1723.
43 Ibid. See Reports of December 18 and 25, 1722, for information about Hop's condolence visit to the king and the regent following the death of the duchess of Orléans.
44 Ibid. Marie Jeanne-Baptiste of Savoy-Nemours (1644–1724), Louis XV's great-grandmother on his mother's side, was known as Madame Royale. Report of March 31, 1724.
45 Ibid. Reports of March 31, April 7 and 14, 1724. See also reports of March 31, April 7 and 14, 1724. NA 1.01.02, 11301, Incoming letters, 1724. See Jean-Baptiste

Bonnart's engraving of "Homme en grand deuil," illustrated in Gérard Sabatier and Béatrix Saule, eds, *Le roi est mort—Louis XIV-1715*, exh. cat. Château de Versailles (Paris: Éditions Tallandier, 2015), 217, fig. 139.

46 Report of May 13, 1720. NA 1.10.97, 1282, 64.
47 See the report of April 8, 1724. NA 1.10.97, 1282, 65.
48 Report of December 12, 1721. NA 1.10.97, 1282, 64.
49 Ibid. Report of December 22, 1721.
50 Report of December 24, 1723. NA 1.10.97, 1282, 65.
51 Ibid. Reports of June 23, July 7, 14, and 31, August 4 and 7, 1724.
52 Ibid. The king left for Fontainebleau on August 23, 1724, and remained there until early December. According to Hop the king had no other amusement than to go hunting on a daily basis for which Fontainebleau was better situated than Versailles. This was also the reason that the king had taken a dislike to Versailles and why he tried to prolong his stay at Fontainebleau as long as possible despite the fact that the provisions were running out. Report of November 23, 1724. See also those of August 11, 18, 21, September 21, November 26, and December 1, 1724.
53 Ibid. Report of August 21, 1724.
54 Ibid. Report of June 16, 1724, and January 19, 1725.
55 *Lettre du Roy, écrite à Monseigneur le Cardinal de Noailles Archevêque de Paris pour faire chanter le Te Deum dans l'Église de Nostre-Dame, en action de graces de la cessation de la contagion dans le Royaume* (Paris: chez Jean-Baptiste Delespine, 1723). NA 1.01.02, 6802. This was received in The Hague on October 7, 1723.
56 See, for instance, the detailed description of the regent's death in the report of December 6, 1723. NA 1.10.97, 1282, 65.
57 Ibid. Reports of February 9 and 12, 1723.
58 Ibid. Report of October 19, 1724.
59 Ibid. Report of February 23, 1725.
60 Reports of October 6, and November 24, 1719. NA 1.10.97, 1282, 64.
61 See, for instance, reports of December 31, 1723, and January 3, 1724. NA 1.10.97, 1282, 65.
62 Ibid. Report of September 28, 1722.
63 Ibid. Report of September 30, 1722. In his report of October 9, 1722, Hop has received the permission from the States General to travel to Rheims. In order to arrive on time and be prepared for the ceremony the diplomat had people working day and night on his equipage. The *introducteur* has invited Hop to the *fête royale* on the day of the coronation but it had been decided that as a Protestant he could not attend the coronation in the cathedral in Rheims in his official role but rather incognito. A full report of the coronation followed on October 26, 1722.

64 The medal, valued at circa two Louis d'Or, was given to him by the bishop of Fréjus on behalf of the king. Report of May 28, 1723. NA 1.10.97, 1282, 65. The States General allowed Hop to accept this medal on June 1, 1723. See NA 1.01.02, 12011, Outgoing letters, 1723.
65 Report of November 9, 1722. NA 1.10.97, 1282, 65.
66 Ibid. Report of December 6, 1723.
67 Ibid. Report of January 3, 1724.
68 Ibid. Report of April 8, 1724.
69 Ibid. It was addressed to Isaäc van Hoornbeek (1655-1727), as grand pensionary, the most important official of the Republic and dated April 8, 1724.
70 In 1724 the council consisted of the king himself, the duke of Orléans, the duke of Bourbon, the marshal of Villars, the bishop of Fréjus and the count of Morville.
71 Report of March 14, 1725. NA 1.10.97, 1282, 65.
72 Ibid. Reports of April 2 and 6, 1725.
73 Ibid. Hop first mentioned her name in a report of April 13, 1725.
74 Ibid. Princess Amelia Sophia Eleanor, a daughter of the future George II of England, had been mentioned as a possible candidate, despite the fact that she was not Roman Catholic. Reports of March 14 and 30, 1725.
75 Ibid. Report of September 16, 1725.
76 Ibid. Report of September 20, 1725.
77 Report of July 19, 1720. NA 1.10.97, 1282, 64.
78 See, for instance, a resolution addressed to Hop by the States General of May 29, 1724, regarding the merchant Pieter Daniel de la Motte to prevent his goods from being confiscated in Bordeaux. NA 1.01.02, 12012.
79 Reports of June 28 and July 1, 1720. NA 1.10.97, 1282, 64.
80 Ibid. See, for instance, the reports of August 26, 1720, July 4 and 7, 1721, and October 6, 1721.
81 Ibid. See reports of June 9 and 16, 1719, April 29, 1720, and of June 13, 1721. Hop dealt with the issue alone since the houses of the British and Swedish ambassadors were not situated along the route of the procession.
82 Hop requested to be recalled on September 7, 1725. See the letter of the States General addressed to the French king of September 11, 1725. NA 1.01.02, 12013, Outgoing letters, 1725.
83 Report of November 3, 1725. NA 1.10.97, 1282, 65.
84 Hop received the medals in 1725, and the snuffbox, valued at 7,209 livres, in 1726. Both gifts are listed in Présents du Roy, 61, vol. 2097, Sur les présents faits de la part du Roi Louis XV dans les Département des Affaires étrangères de 1715 en 1752, fol. 109. A microfilm of this document is in the Wallace Collection, London. See also an undated report. NA 1.10.97, 1282, 57. For the snuffbox see Serge Grandjean,

"Une tabatière royale de Gouers," *La revue du Louvre et des musées de France*, 29, no. 4 (1979), 294–7, figs. 1–3. See also Kisluk-Grosheide and Rondot, *Visitors to Versailles*, 2018, 147, 326, cat. no. 55.

85 Hop gave a consignment of 857 livres to a silversmith so that the *introducteur* could have something made of his choice, as well as half that amount to the secretary of the *introducteurs*. NA 1.10.97, 1282, 65.

86 Blok and Molhuysen, column 602, entry by C.H.Th. Bussemaker about Cornelis Hop.

Part Four

Versailles Now

13

Melancholy, Nostalgia, Dreams: Adventures in the *Grand Cimetière Magique*

Mark Ledbury

One of the more perplexing and enduring fictions of Versailles "after Versailles" in the English-speaking world is Eleanor Jourdain and Charlotte Anne Moberly's *An Adventure*, the story of a bizarre historical time-slip and subsequent fleeting encounter between two Edwardian ladies and the entourage of Marie-Antoinette and various characters populating the Trianons on the fateful October day in 1789 when Versailles ceased to be the home of the Monarchy and seat of power.[1] The tale has had significant fall-out in culture, producing a vast variety of paratexts, inspiring many dramatizations, perhaps most notably the 1991 opera, "Ghosts of Versailles" by John Corigliano and William Hoffman, but also including a BBC Radio production, and a TV drama, "Miss Morison's Ghosts," in 1981 (my first introduction to the story). The queer, melancholy encounter at the heart of *An Adventure*, is, I would argue, a brilliantly illuminating historical fantasy and the direct forbear of a swathe of diverse late-twentieth-century revisitings of the last days of Versailles as a living entity, from the extraordinarily successful Japanese manga, *Rose of Versailles*, historian and novelist Chantal Thomas's informed and acclaimed book *Les Adieux à La Reine* to the revealing confection of Sophia Coppola's *Marie-Antoinette*.[2] It is also, more surprisingly, an influence on museological decision-making at the site, specifically, I will argue, on the choice and the presentation of contemporary art which has had temporary, high-profile outings at Versailles over the last ten years.

    An Adventure itself has a complex publishing history, first published in 1911, and then reprinted with its fullest documentation in 1913, before further and "complete" editions emerged which actually curtailed the 1913 text.[3] If read at all, these days, it is regarded as an oddity, but has a certain emblematic value to all those seeking to explore what we might call the afterlives of Versailles and the current resonance of the site. *An Adventure* has been endlessly fact-checked, railed against, and ridiculed—and the whole affair given a thoughtful historical and cultural analysis in essays by Terry Castle and a recent book by Mark Lamont.[4] My questions though, as this volume seeks to understand Versailles then and now, will be more specifically concerned with the reasons why these two highly educated women (one of whom, Eleanor Jourdain, wrote extensively and in a scholarly manner on the French drama and other topics),[5] and indeed visitors to Versailles in general, were visiting Versailles in the first place, a century after the *Domaine* ceased to be the home of French power? What was Versailles in the historical imagination of the turn of the twentieth century, and, I want further to ask, what is it at the beginning of the twenty first? The Debunkers of Moberly and Jourdain's tale insisted the women's encounter could be explained in some ways by the encounter with a costume party or masquerade (specifically, the homosocial costume parties of the aristocrat, Henri de Montesquiou).[6] I would argue that, in fact, the book is itself such a masquerade; or, rather, that Jourdain and Moberly tapped in to a desire to *live* Versailles, rather than visit it, to experience the site through association and dream, rather than through museological or historical display. This desire, I argue, animates in specific ways the contemporary art program that has brought visitors and controversy to the *Domaine* in recent years.

The Château and the Museum: Nineteenth-Century Versailles and Its Discontents

What was Versailles, when Eleanor Jourdain and Charlotte Anne Moberly visited it in 1901 and 1902? This isn't as daft a question as it might sound. The physical structures and overall cartography of the site were indeed recognizable both to the ancien régime and to the twenty-first century, but as far as what the "stuff" of Versailles was, this is a different matter. Most visitors to the Versailles complex in the earlier nineteenth century, certainly after the 1830s, when it became "visitable," came to see a museum. Specifically, they experienced the elaborate, complex, and very visual museum of French history that was established by Louis-Philippe. It is salutary reading to take in hand a guidebook from the 1830s, written by historian, critic, and journalist Jules Janin, who sets out to describe:

The masterpiece of king Louis-Philippe I, at once so royal and so popular. No sooner had the doors of the new Versailles opened, then suddenly all France rushed within these noble walls, where was rediscovered, God knows with such passionate enthusiasm, all the glories, all the victories, all the great men of peace and war![7]

Janin's evocation of wild popular enthusiasm for Versailles turns on its head the trope of the Parisian mob invading Versailles, and makes the inrushing crowd an adoring and enthused one. Despite this perhaps sycophantic hyperbole, no one could be in any doubt that the Versailles of 1837 was the Versailles of Louis Philippe's particular vision, a museum of visual history of France.

Despite its preamble describing the approaches to the domain and the Château's exterior, the heart of Janin's guide, as of most guidebooks of that era, is an itinerary that takes the visitor through the rooms dedicated to French history. These are processions of painted evocations of kings and Royal moments, battles and treaties, coronations and events from Clovis onward, mostly rendered by (in many cases now obscure) nineteenth-century painters. Ordered, dynastic, certainly, but stretching both back before the creation of Versailles and beyond to the heroic years of the Revolutionary wars, as well as the Empire, this was a museum whose bounds were far more capacious than the 150-odd years of the Château as lived experience from Louis XIII to Louis XVI. The rooms were museologically displayed, chronologically coherent and entirely the product of the then contemporary historical imagination. Legions of contemporary artists contributed to the creation of Louis Philippe's museum, though these contemporary artists were to an extent subordinate to their subjects – the events and personalities that made a nation. The new incarnation of Versailles both depended on and occulted the life and material reality of the ancien-régime *Domaine*. The Museum was, in a sense, the museological parasite thriving on the skeleton of the site.

This Orleanist moment of 1837 might represent the high point of a *juste milieu*, popular-nationalist vision of Versailles, tamed and ordered as a museum, serving popular and elite purposes, dedicated to a vision of France much larger than that of the Bourbon dynasty that had built and inhabited it. Remarkably, though, this ideologically freighted vision of a grand France, built on the achievements of successive French monarchs from Clovis, and reimagined by Louis-Philippe, survived and trumped the complex political history of Versailles as a living entity, even after the end of the Orleanist Monarchy in 1848. This turbulent lived history of the site most notably included the events of the Franco-Prussian War and Commune, which saw among other events the takeover of the Château by Prussian forces in 1870, the national humiliation of the Treaty of Versailles of 1871 and the crowning of the German Kaiser Wilhelm I in January 1871, followed by the disastrous course of events leading to the fratricidal civic violence that placed Paris and Versailles once again at political odds as rival factions and sections of government and parliament moved to Versailles and back.

In 1872, with France barely beginning to recover from the traumas of the previous two years, the savvy (and brave) European visitor armed with the first edition of Baedeker's *Guide to Paris and Its Environs* was thus advised about Versailles:

> Notwithstanding its population of 30,000 inhabitants, its extensive Palace, erected in 1660—1710 by Mansard, its gardens, villas, etc., Versailles has little to attract the stranger beyond the incomparable **Musee Historique, founded by Louis Philippe, and occupying an almost interminable suite of apartments in the palace. In 1832 these rooms were entirely refitted, and adorned with historical pictures brought from the Louvre and other palaces, the deficiencies being supplied by works of the most eminent living artists [...] The gallery of Versailles may be regarded as a collection of modern pictures and sculptures. The historical object, however, was always predominant, to serve which, numerous works were received often without regard to their merits as works of art. The critical eye, therefore, will not fail to detect very inferior productions intermingled with the efforts of transcendent genius.[8]

It is strange to note both the extraordinary brevity of the evocation of the *Domaine* itself, its gardens and its buildings, and the imprecision and dismissiveness of its author, Delafontaine's, tone. However, what is most notable here is the recommendation to visitors, even at this point in French history, to take in a "modern art gallery," the intact Orleanist vision of a museum of French history, told primarily through encounters with visual art.

Of course, while the first Baedeker guides to Paris were ushering in a new era of caustic tourist-focused guidebooks, a simultaneous wave of new historical and art-historical erudition also began to bloom in the last decades of the nineteenth century in France. The first person who might be considered the chief curator of Versailles as a whole, Eudore Soulié, published first a guide and then an extensive three-part catalogue of the then museum under the Second Empire.[9] He also attempted to shield the Château and grounds from the successive impositions of the Prussians and the French government, and his life's work was summarized and saluted in a publication prepared after his death and rewritten by Louis Dussieux in 1885, and which used a rich series of citations from the copious "Maison du Roi" series in the National Archives to try to counter the misapprehensions and gaps in understanding of Versailles as a living entity in the ancien régime.[10]

However, even the weight of this historical investigation of Versailles as lived experience in the ancien régime did not displace the dominant museological vision of Versailles: As late as 1896, Chief Curator of Versailles Pierre de Nolhac, who perhaps did more than anyone before William Newton to reconstruct the life of the Château, archivally, wrote a guidebook to Versailles which emphasized and celebrated Versailles the museum of French history. He achieved this even while nuancing and expanding this museological vision in a connoisseurial manner (and often dismissing the researches of his forebears, including Soulié). Nolhac claimed that the Château could be viewed as a historical survey of French fine and decorative art:

> Despite the many destructions and restorations which have disfigured the Château, the works of marble, wood, and bronze still remain there in sufficiently large number to constitute, by virtue of securely dated and excellent examples a complete history of decoration in France at the time of its greatest flourishing.[11]

Despite the fact that Nolhac introduced a new emphasis on an aesthetic history, attempting to raise the quality of furniture and paintings displayed in the *Domaine*, and to create a design history of what he considered the glorious moment in French culture, his guide still gives the majority of its space to the collections of the Museum as understood by the public in the nineteenth century, and defined by Nolhac thus:

> The Museum of Versailles is a museum of national history unique in Europe for its character and its scope. The inscription placed on the face of the modern pavilions of the great Court, "to all the glories of France," will give perhaps an incomplete idea of the collections that the Château contains: in fact, aside from the commemoration of the deeds of the truly glorious men of the country, we have sought to bring together the greatest possible number of monuments of art that report the nation's past from many sides. In some parts, Versailles is a great school of popular patriotism; in others, it is for the curious visitor? a lively evocation of past reigns and an incomparable source of information for the historian.[12]

Nolhac, here, emphasizes once again what Janin's had seen in 1837 as a double role for Versailles as both a patriotic project and a connoisseurial one, a popular and an elite space, a public and a historian's domain. Neither man doubted that Versailles could and should be *read*, and constituted a historical document, a history of a nation's taste, government, and culture. This was of course a heavy burden for any site to bear.

The Melancholy Versailles

But neither the patient archival work of Soulié and his successors, nor the expert historical eye and poetic pen of Nolhac were enough, it seems, to reanimate Versailles for the particular historical sensibilities of the *fin de siècle*. Visitors seemed unable either to accept the populist or the connoisseurial challenge; enthusiasm for the grand museum of French glories waned, and visitors seemed to focus not on the founding fame but the melancholy end of Versailles; not the grand moments of its foundation and the business of its running, or indeed the splendours of its heyday as taste-setter to the world in the arts, but rather the moment of its crumbling and violent submission. This imaginary had at its heart the Trianons, not the Château, Marie-Antoinette and not Louis XIV. This melancholy "end-of-days" Versailles as it was reconstructed and emphasized in wider culture at the turn of the twentieth century was a counterweight to the cold anachronistic splendor of Louis XIV's monument. Furthermore, it provided an antidote to the bombastic celebration of French national might that had characterized Louis-Philippe's and Louis-Napoléon's hubristic museological enterprise, now hollowed out by humiliations of the surrender to Prussia.[13]

And there was no better summing up of the Trianons' hold on the fin-de-siècle imagination than the eloquent words of a thoughtful, popularizing history of the French Revolution, published in English by Justin H McCarthy in 1890. His chapter entitled "Trianon" in the first volume opens:

> There are certain words which have the power to move all hearers with a profound degree of emotion, and to call up very vivid pictures in the minds of the Imaginative. Perhaps of all such spell-words, no one is better to conjure with than the word "Trianon." [...] That fairy palace, those gracious gardens, the chosen toy, the dearest trinket of the most beautiful and the most ill-starred of queens, arises more or less vaguely, like the shadow-palace of a dream, before the mental vision of the historically sentimental ... and the centre of all this the

enchanting Queen herself. Such is the phantasmagoric image which the word Trianon calls up to the large proportion of persons to whom history is always half romance.[14]

McCarthy's assertions, glib as they might seem, are borne out by a glance at the literature of the turn of the century. Gustave Geffroy, connoisseur and homme de lettres, wrote a guide to Versailles in the series "Les Musées Européens," in 1900, in which observes "the whole of Versailles is a grand museum, and it is also a grand, magical graveyard of the Bourbons ... The park is a splendid necropolis, lined with sombre trees, that lead one to believe that underneath all the pathways and outdoor rooms lie ranks of tombs." Geffroy's words, like Atget's famous photographs, emphasize not a splendid living museum of French glory but a mysterious, melancholy, spectral place.[15]

Even the most erudite of the insiders and connoisseurs seem to have made Versailles's story more closely enmeshed with that of Marie-Antoinette. Pierre de Nolhac's book, *Versailles au temps de Marie-Antoinette*, an explicitly "documentary" study of the distribution of the Apartments, takes its bookend dates not the change of reigns between monarchs, but from the arrival of the dauphine Marie-Antoinette. And even Nolhac finds a way of bringing the October 5/6, 1789, to mind, in the guise of debunking myths about the routes taken by the king and queen to reach each other on those days.[16] Nolhac's study, ostensibly based on inventories and lists, also cites extensively the memoirs of Hezecques, *Souvenirs d'un page de la cour de Louis XVI* a voice distinctly nostalgic and even pro-Marie-Antoinette.[17]

An Adventure: Ghosts, Dreams, and the Affective Versailles

So when Charlotte Anne Moberly and Eleanor Jourdain visited Versailles, they were, like many others, faced with the "interminable" rooms of the Louis-Philippe/Second Empire Museum, and the vastness of the those imposing, "embalmed" spaces of Louis XIV. They chose, specifically, to reject these in favor of the petit Trianon, initiating an act of escapism, a search for a more emotive, more personal experience, which they found in the Trianons, wandering round that *grand cimetière magique*, culturally as well as psychically primed for supernatural encounters with the doomed queen and her entourage.

Miss Morison and Miss Lamont, I would argue, are not synonyms used to disguise real identities, but characters in an elaborate fiction: One of the two,

Miss Morison, is the first voice of narration in *An Adventure* and her account of the August 1901 visit to Versailles begins thus:

> Both of us thought it might prove to be a dull expedition. We [...] walked through the rooms and galleries of the Palace with interest, though we constantly regretted our inability through ignorance to feel properly the charm of the place.[18]

This of course is a bizarrely bad-faith introduction, given at least Eleanor Jourdain's thorough knowledge of and engagement with ancien-regime culture, the level of the two women's education and their acute historical and biographical instincts. But the point of this introduction is to place the narrators in the position of those who only knew Versailles through school-age reading and historical novels. The rapidity and vapidity of their tour through the Château and museum is admirably conveyed in these short sentences. We should note though that this (feigned) lack of knowledge and thus interest makes clear that the museological experience as imagined by Louis-Philippe and subsequent curators had failed in its aims. It was not performing that "popular historical" function of the museum that had been intended. Sitting in the Hall of Mirrors, Miss Morison feels the "sweet air" blowing in through the open windows, and decides on a whim that they should visit the Trianons, about which she has, she claims, only the vaguest of schoolgirl knowledge.

Baedeker in hand (presumably the 13th edition of 1898, revised and now with more detailed descriptions of Versailles), the two women find themselves mysteriously lost on the path to the Petit Trianon. Having passed, but declined to visit, the *Grand Trianon*, they stray from the path and, as Miss Morison reports, "from the moment we left the lane an extraordinary depression had come over me, which, in spite of every effort to shake off, steadily deepened" (4). From here, the gloom and anxiety become predominant, the high point of which is the encounter with the "hideous" pock-marked face of the man that they later assume to have been the comte de Vaudreuil. While in the English garden in front of the Petit Trianon, Miss Morison then has the most significant encounter of her time there—the woman she describes sketching, in "old fashioned" dress, the woman she would later identify as Marie-Antoinette.

The encounter, as Miss Morison explicitly says, is dream-like, and unsettlingly so, but as the two women, confused and bemused, exit the cour d'honneur of the Petit Trianon and find themselves in a carriage, back for tea at a hotel and then onto the station to return to Paris. "Was Marie Antoinette really much at Trianon, and did she see it for the last time long before the fatal drive to Paris accompanied by the mob?" they pondered as the two friends returned to Paris by train.[19] The fascination with the fateful "endgame" of October 1789 makes its first, surprising eruption here—nothing so far, in the account, has placed the women's experiences at this historical moment—but again, we learn that this rich, strange affective experience seems for Miss Morison at least, to have the unfortunate queen as its trigger. Later, Miss Morison asks for Miss Lamont's version of events, and the women realize they had similar emotional and physical experiences of the day, and Miss Morison, in the narrative, then asks Miss Lamont to recount the day from her point of view.

Where Miss Morison had mentioned that she had read McCarthy's *French Revolution* before the encounter,[20] Miss Lamont claims she returned to London to teach the French Revolution,[21] and at that point realized that the two women's visit had taken place on August 10, which as she puts it, with suspect understatement, "had a special significance in French history." Adding up their experiences, the two women correspond and come up with a theory:

> We wondered whether we had inadvertently entered within an act of the Queen's memory when alive, and whether this explained our curious sensation of being completely shut in and oppressed. What more likely, we thought, than that during those hours in the Hall of the Assembly, or in the Conciergerie, she had gone back in such vivid memory to other Augusts spent at Trianon that some impress of it was imparted to the place?
>
> (23–4)

If we understand this tale as a fiction of Versailles, we are here present at a doubling or tripling of the mise-en-abyme. Firstly, as I want to insist, Miss Morison and Miss Lamont, conjured up by Moberly and Jourdain, are not simply pseudonyms, but characters, imagined beings of a sensitive, inquisitive but not connoisseurial disposition; these fictional women themselves conjure up a fitful and nostalgic cast of characters, principal among whom is Marie-Antoinette, who herself, in their imagining, is imprisoned and awaiting her fate in Paris and they wander in to her (Marie-Antoinette's) own nostalgic dream of Versailles. The women don't just see a vision of Marie-Antoinette, but they affectively associate with her fear, incarceration and melancholy, as well as her nostalgia. Indeed, one conclusion to come to from the fact that one of them (Miss Morison) saw Marie-Antoinette and one of them (standing right next to her) did not would be that Miss Lamont *became* for an instant Marie-Antoinette, and in that guise herself saw characters, messengers, familiars that were unseen by Miss Morison. Indeed, in the "responses to questions" in the 1913 edition, this is stated explicitly:

> There is an incoherence about both the large and small incidents which seems to require combination within a single mind, and the only mind to which they could all have been present would have been that of the Queen. Our theory of 1901, that *we had entered within the working of the Queen's memory when she was still alive*, is now enlarged. We think that the two first visits to Trianon (August 10th, 1901, and January 2nd, 1902) were part of one and the same experience; that quite mechanically we must have seen it as it appeared to her more than a hundred years ago, and have heard sounds familiar, and even something of words spoken, to her then.[22]

This affective experience is for them, the true and only heart of their visit to Versailles, it is riveting, and proved to be enduringly compelling for their readers, and in a sense this "heart" of the tale got lost in the endless fact-checking and debunking of their imaginative experience.

In the elaborate pages that follow the first narrative of in *An Adventure*, Miss Lamont returns to Versailles the following winter, January 2, 1902, encouraged by Miss Morison to check on locations and facts. She notices some strange differences, but it is only when she crosses the little bridge to the *Hameau*, "the old feeling returned in full force; it was as if I had crossed a line and was suddenly in a circle of influence" (27). She becomes lost and disoriented in the dense wood and maze of paths, and again encounters various male and female characters whose interactions with her are dream-like and oppressive:

> Then, meaning to go to the Belvedere, I turned back by mistake into the park and found myself in a wood, so thick that though I had turned towards the Hameau I could not see it.
>
> (28)

Her attempts to make sense of this latest set of encounters in conversation with her friends in Paris on her return result in the following discussion:

> A second tradition they mentioned interested me very much. It was that on October 5th, 1789—which was the last day on which Marie Antoinette went to Trianon—she was sitting there in her grotto, and saw a page running towards her, bringing the letter from the minister at the palace to say that the mob from Paris would be at the gates in an hour's time. The story went on that she impulsively proposed walking straight back to the palace by the short cut through the trees.
>
> (31)

Here, *An Adventure* returns its reader to by now familiar ground: the experience of the October 5/6, 1789, is once again a key—the absolute touchstone of the events of which Miss Lamont is trying to make sense—and in some sense it is the key (as it turns out) to the very complex explicatory framework that the women then concoct to situate themselves, archivally and historically, and prove that their experiences may have had a basis in historical reality.[23] This framework, however, acknowledges that their theory only holds if, indeed, Marie-Antoinette was at Trianon on the fateful October 5.

The "imagined" Versailles of Jourdain and Moberly, then, does not revolve around the rich lived experience of the "high moments" of the ancien-régime Château but focuses intensely on the Revolutionary end-point of Versailles, and the fantasies, terror, and melancholy it inspired. The Misses Morison and Lamont finally "become" Marie-Antoinette, identifying with the affective life of the queen in danger. This is a disconcerting, perplexing, out-of-body experience of Versailles, for sure, but one which leads to a fresh and personal visit, as the two ladies have drifted off the guidebook's path, away from the historical and connoisseurial frame of the main Château, to be touched and moved by the goings on beyond the grave in the *grand cimetière magique*.

Reading this strange tale "museologically" may seem itself bizarre. But the heart of *An Adventure* is the fantasy of a less connoisseurial and more direct, affective engagement with a site, whose overlapping, complex lived experiences are suddenly brought into simultaneous existence rather than organized in an exhausting, or impossible way as a suite of rooms or decorative styles or historical evocations of glory. Marie-Antoinette distills the follies, luxuries, appeal, and melancholy of the entire ancien régime, as well as the fundamental crux of modernity's narratives as reimagined by the fin-de-siècle: extravagance vs. virtue, the monarchy vs. the mob. We might speculate that *An Adventure's* recipe for the revival of Versailles borrows something from the very 1900 *Exposition Universelle* that is mentioned at the beginning of Miss Lamont's account. Versailles becomes a new kind of new tourist fantasy—not, as in 1900, a colonial theme park, but a lost continent of manners, mores, and costumes.

I want to argue that *An Adventure*, a tale of being distracted from an organized, museological experience and wandering into a different, very personal set of encounters, can illuminate our current understanding of museums and their desired effects in the postmodern, Biennale era, and specifically might help us understand Versailles's particular dilemmas and solutions today.

The Continuing "Adventure": Contemporary Art in Versailles

The larger and overtly political process of the twentieth-century conversion of Versailles from Louis-Philippe's museum to a new *Domaine* has been brilliantly outlined by Fabien Opperman, whose study focused on the refurnishing of the ancien-régime rooms via diplomacy and philanthropy.[24] Other historians, including Gérard Sabatier and Alexandre Gady, have charted the complex twentieth-century political history of the palace as a site, as part of a wider understanding of the history of modern France.[25] But what of the museological experience of the site now?

In looking for the legacies of *An Adventure*, it is instructive to explore the commissions of contemporary art that have, for ten years since 2008, marked the life of Versailles as museum. In particular, I will examine their attempts to "disrupt" or interrupt the sequence of Versailles's enfilades or gardens as an attempt to evoke both the uncanny, fantasy, and Trianon-focus, of *An Adventure*. Many of the artists commissioned to make work for Versailles, or invited to show retrospectives there, were surprisingly disruptive. At the very least they delighted in the juxtaposition of the spaces and geometries of the principal spaces of the Château with their own bizarre collections, which, with remarkable consistently, have evoked a fantasy Versailles where a spectator is invited to wander and dream.[26]

The irony is that these projects mostly invade and inhabit the Château (propre) while the Grand Trianon is now the centre of a more orthodox museology and the Petit Trianon has been preserved and renovated as a "pristine" quasi-authentic and self-sufficient object. However, often over the last ten years, contemporary artists have effectively "Trianonised" the main Château and gardens, stressing those aspects in culture—play, apparition, surprise, even falsity, performance—that were the dominant and attractive features of the Petit Trianon and its grounds not only for its original inhabitants, but in the imaginations Moberly and Jourdain and many subsequent visitors.

The curators of the first of the major contemporary exhibitions at Versailles, the Jeff Koons retrospective in 2008, defined their aim in this way:

> To (re) discover a site; to call upon the know-how of the estate's staff, in particular its gardeners; to have the thrill of working with a living artist, and enjoy all the resulting emotions, failures and surprises—and to give pleasure. ... to reveal a different Versailles, a Versailles of today, a living monument seen from the way people use it.[27]

With its menagerie, its farmyard, its flora and fauna transformed into shiny surface, as well as its deployment of great musico-dramatic talent in oddly monumental ways (think *Michael Jackson and Bubbles*), the Koons exhibition certainly celebrated play, sensuality, and the emotive present. It fully participated in both the ludic and the spectral aspects of *An Adventure* and its *Trianonization* of the main Château. Perhaps no work exemplified this more than *Split Rocker* (2000), described as "combining innocence and monstrousness" (Figure 13.1)— a surrogate indeed, for Marie-Antoinette herself, one is almost tempted to say— and at the very monumental transplantation of the spirit of both the child-like play of the Trianon garden and the notion of folly into Louis XIV's Orangery.

Perhaps Koons had already prepared the way, but the adventurous and humorous interventions in the palace by Murakami, much talked about in terms of commentary on the "Brand" of Versailles, and discussed in these terms by the catalogue essay, "Murakami's conquest of ubiquity."[28] Meredith Martin has explored the interesting conjunctions between Murakami's kitsch visions and the overt commercialism of Versailles's own culture in the ancien régime in a suggestive review of the controversies surrounding this particular exhibition in Artforum.[29] However, we might take our cue from the artist and

Figure 13.1 Photograph of the Installation of Jeff Koons, *Split Rocker*, in Versailles: Photo: Jean Marc Fondeur, Flickr, Creative Commons License CC-BY-SA.

see the intervention as part of the "unreal" turn initiated by *An Adventure*: As Murakami himself said:

> In many respects, everything is transmitted to us as a fantastic tale coming from a very distant kingdom. Just as French people can find it hard to recreate in their minds an accurate image of the Samurai period, the history of this palace has become diminished for us in reality.
>
> So it is probable that the Versailles of my imagination corresponds to an exaggeration and a transformation in my mind so that it has become a kind of completely separate and unreal world. That is what I have tried to depict in this exhibition.
>
> ....
>
> With a broad smile I invite you all to discover the wonderland of Versailles.[30]

It is the emphasis on the mis-remembered, fairy-tale Versailles, the drift from a "diminished" sense of history into a fantasy, a wonderland of strange encounters, that interests me here. It implies that the artist, the show's curators and even the curatorial team at Versailles were aware of a desire for an "out of body" experience of Versailles. Here, we sense the impact not just of *The Rose of Versailles* but of a raft of brilliant deployments of anachronism, among which I would include Sophia Coppola's *Marie Antoinette* (2006). The hazy, irreal sunrise scenes, confusions, party scenes, in that film with their eerie mixture of luxury and foreboding, echo precisely that strange and unreal mixture of freedom and doom that pervades *An Adventure*. Coppola's canny tapping into the consumerism and excess of the late ancien régime are also evoked and explored by Murakami. Enlisting Murakami, for Nolhac's successors at Versailles, was an exercise in making strange that collided the popular and the connoisseurial, but in ways not dreamt of by Nolhac. Murakami's *Superflat Flowers* in the salon de la Paix, or his *Flower Matango* (Figure 13.2) in the galerie des Glaces, makes plastic that sense of sweet air and the presence of the gardens that "invaded" the galerie on Ms Morison and Ms Lamont's visit, and triggered their wandering adventures. No-one sensitive to the importance of flowers to Marie-Antoinette and her entourage would have escaped noticing that explosive profusion of *Flower Matango* also brought a vestige, a trace of the extravagant passion for flora of the queen into the most public, dazzling, and Louis-quatorziènne of the Château's official spaces.

Such an echo of *An Adventure* — an airy, Marie-Antoinette fantasy of Versailles, creating an interruption, if not a transformation, of the museological

Figure 13.2 Installation photograph of the Versailles exhibition of Takahashi Murakami, *Flower Matango, 2001–6*, fiberglass, iron, oil, and acrylic paint, 315 × 204.7 × 263 cm. Photo: Dimitry B/Flickr, Creative Commons License CC-BY-SA.

spaces of the Château — was also on the mind of Juana Vasconcelos, whose artist's statement on her 2012 exhibition at Versailles explicitly conjures this up:

> When I walk through the salons of the Château and its Gardens, I sense the energy of a space with revolves between reality and dream, the quotidian and the magical, the festive and the tragic. I still hear the echo of Marie-Antoinette's footsteps, the music and the festive ambiance of the salons. How would life be at Versailles if this exuberant and grandiose universe was transferred to our own time?[31]

From Mary Poppins to Marilyn Monroe and Amalia Rodrigues, Vasconcelos introduces powerful fantasy surrogates for the young dauphine and doomed queen, as well as reminiscences of her predecessor Queen Marie Leszczinska, throughout the exhibition. She insistently (and controversially) brings a set of emotional and reproductive "issues of the feminine" to the fore in both a monumental and a provocative way. *Marilyn* (2011) (Figure 13.3) was described as a "un ode aux conquêtes de la femme dans les domaines public et privé." [an ode

Figure 13.3 Joana Vasconcelos, *Marilyn (PA)*, 2011. Pans and lids made of stainless steel, cement (2×) 290 × 157 × 410 cm. Collection of the artist; Courtesy Nathalie Obadia Gallery, Paris/Brussels and Haunch of Venison, London Work produced with the support of Silampos. Photo: Ben Harvey, Creative Commons License CC-BY-SA.

to the conquest of woman in both the private and public domains.] Her surreal and elegant ceramics *Le Dauphin et la Dauphine* (2011) for the Chambre du grand couvert continue a dialogue of consumption and desire that pitch audiences firmly into the late ancien-régime world even as they evoke surrealism.

Even the heroic and seemingly hyper-masculine modernist traditions of hard steel and minimalism that informed Anish Kapoor's work in his installation at Versailles hinted at the "Trianonisation" of the main gardens. The installation, *Dirty Corner* (Figure 13.4) that became infamous for its graffiti and its nickname, "The Queen's vagina," is a case in point.[32] What was this strange earthwork except a kind of chronological and geographical transplantation of the artificial hills and follies of the gardens of the Petit Trianon? Even the extraordinary cost and manpower involved in creating it might remind us of the successions of works carried out by Mique and his equipe to create the landscapes of the Trianon gardens.[33] Was it its association with the queen that made it the center

Figure 13.4 Anish Kapoor, *Dirty Corner*, steel, stone, and concrete, 2015, installation in the park of the Château of Versailles. With graffiti erased. Photo Fred Romero/Flickr, Creative Commons License CC-BY-SA.

of attention, entirely overshadowing other, thoughtful, impressive works by Kapoor in the same installation/exhibition?[34]

In the attacks on the work the ultra-right wing and anti-Semitic royalist graffiti revealed itself to be bizarrely if not entirely unsurprisingly fixated on the end of Versailles and Marie-Antoinette's fate. "La Reine sacrifiée, 2 fois outragée" [The sacrificed queen, twice outraged] ran one of the scrawls. Of course, all this is very far from the mysterious adventures of Ms Morison and Ms Lamont, but along with much else in the ten-year history of contemporary art at Versailles, Kapoor's installation was haunted by the destiny of Marie-Antoinette.

Olafur Eliasson's 2016 installations conceived of Versailles as an unreal space, a place of "drift from grandeur." And Eliasson's *Fog Assembly* (Figure 13.5) and even "Deep Mirrors" contrived to dissolve into uncertainty the grand certainties of the palace, and create a sense of reverie, even disorientation, that are the absolute hallmarks of *An Adventure*. His description of the ideal spectator seems to have Miss Morison and Miss Lamont as the ideal model:

> *The Versailles that I have been dreaming up* is a place that empowers everyone. It invites visitors to take control of the authorship of their experience instead of simply consuming and being dazzled by the grandeur. It asks them to exercise

Figure 13.5 Olafur Eliasson, *Fog Assembly*, 2016, View of the installation in the Domaine de Versailles, 2016. Photo: Fred Romero/Flickr, Creative Commons License CC-BY-SA.

their senses, to embrace the unexpected, to drift through the gardens, and to feel the landscape take shape through their movement.³⁵

(my emphasis)

What are we to make of the striking conjunction between the early-twentieth-century fabrication of Jourdain and Moberly and the persistent aim of so many leading contemporary artists today? We might argue that for reasons rooted in contemporary culture and its discontents, a swathe of artists have been seduced or induced into self-definition as Marie-Antoinette, as surely as Miss Morison and Miss Lamont were a century earlier, craving the freedoms and the sweet air, wishing to disrupt the overwhelming museological enfilade with perceptual play, hoping, perhaps, to turn Versailles into the Petit Trianon. And it may well be true that Versailles plays better today as empowering fantasy space than as overpowering museological one.

I might even argue that the specific choices of many contemporary artists this century, and indeed the project of contemporary art at the site, continue Marie-Antoinette's long and posthumous revenge both on the ancien-régime restrictions of the Château and the revolutionary throng that compelled her departure in October 1789, and that these temporary exhibitions of contemporary artists are moments of a haunting of the Château. Of course this conclusion might provoke many political questions—Is Versailles as a site now so hopelessly devoted to a kind of nostalgic fantasy of monarchy as luxury brand that it, too, has abandoned its mission to convey the complexity of the ancien regime's complex system of government and the continuing political story of Versailles in the nineteenth, twentieth, and twenty-first centuries? What is the purpose of the site as museological domain? Can Versailles, should Versailles, continue to tell meaningful stories of French history, as Louis Philippe hoped it might, or has it finally come to resemble the melancholic dream space of *An Adventure*?

Notes

1   First Published: Anon., [C. A. E Moberly and Eleanor F Jourdain], *An Adventure* (London: Macmillan, 1911); The most recent edition is C. A. E. Moberly, Eleanor F. Jourdain and Michael H. Coleman, *The Ghosts of the Trianon: The Complete An Adventure* (Wellingborough, Northamptonshire, England; New York: Aquarian Press; Distributed in the United States by Sterling, 1988).

2   Riyoko Ikeda, *The Rose of Versailles* (First published, 1976, English version, Tokyo: Sanyusha, 1981); Chantal Thomas, *Les Adieux à La Reine: Roman* (Paris: Points, 2011); Benoit Jacquot et al. "Les Adieux à La Reine: Un Film de Benoit Jacquot" : Dossier : Scénario Intégral de Benoit Jacquot et Gilles Taurand, *L'avant scène. Cinéma*, 601, mars 2013; Ian Curteis and John Bruce, *Miss Morison's Ghosts*, London: ITV, 1981; The BBC adapted Curteis's drama for Radio in 2004 and revived it in 2016; John Corigliano and William M Hoffman, *The Ghosts of Versailles: A Grand Opera Buffa in Two Acts* (New York and Milwaukee, WI: G. Schirmer; Distributed by Hal Leonard, 1991).

3   A series of editions and studies of the text propelled interest through the first five decades of the century. After the first editions and reprints of 1911, an expanded edition with appendices and maps followed in 1913; C. A. E. (Charlotte Anne Elizabeth) Moberly and Eleanor F. (Eleanor Frances) Jourdain, *An Adventure, with Appendix and Maps* (London: Macmillan, 1913); there were editions in every decade, notably *An Adventure*, 4th ed., with further additional matter (London: Faber & Faber Limited, 1931); *An Adventure; with a Preface by Edith Oliver and a Note by J.W. Dunne* (London: Faber, 1951). Skeptical and explicatory studies included J. R. Sturge-Whiting, *The Mystery of Versailles: A Complete Solution* (London: Rider & Co, 1937); A. O. Gibbons, ed., *The Trianon Adventure: A Symposium* (London: Museum Press, 1958); Lucille Iremonger, *The Ghosts of Versailles: Miss Moberly and Miss Jourdain and Their Adventure: A Critical Study* (London: White Lion Publishers, 1975).

4   Terry Castle, "Contagious Folly: 'An Adventure' and Its Skeptics," *Critical Inquiry* 17, no. 4 (July 1991): 741–72; "Contagious Folly: *An Adventure* and Its Skeptics," in *Questions of Evidence: Proof, Practice, and Persuasion across the Disciplines*, ed. James Chandler, Arnold Davidson, and Harry Harootunian (Chicago, IL: University of Chicago Press, 1994), 11–42. See also her development of this analysis in "Marie-Antoinette Obsession," in *Marie Antoinette: Writings on the Body of a Queen*, ed. Dena Goodman and Thomas E. Kaiser (New York: Routledge, 2013), 199–238. See also Mark Lamont, *The Mysterious Paths of Versailles: An Investigation of a Psychical Journey Back in Time* (Bloomington, Indiana: Xlibris Corp, 2016).

5   Eleanor Frances Jourdain, *An Introduction to the French Classical Drama* (Oxford: Clarendon Press, 1912); Eleanor Frances Jourdain, *The Drama in Europe in Theory and Practice* (London, 1924). Charlotte Ann Moberly was also an author and intellectual, author of a biography of her Father, the distinguished cleric and Headmaster of Winchester School, George Moberly. Both Moberly and Jourdain were pioneers of women's education at St Hugh's College in Oxford. See Penny Griffin, ed., *St Hugh's: One Hundred Years of Women's Education in Oxford* (Oxford: Palgrave Macmillan, 1986).

6   The specific association with Henri de Montesquiou was made by Philippe Jullian, in Philippe Jullian, *Robert de Montesquiou, Un Prince 1900. [With Plates, Including Portraits, Illustrations and a Bibliography]* (Paris: Perrin, 1965).

7   Jules Janin, *Versailles et Son Musée Historique, Ou Description Complète et Anecdotique de La Ville, Du Palais, Du Musée, Du Parc et Des Deux Trianons: Précédé d'un Itinéraire de Paris à Versailles, et Orné de Plans et de Vues Gravées Sur Bois/[Par Jules Janin]* (Paris: E Bourdin et Cie, 1837), "introduction," np.

8   Karl Baedeker (Firm), *Paris and Northern France: Handbook for Travellers* (Coblenz: K. Baedeker, 1872), 182. The Author of this book is given as A. Delafontaine. See Edward Mendelson, "Baedeker's Universe," *Yale Review* 74 (Spring 1985): 386–403.

9   Eudore Soulié, *Notice Des Peintures et Sculptures Composant Le Musée Impérial de Versailles* (Versailles, 1854); *Notice Du Musée Impérial de Versailles*, 2nd edn. 3 vols. (Paris: C. de Mourgues Frères, 1859–61).

10 Louis Dussieux, *Le Château de Versailles: Histoire et Description*, 2nd edn. 2 vols. (Versailles: Bernard, 1885).

11 Pierre de Nolhac and André Pératé, *Le Musée National de Versailles, Description Du Château et Des Collections* (Paris: Braun, 1896), 9.

12 Nolhac and Pératé, 37.

13 There is of course an extensive bibliography on fin-de-siècle nostalgia for the ancien régime, with which *An Adventure* intersects, but in which it is not fully participant. See especially Eugen Weber, *Fin de siècle: la France à la fin du XIXe siècle*, Nouvelles études historiques (Paris: Fayard, 1986); Diane Fourny, "The Eighteenth Century or 'Fin-de-Siècle' Beginnings," *L'Esprit Créateur* 32, no. 4 (1992): 7–19.

14 Justin Huntly McCarthy, *The French Revolution* (London, Chatto, 1890), 1:168–9
15 Gustave Geffroy, *Les musées d'Europe: Versailles* (Paris : Eds. Nilsson, 1900), I–II
16 Pierre de Nolhac, *Le Château de Versailles Au Temps de Marie-Antoinette: 1770–1789* (Versailles: Aubert, 1889), 41.
17 Félix de France d'Hézecques, *Souvenirs d'un Page de La Cour de Louis XVI* (Paris: Didier et Cie, 1873) Available online: https://gallica.bnf.fr/ark:/12148/bpt6k49961n
18 C. A. E. Moberly and Eleanor F Jourdain, *An Adventure, with Appendix and Maps* (London, Macmillan, 1913), 3. This will be the edition from which all further citations are taken.
19 *An Adventure* (1913), 11.
20 *An Adventure*, 2.
21 *An Adventure*, appendix B2, 204: "Curiously enough, the next morning I had to give one of a set of lessons on the French Revolution for the Higher Certificate."
22 *An Adventure* (1913) 107–8. (my emphasis)
23 This is chronicled in the largest single chapter of the book, "Results of Research," 41–104.
24 Fabien Oppermann, "Le remeublement du Château de Versailles au XXe siècle, entre action scientifique et manoeuvres politiques," *Bibliothèque de l'École des chartes* 170, no. 1 (2012): 209–32.
25 Among many stimulating and informed discussions of Versailles's complex "reception history" one might cite Gérard Sabatier, "Versailles, un imaginaire politique," *Publications de l'École Française de Rome* 82, no. 1 (1985): 295–324; Alexandre Gady, *Versailles la fabrique d'un chef-d'oeuvre* (Paris; Versailles: Passage; Château de Versailles, 2014); and especially Pierre Arizzoli-Clémentel, Alexandre Gady, and Michel Baridon, eds, *Versailles* (Paris: Citadelles & Mazenod, 2009), with its rye and suggestive discussions of Versailles in the nineteenth and twentieth centuries, including expert studies by Thomas Gaehtgens and others. Especially fertile for my thinking is the discussion of Versailles between Gady, Aurélie Julia and Michel Crépu, "le Miroir de tous les phantasmes," *Revue Des Deux Mondes* (July 2013): 141–9.
26 In date order, at the time of writing this chapter, the exhibitions were the following: Jeff Koons, September 2008–January 2009; Vielhan, September–December 2009; Murakami, 2010; Venet, 2011; Joana Vasconcelos, 2012; Penone, 2013; Lee Ufan 2014; Anish Kapoor, 2015; Olafur Eliasson, 2016.
27 Xavier Barral, Elena Geuna, and Laurent Le Bon, eds, *Jeff Koons, Versailles* (Paris: Xavier Barral, 2008), 129.
28 See Jean-Jacques Aillagon, Fabrice Bousteau, and Takashi Murakami, *Murakami Versailles*, exhibition catalogue (Paris: Editions Xavier Barral, 2010), 160–1.

29 "Amassed Ornaments: Meredith Martin on Contemporary Art at Versailles." Available online: http://link.galegroup.com/apps/doc/A252292963/EAIM?sid=googlescholar (accessed September 14, 2018).
30 As cited from the review of the exhibition, "Murakami Versailles Exhibition," *Design Milk*, October 6, 2010. Available online: https://design-milk.com/murakami-versailles-exhibition/ (accessed September 14, 2018).
31 Juana Vasconcelos, "Introduction." Available online: http://www.vasconcelos-versailles.com/t_vasconcelos.php (accessed September 14, 2018).
32 For an interesting, if polemical, summary of the "Queen's Vagina" affair, see Thierry Lefebvre, "Pour Kapoor," *Sociétés & Représentations* 41 (June 2016): 203–11.
33 Ibid., 208.
34 For details of all the works installed, see Alfred Pacquement, ed., *Anish Kapoor Versailles* (Paris, Éditions RMN-Grand Palais, 2015).
35 "Olafur Eliasson | Versailles," *Olafur Eliasson | Versailles*. Available online: http://olafureliasson.net/versailles (accessed September 14, 2018).

14

American Versailles: From the Gilded Age to Generation Wealth

Robert Wellington

When Donald Trump was elected president in November 2016, people began to wonder what aspects of the signature Trump style he would bring to the White House, not least his famously flashy taste for interior decoration. Many were quick to compare the glittering décor of Trump's homes with the palace of the Sun King Louis XIV. Kate Wagner, creator of the popular satirical blog *McMansion Hell*, asked "Whose Style Is That? Louis XIV or Donald Trump?" (Figure 14.1).[1] There might seem to be some similarities at a cursory glance: the acres of marble, gilt capitals on columns, fountains, and painted ceilings in Trump's residences nod in the direction of the Sun King's palace. Putting questions of accurate period style aside, it is worth considering the broader implications of those comparisons. Trump's opponents are keen to point to his homes as evidence of an unscrupulous and self-serving man with despotic tendencies. Popular wisdom holds that there is a direct link between the grandiose decoration of French Royal palaces and the absolutist rule rejected by the people of France in the 1789 French Revolution; Versailles has come to represent a gilded style of tyrannical opulence for the privileged few at the cost of the many.

The comparison between the Sun King's style and that of the forty-fifth US president is superficial at best, but there is in fact a long-established taste for the art and design of old-regime France in American high society. This chapter aims to find the inspiration for Donald Trump's Manhattan penthouse and his country club, Mar-A-Lago, not directly in the palace of Versailles but rather through the lens of an American tradition for the newly rich to signal their social ascension by quoting and collecting the art and design of old-regime France. From the decoration of the White House in the early nineteenth century to homes and hotels of the Gilded Age robber barons, the pseudo-French palace style that has come to be associated with President Trump echoes established patterns

Figure 14.1 The apartment of Donald and Melania Trump, Trump Tower, New York. Photo: Sam Horine.

of interior decoration to signal financial success among certain American entrepreneurs.

Even before Donald Trump was elected president, the media began to speculate on how a man famous for his love of lavish gilding would put his mark on the White House. During his campaign for office, the *New York Times* posed the question "how will Trump redecorate the White House?"[2] The popular press turned to Trump's Manhattan Penthouse in Trump Tower to find clues for how to answer that question. Louis XIV's Palace of Versailles was taken unquestionably and uncritically to be the inspiration for Trump's home décor by the popular press.[3] The speculation redoubled after President Trump's inauguration. When a photograph was released of Trump in the Oval Office with a backdrop of yellow-gold silk curtains, some believed that this foreshadowed a new pseudo-palatial style for the official residence of the American president.[4]

These first changes to the Oval Office incorporated furnishings commissioned under previous presidents from both sides of the political divide—the gold curtains from the Clinton era, and the starburst carpet designed by Nancy Reagan.[5] Journalists were eager to find evidence of Trump's personal taste in these alterations. "Gone are departing commander-in-chief Barack Obama's crimson curtains, which have been replaced with gold drapes, a dominant color in Trump's over-the-top Trump Tower penthouse," wrote Christian Gollayan for the *New York Post*.⁶ "How much more gold might things get at the White House? Judging from Trump's personal properties and private plane, one can only guess," Janie Campbell opined for the *Huffington Post*.⁷

Commentators soon began to take the comparison between Donald Trump and Louis XIV beyond questions of design to compare the American president's far-right political ideology with the absolutist rule of the French king.⁸ The all-too-convenient slippage between conspicuous richness of the Sun King's palace and the glittering finishes favored by Donald Trump quickly became a rhetorical tool for Trump's critics to question the president's commitment to the democratic principles of the US Constitution. Peter York, author of *Dictator Style: Lifestyles of the World's Most Colorful Despots*, made the link between Trump's taste for interior decoration and a critique of his political ideology explicit in an article titled "Trump's Dictator Chic."⁹ The second of York's style rules for "dictator chic" is: "Think French." "There may never have been an interior style quite as lavish as 18th-century France—a look that allows for deep, curvy marble chimney-pieces, chairs covered in gilding and furniture slathered with ormolu," he writes. Neither Trump nor French decorative arts fare well in this comparison. While the American president is compared to autocratic and authoritarian rulers, the superlative decorative arts of the age of Bourbon kings become gaudy and kitsch.¹⁰

While many are quick to point to Versailles as the model for Trump's apartment, there are no direct quotations of that famous palace to be found. It is easy for a historian of French decorative arts to point out the errors of reference in Trump's interior to the designs that have been said to inspire it. The proportions are all wrong: the columns are wide and squat, the entablature above the gilt capitals too narrow, and the cornice below the painted ceiling far too wide. Not to mention the heavily gilt Louis XV-inspired armchairs that have none of the sinuous appeal of their eighteenth-century forbears. Proportion governs elegance in the palace of the Bourbon kings, and such errors would have been considered extremely poor taste then, as they are now.

The idea of good taste (*bon goût*) in the proportions of a building and its interiors was a much-discussed subject at the time of Louis XIV. Those who belonged to the fashionable society of the Paris salons would demonstrate their inherent understanding of the agreed-upon standards of *bon goût* at their meetings. Indeed, the pretentious displays of innate taste by those *salonniers* were roundly mocked by Moliére his plays.¹¹ By the end of the century Antoine Furetière's *Dictionnaire Universel* (1690) described the word taste (*goust*) as a term "used figuratively for critical jugements" (*des judgements de l'esprit*), giving the example of the treatise on good taste (*Traitté du bon goust*) in Blondel's book of Architecture.[12] The question of *bon goût* in architecture would occupy the Académie Royale d'Architecture throughout the late seventeenth and eighteenth centuries. Académians disputed whether *bon goût* in architecture was based in rules of proportion of the part to the whole, or by splendid individual elements.[13] In 1734 the Académie decreed that *bon goût* depended on three things: *Ordonnance* (the relationship of the part to the whole), *Proportion* (appropriateness of dimensions according to function), and *Consonance* (established rules where everything is in its rightful place).[14] By the end of the eighteenth century, Enlightenment philosophers questioned the foundations of such judgments. David Hume was perhaps the last to evoke the expert with his idea that a judgment of beauty depends on the practiced and refined sensibilities of a "true judge."

Far from conforming to a set of agreed rules of proportion and distribution, nor channeling the practiced and refined sensibilities of the true judge, Trump's interiors select from ancien-régime style in a piecemeal and incoherent way. Mixed references to interiors and furniture in the Louis XIV and Louis XV styles show that this is not an attempt to recreate a specific period. This style is better described as pseudo-French grand manner. It is a mode of design employed by those like Trump who build dream homes that reference the age of the Bourbon kings around the world today. Such buildings and interiors are less interested in an accurate quotation of French period styles, nor the demonstration of a refined understanding of *consonance* in the distribution of decorative elements, but more in creating a fantasy of luxury and decadence; an imagined world that hints to royal riches. It is less likely that Trump and his designers were aiming to imitate old-regime France in this penthouse, and more likely to have been inspired by the echoes of that aristocratic style that became fashionable private mansions and public hotels made for the new rich of Gilded Age America.

Alva Vanderbilt, one of the most flamboyant patrons of the Gilded Age, has been credited with bringing old-regime French style to New York in the 1880s.[15] She used her husband's fortune to commission Richard Morris Hunt to design a mansion at 660 Fifth Avenue (occupying the entire block between 51st and 52nd streets) with finials and turrets of a French renaissance pile, inspiring the moniker, the Petit Château.[16] The French firm Jules Allard and sons were hired to create magnificent interiors in period French styles, including a spectacular neo-rococo salon that started a trend for the era in New York.[17]

Alva's architect, Richard Morris Hunt, was the first American to be admitted to the École des Beaux-Arts in Paris, a school that instilled a deep respect for historical tradition—particularly the magnificent styles of early modern France.[18] The École des Beaux-Arts fueled an international taste for historicism in architecture and design in the late nineteenth and early twentieth centuries. Hunt might be credited with bringing the style to East Coast America, and while many of the private mansions including the Petit Château were destroyed, his design for the Fifth Avenue façade of the Metropolitan Museum of Art remains as a testament to the ideals of the time. Alva worked with Hunt again on a Queen Anne-style mansion in Long Island, the charmingly named Idle Hour. But she wanted a "Summer cottage" in fashionable Newport, and it was here that she worked with Hunt on Marble House, a Louis XIV-inspired pavilion next to the sea.[19]

Marble House is perhaps the best preserved of Hunt's private commissions. Its exterior combines the designs of the two Trianons built for Louis XIV and Louis XV as retreats in the parklands surrounding the palace of Versailles to escape the crowds. Indeed, as Mark Ledbury has shown in his chapter for this book, the Petit Trianon proved to be very popular with nineteenth-century visitors, and was very influential in shaping taste.[20] Like many of the Beaux-Arts buildings of the age, it is a mix of period styles, with a vast Gothic room, and bedrooms decorated in various period styles. But it is the age of Louis XIV that Alva and Hunt evoked most of all at Marble House.

The main entrance opens to the Stair Hall (Figure 14.2), dressed throughout in a yellow sienna marble, with bronze balustrades modeled after those of the Petit Trianon. The mezzanine of the staircase incorporates a copy of Bernini's famous bust of Louis XIV located between two windows (a subtle reference, perhaps to the bust that once sat the center of the Ambassador's staircase at Versailles). Above the arched windows are portrait medallions by Karl Bitter celebrating the architects responsible for this building. Hunt is on the left, with Louis XIV's architect Jules Hardouin-Mansart opposite him. One of Hunt's designs for the staircase shows the portrait of Louis XIV as an integral part of this scheme, but the portrait medallions either side are not the architects who were finally chosen to be commemorated. The double portrait to the right was perhaps William and Alva Vanderbilt, and on the left may have been the founder of the dynasty, Cornelius Vanderbilt. Whether Alva decided that such a direct comparison between the Bourbon King and the Vanderbilt family was a step too far, we may never know for sure.

Figure 14.2 Richard Morris Hunt, Elevation of the Marble Staircase, Marble House, Newport. Photo: Gavin Ainsworth.

The dining room at Marble House also features a portrait of Louis XIV, intended from the start to be the focus of the decorative scheme. Jules Allard and sons likely supplied the ceiling—an original from an eighteenth-century French building—as the firm was known for its skill at incorporating and expanding preexisting antique elements in their designs. Here, they have added the sun devise either side of the central painting to continue the Louis XIV theme. The mantle surrounding the fireplace is a copy of the one found in the Salon d'Hercule at Versailles, designed for Louis XIV by Robert de Cotte in 1710. The combination of red marble pilasters and gilt capitals also derives from the same source, as is the rhythm of paired pilasters and over layered pilasters forming an aedicule around the chimneybreast.

It is no accident that Alva Vanderbilt and her Gilded Age contemporaries quoted Versailles in their mansions. That French art and architecture was (and to some extent still is) emulated by the superrich, attests to the enduring success of a plan set in motion by Louis XIV's leading minister, Jean-Baptiste Colbert, to make France a world leader in manufacturing luxury. Soon after he purchased the office of *Surintendant des batiments du roi* in 1663, Colbert began to reinvigorate the French luxury industry, founding manufactories for tapestry and furniture, glass, lace, textiles—everything that would be needed for the decoration of noble residences.[21] In 1665 he became *Contrôleur général des finances* too, enabling him to impose restrictions on the importation of foreign goods to boost the French economy and to ensure that French aristocrats would buy local. These policies had far-reaching effects, and by the end of Louis XIV's reign French fashion and design were envied and emulated across Europe.

With this in mind it is possible to see the dual function of the Hall of Mirrors at Versailles. It was a statement of royal magnificence and glory: its impressive scale and shimmering, reflective surfaces served to dazzle and disorientate visitors to Versailles then and now.[22] The cycle of the Louis XIV's history on the ceiling painted by Charles Le Brun detailed the political and military acts that made such a display of magnificence possible. But it was also an advertisement for the new luxury industries that Colbert had helped to establish in France, with exquisite silver furniture from the Gobelins manufactory, and mirrors and windows from made in Paris at the Saint-Gobain *Manufacture Royale de glaces de miroirs*. The palace of Versailles was not only an opulent display of material wealth of the French monarchy, but also a spectacular advertisement for the luxury industries in France that was aimed at seducing visitors to Versailles to part with their money in France. So successful was this strategy that Versailles immediately became the model for palace architecture and royal representation and continued to inspire noble and wealthy patrons in the centuries that followed.

As the Vanderbilts and their ilk marked their ascent by emulating the style of Old-World aristocracy, many old European families could no longer sustain the cost of their lavish lifestyles on funds brought in by the family estate. Families who could no longer afford to keep a London house would stay in the city at one of the new luxury hotels that had opened at the end of the nineteenth century.

The luxury hotel is undoubtedly an American invention,[23] but when Le Grand Hôtel, Paris, opened in 1862 it provided a new palatial model that would come to be emulated across the world.[24] The 1890s ushered in a new age of the luxury hotel with the buildings decorated and furnished in same manner as grand aristocratic residences, to provide a home-from-home for their wealthy clientele.[25] César Ritz established his first hotel in a Louis XIV building in the Place Vendôme, Paris. Guests entered the hotel through a façade designed by Louis XIV's architect Jules Hardouin-Mansart, and inside they found the converted aristocratic townhouse furnished with the same kind of wall hangings and antiques found in a Gilded Age mansion.

This new luxe palatial style for hotels was brought to the east coast of America in the 1890s at the Waldolf-Astoria.[26] Situated among the Gilded Age mansions of Fifth Avenue, the Waldorf-Astoria was founded by two scions of the Astor family.[27] The hotel, razed in 1929 to make way for the Empire State Building, was built on the site of two Astor mansions. When the construction of the second building (the Astoria) was planned in 1890, the *New York Times* announced: "The style of the architecture will be that of French Renaissance, and the building itself, Mr. Hardenberg [architect] says, will be something of a copy of the Grand Hotel in Paris on a smaller scale."[28] Much like Alva Vanderbilt's Petit Château, the hotel featured a mix of period rooms, including a Henri IV drawing room, a Louis XIV bedroom, and a Marie-Antoinette parlour. The latter was decorated with an antique bust of the tragic French queen, and a clock that she had purportedly owned.[29] The Waldorf-Astoria marked the translation of the style of the private Gilded Age mansion to the public hotel, albeit one aimed at the upper echelons of society.

The first decades of the twentieth century saw a widespread adoption of the palatial hotel style in New York City and beyond. Among those were the Plaza (1907), Vanderbilt Hotel (1910–13), and the Commodore (1916–19).[30] It is via the mediation of Gilded Age style adapted for the public sphere in the age of twentieth-century capitalism that we can best understand Trump's design style. Trump's Manhattan penthouse and the ballroom at Mar-a-Largo are far closer in style to the famous Palm Court at the Plaza Hotel (Figure 14.3) than it is

Figure 14.3 The Palm Court, Plaza Hotel, New York. Photo John Wisniewski. Creative Commons License CC-BY.

to the palace of Versailles. Design features that bear a distant relationship to those found in the French palace, such as white marble pilasters with gilt capitals surmounted by a giant cornice, can be found in both the Palm Court and Trump's apartment, for example. It is surely no coincidence that Donald Trump purchased and redeveloped the Commodore in 1975 and the Plaza in 1988.[31]

In his memoir, *Trump: The Art of the Deal*, ghost-written by Tony Schwartz, Trump's comments on the renovation of the Commodore reveal that he had little interest in preserving the Gilded Age splendour of the original building. Instead, he worked with architect Der Scutt "to create something that looked absolutely brand-new [...] a sleek, contemporary look, something with sparkle and excitement that would make people stop and take notice."[32] Likewise, when Scutt came to design Trump Tower, the centerpiece of the design was a marble-clad atrium with brass fittings, reflective glass, and a wall of water (Figure 14.4). The lavish use of reflective, gold-hued materials in that atrium recall colours and surfaces of the Sun King's palace, but little comparison can be made in terms of decorative style. There's no mistaking the period in which Scutt's atrium was designed, which exhibits all of the brash ebullience of New York City in the economic boom of the 1980s. The design is almost indistinguishable from that of luxury hotels of the same period.

Trump differs most from arrivistes of the Gilded Age in his disregard for traditional New York High Society. He had no interest in attracting "old-money New Yorkers" to Trump Tower and instead he wanted to appeal to a new clientele of rich, but less socially elevated people, who many not make it through the strict vetting process of cooperative buildings.[33] Trump Tower attracted a new generation of wealthy clients, from Arab oil millionaires to Hollywood celebrities. This coincided with beginning of new age of highly visible consumption. For Trump it was all about the price tag. Part of the success of Trump Tower was the fact that it soon gained a reputation for being expensive and this appealed to a certain kind of buyer who was keen to cultivate the appearance of wealth.

In *Trump: The Art of the Deal*, Trump tells the reader how he decided to double the space of his original penthouse in Trump Tower after a visit to the apartment of billionaire Saudi arms dealer, Adnan Khashoggi:

> In the middle of 1985, I got an invitation [...] to come to his apartment in Olympic Tower. [...] I was impressed by the huge size of its rooms. Specifically, it had the biggest living room I'd ever seen. [...] I decided to take over one of the other apartments on the top three floors [of Trump Tower] and combine it with mine. It has taken almost two years to renovate, but I don't believe there is any

246 *The Versailles Effect*

Figure 14.4 Atrium, Trump Tower, New York. Photo: Sebastian Bergmann/Wikimedia Commons: https://commons.wikimedia.org/wiki/File:Trump_Tower_-_the_atrium.jpg

apartment anywhere in the world that can touch it. And while I can't honestly say that I need an eighty-foot living room, I do get a kick out of having one.[34]

Adnan Khashoggi's 18,000 square foot apartment inspired Trump to make his own home larger and more extravagant.[35] The Manhattan penthouse has become central to Trump's public persona, it gave him "visibility and credibility and prestige."[36] The penthouse has long played a role in the Trump brand, featuring often in the television series *The Apprentice* when contestants are brought to the host's home to see what success looks like. "If you're really successful," Trump tells his protégés, "you'll all live just like this."[37] To quote contributing editor of *Vanity Fair*, Fran Lebowitz, Donald Trump is "a poor person's idea of a rich person. All that stuff he shows you in his house—the gold faucets—if you won the lottery [or perhaps a reality TV show], that's what you'd buy."[38] This bears out in awed responses of the contestants on the apprentice. "This is like rich. Really, really rich," one exclaims.[39] To Trump and his acolytes, success, it seems, looks less like the palace of the Sun King, and more like a luxury hotel designed in a pseudo-French grand manner.

While Trump's apartment makes no direct reference to Versailles, other buildings have appeared in recent years that do. The *Château de Versailles*, this time in Vaughan, Toronto, was built by two Canadian entrepreneurs over five years and finished in 2012 for their wedding.[40] The building was inspired directly by the couple's love for Versailles to which they made an annual pilgrimage. While they may have aimed to achieve a style that evoked the famous French Château, the Canadian couple did not faithfully recreate any particular period style. A promotional video published when the house was placed on the market in 2013 shows a marble-clad entrance hall decorated with murals inspired by the paintings on display at the original Château de Versailles, including a portrait of Queen Marie Leszczyńska after Louis Tocqué.[41] Other references in the Versailles at Vaughan are more generic: chandeliers, painted ceilings, boiseries, elaborate curtains. But it is hard to find an inspiration at the real Versailles for the "heated Ferrari room" that this mansion boasts as its ultimate luxury.

The astute observer will recognize copies of Antoine Coysevox's two winged horses commissioned by Louis XIV not for Versailles, but for the Château de Marly, flanking the elaborate entry gates. The horses are surmounted by Mercury and Fame and celebrate Louis XIV's renown but detached from their original context these copies come to mean something quite different. They are stripped of the signification of the fame and power of a ruler who was once thought divinely appointed to that role, and instead they become a status symbol for financial success for "generation wealth," to borrow a term coined by photographer and filmmaker Lauren Greenfield.[42]

One of the centerpieces of Greenfield's project to document the American obsession with money and "conspicuous consumption" is another "Versailles" built by timeshare property developers David and Jackie Siegel in Orlando Florida.[43] This building, which remains unfinished at time this chapter was published, was brought to the world's attention by Greenfield's 2012 documentary, *Queen of Versailles*.[44] In that film, David Seigel recalled that the design for his new home was inspired by both the seventeenth-century French palace and the Paris Las Vegas Hotel. The design for their 90,000 square foot (approximately 8,360 square meter) mansion, which includes fourteen bedrooms, thirty-two bathrooms, eleven kitchens, a cinema, a roller-skating rink, a bowling alley, a thirty-car garage, three levels, and two elevators was first sketched on the back of an envelope when the couple stayed across the road at Bellagio Hotel and Casino. While they named their mansion Versailles to recall the famously opulent French palace, what they are building is less a recreation of historical French design, and more a private luxury hotel.

While the building and its amenities have a closer connection with five-star Las Vegas casino hotels than it does to a real French palace, the Siegel's dream of living like royalty is signaled with references to royal symbols. The interlaced Ls of Louis XIV's cypher found throughout his palace, replaced here with an "S" for Seigel on the spandrels and balustrades in designs for the entrance hall and staircase. A fantasy portrait of the Siegel family shows David in kingly regalia and Jackie crowned, making the dream of royal riches explicit. The Siegels have long been collecting "French antiques" to decorate their new home. The cursory glance around their warehouse in this film reveals little of real value to the serious collector of decorative arts among these items; most are reproductions of mixed style and quality.

Greenfield's documentary captures the financial instability of the newly rich of generation wealth. The economic crisis of 2008 forced the Seigels to put their unfinished mansion on the market when they could no longer afford the loans needed to complete this ostentatious building. For Greenfield, her project revealed that "real social mobility has been replaced by a kind of fictitious social mobility—bling, surface image."[45] Trump's unexpected presidential win is for her "the apotheosis of Generation Wealth."[46] While Trump has traded on his reputation of being super-rich as a result of his business acumen, the extent of his financial success has long been in question.[47] Without the release of his tax returns, it is impossible to verify his claim to being a billionaire. A claim that is so central to his brand, he has sued the writer of an unauthorized biography who suggested that he had vastly exaggerated his financial worth.

The Vanderbilts and their Gilded Age contemporaries surrounded themselves with the very best porcelain, furniture, tapestries, sculptures, and paintings created for the nobles of the French Court in the seventeenth and eighteenth centuries. In doing so they defined a rich style that I would argue has come to represent the last word in chic and the ultimate cultural capital for those who fought their way to the top. Those wealthy industrialists sought to attain social prestige by association with authentic objects that belonged to a lost world of old-regime France. The interiors made by the Seigels and Trump mimic the only the most superficial aspects of French Court art and design, and the exuberant recreations and displays of it by tycoons of America's Gilded Age to signify capital wealth. This is evident in the additions Trump made to his private club Mar-a-Lago, in Palm Beach, Florida, in the 1990s.

Trump purchased Mar-a-Lago in 1985 as a private residence that he, his family, and business associates enjoyed for a decade before the complex was transformed into a private club and spa.[48] The villa was one of the most prestigious estates in Palm Beach, built by American cereal heiress and businesswoman, Marjorie Merriweather Post, in the 1920s.[49] It is a quintessential example of architectural historicism from the early twentieth century. Post's interior designer, Joseph Urban, whose clients included Emperor Franz Joseph and the Khedive of Egypt, created a Moorish style villa for his patron.[50] In the blend of quotations typical of historicism, the ceiling of the main salon is a copy of that found in the Academia in Venice, and the villa was decorated with antiques, albeit of varying style and quality.

Like many of her Gilded Age contemporaries, Post was also an avid collector of objects from old-regime France. She would often wear a pair of pear-shaped diamond earrings at her extravagant entertainments at Mar-a-Lago that were said to be the very same jewels that were sewn into the Marie-Antoinette's pocket when she made the failed flight to Varennes during the French Revolution.[51] The French Drawing Room of Post's house in Washington, DC, Hillwood—now a museum—is lined with Louis XVI boiseries, and is replete with the very best objects from the same period. Mar-a-Lago and Hillwood were created to frame a private collection of historical importance. This is a quite separate vision from the pseudo-French, grand manner hotel style that Trump brought with his renovations to Mar-a-Lago.

When Trump transformed Mar-a-Lago into a private club, he added what some have described as a "Louis XIV style" ballroom (Figure 14.5) decorated with a reported $7 million of gold leaf.[52] In truth, the Donald J. Trump Grand Ballroom, as it is called, has very little to do with the style of the Sun King. The proportions of squat columns and wide lintels make for an awkward composition. The mix of period references is jarring, the ceiling of the large bay window area vaguely recalls rococo motifs of the salon de la princesse at the Hôtel de Soubise, but the correspondence is not close enough to recognize a direct quotation. This large room is better understood in the tradition of the vast function rooms of luxury hotels.

I first started looking at the interior design of Donald Trump's private houses in 2015 when he was running for office, but few thought he would win the election. While Trump may have long harbored presidential ambitions,[53] the design of his Manhattan apartment in the 1980s, and the Ballroom at Mar-a-Lago in the 1990s were conceived as part of the Trump luxury brand. Trump style was developed to promote an image of personal success won through canny business dealings: the American dream. The message is a simple one: if you make the

Figure 14.5 Palm Beach, Florida—March 13: The Donald J. Trump Ballroom at the Mar-A-Lago Club in Palm Beach where Republican presidential candidate Donald Trump spoke after the Florida primary, March 13, 2016, in Palm Beach, Florida. Photo by Brooks Kraft/Getty Images.

right deals, you can live like a king—all comfort, no responsibility. The forms that represent monarchic power were stripped of their stately function. All that changed when Trump was elected, and began to use his Manhattan penthouse, and private club in Florida as a backdrop for official presidential functions. Mar-a-Lago has become the winter White House, and the codes of luxury have reverted once more to symbols of power.[54] Ironically, the woman who built Mar-a-Lago, Marjorie Merriweather Post, had intended her villa to become an official Florida residence for the American president. She left the estate to the federal government on her death in 1973, but they eventually gave it back to her daughters, when it was deemed too expensive to maintain.

If Donald Trump's Manhattan penthouse and his country club, Mar-a-Lago, recall for many the palace of Versailles, what they perceive is a faint echo of the original mediated by the grandiose private houses and public hotels built by the robber barons of the Gilded Age. The phenomenon of conspicuous consumption that Thorstein Veblen recognized in the late nineteenth century has risen exponentially in the age of generation wealth. Today the new rich mark their ascension (real or fictional as it may be) with visible displays of gold and diamonds, but also luxury brands—many of them French. That Paris is still considered the capital of fashion, and French decorative arts still copied by Trump and his ilk attests to the enduring success of Colbert's plan to make France the center of luxury production. Donald Trump's call for greater support for American industry and manufacturing in his election campaign and inauguration speech is perhaps the closest comparison we could make between him and Louis XIV. But if he was ever inspired by the Sun King (and he has made no public admission to this) he would do well to provide government support for contemporary artists, designers, and intellectuals to reaffirm, or perhaps reposition America as a world leader in the arts and sciences. Perhaps then Trump would be able to fulfil his promise to "make America great again."

Notes

1   Kate Wagner, "Whose Style Is That? Louis XIV or Donald Trump? An Interior Design Guide to the New President," *Curbly*, January 19, 2017. Available online: https://www.curbly.com/trump-is-a-living-mcmansion (accessed September 26, 2018). See also, http://mcmansionhell.com/tagged/donald-trump (accessed September 26, 2018).

2 Patricia Leigh Brown, "How Will Trump Redecorate the White House?," *New York Times*, March 17, 2016. Available online: https://www.nytimes.com/2016/03/20/opinion/sunday/how-will-trump-redecorate-the-white-house.html?_r=0 (accessed September 26, 2018).

3 Idem see also: Edward Goldman, "Louis XIV to Donald Trump: 'You Are Fired,'" *Huffington Post*, March 22, 2016. Available online: https://www.huffingtonpost.com/edward-goldman/louis-xiv-to-donald-trump_b_9526572.html (accessed September 26, 2018).

4 Robert Wellington, "Going for Gold: Trump, Louis XIV and Interior Design," *Conversation*, January 23, 2017. Available online: https://theconversation.com/going-for-gold-trump-louis-xiv-and-interior-design-71698 (accessed October 2, 2018); Robert Wellington "Trump's Display of Wealth, Power Falls Short," *Canberra Times*, March 13, 2017, 17.

5 These curtains came from the White House furnishings archive. They were originally commissioned and hung in the Oval office during the Clinton presidency: "Oval Office History," *The White House Museum*. Available online: http://www.whitehousemuseum.org/west-wing/oval-office-history.htm (accessed September 18, 2018).

6 Christian Gollayan, "Trump Has Already Redecorated the Oval Office," *New York Post*, January 23, 2017. Available online: https://nypost.com/2017/01/23/trump-has-already-redecorated-the-oval-office/ (accessed September 26, 2018).

7 Janie Campbell, "Donald Trump Already Redecorated the Oval Office, and of course the Curtains Are Gold," *Huffington Post*. Available online: https://www.huffingtonpost.com/entry/donald-trump-gold-curtains-oval-office_us_5882b0a4e4b096b4a231dde1 (accessed September 26, 2018.)

8 Shellie Karabell, "What Louis XIV Can Teach Donald Trump," *Forbes*, February 14, 2016; Linda Kiernan, "Trump's White House Might Look like a Royal Court, but He's no Louis XIV," *Conversation*, June 23, 2017. Available online: https://theconversation.com/trumps-white-house-might-look-like-a-royal-court-but-hes-no-louis-xiv-79362 (accessed September 26, 2018); Ed Simon, "Donald Trump: L'Etat, C'est Moi!," *History News Network*, June 5, 2018. Available online: https://historynewsnetwork.org/article/169215 (accessed September 26, 2018).

9 Peter York, "Trump's Dictator Chic," *Politico*, March/April 2017. Available online: https://www.politico.com/magazine/story/2017/03/trump-style-dictator-autocrats-design-214877 (accessed September 27, 2018); Peter York, *Dictator Style: Lifestyles of the World's Most Colorful Despots* (San Francisco, CA: Chronicle Books, 2016).

10 See Kimberly Chrisman-Campbell's excellent commentary on this subject: Kimberly Chrisman-Campbell, "How Gold Went from Godly to Gaudy," *Atlantic*, December 2, 2016. Available online: https://www.theatlantic.com/entertainment/

archive/2016/12/the-midas-touch-gold-trump-gouthiere/509036/ (accessed September 26, 2018).
11 Faith E. Beasley, *Salons, History and the Making of Seventeenth-Century France: Mastering Memory* (Aldershot and Burlington: Ashgate, 2006), 45–7.
12 Antoine Furetiere, *Dictionnaire universel, contenant généralement tous les mots françois tant vieux que modernes …* (Le Haye: A and R Leers, 1690).
13 For the history of *bon goût* relating to ancien-régime architecture see Hanno-Walter Kruft, *A History of Architectural Theory: From Vitruvius to the Present*, trans. R. Taylor, E. Callander, and A. Wood (New York: Princeton Architectural Press, 1994), 141 ff.
14 Ibid., 143–4.
15 Wayne Craven, *Gilded Mansions: Grand Architecture and High Society* (New York: W. W. Norton & Company, 2009), 107–26; Michael C. Kathrens, *Great Houses of New York, 1880–1930* (New York: Acanthus Press, 2014); James T Maher, *The Twilight of Splendor: Chronicles of the Age of American Palaces* (Boston, MA: Little Brown, 1975).
16 Paul R. Baker, *Richard Morris Hunt* (Cambridge, MA: MIT Press, 1986), 266 ff.
17 On Jules Allard and Sons, see Craven, *Gilded Mansions*, 268–9.
18 On Hunt at the École des Beaux-Arts, see Baker, *Richard Morris Hunt*, 266 ff.
19 Craven, *Gilded Mansions*, 161–70; Barker, *Richard Morris Hunt*, 352–62; Richard Cheek and Tom Gannon, *Newport Mansions: The Gilded Age* (Newport, RI: The Preservation Society of Newport County, 2006).
20 Mark Ledbury, "Melancholy, Nostalgia, Dreams: Adventures in the Grand Cimetière Magique," in *The Versailles Effect*, 215, 236.
21 On Colbert, see Georges Mongrédien, *Colbert: 1619–1683* (Paris: Hachette, 1963); Colbert 1619–83, exhibition catalogue (Paris: Hotel de la Monnaie, 1983); and Florian Knothe, *The Manufacture des meubles de la couronne aux Gobelins under Louis XIV* (Turnhout, Belgium: Brepols, 2016).
22 On the visitors to Versailles, see the recent catalogue from the Versailles/Met exhibitions: Bertrand Rondot and Daniëlle Kisluk-Grosheide, *Visitors to Versailles*, exhibition catalogue (New York; New Haven, CT; and London: Yale University Press; The Metropolitan Museum of Art, 2018).
23 A. K. Sandoval-Strausz, *Hotel: An American History* (London and New Haven, CT: Yale University Press, 2009).
24 Le Grand Hôtel was built under Napoleon III and Baron Haussman. It opened in 1862 in anticipation of the 1867 Exposition Universelle. Alexandre Tessier, *Le Grand Hôtel: L'invention du luxe hôtelier 1862–1972* (Rennes: Presses universitaires de Rennes, 2012).
25 The Savoy, London opened in 1889, the Waldorf New York first opened in 1893, soon followed by the Astoria in 1897 (the two were merged shortly after to become

26 William Alan Morrison, *Waldorf Astoria* (Charleston, SC: Arcadia, 2014). See also Valerie Wingfield, "The Waldorf-Astoria Hotel," *New York Public Library Blog*, November 4, 2014. Available online: https://www.nypl.org/blog/2014/11/04/waldorf-astoria-hotel (accessed September 28, 2018).

Waldorf-Astoria linked by a covered alley), the newly renovated Claridges, London, opened in 1898, and the Ritz, Paris, in the same year.

27 The Astors rose on the back of the fur trade and were early investors in New York City real estate. By the mid-nineteenth century they were the wealthiest family in America, but this was soon to be eclipsed by the new generation of railroad millionaires such as the Vanderbilts. See Axel Madsen, *John Jacob Astor: America's First Multimillionaire* (New York: Wiley and Sons, 2001).
28 *New York Times*, May 29, 1890, cited in Wingfield, "The Waldorf-Astoria Hotel."
29 Morrison, *Waldorf Astoria*, 14.
30 Both Vanderbilt Hotel and the Commodore were designed by the architectural firm Warren and Wetmore. Whitney Warren, born into New York High Society, trained at the École des Beaux-Arts. The firm became preferred architects of the Vanderbilt's New York Central Railroad company. Peter Pennoyer and Anne Walker, *The Architecture of Warren and Wetmore* (New York: W. W. Norton & Company, 2006).
31 Robert E. Tomasson, "Deal Negotiated for the Commodore," *New York Times*, May 4, 1975, Robert J. Cole, "Plaza Hotel Is Sold to Donald Trump for $390 Million," *New York Times*, March 27, 1988.
32 Tony Schwartz and Donald Trump, *Trump: The Art of the Deal* (New York: Ballentine Books, 1987), 123–4.
33 Ibid., 181.
34 Ibid., 186–7.
35 The apartment was sold in 2000: Deborah Schoeneman, "Olympic Tower Condo Sold by Khashoggi for Just $12 Million," *Observer*, April 10, 2000. Available online: https://observer.com/2000/04/olympic-tower-condo-sold-by-khashoggi-for-just-12-million/ (accessed September 28, 2018).
36 Schwartz and Trump, *Trump*, 191.
37 "Meet the Billionaire," *The Apprentice*, season 1, episode 1, NBC, 2004.
38 Emily Jane Fox, "Let Fran Lebowitz Soothe All Your Election-Related Worries," *Vanity Fair*, October 20, 2016. Available online: https://www.vanityfair.com/news/2016/10/fran-lebowitz-trump-clinton-election (accessed October 1, 2018).
39 "Meet the Billionaire," *The Apprentice*, season 1, episode 1, NBC, 2004.
40 Tim Kelly, "Versailles Mansion in Vaughan Yours for $17.8M," *YorkRegion.com*. Available online: https://www.yorkregion.com/news-story/4148941-versailles-mansion-in-vaughan-yours-for-17-8m/ (accessed September 18, 2018).
41 Ibid.

42 Lauren Greenfield is the director of award-winning documentary, *Queen of Versailles* (2012). Generation Wealth is the title of the "multi-platform project that Lauren Greenfield has been working on since 2008 and is being released in 2017 as a museum exhibition, a photographic monograph, and a documentary film." http://www.generation-wealth.com/ (accessed September 26, 2018).
43 I use the Thorstein Veblen's term "conspicuous consumption" to draw comparison between the new rich of the Gilded Age and those of today. See Thorstein Veblen, *The Theory of the Leisure Class* (1899).
44 *Queen of Versailles* directed by Lauren Greenfield, Evergreen Pictures, 2012.
45 From an interview with Lauren Greenfield published in: Gillian B. White, "Getting to the Bottom of Americans' Fascination with Wealth," *Atlantic*, May 16, 2017. Available online: https://www.theatlantic.com/business/archive/2017/05/greenfield-generation-wealth/526683/ (accessed September 26, 2018).
46 Ibid.
47 David A. Fahrenthold and Robert O'Harrow Jr., "Trump: A True Story," *Washington Post*, August 10, 2016. Available online: https://www.washingtonpost.com/graphics/politics/2016-election/trump-lies/?utm_term=.ef49853b8c6e (accessed September 26, 2018); Jonathan Greenberg, "Trump Lied to Me about His Wealth to Get onto the Forbes 400. Here Are the Tapes," *Washington Post*, April 20, 2018. Available online: https://www.washingtonpost.com/outlook/trump-lied-to-me-about-his-wealth-to-get-onto-the-forbes-400-here-are-the-tapes/2018/04/20/ac762b08-4287-11e8-8569-26fda6b404c7_story.html?utm_term=.9005250bff4e (accessed October 1, 2018).
48 Mark Seal, "How Donald Trump Beat Palm Beach Society and Won the Fight for Mar-a-Lago," *Vanity Fair*, February, 2017. Available online: https://www.vanityfair.com/style/2016/12/how-donald-trump-beat-palm-beach-society-and-won-the-fight-for-mar-a-lago (accessed October 1, 2018).
49 *New York Times*, "Mrs. Marjorie Merriweather Post Is Dead at 86," September 13, 1973. Available online: https://www.nytimes.com/1973/09/13/archives/mrs-marjorie-merriweather-post-is-dead-at-86-a-rich-working-woman.html?_r=0 (accessed October 1, 2018).
50 On Joseph Urban, see Arnold Aronson, ed., *Architect of Dreams: The Theatrical Vision of Joseph Urban* (New York: Miriam and Ira D. Wallach Art Gallery, Columbia University, 2000). Available online: http://www.columbia.edu/cu/lweb/eresources/archives/rbml/urban/architectOfDreams/index.html (accessed October 1, 2018).
51 *New York Times*, "Mrs. Marjorie Merriweather Post Is Dead at 86."
52 Sam Dangremond, "A History of Mar-a-Lago, Donald Trump's American Castle," *Town and Country*, December 22, 2017. Available online: https://www.townandcountrymag.com/style/home-decor/a7144/mar-a-lago-history/ (accessed October 1, 2018).

53 Ivan Couronne, "For Trump, the White House Is a Long-Held Ambition," *Times of Israel*, March 17, 2017. Available online: https://www.timesofisrael.com/for-trump-the-white-house-is-a-long-held-ambition/ (accessed October 1, 2018); Maggie Haberman and Alexander Burns, "Donald Trump's Presidential Run Began in an Effort to Gain Stature," *New York Times*, March 12, 2016. Available online: https://www.nytimes.com/2016/03/13/us/politics/donald-trump-campaign.html (accessed October 1, 2018).

54 Lily Rothman, "The Mar-a-Lago Club Was a 'Winter White House' Even before President Trump Got There," *Time*, February 16, 2017. Available online: http://time.com/4661763/mar-a-lago-donald-trump-marjorie-post/ (accessed October 1, 2018); Kerry Gruson, "Post Home for Sale for $20 Million," *New York Times*, July 16, 1981. Available online: https://www.nytimes.com/1981/07/16/garden/post-home-for-sale-for-20.html (accessed October 1, 2018).

Bibliography

Académie des inscription et belles-lettres. *Médailles sur les principaux évènements du règne entier de Louis le Grand, avec des explication historiques*. Paris: Imprimerie Royale, 1702.

Adamson, John, ed. *The Princely Courts of Europe*. London: Weidenfeld and Nicholson, 1998.

Aillagon, Jean-Jacques, Fabrice Bousteau, and Takashi Murakami. *Murakami Versailles*, exhibition catalogue. Paris: Editions Xavier Barral, 2010.

Akkerman, Nadine and Birgit Houben, eds. *The Politics of Female Households: Ladies-in-Waiting across Early Modern Europe*. Leiden: Brill, 2013.

Albanel, Christine, Antoine Amarger, and Jeanne Faton. *La Galerie des Glaces. Histoire et restauration*. Dijon: Faton, 2007.

Ames, Winslow. "Bouchardon and Company." *Master Drawings* 13, no. 2 (1975): 397.

Amussen, Susan Dwyer. *Caribbean Exchanges: Slavery and the Transformation of English Society, 1640–1700*. Chapel Hill: University of North Carolina Press, 2007.

Andurand, Olivier. "Fluctuat nec mergiture, les hésitations du cardinal de Noailles." *Cahiers de recherches médiévales et humanistes* 24 (2012): 267–98.

Anon. *Explication des peintures, sculptures et autres ouvrages de Messieurs de l'Académie royale …*. Paris: Jacques Collombat, 1742. https://gallica.bnf.fr/ark:/12148/btv1b8442784w/f9.image.

Anon. (L'Abbé Jean de Vayrac). *Journal du voyage du roi à Rheims contenant ce qui s'est passé de plus remarquables à la cérémonie de son sacre*, 2 vols. La Haye: Rutgert Alberts, 1723.

Anon. *Le papillotage, ouvrage comique et moral*. Rotterdam: E. D. V. W et Cie, 1769.

Anon. *Mémoire d'un Protestant condamné aux galères de France pour cause de religion (1700–1713)*. Amsterdam, Rotterdam: Beman, 1757.

Anon. *Recueil de plusieurs oraisons funèbres de Louis XIV*, 2 vols. Paris: n.p., 1716.

Anon. [C. A. E. Moberly and Eleanor F Jourdain]. *An Adventure*. London: Macmillan, 1911.

Anon. "Arrivé, Séjour & Départ des Ambassadeurs de Moscovie." *Mercure Galant* (September 1687): 329–37.

Anon. "Description de la Galerie, du Sallon, & du grand Apartement de Versailles, & tout ce qui s'y passe les jours de Jeu." *Mercure Galant* (December 1682): 1–73.

Anon. "Description de l'escalier de Versailles." *Mercure Galant* (September 1680): part II: 276–320.

Anon. "Description des deux salons peints par Le Brun qui sont aux deux bouts de la Grande Galerie du Château de Versailles." *Mercure Galant* (April 1687): 14–57.

Anon (LB). *Escalier des ambassadeurs*. Paris, 1725.

Anon. "Explication de la Galerie de Versailles." *Mercure Galant* (December 1684): 3–85.

Anon. "Journal de ce qui s'est passé à Versailles depuis l'instant de l'arrivée de Monsieur le comte et de Madame la comtesse du Nord, jusqu'à celui de leur départ." *Bulletin du Centre de recherche du Château de Versailles*. Available online: http://journals.openedition.org/crcv/12396 (accessed September 13, 2018).

Anon. *The Most Christian Turk: Or a View of the Life and Bloody Reign of Lewis XIV....* London: Henry Rhodes, 1690.

Anon. "Mrs. Marjorie Merriweather Post Is Dead at 86." *New York Times*, 13 September 1973. Available online: https://www.nytimes.com/1973/09/13/archives/mrs-marjorie-merriweather-post-is-dead-at-86-a-rich-working-woman.html?_r=0 (accessed October 1, 2018).

Anon. "Nottes sur le voyage de M. le comte et de Mme la comtesse du Nord en France au mois de may 1782." *Bulletin du Centre de recherche du Château de Versailles*. Available online: http://journals.openedition.org/crcv/12398 (accessed September 13, 2018).

Anon. "Olafur Eliasson | Versailles." *Olafur Eliasson | Versailles*. Available online: http://olafureliasson.net/versailles (accessed September 14, 2018).

Anon. "Voyage des Ambassadeurs de Siam." *Mercure Galant* (September 1686), 2: 339–75, and (November 1686): 272–308.

Arizzoli-Clémentel, Pierre, Alexandre Gady, and Michel Baridon, eds. *Versailles*. Paris: Citadelles & Mazenod, 2009.

Arneth, Alfred de and A. Geoffroy, eds. *Correspondance secrète entre Marie-Thérèse et le comte de Mercy-Argenteau*, 3 vols. Paris: Firmin-Didot Frères, 1875.

Aronson, Arnold, ed. *Architect of Dreams: The Theatrical Vision of Joseph Urban*. New York: Miriam And Ira D. Wallach Art Gallery, Columbia University, 2000. Available online: http://www.columbia.edu/cu/lweb/eresources/archives/rbml/urban/architectOfDreams/index.html (accessed October 1, 2018).

Asséo, Henriette. "Travestissement et divertissement: bohémiens et égyptiens à l'époque modern." *Les Dossiers du Grihl* 2 (2009). Available online: https://doi.org/10.4000/dossiersgrihl.3680 (accessed October 10, 2018).

Aulanier, Christiane. *Histoire du Palais et du Musée du Louvre, vol. 5, La petite galerie: Appartement d'Anne d'Autriche; salles romaines*. Paris: Musées Nationaux, 1955.

Auslander, Leora. *Taste and Power: Furnishing Modern France*. Los Angeles: University of California Press, 1996.

Bachaumont, Louis Petit de et al. *Mémoires secrets pour servir à l'histoire de la république des lettres en France*, 36 volumes, London: John Adamson, 1780–9.

Bachelier, Jean-Jacques. *Memoire Historique sur la Manufacture Nationale de Porcelaine de France*, edited by Gustave Gouellain. Paris: R. Simon, 1878.

Baedeker, Karl (Firm). *Paris and Northern France: Handbook for Travellers*. Coblenz: K. Baedeker, 1872.

Bajou, Thierry. *La Peinture à Versailles. XVIIe siècle*. Paris: Réunion des Musées nationaux, Buchet/Chastel, 1998.

Baker, Paul R. *Richard Morris Hunt*. Cambridge, MA: MIT Press, 1986.

Bamford, Paul. *Fighting Ships and Prisons: The Mediterranean Galleys of France in the Age of Louis XIV*. Minneapolis: University of Minnesota Press, 1973.

Barine, Arvède. *Madame, Mother of the Regent: 1652-1722*, translated by Jeanne Mairet. New York: G.P. Putnam's Sons, 1909.

Barral, Xavier, Elena Geura, and Laurent Le Bon, eds. *Jeff Koons, Versailles*. Paris: Xavier Barral, 2008.

Barriére, Dominique. *Villa Aldobrandina Tusculana*. Rome: np, 1647.

Beasley, Faith E. *Salons, History and the Making of Seventeenth-Century France: Mastering Memory*. Aldershot and Burlington: Ashgate, 2006.

Beauvais, Lydia. *Musée du Louvre. Inventaire général des dessins de Charles Le Brun*. I-II, Paris: RMN, 2000.

Beauvais, Lydia. "The Thirty Paintings Explained: An Allegorised History of the First Eighteen Years of Louis XIV's Reign." In *The Hall of Mirrors History and Restoration*, edited by Christine Albanel, Pierre Arizzoli-Clémentel, and Pierre Coppey. Dijon: Faton, 2007.

Bell, Esther. "A Curator at the Louvre: Charles Coypel and the Royal Collections." Issue 2: *Louvre Local, Journal18* (Fall 2016). http://www.journal18.org/986

Bély, Lucien. *La société des princes, XVIe-XVIIIe siècle*. Paris: Fayard 1999.

Beretta, Marco. "Material and Temporal Powers at the Casino Di San Marco (1574-1621)." In *Laboratories of Art: Alchemy and Art Technology from Antiquity to the Eighteenth Century*, edited by Sven Dupré, 129-56. New York: Springer, 2014.

Beretta, Marco. "Transmutations and Frauds in Enlightened Paris: Lavoisier and Alchemy." In *Fakes!? Hoaxes, Counterfeits and Deception in Early Modern Science*, edited by Marco Beretta and Maria Conforti, 69-108. Sagamore Beach: Science History Publications, 2014.

Berger, Robert and Thomas Hedin. *Diplomatic Tours in the Gardens of Versailles under Louis XIV*. Philadelphia: University of Pennsylvania Press, 2008.

Berger, Robert W. "André Félibien: Description de la grotte de Versailles (Description of the Grotto of Versailles). The Original French Text with Facing English Translation, Introduction and Notes." *History of Gardens and Designed Landscapes* 36, no. 2 (2015): 89-133.

Berger, Robert W. *Versailles: The Château of Louis XIV*. University Park: Penn State Press, 1985.

Bettag, Alexandra. *Die Kunstpolitik Jean Baptiste Colberts unter besonderer Berücksichtigung der Académie Royale de Peinture et de Sculpture*. Weimar: VDG, 1998.

Bindman, David, Bruce Boucher, and Helen Weston. "The Theater of Court and Church: Blacks as Figures of Fantasy." In *The Image of the Black in Western Art*, edited by David Bindman and Henry Louis Gates, Jr., 3 vols. 17–77, Cambridge, MA: Harvard University Press, 2011.

Bischoff, Cordula. "Women Collectors and the Rise of the Porcelain Cabinet." In *Chinese and Japanese Porcelain for the Dutch Golden Age*, edited by Jan van Campen and Titus Eliëens, 171–89. Zwolle: Waanders, 2014.

Blok, Petrus Johannes and Philip Christiaan Molhuysen, eds. *Nieuw Nederlandsch biografisch woordenboek*, vol. 2. Leiden: np, 1912.

Blondel, Jacques-François. *Architecture Françoise ou recueil des plans, élévations, coupes et profils*, 4 vols. Paris: Jombert, 1756.

Blunt, Anthony. *Art and Architecture in France, 1500–1700*. Harmondsworth: Penguin, 1953.

Blunt, Anthony. "The Early Works of Charles Le Brun." *The Burlington Magazine* 85, no. 496 (1944): 165–94.

Bosworth, Welles. "The Rockerfeller Donation for the Restoration of Versailles, Fontainebleau, and Rheims." *The American Magazine of Art* 16, no. 11 (1925): 586–90.

Bottineau, Yves. *Versailles, miroir des princes*. Paris: Arthaud, 1989.

Bourgine, Xavier. "La fréquentation des musées et monuments parisiens poursuit sa hausse en 2018." *Le Monde*, January 15, 2019.

Boze, Claude Gros de. *Histoire de l'académie royale des inscriptions et belles-lettres depuis son etablissement, avec les eloges des academiciens morts depuis son renouvellement*, 3 vols. Paris: np, 1740.

Bresc-Bautier, Geneviève and Étienne Revault, eds. *La galerie d'Apollon au Louvre*. Paris: Gallimard, 2004.

Bresc-Bautier, Geneviève, Yannick Lintz, Françoise Madrus, and Guillaume Fonkenell, eds. *Histoire du Louvre*, 3 vols. Paris: Fayard & Louvre éditions, 2016.

"Brevets de logements sous la grande galerie du Louvre accordés à des artistes et à des artisans." Paris, n.d. Archives nationales (A.N. O^1 1672).

Brice, Germain. *Description nouvelle de ce qu'il y a de plus remarquable dans la ville de Paris*. Paris: Chez Le Gras, 1684.

Brown, Patricia Leigh. "How Will Trump Redecorate the White House?" *New York Times*, March 17, 2016. Available online: https://www.nytimes.com/2016/03/20/opinion/sunday/how-will-trump-redecorate-the-white-house.html?_r=0 (accessed September 26, 2018).

Brunon, Hervé and Monique Mosser. *L'Imaginaire des Grottes dans les Jardins Européens*. Paris: Éditions Hazan, 2014.

Burchard, Wolf. *The Sovereign Artist: Charles Le Brun and the Image of Louis XIV*. London: Paul Holberton Publishing, 2016.

Burke, Peter. *The Fabrication of Louis XIV*. New Haven, CT and London: Yale University Press, 1992.

Cailleux, Jean. "Some Family and Group Portraits by François de Troy (1645–1730)." *The Burlington Magazine* 113, no. 817 (1971): 1–18.

Callières, François de. *De la manière de négoicier avec les souverains*, 2 vols, New edn. London: Jean Nourse, 1750.

Campan, Madame. *Mémoires de Madame Campan, première femme de chambre de Marie-Antoinette*, edited by Jean Chalon. Paris: Mercure de France, 1988.

Campbell, Janie. "Donald Trump Already Redecorated the Oval Office, and of Course the Curtains Are Gold." *Huffington Post*. Available online: https://www.huffingtonpost.com/entry/donald-trump-gold-curtains-oval-office_us_5882b0a4e4b096b4a231dde1 (accessed September 26, 2018).

Cassidy-Geiger, Maureen, ed. *Fragile Diplomacy: Meissen Porcelain for European Courts ca.1710–63*. New Haven, CT and London: Yale University Press, 2007.

Castellucio, Stéphane. "La Galerie des Glaces: les réceptions d'ambassadeurs." *Versalia* 9 (2006): 24–52.

Castelluccio, Stéphane. *Le Garde-Meuble de la Couronne et ses intendants du XVIe au XVIIIe siècle*. Paris: CTHS (Comité des travaux historiques et scientifiques), 2004.

Castex, Jean-Gérald. "La difusión de la Escalera de los Embajadores." In *Dibujar Versalles. Bocetos y cartones de Charles Le Brun (1619–1690) para la Escalera de los Embajadores y la Galería de los Espejos*, exhibition catalogue, edited by Bénédicte Gady, 124–9. Barcelona: Caixa Forum, 2016.

Castle, Terry. "Contagious Folly: 'An Adventure' and Its Skeptics." *Critical Inquiry* 17, no. 4 (July 1991): 741–72.

Castle, Terry. "Contagious Folly: *An Adventure* and Its Skeptics." In *Questions of Evidence: Proof, Practice, and Persuasion across the Disciplines*, edited by James Chandler, Arnold Davidson, and Harry Harootunian, 11–42. Chicago, IL: University of Chicago Press. 1994.

Castle, Terry. "Marie-Antoinette Obsession." In *Marie Antoinette: Writings on the Body of a Queen*, edited by Dena Goodman and Thomas E. Kaiser, 199–238. New York: Routledge, 2013.

Cheek, Richard and Tom Gannon. *Newport Mansions: The Gilded Age*. Newport, RI: The Preservation Society of Newport County, 2006.

Childs, Adrienne L. "A *Blackamoor's Progress*: The Ornamental Black Body in European Furniture." In *ReSignifications: European Blackamoors, Africana Readings*, edited by Ellyn Toscano and Awam Amkpa, 117–26. Rome: Postcart, 2017.

Chilton, Meredith, ed. *Fired by Passion: Vienna Baroque Porcelain of Claudius Innocentius du Paquier*, 3 vols. Stuttgart: Arnoldsche Art Publishers, 2009.

Chrisman-Campbell, Kimberly. "Dressing to Impress: The Morning Toilette and the Fabrication of Femininity." In *Paris: Life & Luxury in the Eighteenth Century*, edited by Charissa Bremer-David, 52–73. Los Angeles: The J. Paul Getty Museum, 2011.

Chrisman-Campbell, Kimberly. "How Gold Went from Godly to Gaudy." *Atlantic*, December 2, 2016. Available online: https://www.theatlantic.com/entertainment/archive/2016/12/the-midas-touch-gold-trump-gouthiere/509036/ (accessed September 26, 2018).

Clark, Ronald W. *Benjamin Franklin: A Biography*. New York: Random House, 1983.

Clément, Pierre. *Lettres, instructions et mémoires de Colbert*, 8 vols. Paris: Imprimerie impériale, 1861–82.

Colas des Francs, Nathalie. *Madame de Polignac Intime de Marie-Antoinette*, 2nd edn. Paris: Tallandier, 2013.

Cole, Robert J. "Plaza Hotel Is Sold to Donald Trump for $390 Million." *New York Times*, March 27, 1988.

Collas, Émile. *La Belle-fille de Louis XIV*. Paris: Emile Paul frères, 1920.

Corigliano, John and William M. Hoffman. *The Ghosts of Versailles: A Grand Opera Buffa in Two Acts*. New York; Milwaukee, WI: G. Schirmer; Distributed by Hal Leonard, 1991.

Couronne, Ivan. "For Trump, the White House Is a Long-Held Ambition." *Times of Israel*, March 17, 2017. Available online: https://www.timesofisrael.com/for-trump-the-white-house-is-a-long-held-ambition/ (accessed October 1, 2018).

Cowan, Pamela. *A Fanfare for the Sun King: Unfolding Fans for Louis XIV*. London: Third Millennium Publishing, 2003.

Craven, Wayne. *Gilded Mansions: Grand Architecture and High Society*. New York: W. W. Norton & Company, 2009.

Crawford, Katherine. *Perilous Performances: Gender and Regency in Early Modern France*. Cambridge, MA and London: Harvard University Press, 2004.

Curteis, Ian and John Bruce. *Miss Morison's Ghosts*. London: ITV, 1981.

Dabydeen, David. *Hogarth's Blacks: Images of Blacks in Eighteenth-Century English Art*. Athens: University of Georgia Press, 1987.

Dangeau, Philippe de Courcillon, duc de. *Journal du marquis de Dangeau*, edited by Eudore Soulié, 19 vols. Paris: Firmin Didot, 1854–60.

Dangremond, Sam. "A History of Mar-a-Lago, Donald Trump's American Castle." *Town and Country*, December 22, 2017. Available online: https://www.townandcountrymag.com/style/home-decor/a7144/mar-a-lago-history/ (accessed October 1, 2018).

Derringer, Jaime. "Murakami Versailles Exhibition." *Design Milk*, October 6, 2010. Available online: https://design-milk.com/murakami-versailles-exhibition/ (accessed September 14, 2018).

Descartes, René. *The Philosophical Works*. Cambridge: Cambridge University Press, 1975–76.

Diderot, Denis, Friedrich Melchior Grimm, Jakob Heinrich Meister, and Guillaume-Thomas Raynal, Meister. *Correspondance littéraire, philosophique et critique,*

Novembre 1774. Edited by Maurice Tourneux, 16 vols. Reprint, Lichtenstein: Kraus Reprint, 1968 [1813].

Didier, Frédéric. "Les appartements de Monsieur et de Madame à l'extremité de l'aile du Midi en 1787." *Versalia* 21 (2018): 59–80.

Duindam, Jeroen. *Vienna and Versailles: The Courts of Europe's Dynastic Rivals, 1550–1780*. Cambridge: Cambridge University Press, 2007.

Duindam, Jeroen, Tülay Artan, and I. Metin Kunt, eds. *Royal Courts in Dynastic States and Empires: A Global Perspective*. Leiden: Brill, 2011.

Dussieux, Louis. *Le Château de Versailles: Histoire et Description*, 2 vols, 2nd edn. Versailles: Bernard, 1885.

Dyer, Geoff. "Eugene Atget, Mute Witness." *Aperture* 206 (2012): 66–73.

Eamon, William, *Science and the Secrets of Nature: Books of Secrets in Medieval and Early Modern Culture*. Princeton, NJ: Princeton University Press, 1994.

Earle, Tom and Kate J. P. Lowe. *Black Africans in Renaissance Europe*. Cambridge: Cambridge University Press, 2005.

Edité par Ministère de la Culture. *Colbert 1619–1683*, exhibition catalogue. Paris: Hotel de la Monnaie, 1983.

El Hamel, Chouki. *Black Morocco: A History of Slavery, Race, and Islam*. Cambridge: Cambridge University Press, 2013.

Elias, Norbert. *The Court Society*, translated by Edmund Jephcott. New York: Pantheon Books, 1983.

Ellis, Harold A. *Boulainvilliers and the French Monarchy: Aristocratic Politics in Early Eighteenth-Century France*. Ithaca, NY and London: Cornell University Press, 1988.

Eriksen, Sven and Geoffrey de Bellaigue. *Sèvres Porcelain: Vincennes and Sèvres 1740–1800*. London and Boston, MA: Faber and Faber, 1987.

Évrard, Fernand. *Versailles, ville du roi*. Paris: Leroux, 1935.

Fahrenthold, David A. and Robert O'Harrow Jr. "Trump: A True Story." *Washington Post*, August 10, 2016.

Falaky, Fayçal. "From Barber to Coiffeur: Art and Economic Liberalisation in Eighteenth-Century France." *Journal for Eighteenth-Century Studies* 36, no. 1 (2013): 35–48.

Félibien, André. *Description de la Grotte de Versailles*. Paris: Imprimerie royale, 1676.

Félibien, André. *Description sommaire du chasteau de Versailles*. Paris: Charles Savreaux, 1674.

Féraud, Jean-François. *Dictionnaire Critique de La Langue Française*. Marseille: Chez Jean Mossy Pere et Fils, 1787–88.

Ferrero, Larrie D. "Bernard Renau d'Elissagary." *Neptunia* 225 (2009).

Foletier, François de Vaux de. *Les Tsiganes dans l'ancienne France*. Paris: Connaissance du Monde, 1961.

Fonkenell, Guillaume. *Building the Louvre: A Richly Illustrated History*. Paris: Louvre Éditions, 2017.

Forty, Adrian. "Versailles—A Political Theme Park." In *Architecture and the Sites of History: Interpretations of Buildings and Cities*, edited by Iain Borden and David Dunster, 54–5. New York: Watson Guptill, 1995.

Foulkes, Fiona. "'Quality Always Distinguishes Itself': Louis Hippolyte LeRoy and the Luxury Clothing Industry in Early Nineteenth-Century Paris." In *Consumers and Luxury: Consumer Culture in Europe, 1650–1850*, edited by Maxine Berg and Helen Clifford, 183–205. Manchester: Manchester University Press, 1999.

Fourny, Diane. "The Eighteenth Century or 'Fin-de-Siècle' Beginnings." *L'Esprit Créateur* 32, no. 4 (1992): 7–19.

Fox, Emily Jane. "Let Fran Lebowitz Soothe All Your Election-Related Worries." *Vanity Fair*, October 20, 2016. Available online: https://www.vanityfair.com/news/2016/10/fran-lebowitz-trump-clinton-election (accessed October 1, 2018).

Friedman, Ann. "The Evolution of the Parterre d'eau." *Journal of Garden History* 8, no. 1 (1988): 1–30.

Froulay, Marquise de Créquy Victoire Renée Caroline de. *Souvenirs de la Marquise de Créquy, 1710 à 1803*. Paris: Michel Lévy, 1867.

Fuhring, Peter, Louis Marchesano, Rémi Mathis, and Vanessa Selbach, eds. *A Kingdom of Images: French Prints in the Age of Louis XIV*. Los Angeles, CA: Getty Research Institute, 2015.

Furcy-Raynaud, Marc, ed. *Correspondance de M. d'Angiviller*. Paris: J. Schemit, 1906–07.

Furcy-Raynaud, Marc, ed. *Correspondance de M. de Marigny avec Coypel, Lépicié et Cochin*. Nouvelles archives de l'art français, 3rd series, no. 20. 1904.

Furetière, Antoine. *Dictionnaire universel, contenant généralement tous les mots françois, tant vieux que modernes …*, 3 vols. The Hague, Netherlands: Arnout et Reinier Leers, 1690.

Gadhoum, Sonia. "Presence réelle et mythique dans le Dictionnaire universel d'Antoine Furetière." In *L'Afrique au XVIIe siècle, mythes et réalités …*, edited by Alia Baccar Bornaz, 23–30. Tübingen, Germany: Gunter Narr Verlag, 2003.

Gady, Alexandre. "La Escalera de los Embajadores, Una obra maestra por adaptación." In *Bocetos y cartones de Charles Le Brun (1619–1690) para la Escalera de los Embajadores y la Galería de los Espejos*, edited by Bénédicte Gadyexhibition catalogue, 43–51. Barcelona: Caixa Forum, 2016.

Gady, Alexandre. *Versailles la fabrique d'un chef-d'oeuvre*. Paris; Versailles: Passage; Château de Versailles, 2014.

Gady, Alexandre, Aurélie Julia, and Michel Crépu. "le Miroir de tous les phantasmes." *Revue Des Deux Mondes* (July 2013): 141–9.

Gady, Bénédicte. "From Sketches to Cartoons: Analysis of (and Doubts about) Charles Le Brun's Working Procedures for the Grands Décors." In *The Gallery of Charles XI at the Royal Palace of Stockholm—in Perspective*, 175–84. Stockholm: Nationalmuseum and Stockholm University, 2016.

Gady, Bénédicte. "La escalera es un sueño." In *Dibujar Versalles. Bocetos y cartones de Charles Le Brun (1619–1690) para la Escalera de los Embajadores y la Galería de los Espejos*, edited by Bénédicte Gady, exhibition catalogue, 61–71. Barcelona: Caixa Forum, 2016.

Gady, Bénédicte. "La Galería de los Espejos, un cambio de escala y de discurso." In *Dibujar Versalles. Bocetos y cartones de Charles Le Brun (1619–1690) para la Escalera de los Embajadores y la Galería de los Espejos*, edited by Bénédicte Gady, exhibition catalogue. Barcelona: Caixa Forum, 2016.

Gady, Bénédicte. *L'ascension de Charles Le Brun: liens sociaux et production artistique*. Paris: Éditions de la Maison des sciences de l'homme, 2010.

Gady, Bénédicte. "Los cartones de Charles Le Brun, un testimonio único de la fabricación de las grandes decoraciones." In *Dibujar Versalles. Bocetos y cartones de Charles Le Brun (1619–1690) para la Escalera de los Embajadores y la Galería de los Espejos*, edited by Bénédicte Gady, exhibition catalogue. Barcelona: Caixa Forum, 2016.

Gady, Bénédicte and Nicolas Milovanovic, eds. *Charles Le Brun (1619–1690)*, exhibition catalogue, Lens: Louvre-Lens. Paris: Lienart éditions, 2016.

Geffroy, Gustave. *Les musées d'Europe: Versailles*. Paris: Eds. Nilsson, 1900.

Gehlen, Stefan. "'Portée en chaise par ses Turcs:' Turquerie und 'Kammertürken am Hof Sophie Charlottes." In *Sophie Charlotte und ihr Schloss: Ein Musenhof des Barock in Brandenburg-Preussen*, edited by Gerd Bartoschek, 106–12. Munich: Prestel, 1999.

Gerber, Matthew. *Bastards: Politics, Family, and Law in Early Modern France*. New York: Oxford University Press, 2012.

Germann, Jennifer G. *Picturing Marie Leszczinska (1703–1768): Representing Queenship in Eighteenth-Century France*. London and New York: Routledge, 2015.

Germer, Stefan. *Kunst, Macht, Diskurs. Die intellektuelle Karriere des André Félibien im Frankreich von Louis XIV*. Munich: Wilhelm Fink, 1997.

Gibbons, Arnold Osborne, ed. *The Trianon Adventure: A Symposium*. London: Museum Press, 1958.

Gillespie, Charles Coulston. *Science and Polity in France at the End of the Old Regime*. Princeton, NJ: Princeton University Press, 1980.

Goldman, Edward. "Louis XIV to Donald Trump: 'You Are Fired.'" *Huffington Post*, March 22, 2016. Available online: https://www.huffingtonpost.com/edward-goldman/louis-xiv-to-donald-trump_b_9526572.html (accessed September 26, 2018).

Gollayan, Christian. "Trump Has Already Redecorated the Oval Office." *New York Post*, January 23, 2017. Available online: https://nypost.com/2017/01/23/trump-has-already-redecorated-the-oval-office/ (accessed September 26, 2018).

Goodman, Dena, ed. *Marie-Antoinette: Writings on the Body of a Queen*. New York: Routledge, 2003.

Grandjean, Serge. "Une tabatière royale de Gouers." *La revue du Louvre et des musées de France* 29, no. 4 (1979): 294–7.

Grant, Sarah. *Female Portraiture and Patronage in Marie-Antoinette's Court: The Princesse de Lamballe*. London: Routledge, 2018.

Greenberg, Jonathan. "Trump Lied to Me about His Wealth to Get onto the Forbes 400. Here Are the Tapes." *Washington Post*, April 20, 2018. Available online: https://www.washingtonpost.com/outlook/trump-lied-to-me-about-his-wealth-to-get-onto-the-forbes-400-here-are-the-tapes/2018/04/20/ac762b08-4287-11e8-8569-26fda6b404c7_story.html?utm_term=.9005250bff4e (accessed October 1, 2018).

Greenfield, Lauren. *Generation Wealth*. Available online: http://www.generation-wealth.com/ (accessed September 26, 2018).

Greenfield, Lauren. *Queen of Versailles*. Evergreen Pictures, 2012.

Griffin, Penny, ed. *St Hugh's: One Hundred Years of Women's Education in Oxford*. Oxford: Palgrave Macmillan, 1986.

Grimaldi-Hierholtz, Roseline. *Les Trinitaires de Fontainebleau et d'Avon*. Fontainebleau: Centre d'études culturelles civiques et sociales de Seine-et-Marne, 1990.

Gruson, Kerry. "Post Home for Sale for $20 Million." *New York Times*, July 16, 1981. Available online: https://www.nytimes.com/1981/07/16/garden/post-home-for-sale-for-20.html (accessed October 1, 2018).

Guiffrey, Jules. "Brevets de logements dans la Galerie du Louvre." In *Nouvelles Archives de l'Art Français*, 63–4. Paris: Charavay Frères, 1873.

Guiffrey, Jules. *Comptes des bâtiments du roy, sous le règne de Louis XIV*, 5 vols. Paris: Imprimerie Nationale, 1881–1901.

Guiffrey, Jules. *Inventaire général du mobilier de la couronne sous Louis XIV (1663–1715)*. 2 vols. Paris: J Rouam, 1885–6.

Guyot, Joseph-Nicolas. *Traité des Droits, Fonctions, Franchises, Exemptions, Prérogatives et Privilèges Annexés en France à chaque Dignité, à chaque Office & à chaque État, soit Civil, soit Militaire, soit Ecclésiastique*, 4 vols. Paris: Visse, 1787.

Haberman, Maggie and Alexander Burns. "Donald Trump's Presidential Run Began in an Effort to Gain Stature." *New York Times*, March 12, 2016. Available online: https://www.nytimes.com/2016/03/13/us/politics/donald-trump-campaign.html (accessed October 1, 2018).

Hanley, Sarah. *The Lit de Justice of the Kings of France: Constitutional Ideology in Legend, Ritual, and Discourse*. Princeton, NJ: Princeton University Press, 1983.

Hedin, Thomas. *The Sculpture of Gaspard and Balthazard Marsy: Art and Patronage in the Early Reign of Louis XIV, with a Catalogue Raisonné*. Columbia: University of Missouri, 1983.

Hellman, Mimi. "The Joy of Sets: The Uses of Seriality in the French Interior." In *Furnishing the Eighteenth Century: What Furniture Can Tell Us about the European and American Past*, edited by Dena Goodman and Kathryn Norberg, 129–53. New York and London: Routledge, 2006.

Hézecques, Félix de France de. *Souvenirs d'un Page de La Cour de Louis XVI*. Paris: Didier et Cie, 1873.
Hitzel, Frédéric. "Turcs et turqueries à la cour de Catherine de Médicis." In *Les Musulmans dans l'histoire de l'Europe: Tome 1. Une intégration invisible*, edited by Jocelyne Dakhlia and Bernard Vincent, 33–54. Paris: Albin Michel, 2011.
Hoffmann, Klaus. "Johann Friedrich Böttger—Stationen seines Lebens." In *Johann Friedrich Böttger: Die Erfindung des europäischen Porzellans*, edited by Willi Goder, Klaus Hoffmann, Rolf Sonnemann, and Eberhard Wächtler, 71–98. Leipzig: Staatliche Kunstsammlungen Dresden, 1982.
Hoffmann, Roald. "Meissen Chymistry." *American Scientist* 92, no. 4 (2004): 312–15.
Horowski, Leonhard. "'Such a Great Advantage for My Son:' Office-Holding and Career Mechanisms at the Court of France, 1661 to 1789." *The Court Historian* 8 (2003): 125–75.
Hyde, Elizabeth. *Cultivated Power: Flowers, Culture, and Politics in the Reign of Louis XIV*. Philadelphia: University of Pennsylvania Press, 2005.
Ikeda, Riyoko. *The Rose of Versailles*. First published, 1976, English version, Tokyo: Sanyusha, 1981.
Ingamells, John. *The Wallace Collection: Catalogue of Pictures*. London: The Trustees of the Wallace Collection, 1989.
Iremonger, Lucille. *The Ghosts of Versailles: Miss Moberly and Miss Jourdain and Their Adventure: A Critical Study*. London: White Lion Publishers, 1975.
Isambert, François André and Alphonse Taillandier, eds. *Recueil général des anciennes lois françaises*, 29 vols. Paris: Belin-Leprieur, 1821–33.
Isom-Verhaaren, Christine. *Allies with the Infidel: The Ottoman and French Alliance in the Sixteenth Century*. London: Tauris Academic Studies, 2011.
Jacquiot, Josèphe. *Médailles et jetons de Louis XIV, d'après le manuscrit de Londres (ADD 31908)*, 4 vols. Paris: Académie des Inscriptions et Belles Lettres, 1968.
Jacquot, Benoit et al. "Les Adieux a La Reine: Un Film de Benoit Jacquot: Dossier: Scénario Intégral de Benoit Jacquot et Gilles Taurand." *L'avant scène. Cinéma*. 601, March 2013.
Jal, Augustin. *Dictionnaire critique de biographie et d'histoire: errata and supplement pour tous les dictionnaires historiques d'après des documents authentiques inédits*, 2nd edn. Paris: Henri Plon, 1872.
Janin, Jules. *Versailles et Son Musée Historique, Ou Description Complète et Anecdotique de La Ville, Du Palais, Du Musée, Du Parc et Des Deux Trianons: Précédé d'un Itinéraire de Paris à Versailles, et Orné de Plans et de Vues Gravées Sur Bois Par Jules Janin*. Paris: E Bourdin et Cie, 1837.
Jean-Francois, Autier (dit Leonard). *Souvenirs de Léonard*. Paris: Alfonse Levavasseur et cie, 1838.
"John Vanderlyn's View of Versailles: Spectacle, Landscape, and the Visual Demands of Panorama Painting: Early Popular Visual Culture: Vol 12, No 1." Available online:

https://www-tandfonline-com.ezproxy1.library.usyd.edu.au/doi/abs/10.1080/17460654.2013.876922 (accessed November 29, 2018).

Jones, Colin. *The Great Nation: France from Louis XV to Napoleon*. London: Penguin Books, 2003.

Jourdain, Eleanor Frances. *The Drama in Europe in Theory and Practice*. London: Methuen, 1924.

Jourdain, Eleanor Frances. *An Introduction to the French Classical Drama*. Oxford: Clarendon Press, 1912.

Jullian, Philippe. *Robert de Montesquiou, Un Prince 1900. With Plates, Including Portraits, Illustrations and a Bibliography*. Paris: Perrin, 1965.

Kaiser, Thomas E. "Louis le Bien-Aimé and the Rhetoric of the Royal Body." In *From the Royal to the Republican Body: Incorporating the Political in Seventeenth- and Eighteenth-Century France*, edited by Sara E. Melzer and Kathryn Norberg, 131–61. Berkeley: University of California Press, 1998.

Kaiser, Thomas E. "Madame de Pompadour and the Theatres of Power." *French Historical Studies* 19, no. 4 (1996): 1025–44.

Kaiser, Thomas E. "Scandal in the Royal Nursery: Marie-Antoinette and the 'Gouvernantes des Enfants de France.'" *Historical Reflections* 32 (2006): 403–20.

Kaplan, Paul. "Black Turks: Venetian Artists and Perceptions of Ottoman Ethnicity." In *The Turk and Islam in the Western Eye, 1450–1750: Visual Imagery before Orientalism*, edited by James G. Harper, 41–66. Aldershot and Burlington: Ashgate, 2011.

Kaplan, Paul. "Titian's 'Laura Dianti' and the Origins of the Motif of the Black Page in Portraiture." *Antichità viva* 21 (1982): 10–18.

Karabell, Shellie. "What Louis XIV Can Teach Donald Trump." *Forbes*, February 14, 2016.

Kathrens, Michael C. *Great Houses of New York, 1880–1930*. New York: Acanthus Press, 2014.

Kaufmann, Georg, *Bemalte Wandfliesen. Bunte Welt auf kleinen Platten. Kulturgeschichte, Technik und Dekoration der Fliesen in Mitteleuropa*. Leipzig: Duncker und Humblot, 1880.

Kelly, Tim. "Versailles Mansion in Vaughan Yours for $17.8M." *YorkRegion.com*. Available online: https://www.yorkregion.com/news-story/4148941-versailles-mansion-in-vaughan-yours-for-17-8m/ (accessed September 18, 2018).

Kiernan, Linda. "Trump's White House Might Look Like a Royal Court, but He's No Louis XIV." *The Conversation*, June 23, 2017. Available online: https://theconversation.com/trumps-white-house-might-look-like-a-royal-court-but-hes-no-louis-xiv-79362 (accessed September 26, 2018).

Kisluk-Grosheide, Daniëlle and Bertrand Rondot, eds. *Visitors to Versailles. From Louis XIV to the French Revolution*, exhibition catalogue. The Metropolitan Museum of Art, New York, 2018.

Klidis, Artemis. *François Girardon, Bildhauer in königlichen Diensten 1663–1700.* Weimar: VDG, 2001.

Knothe, Florian. *The Manufacture des meubles de la couronne aux Gobelins under Louis XIV: A Social, Political and Cultural History.* Brussels: Brepols, 2016.

Kruft, Hanno-Walter. *A History of Architectural Theory: From Vitruvius to the Present*, translated by R. Taylor, E. Callander, and A. Wood. New York: Princeton Architectural Press, 1994.

Kwass, Michael. "Big Hair: A Wig History of Consumption in Eighteenth-Century France." *The American Historical Review* 11, no. 3 (2003): 631–59.

Laborde, Marquis Léon de. *Répertoire alphabétique manuscrit de noms d'artistes et artisans des XVIe, XVIIe et XVIIIe siècles relevés dans les anciens registres de l'état civil parisien (XVIIe-XVIIIe siècle), dit Fichier Laborde.* Nouvelles acquisitions françaises, B.N.F., Ms., Paris, 1871.

La Fontaine, Jean de. *Recueil des poesies chrestiennes et diverses.* Paris, 1671.

La Font de Saint Yenne, Étienne. *L'Ombre du grand Colbert, le Louvre, et la ville de Paris …*, nouvelle edition. Paris: np, 1752.

La galerie des Glaces: Charles Le Brun maître d'œuvre, exhibition catalogue, edited by Alexandre Maral and Nicolas Milovanovic. Versailles: musée national du Château, 2007.

La Gorce, Jérôme de. "Le Premier grand spectacle équestre donné à Versailles: le carrousel des galants maures." In *Les Ecuries royales du XVIe au XVIIe siècle*, edited by Daniel Roche, 276–85. Versailles: Association pour l'académie d'art équestre de Versailles, 1998.

Lamont, Mark. *The Mysterious Paths of Versailles: An Investigation of a Psychical Journey Back in Time.* Bloomington: In Xlibris Corp, 2016.

Landweber, Julia. "French Delight in Turkey: The Impact of Turkey on the Construction of French Identity, 1660–1789." PhD diss., Rutgers, The State University of New Jersey, 2001.

Lange, Liliane. "La grotte de Thétis et le premier Versailles de Louis XI." *Art de France* 1 (1961): 133–48.

Larsson, Lars Olaf. "Versailles als Schauplatz. Die bildende Kunst im Dienste der Repräsentation im Schloss und Garten von Versailles." In *Die Inszenierung des Absolutismus. Politische Begründung und künstlerische Gestaltung höfischer Feste im Frankreich Ludwigs XIV*, edited by Fritz Reckow, 51–69. Erlangen: Universitätsbund Erlangen-Nürnberg, 1992.

Lastic, Georges de. "Nicolas de Largillière: heurs et malheurs d'un chef-d'oeuvre." *L'Oeil* 365 (1985): 36–45.

Le Comte, Florent. *Cabinet des singularitez d'architecture, peinture, sculpture et graveure ….* Paris: Étienne Picart and Nicolas Le Clerc, 1699–1700.

Le Duc, Geneviève. *Porcelaine tendre de Chantilly au XVIIIe siècle.* Paris: Hazan, 1996.

Le Guillou, Jean-Claude. "L'appartement de Madame Sophie Au Château de Versailles. Formation et Métamorphoses, 1774–1790." *Gazette des Beaux-Arts* 97 (1981): 201–18.

Le Roi, Joseph-Adrien. *De l'état de Versailles Avant 1789*. Versailles: Imprimerie de Aubert, 1871.

Lebigre, Arlette. *La Duchesse de Longueville*. Paris: Perrin, 2004.

Lebrun, François. "Turcs, barbaresques, musulmans, vus par les français du XVIIe siècles, d'apres le 'Dictionnaire' de Furetière." *Cahiers de Tunisie* 44, no. 3–4 (1991): 69–74.

Lefebvre, Thierry. "Pour Kapoor." *Sociétés & Représentations* 41 (2016): 203–11.

Louis XIV (1638–1715 ; roi de France). *Lettre du Roy, écrite à Monseigneur le Cardinal de Noailles Archevêque de Paris pour faire chanter le Te Deum dans l'Église de Nostre-Dame, en action de graces de la cessation de la contagion dans le Royaume*. Paris: chez Jean-Baptiste Delespine, 1723.

Lever, Évelyne, ed. *"Que je suis heureuse d'être ta femme": lettres intimes, 1778–1782*. Paris: Tallandier, 2009.

Lombard-Jourdan, Anne. "Des Malgaches à Paris sous Louis XIV: exotisme et mentalités en France au XVIIe siècle." *Archipel* 9, no. 1 (1975): 79–90.

Louis, XIV, *Manière de montrer les jardins de Versailles par Louis XIV*, [Versailles 1689]. Edited and reprinted. Paris: Simone Hoog, 1982.

Love, Ronald S. "Rituals of Majesty: France, Siam, and Court Spectacle in Royal Image-Building at Versailles in 1685 and 1686." *Canadian Journal of History* 31 (1996): 171–98.

Lugo-Ortiz, Agnes and Angela Rosenthal, eds. *Slave Portraiture in the Atlantic World*. New York: Cambridge University Press, 2013.

Luttervelt, Remmet van. "De ontvangst van Cornelis Hop als Nederlandsch ambassadeur te Parijs." *Jaarverslag van het Koninklijk Oudheidkundig Genootschap* (1948/9, pub. 1950): 80–104.

Luynes, Charles Philippe d'Albert, duc de. *Mémoires du duc de Luynes sur la cour de Louis XV, 1735–1758*, edited by Louis Dussieux and Eudore Soulié, 17 vols. Paris: Firmin Didot Frères, 1860–5.

Mabille, Gérard. "La galerie d'Apollon dans l'histoire des galeries royales françaises." In *Le galerie d'Apollon au palais du Louvre*, edited by Genevieve Bresc-Bautier and Étienne Revault, 12–21. Paris: Gallimard, 2004.

Madsen, Axel. *John Jacob Astor: America's First Multimillionaire*. New York: Wiley and Sons, 2001.

Maher, James T. *The Twilight of Splendor: Chronicles of the Age of American Palaces*. Boston, MA: Little Brown, 1975.

Maintenon, Françoise d'Aubigné, Madame de. *Lettres de Madame de Maintenon*, nouvelle edition, 9 vols. Chez Antoine Philibert, 1758.

Marchesano, Louis. "The Impostures Innocentes: Bernard Picart's Defense of the Professional Engraver." In *Bernard Picart and the First Global Vision of Religion*, edited by Lynn Hunt, Margaret Jacob, and Wijnand Mijnhardt, 105–37. Los Angeles, CA: Getty Research Institute, 2010.

Marchesano, Louis and Christian Michel. *Printing the Grand Manner: Monumental Prints in the Age of Louis XIV*. Los Angeles, CA: Getty Research Institute, 2010.

Marolles, Michel de. *Livre des peintres et graveurs*. Paris: np, 1677.

Marteilhe, Jean. *Mémoire d'un Protestant condamné aux galères de France pour cause de religion ….* Rotterdam: J.D. Beman & fils, 1757.

Martin, Germain. *La grande industrie sous le règne de Louis XIV (plus particulièrement de 1660 à 1715)*. Paris: Rousseau, 1899.

Martin, Meredith. "Amassed Ornaments: Meredith Martin on Contemporary Art at Versailles." Available online: http://link.galegroup.com/apps/doc/A252292963/EAIM?sid=googlescholar (accessed September 14, 2018).

Martin, Meredith. "Mirror Reflections: Louis XIV, Phra Narai, and the Material Culture of Kingship." *Art History* 38, no. 4 (2015): 652–67.

Martin, Meredith. "Special Embassies and Overseas Visitors." In *Visitors to Versailles. From Louis XIV to the French Revolution*, edited by Danièlle Kisluk-Grosheide and Bertrand Rondot, 108–21. New York: Metropolitan Museum of Art and Yale University Press, 2018.

Martin, Meredith and Gillian Weiss. "A Tale of Two Guns: Maritime Weapons between France and Algiers." In *The Art of Travel: The Mobility of People and Things in the Early-Modern Mediterranean*, edited by Elisabeth Fraser. New York: Routledge, 2019. https://www.google.com.au/books/edition/The_Mobility_of_People_and_Things_in_the/SHGlDwAAQBAJ?hl=en&kptab=editions&gbpv=1.

Martin, Meredith and Gillian Weiss. "'Turks' on Display at Versailles during the Reign of Louis XIV." *L'Esprit Créateur* 53, no. 4 (2013): 98–112.

Martin, Morag. *Selling Beauty: Cosmetics, Commerce, and French Society, 1750–1830*. Baltimore, MD: Johns Hopkins University Press, 2009.

Maskill, David. "The Neighbor from Hell: André Rouquet's Eviction from the Louvre." *Louvre Local, Journal18* 2 (2016). Available online: http://www.journal18.org/822.

Mathorez, Jules. *Les Etrangers en France sous l'ancien régime: histoire de la formation de la population française*, 2 vols. Paris: Edouard Champion, 1919.

McCarthy, Justin Huntly. *The French Revolution*, vol. 1. London: Chatto, 1890.

McClellan, Andrew. *Inventing the Louvre: Art, Politics, and the Origins of the Modern Museum in Eighteenth-Century Paris*. Berkeley: California University Press, 1994.

McGrath, Elizabeth. "Caryatids, Page Boys, and African Fetters: Themes of Slavery in European Art." In *The Slave in European Art: From Renaissance Trophy to Abolitionist Emblem*, edited by McGrath and Jean Michel Massig, 3–38. London: Warburg Institute, 2012.

Mendelson, Edward. "Baedeker's Universe." *Yale Review* 74 (1985): 386–403.

Mercier, Louis-Sebastien. *Tableau de Paris* 97. Amsterdam: np, 1783.
Merrick, Jeffrey. "Fathers and Kings: Patriarchalism and Absolutism in Eighteenth-Century French Politics." *SVEC* 308 (1993): 281–303.
Merrick, Jeffrey W. *The Desacralization of the French Monarchy in the Eighteenth Century*. Baton Rouge and London: Louisiana University Press, 1990.
Mersenne, Marin. *Correspondance du P. Marin Mersenne, religieux minime (1617–1648)*, edited by Mme Paul Tannery and Cornélis de Waard, 17 vols. Paris: G. Beauchesne, 1932–88.
Merton, Robert K. and Elinor G. Barber. *The Travels and Adventures of Serendipity. A Study in Historical Semantics and the Sociology of Science*, [written in 1958]. Princeton, NJ: Princeton University Press, 2004.
Michel, Christian. *The Académie Royale de Peinture et de Sculpture: The Birth of the French School, 1648–1793*, translated by Chris Miller. Los Angeles, CA: Getty Publications, 2018.
Michel, Christian. *Charles-Nicolas Cochin et l'art des Lumières*. Rome: École française de Rome, 1993.
Milovanovic, Nicolas. "Astronomie et astrologie dans les grands décors français du xviie siècle: de Vaux-le-Vicomte à Versailles." *Revue de l'art* 140 (2003): 29–40.
Milovanovic, Nicolas. "Les plafonds des Grands Appartements du Château de Versailles: un traité du bon gouvernement." *Monuments et mémoires de la Fondation Eugène Piot* 78 (2000): 85–139.
Moberly, Charlotte Anne Elizabeth and Eleanor Frances Jourdain. *An Adventure*, 4th edn, with further additional matter. London: Faber & Faber Limited, 1931.
Moberly, Charlotte Anne Elizabeth and Eleanor Frances Jourdain. *An Adventure, with Appendix and Maps*. London: Macmillan, 1913.
Moberly, Charlotte Anne Elizabeth and Eleanor Frances Jourdain. *An Adventure; with a Preface by Edith Oliver and a Note by J.W. Dunne*. London: Faber, 1951.
Moberly, Charlotte Anne Elizabeth, Eleanor Frances Jourdain, and Michael H. Coleman. *The Ghosts of the Trianon: The Complete An Adventure*. Wellingborough, Northamptonshire, England and New York: Aquarian Press; Distributed in the USA by Sterling, 1988.
Molineux, Catherine. *Faces of Perfect Ebony: Encountering Atlantic Slavery in Imperial Britain*. Cambridge, MA: Harvard University Press, 2012.
Mongredian, Georges. *Colbert: 1619–1683*. Paris: Hachette, 1963.
Montagu, Jennifer. "Le Brun's Early Designs for the Grande Galerie: Some Comments on the Drawings." *Gazette des Beaux-Arts* 120 (1992): 195–206.
Monteclos, J-M. de and Robert Polidori. *Versailles*. Cologne: Könneman, 1996.
Moreau, François. "Égyptiens et égyptiennes à la cour et à la ville: la trace gitane sous Louis XIV." In *Le Théâtre des voyages: une scénographie de l'âge classique*, edited by François Moreau, 445–52. Paris: Presses de l'Université Paris-Sorbonne, 2005.
Morrison, William Alan. *Waldorf Astoria*. Charleston, SC: Arcadia, 2014.

Narbonne, Pierre. *Journal des règnes de Louis XIV et Louis XV: de l'année 1701 à l'année 1744*, edited by Joseph-Adrien Le Roi. Paris: Durand, 1866.

Nelson, Christina and Letitia Roberts. *History of Eighteenth-Century German Porcelain: The Warda Stevens Stout Collection*. New York: Hudson Hills Press, 2013.

Newton, William Ritchey. *La Petite Cour: Services et serviteurs à la Cour de Versailles au XVIII siècle*. Paris: Fayard, 2006.

Newton, William Ritchey. *L'espace du Roi: La Cour de France au Château de Versailles, 1682–1789*. Paris: Le Grand livre du mois, 2000.

Newton, William Ritchey. *Vivre à Versailles: Derrière la façade, la vie quotidienne au Château*, 2nd edn. Paris: Flammarion, 2014.

Nicot, Jean. *Thresor de la langue francoyse tant ancienne que moderne …*. Paris: D. Douceur, 1606.

Nolhac, Pierre de. *Histoire du Château de Versailles au XVIIIe siècle*. Paris: Emile-Paul, 1918.

Nolhac, Pierre de. *Le Château de Versailles Au Temps de Marie-Antoinette: 1770–1789*. Versailles: Aubert, 1889.

Nolhac, Pierre de and André Pératé. *Le Musée National de Versailles, Description Du Château et Des Collections*. Paris: Braun, 1896.

Norberg, Kathryn and Sandra Rosenbaum, eds. *Fashion Prints in the Age of Louis XIV: Interpreting the Art of Elegance*. Lubbock: Texas Tech University Press, 2014.

Notice Du Musée Impérial de Versailles, 3 vols, 2nd edn, Paris: C. de Mourgues Frères, 1859–61.

Nummedal, Tara. *Alchemy and Authority in the Holy Roman Empire*. Chicago, IL: University of Chicago Press, 2007.

Oberkirch, Baronne de. *Mémoires de la baronne d'Oberkirch*, edited by Suzanne Burkard. Paris: Mercure de France, 1989.

Oberkirch, Henriette-Louise de Waldner de Freundstein and Léonce Bernard de Montbrison. *Mémoires de la baronne d'Oberkirch*, 2 vols. Paris, 1869.

Olson, Robert. "The Ottoman-French Treaty of 1740: A Year to Be Remembered?" *Turkish Studies Association Bulletin* 15, no. 2 (1991): 347–55.

Oppermann, Fabien. "Le remeublement du Château de Versailles au XXe siècle, entre action scientifique et manoeuvres politiques." *Bibliothèque de l'École des chartes* 170, no. 1 (2012): 209–32.

Orléans, Elisabeth Charlotte, *Lettres de madame duchesse d'Orléans, née princesse Palatine*, edited by Olivier Amiel. Paris: Mercure de France, 1985.

Ostergard, Derek, ed. *The Sèvres Porcelain Manufactory: Alexandre Brongniart and the Triumph of Art and Industry, 1800–1847*. New Haven, CT: Yale University Press, 1997.

Ovid. *Les Métamorphoses d'Ovide divisées en deux parties, traduites en françois par P. Du Ryer*. Paris: A. Sommaville, 1666.

Pacquement, Alfred, ed. *Anish Kapoor Versailles*. Paris: Éditions RMN-Grand Palais, 2015.

Palmer, Jennifer L. "The Princess Served by Slaves: Making Race Visible through Portraiture in Eighteenth-Century France." *Gender & History* 26, no. 2 (2014): 242–62.

Peabody, Sue. *"There Are No Slaves in France": The Political Culture of Race and Slavery in the Ancien Régime*. New York: Oxford University Press, 1996.

Pennoyer, Peter and Anne Walker. *The Architecture of Warren and Wetmore*. New York: W. W. Norton & Company, 2006.

Pératé, André. *Le parterre d'eau du parc de Versailles sous Louis XIV*. Versailles: L. Bernard, 1899.

Perey, Lucien. *Histoire d'une grande dame au XVIIIe siècle: La Comtesse Hélène Potocka*. Paris: Calmann-Lévy, 1924.

Pernety, Antoine-Joseph. *Dictionnaire portatif de peinture, sculpture et gravure: avec un traité pratique des differentes manieres de peindre, dont la théorie est développée dans les articles qui en sont susceptibles: ouvrage utile aux artistes, aux eleves & aux amateurs*. Paris: Bauche, 1757.

Perrault, Charles and Claude Perrault. *Mémoires de ma Vie par Charles Perrault Voyage à Bordeaux (1669) par Claude Perrault*. Paris: Paul Bonnefon, 1909. https://archive.org/details/mmoiresdemavie00perruoft.

Peters, David. *Sèvres Plates and Services of the 18th Century*, 7 vols. London: The French Porcelain Society, 2005.

Peupler les cieux. Dessins pour les plafonds parisiens au XVIIe siècle. Paris: musée du Louvre, 2014.

Pietsch, Ulrich. "Meissen Porcelain: Making a Brilliant Entrance, 1710 to 1763." In *Triumph of the Blue Swords; Meissen Porcelain for Aristocracy and Bourgeoisie, 1710–1815*, edited by Ulrich Pietsch and Claudia Banz, 11–31. Leipzig: Seeman Verlag, 2010.

Place, Richard. "The Self-Deception of the Strong: France on the Eve of the War of the League of Augsburg." *French Historical Studies* 6, no. 4 (1970): 459–73.

Plantet, Eugène. *Mouley Ismaël, Empereur du Maroc et la Princesse de Conti*. Paris: E. Jamin, 1893.

Polignac, Diane, Comtesse de. *Mémoires sur la vie et le caractere de Mme. La duchesse de Polignac ...*. London: Chez J. Debrett, 1796.

Pommier, Edouard. "Versailles, l'image du souverain." In *Les lieux de mémoires*, 3 vols, edited by Pierre Nora, 193–234. Paris: Gallimard, 1984–86.

Pongo, Marie-Laure Buku. "La seconde ambassade Ottomane, 1742." In *Visiteurs de Versailles, voyageurs, princes, ambassadeurs 1682–1789*, edited by Daniëlle Kisluk-Grosheide and Bertrand Rondot, 186–91. Paris and Versailles: Gallimard, 2017.

Posner, Donald. "Mme. de Pompadour as a Patron of the Visual Arts." *Art Bulletin* 72, no. 1 (1990): 74–105.

Powell, John Hunwick and Eve Trout, eds. *The African Diaspora in the Mediterranean Lands of Islam*. Princeton, NJ: Markus Wiener, 2002.

Préaud, Maxime. *Les Effets du soleil: almanachs du règne de Louis XIV*. Paris: Réunion des musées nationaux, 1995.

Principe, Lawrence. *The Secrets of Alchemy*. Chicago, IL and London: Chicago University Press, 2013.

Principe, Lawrence M. "The End of Alchemy? The Repudiation and Persistence of Chrysopoeia at the Académie Royale des Sciences in the Eighteenth Century." *Osiris* 29, no. 1 (2014): 96–116.

Raunié, Emile, ed. *Chansonnier historique du XVIIIe siècle*, 10 vols. Paris: A. Quantin, 1879–84.

Registre Journal des délibérations et des assemblées de l'Académie Royale des Inscriptions, 1694–1702. Archives et patrimoine historique Institut de France. MS. 8 vols.

Ribeiro, Aileen. *The Art of Dress*. London: Yale University Press, 1995.

Ripa, Cesar. *Iconologie ou la science des emblems devises &c*, 2 vols. Amsterdam: np, 1698.

Ripa, Cesare. *Iconologia overo descrittione dell'imagini universali cavate all antichita et da altri luonghi*. Rome, np, 1603.

Ripa, Cesare and Jean Baudoin. *Iconologie ou explication nouvelle de plusieurs images ... tiréer des recherches et des figures de Cesare Ripa, moralisées par I. Baudoin*, 2 vols. Paris, np, 1644.

Rochbrune, Marie-Laure de. "La porcelain de Vincennes-Sèvres: une arme diplomatique au 18e siècle." *The French Porcelain Society Journal* 3 (2007): 20–34.

Roche, Daniel. *The Culture of Clothing: Dress and Fashion in the "Ancien Régime,"* translated by Jean Birrell. Cambridge: Cambridge University Press, 1994.

Rondot, Bertrand, ed. *Discovering the Secrets of Soft-Paste Porcelain at the Saint Cloud Manufactory ca. 1690–1766*. New Haven, CT and London: Yale University Press, 1999.

Rosenthal, Angela. "Raising Hair." *Eighteenth-Century Studies* 38, no. 1 (Fall, 2004): 1–16.

Rothman, Lily. "The Mar-a-Lago Club Was a 'Winter White House' Even before President Trump Got There." *Time*, February 16, 2017. Available online: http://time.com/4661763/mar-a-lago-donald-trump-marjorie-post/ (accessed October 1, 2018).

Rousset, Jean [de Missy]. *Le ceremonial diplomatique des cours de l'Europe, ou collection des actes, memoires et relations*. Amsterdam: Zacharie Chatelain; The Hague: Pieter de Hondt, 1739.

Rouvroy, Louis de, duc de Saint-Simon. *Mémoires*, 7 vols. Paris: Gallimard, 1986.

Sabatier, Gérard. *Le prince et les arts: stratégies figuratives de la monarchie française, de la Renaissance aux Lumières*. Paris: Champ Vallon, 2010.

Sabatier, Gérard. *Versailles ou le figure du roi*. Paris: A Michel, 1999.

Sabatier, Gérard. "Versailles, un imaginaire politique." *Publications de l'École Française de Rome* 82, no. 1 (1985): 295–324.

Sabatier, Gérard and Béatrix Saule, eds. *Le roi est mort—Louis XIV-1715*, exhibition catalogue, Château de Versailles. Paris: Éditions Tallandier, 2015.

Sahlins, Peter. "Fictions of a Catholic France: The Naturalization of Foreigners, 1685–1787." *Representations* 47 (1994): 85–110.

Saint-Priest, Comte de. *Mémoires: La Revolution et l'Émigration*, edited by baron de Barante. Paris: Calmann-Lévy, 1929.

Sandberg, Brian. "'The Recovering of God's Heritage': Marie de" Medici and French Religious Politics in the Eastern Mediterranean'. In *The Medici and the Levant*, edited by Marta Caroscio and Maurizio Arfaioli. Turnhout: Brepols, 2016.

Sandoval-Strausz, A. K. *Hotel: An American History*. London and New Haven, CT: Yale University Press, 2009.

Schlesinger, H. *La Duchesse de Polignac et son temps*. Paris: Auguste Ghio, 1889.

Schoeneman, Deborah. "Olympic Tower Condo Sold by Khashoggi for Just $12 Million." *Observer*, April 10, 2000. Available online: https://observer.com/2000/04/olympic-tower-condo-sold-by-khashoggi-for-just-12-million/ (accessed September 28, 2018).

Schönfeld, Martin. "'Was There a Western Inventor of Porcelain?" *Technology and Culture* 39, no. 4 (1998): 716–27.

Schwartz, Tony and Donald Trump. *Trump: The Art of the Deal*. New York: Ballentine Books, 1987.

Scudéry, Madeleine de. *La promenade de Versailles*. Paris: Claude Barbin, 1669.

Seal, Mark. "How Donald Trump Beat Palm Beach Society and Won the Fight for Mar-a-Lago." *Vanity Fair*, February, 2017. Available online: https://www.vanityfair.com/style/2016/12/how-donald-trump-beat-palm-beach-society-and-won-the-fight-for-mar-a-lago (accessed October 1, 2018).

Sichel, Edith Helen. *Catherine de' Medici and the French Reformation*. New York: E. P. Dutton, 1905.

Simon, Ed. "Donald Trump: L'Etat, C'est Moi!" *History News Network*, June 5, 2018. Available online: https://historynewsnetwork.org/article/169215 (accessed September 26, 2018).

Singer-Lecocq, Yvonne. *Quand les artistes se logeaient au Louvre 1608–1835*. Paris: Perrin, 1998.

Skilliter, Susan A. "Catherine de' Medici's Turkish Ladies-in Waiting." *Turcica* 7 (1975): 188–204.

Smith, Pamela H. *The Business of Alchemy: Science and Culture in the Holy Roman Empire*. Princeton, NJ: Princeton University Press, 1994.

Soulié, Eudore. *Notice Des Peintures et Sculptures Composant Le Musée Impérial de Versailles*. Versailles: Imprimerie de Montalant-Bougleux, 1854.

Spicer, Joaneath A., ed. *Revealing the African Presence in Renaissance Europe*. Baltimore, MD: Walters Art Museum, 2012.

Staël, Madame de (Anne-Louise-Germaine). *Correspondance Générale*, edited by Béatrice W. Jasinski. Paris: Hachette, 1962.

Stein, Fabian. *Charles Le Brun, la tenture de l'Histoire du Roy*. Worms: Werner, 1985.

Stein, Perrin. "Exoticism as Metaphor: *Turquerie* in Eighteenth-Century French Art." PhD diss., Institute of Fine Arts, New York University, 1997.

Sturge-Whiting, J. R. *The Mystery of Versailles: A Complete Solution*. London: Rider & Co, 1937.

Syndram, Dirk and Ulrike Weinhold, eds. *Böttger Stoneware: Johann Friedrich Böttger and Treasury Art*. Berlin: Deutscher Kunstverlag, 2009.

Tamizey de Larroque, Philippe, ed. *Lettres de Jean Chapelain, de l'Académie Française*, 2 vols. Paris: Imprimerie Nationale, 1880–1883.

Tessier, Alexandre. *Le Grand Hôtel: L'invention du luxe hôtelier 1862–1972*. Rennes: Presses universitaires de Rennes, 2012.

Thomas, Chantal. *Les Adieux à La Reine: Roman*. Paris: Points, 2011.

Thomas, Chantal. *The Wicked Queen: The Origins of the Myth of Marie-Antionette*, translated by Julie Rose. New York: Zone Books, 1999.

Thomas, Robin Lemuel. "Slavery and Construction at the Royal Palace of Caserta." *Journal of the Society of Architectural Historians* 78, no. 2 (2019): 167–86.

Thuillier, Jacques and Claire Constant, eds. *Charles Le Brun 1619–1690. Le décor de l'escalier des Ambassadeurs à Versailles*, exhibition catalogue, Versailles, musée national du Château. Paris: Réunion des musées nationaux, 1990.

Tobin, Beth Fowkes. *Picturing Imperial Power: Colonial Subjects in Eighteenth-Century British Painting*. Durham, NC: Duke University Press, 1999.

Tomasson, Robert E. "Deal Negotiated for the Commodore." *New York Times*, May 4, 1975.

Tricoire, Damien. "Attacking the Monarchy's Sacrality in Late Seventeenth-Century France: The Underground Literature against Louis XIV, Jansenism and the Dauphin's Court Faction." *French History* 31, no. 2 (2017): 152–73.

van Andel, Pek and Danièle Bourcier. *De la sérendipité dans la science, la technique, l'art et le droit. Leçons de l'inattendu*. Paris: Hermann, 2013.

van de Sandt, Udolpho. "La frequentation des Salons sous l'Ancien Régime, la Révolution et l'Empire." *Revue de l'Art* 73 (1986): 43–8.

Van Kley, Dale K. *The Damiens Affair and the Unraveling of the Ancien Régime, 1750–1770*. Princeton, NJ: Princeton University Press, 1984.

Vanuxem, Jacques. "Emblèmes et devises vers 1660–1680." *Bulletin de la Société de l'Histoire de l'Art français* (1954): 60–70.

Vasconcelos, Juana. "Introduction." Available online: http://www.vasconcelos-versailles.com/t_vasconcelos.php

Veblen, Thorstein. *The Theory of the Leisure Class: An Economic Study of Institutions*, [first published, 1899] New York: Modern Library, 1961.

Veinstein, Gilles. "Les Capitulations franco-ottomanes de 1536: sont-elles encore controversables." In *Living in the Ottoman Ecumenical Community: Essays in Honour of Suraiya Faroqhi*, edited by Vera Costantini and Markus Koller, 71–88. Leiden, The Netherlands: Brill, 2008.

Verlet, Pierre. *French Royal Furniture*. London: Clarkson Potter, 1963.

Verlet, Pierre. *Le Mobilier Royal Français*, 4 vols, Rev. edn. Paris: Picard, 1990.

Verlet, Pierre. *Versailles*. Paris: Fayard, 1961.

Versailles. Created by David Wolstencroft, Simon Mirren. With George Blagden, Alexander Vlahos, Stuart Bowman, Evan Williams. 3 series, 2015. http://www.imdb.com/title/tt3830558/ (accessed November 29, 2018).

Versailles. Treasures from the Palace, exhibition catalogue, edited by Béatrice Saule and Lucina Ward. Canberra: National Gallery of Australia, 2016.

Vigée-Lebrun, Elisabeth. *Souvenirs*, edited by Claudine Herrmann, 2 vols. Paris: Des femmes, 1986.

Vitet, Ludovic. *L'Académie Royale de Peinture et de Sculpture*. Paris: Michel Lévy frères, 1861.

Volle, Nathalie et Nicolas Milovanovic, eds. *La Galerie des Glaces après sa restauration. Contexte et restitution*. Paris: École du Louvre, 2013.

Voltaire. "Vers de M. de Voltaire, sur le Louvre." *Mercure de France* (May 1749).

von Arneth, Alfred and M. A. Geffroy, eds. *Correspondance secrète entre Marie-Thérèse et le comte de Mercy-Argenteau*, 3 vols. Paris: Firmin Didot, 1874–5.

Wagner, Kate. "Whose Style Is That? Louis XIV or Donald Trump? An Interior Design Guide to the New President." *Curbly*, January 19, 2017. Available online: https://www.curbly.com/trump-is-a-living-mcmansion (accessed September 26, 2018).

Watanabe O'Kelly, Helen. *Court Culture in Dresden from Renaissance to Baroque*. Basingstoke: Palgrave Macmillan, 2002.

Watelet, Claude-Henri. *Dictionnaire des arts de peinture, sculpture et gravure*. Paris: L.F. Prault, 1792.

Weber, Eugen. *Fin de siècle: la France à la fin du XIXe siècle*. Nouvelles études historiques. Paris: Fayard, 1986.

Weber, Gerold. *Brunnen und Wasserkünste in Frankreich im Zeitalter von Louis XIV. Mit einem typengeschichtlichen Überblick über die französischen Brunnen ab 1500*. Worms: Werner'sche Verlagsgesellschaft, 1985.

Weiss, Allen S. *Mirrors of Infinity: The French Formal Garden and 17th-Century Metaphysics*. New York: Princeton Architectural Press, 1995.

Weiss, Gillian. "Infidels at the Oar: A Mediterranean Exception to France's Free Soil Principle." *Slavery & Abolition* 32, no. 3 (2011): 397–412.

Welch, Ellen R. *A Theater of Diplomacy: International Relations and the Performing Arts in Early Modern France*. Philadelphia: University of Pennsylvania Press, 2017.

Wellington, Robert. *Antiquarianism and the Visual Histories of Louis XIV: Artifacts for a Future Past*. Aldershot and Burlington: Ashgate, 2014.
Wellington, Robert. "Going for Gold: Trump, Louis XIV and Interior Design." *The Conversation*, January 23, 2017. Available online: https://theconversation.com/going-for-gold-trump-louis-xiv-and-interior-design-71698 (accessed October 2, 2018).
Wellington, Robert. "Trump's Display of Wealth, Power Falls Short." *Canberra Times*, March 13, 2017, 17.
White, Gillian B. "Getting to the Bottom of Americans' Fascination with Wealth." *Atlantic*, May 16, 2017. Available online: https://www.theatlantic.com/business/archive/2017/05/greenfield-generation-wealth/526683/ (accessed September 26, 2018).
White House Museum. "Oval Office History." Available online: http://www.whitehousemuseum.org/west-wing/oval-office-history.htm (accessed September 18, 2018).
Whitehead, John. "Royal Riches and Parisian Trinkets: The Embassy of Saïd Mehmet Pasha to France in 1741–42 and Its Exchange of Gifts." *Court Historian* 14, no. 2 (2009): 161–75.
Whitehead, John. *Sèvres at the Time of Louis XV: Birth of the Legend*. Paris: Éditions Courtes et Longues, 2010.
Wildenstein, Georges. *Le peintre Aved: sa vie et son oeuvre, 1702–1766*, 2 vols. Paris: Les Beaux-Arts, 1922.
Williams, Hannah. "Drifting through the Louvre: A Local Guide to the French Academy." In *Eighteenth-Century Art Worlds: Local and Global Geographies of Art*, edited by Stacey Sloboda and Michael Yonan. New York: Bloomsbury, 2019.
Williams, Hannah. "Le Louvre de Demachy, le palais et son quartier au XVIIIe siècle." In *Le Témoin méconnu: Pierre-Antoine Demachy, 1723–1807*, edited by Françoise Roussel-Leriche. exhibition catalogue, 28–39. Versailles: Musée Lambinet, 2014.
Williams, Hannah and Chris Sparks. *Artists in Paris: Mapping the 18th-Century Art World*. Available online: www.artistsinparis.org.
Wimmer, Stefan Jakob. *München und der Orient*. Munich: Kunstverlag Josef Fink, 2012.
Wine, Humphrey. "Madame de Pompadour." In *The Saint-Aubin Livre de caricatures: Drawing Satire in Eighteenth-Century Paris*, edited by Colin Jones, Juliet Carey, and Emily Richardson, 179–90. Oxford: Voltaire Foundation, 2012.
Wingfield, Valerie. "The Waldorf-Astoria Hotel." *New York Public Library Blog*, November 4, 2014. Available online: https://www.nypl.org/blog/2014/11/04/waldorf-astoria-hotel (accessed September 28, 2018).
Wormeley, Katherine Prescott. *The Correspondence of Madame, Princess Palatine, Mother of the Regent; of Marie-Adélaïde de Savoie, Duchesse de Bourgogne; and of Madame de Maintenon, in Relation to Saint-Cyr*. Boston, MA: Hardy, Pratt & Company, 1902.

York, Peter. *Dictator Style: Lifestyles of the World's Most Colorful Despots*. San Francisco, CA: Chronicle Books, 2016.

York, Peter. "Trump's Dictator Chic." *Politico*, March/April 2017. Available online: https://www.politico.com/magazine/story/2017/03/trump-style-dictator-autocrats-design-214877 (accessed September 27, 2018).

Zega, Andrew and Bernd H. Dams. *Palaces of the Sun King. Versailles, Trianon, Marly: The Châteaux of Louis XIV*. London: Laurence King Publishing, 2002.

Zimmermann, Hans-Joachim. *Der Triumph der Akademie: Eine allegorische Komposition von Charles Le Brun und ihr historisches Umfeld (Sitzungsberichte der Heidelberger Akademie der Wissenschaften, Philosophisch-Historische Klasse)*. Heidelberg: Winter, 1988.

Zysberg, André. *Les Galériens: vies et destins de 60,000 forçats sur les galères de France, 1680–1748*. Paris: Editions du Seuil, 1987.

Index

Note: Page numbers in bold indicate an illustration.

Abbas II, Khedive of Egypt (1874–1944) 249
absolutism 8, 77, 79, 82–3, 112, 121, 237
Académie française 16, 45
Académie Royale d'Architecture 16, 240
Académie Royale de Peinture et de Sculpture 16–17, 26, 33, 45–8, 55, 183
Académie Royale des Inscriptions et Belles Lettres 1, 16, 45–6, 48, 50, 53–5, 63. See also Petite Académie
  as the Académie Royale des Médailles et Inscriptions 50
Académie Royale des Sciences 16, 86
academies 16, 54. See also Académie Française; Académie Royale d'Architecture; Académie Royale de Peinture et de Sculpture; Académie Royale des Inscriptions et Belles Lettres; Académie Royale des Sciences
Adolphe Thiers (1789–1877) 3
Africa
  North 155–6, 158, 165
  West 155, 165
alchemy 79, 85–7
Algerian embassy 155–6
Algiers 155–6
ambassadors 8, 155–6. See also diplomacy
  Algerian embassy 155–6
  Cornelis Hop (1685–1762) 193–207
  Mehmed Saïd Pasha (c. 1597–1761) 177–88
  Persian embassy (1715) 179
  Siamese embassy (1686) 179
Amphitrite (Goddess of the sea) 195
Amsterdam 193, **194**, 207
Angiviller, Charles-Claude Flahaut de la Billaderie, compte d' (1730–1809) 26, 89–90, 139

Angoulême, Louis Antoine, duc d' (1775–1844) 137
Anguire, Guillaume (1628–1708) 51
Anjou, Louis duc d'. See Louis XV
Anne of Austria (Queen of France) (1601–66) 119, 153, 159, 197
  her apartments at the Louvre 197, **198**, **199**
antiquity 105
Apollo 34, 36, 38–40, 64–5, 118–19
Apprentice, The (television series) 247
Archbishop of Paris (during the regency of Louis XV) 114, 115. See also Noailles, Louis-Antoine de (1651–1729)
Archives nationales (Paris) 219
Arnoult, Nicholas (c. 1650–1722) Madame la Princesse de Conty douairière (c. 1695) 163, **164**, 168
Art versus nature 53, 63, 70, 87. See also hair
Artois, Charles-Philippe, comte d' (later Charles X) (1757–1836) 135, 141
Assemblée nationale de France 3, 89–90, 133
Astor family 243
Astoria (hotel) 243
Atget, Eugène (1857–1927) 4
Augustus II (the Strong) Elector of Saxony and King of Poland (1670–1733) 77–9, 88
Austria 178
Aved, Jacques-André-Joseph Aved (1702–66)
  Portrait of Mehmed Saïd Efendi (1742) 8, **183**–8, **185**
Aveline, Pierre (c. 1656–1722) Entrée du Trianon de Porcelaine (c. 1690) 83

Bachelier, Jean-Jacques (1724–1806) 80
Baedeker (guidebooks) 3, 218, 222. *See also* Versailles, guidebooks
Ballin, Claude (the younger) (*c.* 1660–1754) 187
Barbary pirates 155
Barriére, Dominique (1618–1678) *Villa Aldobrandina Tusculana: siue, uarij illius hortorum et fontium prospectus* (1647) 67, 70–1
Bâtiments du roi
    under Colbert (1664–83) 14, 45–8, 50, 67, 242
    under Angiviller (1774–89) 26, 89, 134, 136, 139, 141, 144
    under Marigny (1751–73) 23
Baudet, Étienne (*c.* 1636–1711) *Staircase of the Ambassadors* (*c.* 1679–83) **42**, 47
Baudoin, Jean (1662–98) 50
Beautru de Nogent, comtesse (active 1680s) 167. *See also* Catholics, Catholic conversions
beaux-arts (style) 241. *See also* École des Beaux-Arts
Bénard, Robert (1734–77) *Le Perruquier Barbier* (after J.R. Lucotte) (1762) **97**
Benoist, Antoine (1632–17) 97
Bérain, Jean (1640–1711) 153–4, **154**
Bernini, Gian Lorenzo (1598–1680) *portrait bust of Louis XIV* (after) 241, **242**
Berry, Marie Louise Élisabeth d'Orléans, duchesse de (1695–1719) 197
Bertin, Marie-Jeanne "Rose" (1747–1813) 102–3
Bignon, Jean-Paul, Abbé (1662–1743) 187
Bitter, Karl (1867–1915) portrait medallions of Richard Morris Hunt and Jules Hardouin Mansart 241, **242**
blackness 8, 100, 157, 166. *See also* complexion (skin colour)
Blois, Marie Anne de Bourbon, Mademoiselle de (1666–1739) and slavery 163, 166

Blondel, Jacques-François (1705–74) 16, 240
Blunt, Anthony (1907–83) 6, 33
Body (royal) 53, 112, 114, 116, 120
Bohemia (country) 154
Bombelles, Marie-Angélique Charlotte, marquise de (1762–1800) 140
Bonnart, Henri (1642–1711) 161, 163–5
    "*Dame*," from *Recueil des modes de la cour de France* (1677) **164**, 165
    The Glorious Actions of the Duc of Bavaria Presented to His Sister Madame La Dauphine (1688) 160, **161**
Bonnart, Nicolas (1637–82) *Habit d'Espée en Esté* (*c.* 1678) **96**
Bonnemer, François (1637–89) 47
Bontemps, Louis Alexander (1669–1742) 180
Böttger, Johann Friedrich (1682–1719) 79, 86
Bouchardon, Edmé (1698–1762) 16, 188
Boucher, François (1703–70) 16–17
Boulle, André-Charles (1642–1732) 16
    bureau plat (*c.* 1710) **136**, 139
Bourbon dynasty 2, 6, 8, 53, 111–12, 117–19, 217, 221, 239–40
Bourbon, Louis Henri de Bourbon, duc de (prince de Condé) (1692–1740)
    Chantilly porcelain 89
    as first minister to Louis XV 203–4
    at the formal audience of Cornelis Hop with Louis XV (1719) 198–99
    his quarrel with the comte de Toulouse 200
    Louis XV's fondness for him 202
    rivalry with the House of Orléans 203–4
Bourgogne, Louis duc de (1682–1712) 98, 117–19
Breteuil, François Victor Le Tonnelier de (1686–1743) 204
Bretez, Louis (active 1706–39) *Plan de Paris dessiné et gravé sous les ordres de Michel-Étienne Turgot* (1739) **15**, 17–18
Brionne, Louis de Lorraine, comte de (1725–61) 179–80

Brutus 105
bubonic plague (1720) 202

Cabinet du roi (prints) 65, 67. *See also* print culture
Caesar (Julius) 156
Caffièri, Philippe (c. 1633-1716) 51
Callières, François de (1645-1717) 185
Calliope, Muse of Heroic Poetry 39
Campan, Jeanne Louise Henriette (1752-1822) 99, 101-2
Caribbean 165
Carmelites 159, 168
Casino di San Marco 85
Catherine II of Russia (the Great) (1729-96) 81, 140
Catholicism
  anti-protestant propaganda 159. *See also* Revocation of the Edict of Nantes
  Catholic conversion 157-9, 166-8
  celebration of Catholic holidays in Paris 206
  conquest 156
  Louis XIV's Catholic credentials 160
  Maria Leszcyńska's Catholicism 205
Caze, Madame de la (circle of the princesse de Lamballe) 134
Chaillou, Jean Jacques Amelot de (1689-1749) 182
Chantilly
  Château 202
  porcelain manufactory 89
Chardin, Jean-Siméon Chardin (1699-1779) 186
Chartres, Louise Marie Adélaïde de Bourbon, duchesse de (later the duchesse d'Orléans) (1753-1821) 8, 100
Château de Versailles (Vaughan, Toronto) 247
Chinese Empire as model for European absolutism 83
Choisy, Château de 183
Clérisseau, Charles-Louis (1721-1820) 26
Clermont, Marie Anne de Bourbon, Mademoiselle de (1697-1741) 137
Clinton, William Jefferson (Bill) (b.1946) 238

Clio, Muse of History 39-40
Clovis (c. 466-511) 217
Cochin, Charles-Nicolas (1715-90)
  Death of Louis XIV (1753) 120-1, **121**
  the Reception by Louis XV of Saïd Méhémet Pacha in the Grand Gallery at Versailles (1744-5) 177, **178**, 182
Code Noir 165
coiffeurs 101-5. *See also* hair
Colbert, Jean-Baptiste (1619-83) 14, 19-21, 23, 33, 40, 54
  Ghost of 20-1
  and naval affairs 155
  organization of the arts 45, 47-8, 67, 72, 242, 259
  and slavery 155
collaboration, artistic 46, 48, 50-1, 54-5, 67
Commodore (hotel) 245-5
  Donald J. Trump purchase and redevelopment of 245
Compagnie d'Occident (later Compagnie des Indes) 205
Compagnie de Sénégal 155
complexion (skin color) 157, 166
Condé, Louis de Bourbon, prince de (duc de Bourbon) (1668-1710)
  Egyptian ball held by (1683) 153-5, 167
Congrégation de la Mission 168
conspicuous consumption 248, 251
Constantinople. *See* Istanbul
Construction. *See* Louvre, building of; Versailles, building of
contemporary art at Versailles 215-16, 226-33, **227**, **229**, **230**, **231**, **232**
Conti, Louis François I, prince de (1727-76) 133
Conti, Marie Anne de Bourbon, princesse de (1666-1739)
  rejection of Moulay Ismaïl, sultan of Morocco 167-8
  and slavery 153-7, 163, 166, 168
Coppola, Sophia (b. 1971) *Marie-Antoinette* (film) (2006) 215, 228
Corigliano, John (b. 1938) Ghosts of Versailles (1991) (with William M. Hoffman) 215
Corneille, Jean-Baptiste (1649-95) 47

Cotte, Robert de (1656–1735) 242
Courtois, Pierre (active early 1600s) 15
Coustou, Nicolas (1658–1733) 16
Coypel, Antoine (1661–1722) 16
Coypel, Charles-Antoine (1694–1752) 26
Coypel, Noël (1628–1707) 47
Coysevox, (Charles) Antoine (1640–1720) 47
  copies of his Marly Horses at Château de Versailles (Vaughan, Toronto) 247
Crimean War (1853–6) 2
Cucci, Domenico (*c.* 1635–1705) 51

Dauphin, Louis de France (1729–65) 120, 182
Dauphine, Maria Anna Victoria (1660–90) and slavery 157, 160, **162**, 166
David, Jacques-Louis (1748–1825) *Marie-Antoinette led to her execution* (1793) 105
de La Tour, Maurice-Quentin (1704–88) 186
de Troy, François (1645–1730) *Portrait of Charlotte-Élisabeth de Bavière, princesse Palatine, Duchesse d'Orléans* (1680) **163**, 166–7
Delafosse, Jean-Charles (1734–89) wall lights designed by 139
Della Bella, Stefano (1610–64) *Vues de la villa de Pratolino* (*c.* 1653) 67, 70
Demachy, Pierre-Antoine (1723–1807) 23–6
  Clearing the Colonnade of the Louvre (1764) **24**
  Clearing the Colonnade of the Louvre (1772) **25**
demography 27–8
Denis, Claude (active *c.* 1670–92) 47
Description de la Grotte de Versailles (1676) **64**, **66**, 67, **68**, **69**, 71
Desjardins, Martin (1637–94) 48
Dieu, Antoine (1662–1727) *Cartoon for the tapestry of the Marriage of the duc de Bourgogne* 98
diplomacy. *See also* ambassadors; Hop, Cornelis; Mehmed Saïd Pasha
  Algerian embassy (1684) 155–6
  diplomatic gifts 77, 88, 90, 182, 187, 206
  enslaved people as diplomatic gifts 155
  letters of credential 184–5
  Persian embassy (1715) 179
  Siamese embassy (1686) 179
  tension with Ottomans over enslaved girls a the Court of Catherine de Médicis 158
  Turkish embassy to France 177
Dresden 77, 79, 86
Dreux-Brézé, Michel, marquis de (1700–54) 180
Du Barry, Jeanne Bécu, Comtesse (known as Madame du Barry) (1743–93) 80, 135
Dubois, Guillaume, Abbé (later Cardinal) (1656–1723) 195, 198, 202
Dumesnil, Louis Michel (*c.* 1663–1739) *The Formal Audience of Cornelis Hop at the Court of Louis XV* (*c.* 1720–29) 197, **198**
Dumont, Edmé (1720–75) 26
Duplessis, Jean-Claude (1699–1774) 187
Dupont, Pierre (*c.* 1577–1650) 15
Durameau, Louis Jean-Jacques (1733–96) 26
Dussieux, Louis (1815–94) 219
Dutch Republic
  alliance with France, and Great Britain against Spain (1717) 194
  Dutch colonies 193
  fashion for porcelain 83–4
  and France 193–5, 201
  global trade 84
Duvivier, Benjamin (1730–1819) *medal of the Turkish embassy of 1742* (after Edme Bouchardon) **188**

East India Company (Dutch) 207
École des Beaux-Arts 241
Edelinck, Gérard (1640–1707) 47
Egyptian Ball hosted by the duc de Bourbon (1683) 153–5, **154**, 167
Eisen, Charles-Dominique-Joseph (1720–78) 21
Elements (iconography) 47, 53–4
Eliasson, Olafur (b. 1667)
  Deep Mirrors (2016) 231
  Fog Assembly (2016) 231, **232**

Élisabeth of France (Madame Élisabeth) (1764–94) 103, 140–1
Empire State Building 243
England 160
engraving, techincal description 71
enslaved people 8, 153–69. *See also* Catholicism, Catholic conversions
    Ayche and Fatma 158
    Charles (known as "Sainte-Marie") 159
    as diplomatic gifts 156
    Emmanuel 168
    eroticism 166
    Huceïn (known as "Houssi") 159–60, 166
    Huma (mother to Ayche and Fatma) her petitions for the return of her daughters 158
    Joseph Charles 159
    Louis Élisabeth Ally 167
    Marie-Julie Julistanne 167
    representations of 162–6, **162**, **163**, **164**
    rowing galleys at Versailles 155–7, 159, 166
    Vernacini, Madeleine (known as "The Queen's Moor") 158
    as war prizes 165
    Yasmine 168
    Zoula 157
entertainment
    Egyptian ball (1683) 153–5, **154**, 167
    equestrian carrousels 154
Erato, Muse of Erotic Poetry 40, **41**
Errard, Charles (1606–89) 47
Este Alfonso d' (Duke of Ferrara) (1476–1534) 165
etching, technical description 67–71
Eu, Hôtel d' 141
Europische Mercurius 195
Exposition Universelle (1900) 225

Fagel, François (1659–1746) 200
Falconet, Étienne-Maurice (1716–91) 16
fashion. *See also* hair; hats
    fashion industry 4, 251
    marchand(e) de modes 102, 105
Félibien, André (1619–1715) 53, 65, 67, 71. *See also Description de la Grotte de Versailles* (1676)
Félibien, Jean-François (1658–1733) 39

female agency
    and Catholic conversions 161
    Madame de Ventadour, her role as governess to Louis XV 7, 110, 115–19, 121–2, *see also* Ventadour, Charlotte-Eléonore-Madeleine de La Motte-Houdancourt, duchesse de (1654–1744)
    princesse de Lamballe, her status in the circle of Marie-Antoinette 131, 144, *see also* Lamballe, Marie Thérèse Louise de Savoie-Carignan, princesse de (1749–92)
    and slavery 157–8, 168–9
Feodorovna, Maria (Sophia Dorothea of Würtemberg) (1759–1828) 141
Ferrier, Antoine (active early 1600s) 15
Fiennes, Charles Maximilien, marquis de (1701–50) 205
First World War (1914–18) 3–4
FitzJames, Marie Claudine Sylvie de Thiard de Bissy, duchesse de (1752–1812) 139
Flemming, Jacob Heinrich Graf von (1667–1728) 78
Fleury, André-Hercule, Cardinal de (earlier bishop of Fréjus) (1653–1743) 182–3, 195, 198, 204
Fokke, Simon (1712–84) *The Formal Audience of Cornelis Hop at the Court of Louis XV* (c. 1747–59) 198, **199**
Fontages, Marie Angélique de Scorailles, duchesse de (1661–81) 100
Fontaine, Pierre-François-Léonard (1762–1853) 17
Fontainebleau, Château de
    foreign diplomats at 202, 206
    and John D. Rockerfeller Jr's philanthropy 4
    Louis XV at 203, 205
    marriage of Louis XV and Maria Leszczyńska (1725) 205
    opera-ballet staged at 155
    princesse de Lamballe's apartments 131, 135, 143, 159
Foster, Lady Elizabeth (later Duchess of Devonshire) (1758–1824) 103

France
　as artistic centre 13
　as "free soil" (prohibition of slavery) 156
Franco-Dutch War (1672–78) 84, 193
Franco-Prussian War (1870–1) 218
Franklin, Benjamin (1706–90) 99, 144–5
Franz Joseph of Austria (1830–1916) 249
French East India Company 84
Fresnes, duchesse de. *See* Noailles, Henriette Anne Louise d'Aguesseau de Fresnes, duchesse de (1737–94)
Fronde (1648–53) 13, 159
Fulvy, Jean-Louis Henry Orry, seigneur de (1703–51) 84
Furetière, Antoine (1619–88) 239–40
furniture. *See Garde-Meuble de la Couronne*
furniture making 16, 135

Gabriel, Ange-Jacques (1698–1782) 17
Gabriel, Jacques (1667–1742) 17
Garde-Meuble de la Couronne 7, 134–7, 139, 144
gardens. *See* Versailles, gardens; Trianon de Porcelain, gardens
Gautier-Dagoty, Jean–Baptiste (1740–86) *Marie-Antoinette playing the harp in her room at Versailles* (1777) 103, **104**
Gazette de France 159, 168
Geffroy, Gustave (1855–1926) 221
generation wealth 248, 251. *See* Lauren Greenfield
Germany, representation of 39, 160
Gersaint, Edme-François (1694–1750) 70
Gilded Age (*c.* 1870–1900) 9, 237, 240–45, 249, 251
Ginestous, Madame de (circle of the princesse de Lamballe) 134
Giorgio, Francesco (1466–1540) 38
Girardon, François (1628–1715) 16, 47–8, 65
gloire (glory) 36, 54, 89, 118
Gobelins, Manufacture royale des
　as artistic centre 45–8, 50, 52, 55
　Charles Le Brun as director 33–4
　Jean Hellot as administrator of dyes 86

　lodging at 47
　Louis XIV's visit to, tapestry 34
　silver furniture made at 243
Govaers, Daniel (active 1687–1767) *snuffbox with Miniature Portraits of Louis XV and Marie Leszczyńska* **206**
Governess
　duchesse de Polignac 129, 142
　Madame de Ventadour 109–22
Graces, three 36
Grand Dauphin, Louis de France (1611–1711) 117–18
Grand Hôtel (Paris) 243–4
Grand Trianon 3–4, 9, 201, 203, 222, 226, 241. *See also* Trianon de Porcelain
Grave, Barbara (Dutch rope dancer, active early 1700s) 205
Greenfield, Lauren (b. 1966) *Queen of Versailles* (documentary film) (2012) 248
Grotto of Thetis. *See* Versailles, Grotte de Thétys
Guébriant, Anne marguerite Chabenas de Bonneuil, comtesse de (d. 1824) 134
Guerin, Gilles (1611–78) 65
guidebooks. *See* Versailles, guidebooks
Guinée 155–6
Gustav III, king of Sweden (1746–92) 140–1
gypsies. *See* Roma

Hague, The 193–4, 200
hair
　barbier–perruquiers (guild of barbers and wigmakers) 96, 98, 104
　coiffeurs (hairdressers) 98, 101–5
　fontages 100
　perruque à bourse (bag wig) 98
　pomade 99
　pouf 100–2
　power 96, 98–9, 104
　and social status 7, 95–105
　tête de mouton 100
　à la Titus 105
　à la victime 105
Hallé, Claude-Guy (1652–1732) 47

Hardouin-Mansart, Jules (1646–1708) 17, 48, 54
  Place Vendôme (formerly Place Louis-le-Grand) 243
  portrait medallion by Karl Bitter 241, **242**
hats 98, 102
Hellot, Jean (1685–1766) 86. 88
Henri II (r. 1547–1559) 158
Henri IV (r. 1589–1610) 13, 15, 117–18, 158
Herculaneum 105
Hercules 34, 36, 38–40, 118
Hezecques, Felix de France d' (1774–1835) 221
Hickel, Karl Anton (1745–98) *Portrait of the princesse de Lamballe* (1788) **130**, 136, 139
histoire métallique 54. See also medals
historicism 241, 249
Hoffman, William M. (1939–2017) *Ghosts of Versailles* (1991) (with John Corigliano) 215
Holland, representation of 39
Hop, Cornelis (1685–1762) 3, 193
  grand deuil (deep mourning) for Madame Royale 201
  as administrator for the Dutch East India Company 207
  assistance to Dutch merchants 205
  Coach made for 195
  diplomatic gifts received 206
  first audience with Louis XV at the Palais de Tuileries 194–5, 197
  formal entry into Paris 195
  his letters read by other ambassadors 201
  his opinion of French ministers 204
  his return to Amsterdam (1725) 206
  his secretary Ruijsch 198
  letters of credential 198
  marks of distinction from Louis XV 200
  medal received at Louis XV's coronation 203
  Paris residence 194
  and protestantism 206
  public audience with Louis XV at the Louvre 196–9

  report of marriage of Louis XV and Maria Leszczyńska 205
  tips given coachmen and valets 196
  visit to the Spanish ambassador (etiquette) 201–2
  visit to Versailles (1719) 200
Hop, Jacob (1654–1725) 193–4
  House built for **194**
hotels (commercial) 9, 243–5
  age of the luxury hotel 243
  as Gilded Age mansions 243–5
Houasse, Réne-Antoine (c. 1645–1710) 47
Huguenots 158, 167
  as slaves on royal galleys 167
Huis Ten Bosch, porcelain room at 84
Hume, David (1711–76) 240
Hunt, Richard Morris (1827–95) 240
  Fifth Avenue façade of the Metropolitan Museum of Art 240
  Marble House 241, **242**
  Petit Château 240–1
  portrait medallion by Karl Bitter 241, **242**
hydraulics 47, 63–4. See also Versailles, fountains

Imprimerie Royale 16
Iroquois 156
Islam 156, 161, 166
Istanbul (Constantinople, or the Sublime Porte) 158, 160, 183–5, 187

Jacob, Georges (1739–1814) *Chaise de toilette* (with J-B. S. Rode) (c. 1787) **101**
Janin, Jules Gabriel (1804–74) 216–17
Jansenism 159
Joséphine de Beauharnais, Empress of France (1763–1814) (r. 1805–10) 105
Jourdain, Eleanor (1863–1937) and Charlotte Anne Moberly (1846–1937)
  An Adventure 215, 221–33
  Miss Lamont (character in *An Adventure*) 222–5
  Miss Morison (character in *An Adventure*) 222–5

Miss Morrison's Ghosts (1981) (BBC) 215
Jouvenet, François (the younger) (1664–1749) 47
Jules Allard and sons 240, 242
   use of prexisting antique elements in their interiors 242
Jupiter (god) 37

Kapoor, Anish (b. 1954) *Dirty Corner* (2015) 230, **231**
Khashoggi, Adnan (1935–2017) 245–7
Knights of Malta 158
Koons, Jeff (b. 1955) 226–7
   Michael Jackson and Bubbles 227
   Split Rocker (2000) **227**

La Chapelle, Vincent (*c.* 1690–1745) *Le cuisinier moderne* (1742) **81**
La Fontaine, Jean de (1621–1695) 53
La Muette, Château de 199
Lâge de Volude, Béatrix Stéphanie Renart de Fuchsamberg d'Amblimont (1764–1842) 134, 139
Lamballe, Marie Thérèse Louise de Savoie-Carignan, princesse de (1749–92)
   1789 revolution 143–4
   apartments at Fontainebleau 131, 135, 143
   first apartment at Versailles 131–7, **132, 133**
   her entourage 134
   Hôtel d'Eu 141
   portraits of 130
   resentment of 130
   rivalry with Polignac 130–1, 139–40, 142
   salary 131
   second apartment at Versailles **132**, 137–41
   Superintendent of the Queen's Household 7, 129–30, 133
   third apartment at Versailles 141–3, **142, 143**
   unrealised project for a gallery extension to her apartments at Versailles **140**

Laurent, Girard (active early 1700s) 15
Lavoisier, Antoine-Laurent (1743–94) 86
Law, John (1671–1729) 205
Le Bas, Jacques-Philippe (1707–83) 21
Le Brun, Charles (1619–90) 6, 33
   ceiling of the Hall of Mirrors 193, 243
   design process 6, 33–42, 47–8, 50–1
   as dictator of the arts 6, 33
   education of 50
   Erato, Muse of Lyric Poetry (*c.* 1674) **41**
   Histoire du roi tapestries 54
   Les Quatre Tempéraments (Complexions) de l'Homme, *c.*1674 **51**
   as manager 33–4, 47–8, 51, 55, 72
   Minerva and Three Muses (*c.* 1674) **39**
   Order Restored to the National Finances 34–5
   Plan du premier parterre d'eau de Versailles (workshop of) **49**
   premier peintre 55
   Quatre Elements tapestries 47, 53–4
   Quatre Seasons tapestries 53–4
   Study for the Arcs of the Apollo Gallery (*c.* 1663) **37**
   The King Governs by Himself 34
   Vue en perspective du premier parterre d'Eau de Versailles (workshop of) **49**
Le Clerc, Sébastien (1637–1714) 47
Le Comte, Florent (1655–1712) 70
Le Hongre, Étienne (1628–90) 47
Le Nôtre, André (1613–1700) 48
Le Pautre, Jacques (1653–84) 6, 64, 68–71
   Ballroom at Court during Carnival (1683) (after Jean Bérain) 153, **154**
   guéridons designed by 153–4
   Pillar ornamented with seashells and rocks (plate 9) **66**
   View of the interior of the Grotto of Versailles (plate 2) **64**
   View of the interior of the Grotto of Versailles (plate 7) **66**
Le Vau, Louis (1612–70) 17, 48, 82
League of Augsburg 160
Leibniz, Gottfried Wilhelm (1646–1716) 79
Lemoine, Jean (1638–1713) 47

Léonard (Léonard-Alexis Autié)
  (c. 1751–1820) 102–5
  brothers, Pierre and Jean-François
    Autié 103–4
Leroy, Louis-Hippolyte (1763–1829) 105
Lespagnandelle, Matthieu (1616–89) *Le Flegmatique* (c. 1674) **52**
Levant 156
lisières (leading strings) 109, 114, 118
lit de justice 114, 115
logements 15, 25–8, **28**, 46–7, 50. *See also* Louvre, lodging at
Longueville, Anne Geneviève de Bourbon, duchesse de (1619–79) 159
Lorraine, François de, duc de Guise (1519–63) 158
Louis Napoléon. *See* Napoléon III
Louis-Philippe (r. 1830–48) 133, 216–18, 220
Louis I of Spain (1707–24) 203
Louis XIII (r. 1610–43)
  hair 95
  hunting lodge at Versailles 1
  group portrait with Madame de Ventadour 117–18
  and the Louvre 13
Louis XIV (r. 1643–1715)
  in African costume 154
  allegory of the reign 53–5, 65, 82–3, 247
  as Apollo 64–5
  Catholic conversions 159
  comparison of Versailles to the homes of Donald Trump 9, 237–9
  Court of 7, 45, 158, 160, 166
  criticism of his pro-Ottoman policies 160
  Death 121
  final years 111–12
  hair 95–6, 98
  his gloire 23
  his insignia 65, 248
  king's victories on the ceiling of the Hall of Mirrors 193, 243
  and Le Brun 33–6
  his legitimized children 111, 168
  and Louis XV 109–21
  Manière de montrer les jardins de Versailles (1689) 5, 53

medals 1, **2**, 206
minority (1643–1661) 7, 13, 71
moves Court to Versailles in 1682 13
as patron 14–15, 21, 39–40, 45–7, 63–4, 83
period style (decorative arts) 237–44, 250–1
Persian embassy (1715) 179
Personal reign (1661–1715) 65
portraits of 111, 113, 116–19, 121, **162**
Siamese embassy (1686) 177, 199
and slavery 155–6, 159, 166
as "The Most Christian King" 156
Louis XV (r. 1715–74)
  aversion to Mariana Victoria 204
  changes made to Versailles 38, 80
  childhood seizure 116
  coronation in Rheims cathedral 203
  Court of 179, 200–1
  death from smallpox (1774) 203
  diplomatic gifts presented 88
  as duc d'Anjou 111
  engagement to Maria Leszczyńska 204
  health 203
  interest in science 86–7
  Louis the beloved (*le bien aimé*) 119–20
  minority of 1, 109–22, 194–5, 199–212, 215–24
  official separation from his governess in 1717 109, 112
  passion for hunting 202
  as patron 84–5
  period style (decorative arts) 239–41
  portrait on snuffbox presented to Dutch ambassador Cornelis Hop **206**
  portraits with Madame de Ventadour 112–22, **113, 114, 115, 117, 121**
  portraits of 21, 87–8, 113–15, 137–8, 241–2
  reception of Cornelius Hop, Dutch ambassador 8, 194–5, 197–9
  reception of Mehmet Saïd, Ottoman ambassador 177–8, 181, 188
  regency of 1, 110–11, 113–15
  return to Versailles in 1722 1–2, 120, 200
Louis XVI (r. 1774–92)
  1789 revolution 1–2, 7, 89–90

Court of 102, 133, 140, 165, 217
his interest in science 87
as patron 80, 89–90
period style (decorative arts) 249
Louvois, François Michel Le Tellier, marquis de (1641–91) 48
Louvre
Anne of Austria's apartments 197, **198**, **199**
as artistic centre 6, 13–16, 26–8, 46–7, 50, 55
building of 14, 17, 23, 46
Colonnade 14, 17–18, 21, **22**, 23–5, **24**, **25**
Cour Carré 19–20, 26
Cour Napoléon 18
Département des Arts graphiques 34
Galerie d'Apollon (Apollo Gallery) 36–8, **37**, 54
Grand Galerie 15, 17
lodging at 13, 15–16, 23, 25–8, **28**, 46–7, 50
map of **15**, 17–18
as monument 19
as museum 13, 16–17, 27, 218
Place du Louvre 18
Pyramid 18
Salon carré 17
sanitation 26
Löwenstern, Johann Kunckel von (1630–1703) 79
Ludwigsburg porcelain manufactory 79
luxury brands 4, 251
Luynes, Charles Philippe d'Albert, duc de (1695–1758) 177–8, 180–1

Madagascar 155
Mahmud I, Ottoman Sultan (1696–1754) 177–8
Maintenon, Françoise d'Aubigné, marquise de (1635–1719) as mediator with Louis XIV 116
Maison de Saint-Lazare 168
Manilius, Marcus (first century AD) 37
manufactories. See Chantilly, Manufacture de; Gobelins, Manufacture Royale de; Saint Cloud, Manufacture de; Saint-Gobain, Manufacture Royale de glaces de miroirs; Ludwigsburg porcelain manufactory; Meissen; Sèvres, Manufacture Royale de; Vincennes, Manufacture de
Mar-a-Lago 9, 237, 244, 249–51
as the Winter White House 251
Donald J. Trump Grand Ballroom **250**, 251
Marble House (Newport)
reference to the Ambassadors's Staircase at Versailles 241, **242**
reference to the Salon d'Hercule at Versailles 242
Maria Theresa, Empress of Austria (r. 1745–80) 102, 137
Mariana Victoria d'Espagne (1718–81) 168, 203–4
Marie Leszcyńska, Queen of France (1703–68) 179, 204–6, 229
copy of her portait in Château de Versailles (Vaughan, Toronto) 247
Marie-Antoinette (1755–93) 1–2
circle of 129, 131, 137, 141–3
fin-de-siécle fascination with 220–1
hair 95, 102–5
in *An Adventure* (Jourdain and Moberly) 222
last days at Versailles/Petit Trianon 215, 221–5
as taste-maker 7
Marie-Thérèse, Queen of France (1778–1851) 105, 159
and Catholic conversions 159
Mariette, Pierre-Jean (1694–1774) 70
Marigny, Abel-François Poisson de Vandières, marquis de (1727–81) 23
Marly, Château de 200, 203, 247
Mars 36
Marseille 155, 158–9
bubonic plague (1720) 202
Marsy, Gaspard (*c.* 1624–81) and Balthazard (1628–74) 65
Massé, Jean-Baptiste (1687–1767) 186
portrait miniatures of Louis XV and Maria Leszczyńska attributed to him, on snuff presented to Dutch ambassador Cornelis Hop **206**

Mathieu, Jean-Adam (c. 1698–1753) 186
Maurepas, Jean-Frédéric Phélypeaux, comte de (1701–81) 204
Mauritania 155
Maximilian II Emanuel, Elector of Bavaria (1662–1726) 160
McCarthy, Justin H (1859–1936) 220–21, 223
McMansion Hell (blog) 237
medals
  as diplomatic gifts 206
  histoire métallique 54
  satirical medals against Louis XIV 160
  Turkish embassy of 1742 **188**
  Versailles medal 1, **2**
Médici, Catherine de' (Queen of France) (1519–89) 119
  and Catholic conversions 168
  and slavery 158
Medici, Grand Duke Francesco de' (Grand Duke of Tuscany) (1541–87) 85
Médicis, Ferdinando de' (Grand Duke of Tuscany) (1549–1609) 158
Médicis, Marie de' (Queen of France) (1575–1642) 119
  and Catholic conversions 168
  and slavery 158
Mediterranean 155–6, 158, 165
Mehmed Çelebi Efendi (1670–1732) 180–1
  Audience Given by King Louis XV to Mehmed Çelebi Efendi, Ambassador of Sultan Achmet III, March 16, 1721, at the Tuileries Palace **181**
  embassy to Louis XV 180–1
Mehmed Saïd Pasha (previously Efendi) (c. 1697–1761) 8, 177–88, **178**, **182**
  as grand vizier to Sultan Osman III 188
  embassies to Poland and Sweden 180
  establishes first printing house in Ottoman empire 187
  gifts from Louis XV 187
  French fluency 181
  interest in French painting 186

letters of credential 184–5
medal commemorating his embassy to France **188**
portrait by Aved 183–8, **183**, **185**
promotion of Ottoman language 187
Meissen (porcelain) 77–9, 85, 88–9
Melpomene, Muse of Tragedy 39–40
Menus-Plaisirs du Roi 16
mercantilism 78, 84–5, 242–3
Mercoeur, Laura Mancini, duchesse de (1636–57) 159
Mercoeur, Louis de Bourbon, duc de (later duc de Vendôme) (1612–69) 159
Mercure de France 180
Mercure Galant 53–4, 96, 98, 153, 155
Mercury 37, 118, 247
Mercy-Argenteau, Florimond Claude, comte de (1727–94) 137
Merlin, Monsieur (secretary to the introducteur des ambassadeurs) (active early 1700s) 194
Metamorphoses (Ovid) 63
Metropolitan Museum of Art 241
Metz 166
Meudon, Château de 202–3
Mignard, Pierre (1612–95) 47, 157
  Portrait of Louise de Kéroualle, duchess of Portsmouth (1682) **157**
Minerva 36, 38–40, 119
Mique, Richard (1728–94) 230
Mississippi Bubble 205
Moberly, Charlotte Anne (1846–1937). *See* Jourdain, Eleanor (1863–1937) and Charlotte Anne Moberly (1846–1937)
Molière (Jean-Baptiste Poquelin) (1622–73) 239
Monoyer, Jean-Baptiste (1636–99) 47
Monroe, Marilyn (1926–62) 229–30
Montespan, Françoise-Athénaïs de Rochechouart, Marquise de (1640–1707) 166
Montesquiou, Henri de (active late 1800s) 216
Montesquiou, Pierre de, marshal of France (1640–1725) 196

Moors, enslaved 153–5, 158–9, 161, 165–6, 168
　model galley rowed by at Versailles 155–7, 166
Morocco 155–6, 165
Morville, Charles Jean-Baptiste Fleuriau, comte de (1686–1732) 204
Moulay Isma'il (Ismail Ibn Sharif) sultan of Morocco (c. 1645–1727) 167–8
Murakami, Takahashi (b.1962) 227–9
　Flower Matango 228, **229**
　Superflat flowers 228
Musée d'histoire de la France. *See* Versailles, Musée d'histoire de la France
museology 2–3, 9, 16, 27, 215–22, 225–6, 232
Muses 38–40
Muslims 8, 155–6, 158–61, 167–8
　Muslim converts to Christianity 159, 161, 167–8
Mustafa Pasha, Köprülüzade Fazıl (1637–91) 187

Naiads 195
Nantes, Louise Françoise de Bourbon, duchesse de Bourbon, Mademoiselle de (1673–1743) 163, 166
Napoléon (r. 1804–14) 14
Napoléon III (also known as Louis Napoléon) (r, 1852–70) 220
Narbonne, Pierre (d. 1746) 180
natural philosophy 79, 86
neo-rococo 240, 250
neoclassicism 105, 138, 141
Neptune 37
Nero 105
Netherlands 47, 160
　Republic of the United Netherlands 83
New York City 237–41
Newport 241
Newton, William Ritchey (b. 1945) 7, 219
Noailles, Adrien Maurice, duc de (1678–1766) 180
Noailles, Anne Jules de Noailles, duc de (1650–1708) 159
Noailles, Henriette Anne Louise d'Aguesseau de Fresnes, duchesse de (1737–94) 139

Noailles, Louis-Antoine de (1651–1729) 114, 115
Nolhac, Pierre de (1859–1936) 219–21, 228
Nôtre Dame (cathedral) 168, 202
　Te Deum for end of plague epidemic (1723) 202
nouveau riche 9, 245, 251

Obama, Barack (b. 1961) 238
Oberkirch, Henriette Louise de Waldner de Freundstein, baronne d' (1754–1803) 100, 141
Olympus 37
Orange, House of 83–4
　Prince of Orange 81
Orbay, François d' (1634–97) 82
Orléanist monarchy. *See* Louis Philippe
Orléans, Louis duc d' (1703–52) rivalry with the duc de Bourbon 204
Orléans, Louise Élisabeth (1709–42) 203
Orléans, Philippe II duc d' (1674–1723) 1, 89, 109, 111, 113–15
　as regent 115, 119, 194, 200
　death of 201
　his meeting with John Law 205
　marriage of his daughter to the future king of Spain 203
Osman III (1754–57) 188
Osuna, José Maria Téllez-Girón, seventh duke of (1685–1733) 201–2
Ottomans 8
　diplomatic ranks (Ichoglan/Cadi) 185–6
　embassy to Louis XV (1721) 180–1
　embassy to Louis XV (1742) 179–88
　Franco-Ottoman trade agreement 156, 160, 178
　French assistance for Venetians against the Ottomans in Candia (Crete) 159
　Maximilian II Emanuel of Bavaria, battles against Ottoman forces 160
　Ottoman colonists in North Africa 155
　the Ottoman-Habsburg front 156
　slaves from the Ottoman Empire 165–7
　Treaty with Austria and Russia 178
Ovid 63

Palais Royal 205
Palatine, Élisabeth Charlotte, duchesse d'Orléans, princesse (known as Madame, or Liselotte) (1652–1722) 157, 160, 163, 166
Paris. *See also* Louvre; Tuileries, Palais des
 Artists in Paris maps (Williams and Sparks) **28**
 as printmaking centre of Europe 67
 as the new Rome 24
 City of 20–1
 Commune (1871) 3, 218
 during the Fronde 13
 rue de Rivoli 18
 rue des Poulies 18
 rue du Petit Bourbon 18, 21
 Siege of (1870) 2
 urban planning 18
Paris Las Vegas Hotel 248
parlement de Paris 114–16
Parnassus 36
Patel, Pierre (1605–76) *View of the Château de Versailles and Its Gardens* (1668) 18
Paul I, Emperor of Russia (r. 1796–1801) 140
Pei, Ieoh Ming (1917–2019) 18. *See also* Louvre, Pyramid
Penthièvre, Louis Jean Marie de Bourbon, duc de (1725–93) 130–2
Percier, Charles (1764–1838) 17
Perrault, Claude (1613–88) 14, 17–18, 21
perruque. *See* hair
Petit Château (New York City) 240–1, 244
Petit Trianon 3–5, 9, 222–7, 230, 232, 241
 Belvedere 224
 Hameau 224
Petite Académie. *See* Académie Royale des Inscriptions et Belles Lettres
philanthropy 4, 9
Philip V (King of Spain) (r. 1700–24, 1724–46) 111, 203
Picart, Bernard (1673–1733) 70
Picart, Étienne (1632–1721) 6, 71
 Horses of Apollo Tended by Tritons (plate 17) (after G. and B. Marsy) **68**, 69

Pierre, Jean-Baptiste-Marie (1714–89) 26
Place Vendôme (Paris) 243
Platre, Chalres (known as Bellecour) (active late 1700s) 105
Plaza Hotel 244–5
 Donald J. Trump purchase and redevelopment of 245
 Palm Court **244**, 245
Pluto (god) 37–8
Poincaré, Raymond (President of France) (1860–1934) 4
Polignac, Yolande Martine Gabrielle de Polastron, duchesse de (1749–93)
 apartments at Fontainebleau 131
 rivalry with Lamballe 129–31, 139–40, 142
Polyhymnia, Muse of Eloquence 39–40
Pompadour, Jeanne Antoinette Poisson, marquise de (1721–64)
 and science 87
 hair 100
Pompeii 105
Pons, Charles Louis de Lorrain, prince de (1696–1755) 197
Poppins, Mary (fictional character) 229
porcelain 6–7, 53, 77–91. *See also* Chantilly, Manufacture de; Ludwigsburg porcelain manufactory; Meissen; Saint Cloud, Manufacture de; Sèvres, Manufacture Royale de; Vincennes, Manufacture de; Trianon de Porcelaine
 and alchemy 79, 85–7
 as statecraft 78–9, 82–3, 87–90
 commercial viability 78–9, 85, 90
 hard-paste 77, 86
 porcelain and global trade 84
 porcelain rooms 84
 soft-paste 85
Portsmouth, Louise Renée de Penancoët de Kérouaille, duchess of (1649–1734) 157
Post, Marjorie Merriweather (1887–1973) 249
 Bequest of Mar-a-Lago to the federal government 251
 collection of French antiques 249

earrings with diamonds purportedly owned by Marie-Antoinette 249
French Drawing Room at Hillwood (Washington DC) 249
pouf. See hair
print culture 65, 67, 69–70. *See also* Cabinet du roi
propaganda 46, 50, 53, 70, 89
Protestants 156, 159–60, 206
Prou, Jacques (1655–1706) 47
Provence, Louis Stanislas Xavier, comte de (later Louis XVIII) (1755–1824) 103, 137, 141. *See also* Louis XVIII
Provence, Marie Joséphine de Savoy, comtesse de (1753–1810) 137, 141
Prussia
    Prussian government and France 219
    Prussian troops 3
pseudo-French grand manner 240, 247

Quebec 156

Rambouillet 195
Raphael (Rafaello Sanzio da Urbino) (1483–1520) 50
Reagan, Nancy (1921–2016) 238
Revocation of the Edict of Nantes (1685) 156, 158, 166–7
Revolution, 1789 2, 7, 14, 17, 80, 88–9, 98, 104–5, 135, 143, 220, 237
    Marie-Antoinette's last days at Versailles 215–16, 220–5, 232
    Revolutionary wars 217
    sale of Versailles contents 134, 143–4
Revolution, American Independence 99
Rheims Cathedral 4, 203
Ribeira Grande, Luís Manuel da Câmara, third count of (1685–1723)
    Carriage for his audience at Versailles (1715) 195, **196**
Rigaud, Hyacinthe (1659–1743) (school of) *portrait of the duc de Bourbon (later the prince de Condé)* 167
Ripa, Cesare (*c.* 1560–1622) *Iconologia* 50
Ritz, César (1850–1918) 243
Rockefeller Foundation 4, 9
Rockefeller Jr, John D. (1874–1960) 4, 9

Rodrigues, Amalia (1920–99) 229
Roma (people) 154
Rome 24, 50
Rose of Versailles (manga) 215, 228
Ruijsch (secretary to the Dutch ambassador) (active early 1700s) 198
Russia 81, 100, 140, 178

Sainctot, Nicholas Sixte de (1683–1753) 194–5, 198
Saint Cloud, Manufacture de 89
Saint Geneviève, Abbey of 168, 187
Saint Louis (Louis IX) 156
Saint Yenne, Étienne La Font de (1688–1771) 19–23
    Frontispiece to L'Ombre du Grand Colbert, **22**
Saint-Esprit, Order of 118
Saint-Gobain Manufacture Royale de glaces de miroirs 243
Saint-Nicolas-des-Champs (church) 167
Salon exhibitions 17, 183, 186
salonniers 239. *See also* Louis XIV, Court of; Louis XV, Court of
Sarrazin, Bessigne (active 1600s) 47
Sarrazin, Jacques (1592–1660) 47
Sarrazin, Jean-Pierre (active 1600s) 47
Savonnerie (carpets) 139, 187
Savoy-Nemours, Marie Jeanne Baptiste (known as Madame Royale) (1644–1724) 201
Scudéry, Madeleine de (1607–1701) 53
Scutt, Der (1934–2010)
    design of Trump Tower (New York City) 245, **246**
    renovation of the Commodore 245–6
Seasons (iconography) 53–4
Second Empire 2, 218–19, 221
Seigel, David A. (b. 1935) and Jacqueline (Jackie) (b. 1966) 248–9
    fantasy portrait in royal regalia 248
Seine (river) 15, 17, 18, 36
Sené, Jean-Baptiste Claude (1747–1803) *lyre-backed chair* (1787) **138**
Sève, Gilbert de (*c.* 1615–98) 47
Seven Years War (1756–63) 85, 89
Sèvres, Manufacture Royale de 6–7, 77, 80

appartement du roi 80, 87–8
Cameo service **78**, 81
displayed by Lamballe at the Hôtel d'Eu 141
grand service 81–2
lodging at 87
Manufactory building 84–8, **88**
Perles et Barbeaux service (1781) 80
Riche en couleurs variées service (1784) 80
Rubans bleu céleste service (1769–70) 80
Sibrayque, George (active at Versailles 1672–82) *Afrique* 51–2
Silvestre, Israël (1621–91) 47
Simonneau, Charles (1615–1728) (after Antoine Benoist) *Portraits de Louis le Grand graves suivant ses differentes âges* **97**
slavery. *See* enslaved people
smallpox 202–3
Society of Suriname 193
Solms-Braunfels, Amalia von (1602–75) 84
Soubise, Hôtel de 135, 138, 250
Soulié, Eudore (1817–76) 218–20
Spain, representation of 39
Spinoza, Baruch (1632–77) 79
Staël-Holstein, Anne Louise Germaine de (known as Madame de Staël) (1766–1817) 131, 142–3
Stair, John Dalrymple, second Earl of Stair (1673–1747) 205
States General 193, 198, 200–203, 205, 207
Sublime Porte. *See* Istanbul
Succession 114–5, 118, 120
    primogeniture 110–11
    salic law 111
    Seuccession [sic] du Roy Louis XV … (1715) **113**
Suleiman II (r. 1687–91) 187
Sun (iconography) 36, 64
Sun King. *See* Louis XIV

Tallemant, Abbé Paul 50
Taraval, Hugues (1729–85) 26
taste (*bon gout*) 239–40
Taube, Evert, baron (1739–99) 140

Thalia, Muse of Comedy 39–40
Thetis 63–5
Thomas, Chantal (b. 1945) *Les Adieux à La Reine* (book) (2002) 215
Tiepolo, Lorenzo (Venetian ambassador) (active early 1700s) 195
Time (iconography) 53
Titian (Tiziano Vecelli) (1490–1576) *portrait of Laura Dianti* 165
Titus 105
Tocqué, Louis (1696–1772) copy of his portrait of Maria Leszczyńska at Château de Versailles (Vaughan, Toronto) 247
toilette 100–1, 103–4
Toulouse, Louis Alexandre, comte de (1678–1737) 200
tourism 3–4, 216. *See also* Versailles, tourism
Treaty of Versailles (1871) 3, 218
Trianon de Porcelaine 53, 82–4, **83**. *See also* Grand Trianon
    plants and global trade 84
trianonization of Versailles 8, 220–1, 226
Tritons 195
Trump, Donald J. (b. 1946)
    American art and design 251
    as a luxury brand 250
    his claim to being a billionaire 248–9
    his interior design style 237–8, 244
    his memoir ghost-written by Tony Schwartz 245
    manufacturing 251
    Mar-a-Lago 237, 244, 249–51, **250**
    pseudo-French grand manner 240, 247, 249
    rivalry with Adnan Khashoggi 245–7
    The Apprentice (television series) 247
    Trump Tower apartment 237–8, **238**, 244, 247, 250
Trump Tower 245–6
    atrium 245–6, **246**
    Donald J. Trump's apartment 237–8, **238**, 244, 247, 250
Tschirnhaus, Ehrenfried Walther von (1651–1708) 79
Tuby, Jean-Baptiste (1635–1700) 47–8, 51

Tuileries, Palais des 135–6, 156, **181**, 194–5, 197, 200
Tuscany 158

Urban, Joseph (1872–1933) 249

Valenciennes 205
Vallière, Louise de la (1644–1710) 168
van der Laan, Adolf (1684–1755) *The Formal Entry of Cornelis Hop into Paris* (1719–20) 195–7, **197**
van der Meulen, Adam Frans (1632–90) 47
Vanderbilt family, collection of French historical art and design 249
Vanderbilt Hotel 244
Vanderbilt, Alva (née Smith, later Belmont) (1853–1933) 240–4
Vanderbilt, Cornelius (1794–1877) 241
Vanderbilt, William Kissam (1849–1920) 241
Vasconcelos, Juana (b. 1971) 229–30
  Le Dauphin et la Dauphine (2011) 230
  Marilyn (2011) 229, **230**
Vaudreuil, Joseph Hyacinthe François de Paule de Rigaud, comte de (1740–1817) 222
Vaux-le-Vicomte 33
Veblen, Thorstein (1857–1929) 251
Venetian Republic 159, 193
Ventadour, Charlotte-Eléonore-Madeleine de La Motte-Houdancourt, duchesse de (1654–1744) 7, 109–22
  death 120
  dedication to her in eulogies to Louis XIV 112, 119
  her family, Rohan-Soubise 110, 116, 118
  her suitability as governess 111–12
  images with Louis XV 112–22, **113, 114, 115, 117, 121**
  Louis XIV's thanks 112
  Madame de Ventadour with Louis XIV and his heirs (French School, 1715–22) **117**, 118
  maternal care of Louis XV 112–16, 120
  official separation from Louis XV in 1717 109, 112

Verdier, François (1651–1730) 47
Verneüil, Eusèbe Félix Chaspoux, marquis de (1720–91) 180
Versailles
  aile du Midi 132–3, 141–2, **142**
  American fascination with 237–51
  Americans at 4, 9
  and government 3, 6, 13
  and Louis Philippe I 216–18, 220–2, 226, 233
  and Napoléon III (Louis-Napoléon) 220
  appartement du président de l'Assemblée nationale 133
  as an advertisement for luxury industries 243
  as grand cimetière magique 221, 225
  as theatrical stage 52–3
  avenue de Paris 180
  Bibliothèque de Versailles 132
  building of 14, 17, 23, 33, 46
  chambre du grand couvert 230
  Chapelle royale 139, 159
  Château de Versailles (Vaughan, Toronto) 247
  contemporary art at (20th–21st century) 215–16, 225–33, **227, 229, 230, 231, 232**
  costume drama 4
  Cour de l'Apothicaiererie [sic] 132
  Cour de la Bouche de Mesdames 132, 134
  Cour des Princes 132–3
  courtiers displeasure with 200
  escalier des Ambassadeurs (Ambassadors's staircase) 38–9, **39, 41, 42**, 180, 241, 243
  Egyptian ball (1683) 153–5, **154**, 167
  final days of 220–21
  fountains 47, 53, 200
  Galerie de Pierre 133
  Galerie des glaces (Grand galerie or Hall of Mirrors) 34–6, **35**, 54, 177–80, **178, 179, 182**, 222, 228, 243
  Galerie des glaces as military hospital 3
  gardens 3–4, 18, 47–55, 82
  golden gates 4

Grand canal 82, 155, 166
Grand Commande 49–50
grand parterre 48
grands décors 6, 33–4
Grotte de Thétys 6, 63–72, **64, 66, 68, 69, 162**
guidebooks 5, 53, 65, 216–18, 222
historiography of 1, 215–21, 226
hôtel de la Surintendance des bâtiments 139
hôtel des Affaires Étrangères et de la Marine 132
king's apartments 38
lodging at 7, 131–65, 217
Louis XV's return in 1722 120, 200
Manière de montrer les jardins de Versailles (1689) 53
medal 1–**2**
Ménagerie 53
Musée d'histoire de la France 3, 216–17, 221–2, 226, 233, *see also* museology
Orangerie 227
Parterre d'eau 6, 45–55, **49**
Parterre du Midi 141–2
Pavillon de la Surintendance **132**, 141
Petite galerie du Roi 182
Plan of the Hall of Mirrors, the Salons of Peace and War for the Audience of the Turkish Ambassador in 1742 **179**
private apartments 54
reception of Queen Victoria 2
Opéra 3
rue de la Surintendance 132
salle de la Congrès 3
salle des ambassadeurs 180, 182, 194–5
salles du sénat 133
Salles Empire 142
Salon d'Apollon 178, 180
Salon d'Hercule 242
Salon de Diana 180
Salon de la guerre 177, 180
Salon de la paix 228
Salon de Mercure 180
Salon de Venus 180
sanitation of 5, 145

smallpox outbreak (1722) 200
storm damage 3
the *domaine* 217–18, 226
tourism 1, 3–4, 8, 216
Versailles (Orlando Florida) 248
Victoria, Queen of England (r. 1837–1901) 2
Vigée-Lebrun, Élisabeth (1755–1842) 102, 104
Vignon, Philippe (1638–1749) *Portrait of the sisters Mademoiselle de Blois and Mademoiselle de Nantes* 166–7
Villeroy, François de Neufville, duc de (1644–1730) 120, 195
Vincennes, Château de 84, 199
Vincennes, Manufacture de 84
Voltaire (François-Marie Arouet) (1694–1778) 18–20, 23, 105
Vulcan 37–8

Waldorf-Astoria 243–4
  French Renaissance style decoration of 244
  Henri IV drawing room 244
  Louis XIV ballroom 244
  Marie-Antoinette parlour 244
War of Spanish Succession (1701–14) 113
War of the League of Augsburg (1688–97) 47, 160
Watelet, Claude-Henri (1718–86) 70
West India Company (Dutch) 193
Wettin, House of 77. See also Augustus the Strong, Elector of Saxony and King of Poland
White House 9, 237–9
  Oval Office decoration 238
whiteness 157. See also complexion (skin color)
Wigs. See hair
Wilhelm I (German Kaiser) (1797–1888) 3, 218
Württemberg, Carl Eugen von (1728–93) 79

Yvard, Baudouin (1611–90) 47

Zodiac 37–8

www.ingramcontent.com/pod-product-compliance
Lightning Source LLC
Chambersburg PA
CBHW052150300426
44115CB00011B/1596